NINETEENTH-CENTURY LITERATURE IN TRANSITION: THE 1890s

The 1890s were once seen as marginal within the larger field of Victorian studies, which tended to privilege the realist novel and the authors of the mid-century. In recent decades, the fin de siècle has come to be regarded as one of the most dynamic decades of the Victorian era. Viewed by writers and artists of the period as a moment of opportunity, transition, and urgency, the 1890s are pivotal for understanding the parameters of the field of Victorian studies itself. This volume makes a case for why the decade continues to be an area of perennial fascination, focusing on transnational connections, gender and sexuality, ecological concerns, technological innovations, and other current critical trends. This collection both calls attention to the diverse range of literature and art being produced during this period and foregrounds the relevance of the Victorian era's final years to issues and crises that face us today.

DUSTIN FRIEDMAN is an associate professor in the Department of Literature at American University. He is the author of *Before Queer Theory: Victorian Aestheticism and the Self* (Johns Hopkins University Press, 2019). His other writings have appeared in the journals *Victorian Literature and Culture*, *Modernism/modernity*, *Victorian Studies*, *Feminist Modernist Studies*, *Journal of Modern Literature*, *ELH*, and elsewhere.

KRISTIN MAHONEY is an associate professor in the Department of English at Michigan State University. She is the author of *Literature and the Politics of Post-Victorian Decadence* (Cambridge University Press, 2015) and *Queer Kinship after Wilde: Transnational Decadence and the Family* (Cambridge University Press, 2022). Along with Kate Hext and Alex Murray, she edits the journal *Cusp: Late 19th-/Early 20th-Century Cultures*.

NINETEENTH-CENTURY LITERATURE IN TRANSITION

General Editors:

Gail Marshall, *University of Reading*
Andrew Stauffer, *University of Virginia*
Marion Thain, *King's College London*

This series aims to move beyond existing preconceptions of the British literature of each decade of the nineteenth century ('the reforming thirties', the 'hungry forties', and the 'naughty nineties') in favour of a mode of characterization that considers each ten-year period as a dynamic field of synchronic and diachronic forces, and as sites of energetic tension between what came before and what followed. Viewing the decade as a vivid and relational concept will reinvigorate critical understanding of British literary production and consumption in a century in which unprecedented historical self-reflexivity ensured concepts of a 'century' and a 'decade' became important structures for lived experience.

As literacy increased to near-ubiquity and modern print media emerged, British literature evolved as a set of social practices and expressive modalities. The volumes in this series produce fresh characterizations enabled by attention to recent (particularly digital) methodologies, as well as by examination of nineteenth-century concerns that continue to shape our contemporary world, such as globalization, the refugee crisis, and the changing nature of war. Each volume places British literary history within transnational and global contexts, and, although rooted in the study of literary texts, works within an explicitly interdisciplinary frame of reference.

This series represents a unique and innovative approach to the nineteenth century. It acknowledges the enormity of the changes witnessed by that period, and investigates the ways in which literature colludes with and contests the century's shifting contours.

NINETEENTH-CENTURY LITERATURE IN TRANSITION: THE 1890s

EDITED BY

DUSTIN FRIEDMAN

American University

KRISTIN MAHONEY

Michigan State University

CAMBRIDGE
UNIVERSITY PRESS

CAMBRIDGE
UNIVERSITY PRESS

Shaftesbury Road, Cambridge CB2 8EA, United Kingdom

One Liberty Plaza, 20th Floor, New York, NY 10006, USA

477 Williamstown Road, Port Melbourne, VIC 3207, Australia

314–321, 3rd Floor, Plot 3, Splendor Forum, Jasola District Centre, New Delhi – 110025, India

103 Penang Road, #05-06/07, Visioncrest Commercial, Singapore 238467

Cambridge University Press is part of Cambridge University Press & Assessment, a department of the University of Cambridge.

We share the University's mission to contribute to society through the pursuit of education, learning and research at the highest international levels of excellence.

www.cambridge.org
Information on this title: www.cambridge.org/9781316513255

DOI: 10.1017/9781009063852

First published 2023

Printed in the United Kingdom by TJ Books Limited, Padstow Cornwall

A catalogue record for this publication is available from the British Library.

Library of Congress Cataloging-in-Publication Data
NAMES: Friedman, Dustin, 1982- editor. | Mahoney, Kristin Mary, editor.
TITLE: Nineteenth-century literature in transition : the 1890s / edited by Dustin Friedman, Kristin Mahoney.
DESCRIPTION: Cambridge ; New York, NY : Cambridge University Press, 2023. | Series: Nineteenth-century literature in transition | Includes bibliographical references and index.
IDENTIFIERS: LCCN 2022062168 (print) | LCCN 2022062169 (ebook) | ISBN 9781316513255 (hardback) | ISBN 9781009073349 (paperback) | ISBN 9781009063852 (epub)
SUBJECTS: LCSH: Literature, Modern–19th century–History and criticism. | Eighteen nineties.
CLASSIFICATION: LCC PN761 .N57 2023 (print) | LCC PN761 (ebook) | DDC 809/.034–dc23/eng/20230418
LC record available at https://lccn.loc.gov/2022062168
LC ebook record available at https://lccn.loc.gov/2022062169

ISBN 978-1-316-51325-5 Hardback

Contents

List of Figures   *page* vii
List of Contributors   ix
Acknowledgments   xiii

Introduction. The 1890s: Decade of a Thousand Movements   1
Dustin Friedman and Kristin Mahoney

1   Race and Empire in the 1890s   21
Zarena Aslami

2   Island Dandies, Transpacific Decadence, and the
Politics of Style   41
Lindsay Wilhelm

3   The 1890s and East Asia: Toward a Critical Cosmopolitanism   61
Stefano Evangelista

4   *Indulekha*, or The Many Lives of Realism at the Fin de Siècle   78
Sukanya Banerjee

5   Reading World Religions in the 1890s   97
Sebastian Lecourt

6   Night Lights: The 1890s Nocturne   112
Emily Harrington

7   The Green 1890s: World Ecology in Women's Poetry   132
Ana Parejo Vadillo

8   "Only Nature is a Thing Unreal": The Anthropocene 1890s   170
Elizabeth Carolyn Miller

9   Weird Ecologies and the Limits of Environmentalism   187
Dennis Denisoff

10   Queer Theories of the 1890s   208
     Simon Joyce

11   Eugenics and Degeneration in Socialist-Feminist Novels
     of the Mid-1890s   227
     Diana Maltz

12   The Conservative and Patriotic 1890s   246
     Alex Murray

13   Decadence and the Antitheatrical Prejudice   264
     Adam Alston

14   Religion and Science in the 1890s   285
     Anne Stiles

15   Little Magazines and/in Media History   305
     Lorraine Janzen Kooistra

16   Fin-de-Siècle Visuality (and Textuality) and the Digital
     Sphere   328
     Rebecca N. Mitchell

Index   351

Figures

2.1 "Dandy in His Prime," *Pacific Commercial Advertiser*,
May 5, 1903. *page* 47

2.2 Detail from Hawaii album (Library of Congress). 52

7.1 Laurence Housman, "The Goblins Selling their Wares in the
Market," illustration for Christina Rossetti's *Goblin Market*
(Macmillan & Co, 1893), 3. 136

7.2 Laurence Housman, "The Goblins Harvesting Crops,"
illustration for Christina Rossetti's *Goblin Market*
(Macmillan & Co, 1893), 8. 137

7.3 Laurence Housman, "The Goblins Handling the Harvest,"
illustration for Christina Rossetti's *Goblin Market*
(Macmillan & Co, 1893), 9. 138

7.4 Laurence Housman, "Lizzie Shielding Trees,"
illustration for Christina Rossetti's *Goblin Market* (1893)
(Macmillan & Co, 1893), 52. 141

7.5 Laurence Housman, "The Goblins Abandoning
the Land," illustration for Christina Rossetti's *Goblin Market*
(Macmillan & Co, 1893), 53. 142

7.6 William Hyde, "An Impression," *London
Impressions* (1898). 153

7.7 Book cover for Katharine Tynan's *Shamrocks* (1887). 158

7.8 Book cover for Jane Barlow's *Irish Idylls* (1898). 159

7.9 Book cover for Nora Hopper's *Ballads
in Prose* (1894). 160

9.1 Sidney Simes, untitled cover image for Arthur
Machen's *The House of Souls* (1906). 188

9.2 William T. Horton, second image from
Three Visions, Savoy 2 (April 1896): 75. 196

10.1 Title page for chapter of *The Intermediate Sex*, reflecting
new title and opening.   220

10.2 Material added in revision for *The Intermediate Sex*,
including note on Hirschfeld, running up left-hand side.   222

15.1 Constantin Guys, "A Sketch," *Yellow Book* 5
(April 1895): 261.   312

15.2 Charles Ricketts, "The Marred Face," *Dial* 2 (1892): 1.   318

15.3 Table of Contents, *Evergreen: A Northern Seasonal* 2
(Autumn 1895): 3–4.   321

15.4 Pamela Colman Smith, cover design for
Green Sheaf 4 (1903).   322

16.1 Aubrey Beardsley, "John and Salome" (1894)
from *A Portfolio of Aubrey Beardsley's Drawings
Illustrating "Salome" by Oscar Wilde* (John Lane, 1907).   330

16.2 William Morris, frontispiece from *News from
Nowhere* (Kelmscott Press, 1894).   333

16.3 Selwyn Image, cover of the *Century Guild
Hobby Horse* (1884).   335

16.4 Walter Crane, cover of *The Shepheard's Calender* (1898).   337

16.5 Walter Crane, invitation card (1899).   338

16.6 Evelyn Holden, "Binnorie, O Binnorie,"
Yellow Book 9 (April 1896): 164.   341

16.7 Georgie (Mrs. A. J.) Gaskin, "A Book Plate for
Isobel Verney Cave," *Yellow Book* 9 (April 1896): 257.   342

Contributors

ADAM ALSTON is Senior Lecturer in Modern and Contemporary Theatre at Goldsmiths, University of London. He is the author of *Beyond Immersive Theatre: Aesthetics, Politics and Productive Participation* (Palgrave Macmillan, 2016), coeditor of *Theatre in the Dark: Shadow, Gloom and Blackout in Contemporary Theatre* (Bloomsbury, 2017), and coeditor of a special issue of *Volupté: Interdisciplinary Journal of Decadence Studies* on "Decadence and Performance" (Winter 2021). He runs the Arts and Humanities Research Council (AHRC)-funded Staging Decadence project (www.stagingdecadence.com), and is currently working on a new monograph: *Staging Decadence: Theatre, Performance and the End(s) of Capitalism* (Bloomsbury, 2023).

ZARENA ASLAMI is Associate Professor in the Department of English at Michigan State University. She is the author of *The Dream Life of Citizens: Late Victorian Novels and the Fantasy of the State* (Fordham University Press, 2012). Her current book project, *Sovereign Anxieties: Victorian Afghanistan and the Literatures of Empire*, gathers an imperial archive of Victorian representations of Afghanistan and pays particular attention to how the British imagined Afghan political authority.

SUKANYA BANERJEE is Associate Professor of English at the University of California, Berkeley. She is the author of *Becoming Imperial Citizens: Indians in the Late-Victorian Empire* (Duke University Press, 2010), which was awarded the Northeast Victorian Studies Association (NVSA) Sonya Rudikoff Prize (2012). She is an editor of *New Routes in Diaspora Studies* (Indiana University Press, 2012), and her essays and articles have appeared in journals such as *Victorian Studies, Victorian Literature and Culture,* and *Nineteenth-Century Literature.* She is currently working on a book on the relation between loyalty and modernity in nineteenth-century Britain and its empire.

DENNIS DENISOFF is the McFarlin Chair of Victorian Literature and Culture at the University of Tulsa. In 2022, he was a Distinguished Visiting Research Fellow at Queen Mary – University of London. Recent publications include *Decadent Ecology in British Literature and Art, 1860–1910: Decay, Desire, and the Pagan Revival* (Cambridge University Press, 2022), *Arthur Machen: Decadent and Occult Works* (MHRA, 2018), and he has guest-edited issues on "Global Decadence" for the journal *Feminist Modernist Studies* (2021) and "Scales of Decadence" for the journal *Victorian Literature and Culture* (2021).

STEFANO EVANGELISTA is Professor of English and a Fellow of Trinity College, Oxford. He works on nineteenth-century English and comparative literature and is especially interested in aestheticism and decadence, the reception of the classics, gender, and the relationship between literary and visual cultures. He is the author of *British Aestheticism and Ancient Greece: Hellenism, Reception, Gods in Exile* (Palgrave Macmillan, 2009) and *Literary Cosmopolitanism in the English Fin de Siècle: Citizens of Nowhere* (Oxford, 2021).

EMILY HARRINGTON is Associate Professor of English at the University of Colorado, Boulder. She is the author of *Second Person Singular: Late Victorian Women Poets and the Bonds of Verse* (University of Virginia Press, 2014). Her essays on various Victorian poets have appeared in the journals *Victorian Studies, Victorian Poetry, Nineteenth-Century Literature,* and *Victorian Literature and Culture.* She is currently working on a book project entitled *Ripe Time Pending: Waiting in Victorian Poetry.*

LORRAINE JANZEN KOOISTRA is a Fellow of the Royal Society of Canada and Emerita Professor of English at Toronto Metropolitan University (TMU). A Senior Research Fellow at TMU's Centre for Digital Humanities, her research interests include Victorian illustration studies, little magazines, digital humanities, and digital editing.

SIMON JOYCE is the Sara and Jess Cloud Professor of English at William and Mary (Virginia, USA). He is the author of *Capital Offenses: The Geography of Class and Crime in Victorian London* (University of Virginia Press, 2003), *The Victorians in the Rearview Mirror* (Ohio University Press, 2007), *Modernism and Naturalism in British and Irish Fiction, 1880–1930* (Cambridge University Press, 2014), and, most recently, *LGBT Victorians: Sexuality and Gender in the Nineteenth-Century Archives* (Oxford University Press, 2022).

SEBASTIAN LECOURT is an associate professor in the Department of English at the University of Houston. His research focuses on Victorian literature and questions of secularization, colonialism, and comparativism. He is the author of *Cultivating Belief: Victorian Anthropology, Liberal Aesthetics, and the Secular Imagination* (Oxford University Press, 2018), and his essays have appeared in the journals *PMLA, Representations, Victorian Studies, ELH*, and *Victorian Literature and Culture*. He is currently working on a book entitled *The Genres of Comparative Religion, 1783–1927*.

DIANA MALTZ is Professor of English at Southern Oregon University. She is the author of *British Aestheticism and the Urban Working Classes, 1870–1900: Beauty for the People* (Palgrave Macmillan, 2006) and the editor of *Critical Essays on Arthur Morrison and the East End* (Routledge, 2022). She has also produced critical editions of Arthur Morrison's *A Child of the Jago* (Broadview, 2013) and W. Somerset Maugham's *Liza of Lambeth* (Broadview, 2022). She is presently completing a monograph on socialist-feminist writers associated with the utopian Fellowship of the New Life. She is Past President of the Victorian Interdisciplinary Studies Association of the Western United States.

ELIZABETH CAROLYN MILLER is Professor of English and Environmental Humanities at the University of California, Davis, and the author of *Extraction Ecologies and the Literature of the Long Exhaustion* (Princeton, 2021), which was recently awarded Honorable Mention for the Association for the Study of Literature and Environment book prize. Her previous books are *Slow Print: Literary Radicalism and Late Victorian Print Culture* (Stanford, 2013), which was named Best Book of the Year by the North American Victorian Studies Association and received Honorable Mention for the Modernist Studies Association book prize, and *Framed: The New Woman Criminal in British Culture at the Fin de Siècle* (Michigan, 2008).

REBECCA N. MITCHELL is Professor of Victorian Literature and Culture at the University of Birmingham and has published widely on Oscar Wilde, Victorian fashion, print culture, realism, and George Meredith. Her books include *Victorian Lessons in Empathy and Difference* (Ohio State University Press, 2011), *Fashioning the Victorians* (Bloomsbury, 2018), and, with Joseph Bristow, *Oscar Wilde's Chatterton: Literary History, Romanticism, and the Art of Forgery* (Yale University Press, 2015).

ALEX MURRAY is Reader in Modern Literature at Queen's University Belfast. His fourth monograph, *Decadent Conservatism: Aesthetics, Politics, and the Past*, will be published by Oxford University Press in 2023. He is currently coediting *The Oxford Handbook of Oscar Wilde* and is a founding editor of the journal *Cusp: Late 19th-/Early 20th-Century Cultures*, published by Johns Hopkins University Press.

ANNE STILES is Professor of English and Coordinator of Medical Humanities at Saint Louis University. She is the author of *Children's Literature and the Rise of "Mind Cure": Positive Thinking and Pseudo-Science at the* Fin de Siècle (Cambridge University Press, 2020) and *Popular Fiction and Brain Science in the Late Nineteenth Century* (Cambridge University Press, 2012). She has held long-term grants from the Institute for Research in the Humanities at the University of Wisconsin, Madison (AY 2016–20), the Huntington Library (AY 2009–10), and the American Academy of Arts and Sciences (AY 2006–07).

ANA PAREJO VADILLO is Assistant Dean at the School of Arts, Birkbeck, University of London. She is the General Editor of the journal *19: Interdisciplinary Studies in the Nineteenth Century*. She has published widely on decadence, cosmopolitanism, poetry, and the arts. Her books include *Women Poets and Urban Aestheticism: Passengers of Modernity* (Palgrave Macmillan, 2005), *Michael Field, The Poet: Published and Unpublished Materials* (Broadview Press, 2009) and *Victorian Literature* (Palgrave Macmillan, 2011). Her most recent book is *Michael Field, Decadent Moderns* (Ohio University Press, 2019). She is currently writing a monograph entitled *Poetry in Polygamy* for Oxford University Press. She is also preparing a collection of essays on Michael Field's poetic dramas.

LINDSAY WILHELM is an Assistant Professor in the Department of English at Oklahoma State University. Her research interests include late nineteenth-century literature and science, aestheticism and decadence, and the global nineteenth century. She has published articles on these and related topics in the journals *Victorian Studies, Victorian Literature and Culture*, and *Nineteenth-Century Literature*, and she is currently working on a book project on the intersections of British aestheticism and post-Darwinian science.

Acknowledgments

The editors would like to thank all the contributors for their thoughtful and innovative work. Thank you to Marion Thain and Diana Maltz for their suggestions regarding our introduction. Marion Thain, Gail Marshall, and Andrew Stauffer have been wonderful to work with as series editors, providing helpful guidance concerning the vision for the series as well as useful feedback on the contents of this collection. Bethany Thomas and George Paul Laver at Cambridge University Press have provided tremendous support and assistance. Sarah Potts at Michigan State University performed crucial copyediting work during the final stages of this project.

Introduction
The 1890s: Decade of a Thousand Movements
Dustin Friedman and Kristin Mahoney

The 1890s were not very far in the rearview mirror when Holbrook Jackson published *The Eighteen-Nineties: A Review of Art and Ideas at the Close of the Nineteenth Century* (1913), the first of many early twentieth-century attempts to capture the spirit of the nineteenth century's final decade. Jackson's work is somewhat singular, however, in its effort to take in the enormous range of innovations occurring within literature and the arts at the fin de siècle. Later works, such as Bernard Muddiman's *The Men of the Nineties* (1920), Osbert Burdett's *The Beardsley Period* (1925), and Richard Le Gallienne's *The Romantic '90s* (1926), tend to collapse decadence and the fin de siècle, while Jackson endeavors to engage the divergent and contradictory movements that, for him, were all similarly motivated by "the restless spirit of the time," its sense of "experiment and adventure."[1] Jackson's volume might be dedicated to Max Beerbohm and include a frontispiece of Aubrey Beardsley and a lengthy chapter on Oscar Wilde, but it also turns to Rudyard Kipling, George Bernard Shaw, the Celtic Renaissance, H. G. Wells, and the revival of the art of printing to make the case that this was a "distinctive epoch" (12). Beardsley was "but an incident of the Eighteen Nineties," "but one expression of *fin de siècle* daring, of a bizarre and often exotic courage, prevalent at the time and connected but indirectly, and often negatively, with some of the most vital movements of a decade which was singularly rich in ideas, personal genius, and social will" (17). The period was, Jackson acknowledges, a decadent moment, but it was also many other things, a period "electric with new ideas," operating in myriad forms to facilitate change, the "decade of a thousand 'movements'" (25, 34).

The mythmaking surrounding a period so singular, according to Jackson, could begin sooner than its end and flower before it was even a distant memory. In the preface to the 1927 edition of *The Eighteen-Nineties*, Jackson states that in the years since first publishing this volume, "the Eighteen Nineties has become a legend."[2] The fact that this is possible, he asserts, is because the era was distinct, an "extraordinarily self-contained" period of ten years, making it "possible to interpret . . . in what may be called terms of personality" (12). He has not singled out this period for review. "That decade had," he insists, "singled itself out."[3] In characterizing the art and literature of the period, Jackson pays particular attention to the extent to which the artists and authors of the 1890s were self-aware about their positioning within a unique and vital moment, the ending of one century, the transition into another. "We are actually," he argues, "made more conscious of our standing towards time by the approaching demise of a century" (18). It was not left to historians to establish the defining characteristics of this decade. This process was well underway as the era began. The writers of the 1890s saw themselves in time, of a time, as evidenced by the prevalence of the term "fin de siècle," which according to Jackson indicates "the liveliness of the people of the Nineties to their hour and its characteristics" (21). Side by side with this term marched the moniker "new," operating as a prefix that could move in every direction during a period "so conscious of its own novelty," modifying the New Woman, the New Fiction, the New Hedonism, the New Drama (24). This historical and temporal self-consciousness was accompanied by a revolutionary spirit, "demands for culture and social redemption," "seeking the immediate regeneration of society by the abolition of such social evils as poverty and overwork, and the meanness, ugliness, ill-health and commercial rapacity which characterized so much of modern life" (25–26). This was a decade that experienced itself as a decade, as a distinct moment in time with a distinct ethos, when one way of approaching existence would dissipate so another might begin.

Along with this sensitivity to time, there was something unique also, Jackson and other early writers on the 1890s insist, about the manner in which the authors of the 1890s conceptualized space. A receptivity to national influences outside of Britain is often cited as a marked characteristic of the period. Bernard Muddiman argues that "it is to France if anywhere we can trace the causes of this new attitude" that shaped the 1890s, asserting that it was in particular "a genital restiveness which came over from France" that "started the sex equation" in the literature of the 1890s.[4] Jackson also notes the "profound effect" of French fiction writers on the "imaginations" of the period as well as the influence of German wood-engravers on the English artist Walter Crane (271). Even the enthusiasm for Kipling, that most jingoistic of fin-de-siècle fiction writers, had to do, according to Jackson, with the manner in which he facilitated contact with other places, enabling British readers to experience "the scent and heat, the colour and passion of the East in all its splendours and seductiveness" (280). Osbert Burdett narrowly framed the scene of the 1890s as "set in London," but admitted "its tone was . . . cosmopolitan."[5] And there was something self-contained, too, about this transnational openness and curiosity, brought to a close by the jingoism of the Boer War (1899–1902). W. G. Blaikie-Murdoch noted in his *The Renaissance of the Nineties* (1911) that the war submerged the nation in "patriotic anxiety and ardour," eliminating the prior enthusiasm for aesthetic cultures both domestic and international that marked the period, for "in the main imperialism is the enemy of art."[6] Muddiman notes similarly that French art continued to stimulate the English imagination "until the Boer War, when the imperialism of writers like Kipling became the chief interest" (4). As the century drew to a close, Jackson argues, "pride of race" reached an "unseemly" pitch, and "the nation forgot arts and letters" in favor of "an unseeing pride" and "a strangely inorganic patriotism" (63–64). The fluid national boundaries that marked the 1890s, these writers insist, became again consolidated and guarded as the century came to a close.

There is much we would like to bring forward into this collection from Jackson's *The Eighteen Nineties* and these other early volumes. *Nineteenth-Century Literature in Transition: The 1890s* could be understood as the continuation of the work that Jackson initiated. Working within a series meant to revise conventional visions of the individual decades of the nineteenth century, we hope, like Jackson, to enrich and complement received insights about "the Naughty Nineties," "the Yellow Nineties," or "the Beardsley Period," recognizing the divergent strains of cultural production that operated alongside Wilde and Beardsley. We are interested, of course, in the French-inflected "genital restiveness" that inaugurated this period of sexual anarchy, but we have endeavored to gather together a set of approaches that see beyond that horizon. This collection strives to fulfill the mission of the broader Nineteenth-Century Literature in Transition series and to establish what was particular about one decade in comparison with the others to which this broader series is devoted. In this light, we find compelling Jackson's assertions about historical self-consciousness and temporal awareness on the part of the denizens of the 1890s. If the authors and artists of the 1890s were already characterizing themselves as "fin-de-siècle" during the fin de siècle, then they have already begun to do some of our work for us, to tease out the threads that truly make this a discrete historical period, worthy of consideration as a moment unto itself. And if, as Jackson and his fellow critics of the period insist, this was a period of heightened transnational receptivity, that makes it a particularly fertile ground for doing the kind of "undisciplining" work that seems so necessary at this moment, work that might facilitate a renewed vision of the nineteenth century, one that moves away from nationally siloed treatments of Victorian literature and attends to the cross-currents that made this period so cosmopolitan in tone.

Rethinking the 1890s

Throughout the twentieth century, interest in the 1890s as a decade persisted. The tradition inaugurated by Jackson, Muddiman, and Burdett, which insisted upon the peculiarity and significance of the 1890s, continued into midcentury, facilitated by the publication of anthologies devoted to the decade, such as *The Eighteen-Nineties* (1948) edited by Martin Secker; *Aesthetes and Decadents of the 1890s* (1966) edited by Karl Beckson; *Short Stories of the 'Nineties* (1968) edited by Derek Stanford; and *Poetry of the Nineties* (1970) edited by R. K. R. Thornton. The period has traditionally been thought of as an era of significant cultural and artistic transition between the confident moralism of the high Victorians and the disillusioned pessimism of twentieth-century modernism and thus deserving of critical attention.[7] The establishment of the Eighteen Nineties Society in 1972 along with works such as John Stokes's *In the Nineties* (1989), Margaret Stetz and Mark Samuels Lasner's *England in the 1890s: Literary Publishing at the Bodley Head* (1990), and *The Fin-de-Siècle Poem: English Literary Culture and the 1890s* (2005) edited by Joseph Bristow sustained scholarly interest in the era as a period apart, an era of rapid aesthetic change during the final decades of the twentieth century into the present moment.

We hope the work in this collection will extend this tradition by pointing toward new possibilities for conceptualizing the 1890s as a distinct historical period. There are, of course, several excellent overviews of fin-de-siècle literature and culture, such as *Fin de Siècle/Fin du Globe: Fears and Fantasies of the Late Nineteenth Century* (1992) edited by John Stokes, *Cultural Politics at the Fin de Siècle* (1995) edited by Sally Ledger and Scott McCracken, and *The Cambridge Companion to the Fin de Siècle* (2007) edited by Gail Marshall. These works can help orient students and scholars new to the field, introducing them to major figures, movements, and historical events. However, the aims of this collection, inflected by the particular objectives of the Nineteenth-Century Literature in Transition series, are different. Rather than stressing coverage or genealogies, we have asked our authors to craft innovative scholarly arguments that also exemplify recent critical trends in the field and have encouraged them to reflect on how we might practice literary history moving forward. Accordingly, the chapters brought together here both build upon the insights of previous scholars and introduce into these longstanding conversations new texts, contexts, methodologies, and media. We have encouraged contributors to think critically about the stories we have tended to tell about the period and to incorporate literary forms and movements, such as weird fiction, the nocturne, colonial realism, and socialist novels, that have received less notice in the past. Consequently, some of the more familiar names traditionally associated with the 1890s, such as Thomas Hardy, Bram Stoker, George Bernard Shaw, H. G. Wells, Henry James, and Rudyard Kipling, appear less frequently in these chapters than one might expect. Indeed, some of the figures who do play a central role in these pages – Emma Frances Brooke, O. Chandumenon, and Moncure Conway, to name a few – are likely obscure even to specialists. This has not been done solely to introduce readers to lesser-known and lesser-studied authors of the era, but because new methodologies necessarily summon our attention to new texts and issues. For example, while one might expect to find separate chapters on decadence and theater in a collection on the 1890s, Adam Alston, in Chapter 13, combines the two, arguing that to understand the 1890s properly we must also understand certain understudied theatrical works as central to the decadent project and vice versa, an insight that becomes readily apparent once we move beyond certain antitheatrical prejudices that still dominate literary studies.

The results of this and the other investigations undertaken in this collection have, we believe, been twofold. They enhance our understanding of the nineteenth century's closing years in their full complexity, dynamism, and intellectual ferment; they also make a case, implicitly or explicitly, for the relevance of perspectives from the 1890s regarding issues that still preoccupy us today. What can the alluring artificiality of hothouses and hothouse flowers famously associated with fin-de-siècle decadence tell us about the greenhouse gas effect and humanity's role in climate change, as Elizabeth Carolyn Miller asks in Chapter 8? How, Zarena Aslami queries in Chapter 1, do recent interrogations of the Enlightenment category of "the human" within Black studies force us to confront the pervasiveness of anti-Blackness in 1890s culture and the centrality of racialization within multiple turn-of-the-century discourses? What happens to the era-of-transition narrative when recent advances in digital technology prompt us to see the decade's "little magazines" as a pivotal moment in media history in and of itself rather than an anticipation of modernist innovation, as Lorraine Janzen Kooistra argues in Chapter 15? These are just a few examples of how our authors bring rigorous historical research to bear on pressing presentist concerns with the goal of enhancing both our comprehension of the 1890s and our current moment.

Ultimately, we believe these chapters offer both helpful distillations of current critical trends in fin-de-siècle studies and innovative critical arguments. Rather than providing a synoptic overview of or handbook to the period, they collectively offer a snapshot of issues currently igniting scholarly debate, as well as individually modeling new paths of inquiry that can be followed by others. Our hope is that this volume will be just as useful and informative to those who are already familiar with the field as it is to relative newcomers, insofar as it makes a case for why the 1890s continue to be an area of perennial interest and relevance, even while our comprehension of the decade is changing in response to our own era's shifting cultural and political concerns. The attraction this period holds has much to do with the way authors and artists of the period perceived their historical moment as vexed and apocalyptic – an end as well as a beginning leading into a more keenly modern new world. We believe that the sense of urgency, rapidity, transition, and crisis we associate with the fin de siècle speaks directly to how many of us perceive our dizzying and disorienting present.

The "Naughty Nineties"?: New Perspectives on Gender and Sexuality

The final decade of the nineteenth century has long had a reputation for being the "Naughty Nineties" (a phrase in use since the early twentieth century), a time when bourgeois gender norms and sexual mores came under attack by what decadent writer Vernon Lee called a "queer comradeship of outlawed thought."[8] No two figures have been more emblematic of this "sexual anarchy," to borrow a phrase from Elaine Showalter's landmark study of the era, than the cigarette-smoking, bicycle-riding, sexually liberated New Woman and the effete, aesthetic, and erotically perverse male decadent, epitomized by Oscar Wilde.[9] The New Woman and the decadent formed something of a matched set in the decade's popular imagination, serving as harbingers of either an emancipated or degenerate future, depending on one's perspective.[10] These figures have continued to dominate critical accounts of the Victorian fin de siècle, which became more central to the field of Victorian studies with the advent of feminist and, later, queer criticism in the twentieth century's closing decades. The sexual radicalism commonly associated with the New Woman and the decadent played a prominent role in the establishment and development of these schools of thought, often serving as historical inspirations for their own political goals and commitments. One need only look at groundbreaking work done by scholars such as Joseph Bristow, Richard Dellamora, Ellis Hanson, and Richard Kaye on aestheticist and decadent challenges to normative sexualities; Kathy Alexis Psomiades, Talia Schaffer, and Jill Ehnenn on women's decadent writing; and the revolutionary work on New Woman fiction by Ann Ardis, Ann Heilmann, Sally Ledger, Lyn Pykett, and Margaret Stetz to see how the pressing concerns of the present day led to new, fuller understandings of the cultural significance of the 1890s.[11]

Although it is incontrovertible that the New Woman and the decadent were cultural lightning rods throughout the 1890s, several of our authors suggest that the preeminent role they have occupied in cultural memory has distorted our perception of an era that was only ever partially "naughty" at best. In Chapter 12, Alex Murray highlights the political complexities of the fin de siècle, the subtleties of which are lost if one applies an overly simplistic binary opposition between sexual radicals and their enemies. He shows that, despite its reputation, the 1890s were just as conservative and patriotic as they were subversive and cosmopolitan, and that many of the authors who have been celebrated for their aesthetic experimentalism and unconventional personal lives were also reactionaries, nationalists, and imperialists. Murray reminds us that gender and sexual dissidence need not necessarily align with other progressive political commitments – a useful lesson for our own era, when the most famous transgender celebrity in the United States is a conservative Republican, and a small but vocal faction of so-called gender critical lesbian, gay, and bisexual activists in the UK are currently campaigning against transgender rights.

In Chapter 10, Simon Joyce advises us to look beyond our present-day version of queer politics as a tenuous coalition between two groups that are separate yet somehow related: those who define their identity primarily by their non-normative sexual orientation (i.e., lesbians, gays, bisexuals) and those who primarily define themselves by their non-normative gendered embodiment (i.e., transgender, nonbinary, and genderqueer people). For Joyce, thinking outside this spurious binary can enhance our comprehension of sexual and gender identity in the 1890s. While in our current moment, it is an indication of one's sophistication to insist on the separability of sexual orientation and gender identity, a perspective encapsulated by the well-worn explanatory phrase, "sexuality is who you go to bed with, gender identity is who you go to bed as," Joyce proposes that this separation might have actually been a historical misstep. He looks back to the writings of Edward Carpenter, a socialist, feminist, and early gay rights activist who was influenced by both New Woman authors and German sexologists to conceive of the complex interrelations of gender transitivity and sexual identity. For Joyce, this model of sexual selfhood might be more politically efficacious and personally empowering than the one we have now.

Perhaps Joyce's boldest claim, at least in terms of dominant assumptions of literary and cultural history, is that we cannot learn terribly much about the new models of gender and sexual identity arising in the 1890s by looking to Oscar Wilde: his classical, pederastic model of same-sex relations was already considered by many to be regressively hierarchical. The notion that Wilde might not be central to the decade, especially when it comes to sexuality and gender, goes against the scholarly trend to view him as the very embodiment of the spirit of the age.[12] His outsized personality, the wit and audacity of his writings, as well as the media spectacle of the trials and his subsequent vindication as an early martyr for gay rights, have altogether made him not only a synecdoche for the decade when he rose to fame and fell into infamy, but one of the most famous and widely read authors in the English language. His presence as one of the biggest celebrities of the 1890s undoubtedly helped make the era a hotbed for scholarly investigations into alternative sexualities and genders. Yet the dominance of the Wilde *mythos* – a cultural role the author himself helped to create in his own writings – has tended to crowd out of our cultural memory the period's numerous other writers on sexuality and gender. Consequently, although discussions of Wilde appear frequently in this collection, our authors tend to treat him as part of a larger constellation of thinkers, rather than as somehow exemplary or sui generis.

In this context, the era's most characteristic author may not be Wilde but rather Carpenter. Although today he is not especially well known outside of specialist circles and was even something of a niche figure during the 1890s, perhaps no other author better exemplifies our vision of a "decade of a thousand movements." During the late nineteenth and early twentieth centuries he was an internationally known thinker who combined a Walt Whitman-inspired mysticism with a radical political outlook. In contrast to Wilde's presentation of himself as a solitary genius, Carpenter understood himself to be but a node in a network of progressive activists that included utopian socialists, New Woman feminists, vegetarians and anti-vivisectionists, anti-imperialists, and campaigners for the rights of sexual minorities. In her contribution to this volume (Chapter 11), Diana Maltz discusses the Carpenter-inspired socialist New Woman novelists – authors who, unlike better known New Woman novelists like Sarah Grand, George Egerton, and Mona Caird, were just as committed to socialism as they were to feminism. While critics have long noted the ideological tensions that existed between New Woman and male decadent authors, Maltz builds upon this insight to demonstrate how socialist feminists were inspired by Carpenter's utopian pastoralism to embrace ideas of degeneration and eugenics against a male decadence which they thought to be the very embodiment of middle- and upper-class convention, a hindrance to social and evolutionary advancement. Both Maltz's and Joyce's chapters support Murray's claim that it is impossible to reduce the politics of the 1890s to a progressive/reactionary binary, just as it is misleading to let one major figure stand in for the entire ecosystem of dissident gender and sexual thought at the fin de siècle.

Cosmopolitanism/Patriotic Anxiety: Transnational Contact at the Fin de Siècle

Decadence has to a certain extent managed to define our vision of transnational contact and cosmopolitanism in the 1890s as well. This is in part because, as Stefano Evangelista notes, "decadence has always been regarded as a foreign import," a cultural disease contracted from France, making the very existence of the movement within England a testament to the nation's permeable borders.[13] This has also to do with the essential nature of the decadent sensibility, the fact that as an aesthetic and an approach to living, decadence welcomed contact with alterity. Guided by the Paterian exhortation to be forever courting new impressions, decadent writers and artists opened themselves up to transnational influence in a manner that hovered somewhere between an ethics of curiosity, welcoming contact with strangers, and racial fetishism, subjecting the world outside of England to an appetitive and orientalist gaze. For this reason, some of the strongest scholarship on transcultural contact at the fin de siècle has focused on the decade's aestheticism and decadence. Stephen Arata's *Fictions of Loss at the Victorian Fin de Siècle: Identity and Empire* (1996) discusses how much the concepts of decadence and imperialism were intertwined in the late Victorian imagination.[14] Matthew Potolsky has highlighted the manner in which networks of taste facilitated transnational contact within the "decadent republic of letters," inspiring decadent writers to generate alternative canons that fostered a cosmopolitan sensibility.[15] In a similar vein, Leela Gandhi's *Affective Communities* describes how the aestheticist ethos underwrote bonds between British and colonial subjects at the end of the century, giving close consideration to how the Indian writer Manmohan Ghose drew from his contact with Wilde's circle "a radical reading of 'aestheticism' as a profound and effective rehearsal of anti-imperial 'autonomy.'"[16]

Work like Gandhi's, however, also shows us the rich array of fin-de-siècle radical thinking that circulated around the question of cross-cultural contact. Such thinking extended beyond the borders of the Decadent Movement, within coteries of vegetarians, spiritualists, and sexologists. And, as Sebastian Lecourt's contribution to this volume (Chapter 5) on popular publications on world religions highlights, these conversations were not confined to radical circles but also took place on a mass-market level. The broader attentiveness across British culture to the question of international relationality is an instance of what Ross Forman has described as the consolidation of "the model of acquisitive empire" during this period, as Britain came increasingly to conceptualize itself as "able to select, absorb, domesticate, and recycle the commodities, peoples, languages and methods of other cultures."[17] If this was a heyday for forms of anticolonial theory and activism, it was also, as Tanya Agathocleous and Jason Rudy have recently argued, the moment when "the empire was at its largest, most powerful, and most correspondingly bombastic" and the expansion of Anglophone print culture accelerated communication about the realities of empire, allowing "English language newspapers, books, periodicals, pamphlets, Bibles and other printed matter to circulate within colonies, between colonies, and between colony and metropole."[18] Global contact was increasingly significant and increasingly rapid, making it crucial for modern critics to address transnational exchanges in the 1890s, as well as rendering the 1890s particularly relevant to the longer history of globalization in our present moment.

With the objectives of the Nineteenth-Century Literature in Transition series in mind, particularly the call to examine the nineteenth-century concepts and concerns that shape our contemporary world, we have placed a great deal of emphasis on questions of race, empire, and global circulation. In envisioning futures for the field of nineteenth-century studies, we wish to put the most pressure on the national boundaries that have for so long curtailed work in the field. As Caroline Levine has argued, despite the influence of work in postcolonial, transatlantic, and world literary studies,

Victorian studies continues to reproduce the logic of nation and retains a focus on British authors.[19] The work in this volume heeds Levine's appeal to begin thinking in terms of networks rather than nation in order to attend to transnational conversation during the nineteenth century. We also conceptualized the collection in conversation with Ronjaunee Chatterjee, Amy Wong, and Alicia Christoff's recent call to "undiscipline Victorian studies" and "[unmake] the nostalgia that often undergirds the field's self-definition ... by exploding its limited geographic imaginary."[20] Illuminating the shortcomings of staging our approach to the period in terms of Britishness and Eurocentrism are contributions to this volume on India, China, Japan, and Hawai'i in the 1890s; on fin-de-siècle conceptions of race, empire, and cosmopolitanism; and on comparative religion.

We wanted to foreground how our sense of what the field might be alters when we think about this as a decade that was particularly open in terms of the circulation of culture, a moment when authors across the globe were more in conversation with one another than they had been at any other point in the century. Emily Harrington models this in Chapter 6 in her approach to the transnational circulation of the genre of the nocturne, conveying how the nocturne uniquely expresses preoccupations of the 1890s, such as the relationship between the artificial and the natural. She also emphasizes how our comprehension of these preoccupations is enhanced by engaging with the manner in which this genre was altered and revised when practiced by the Indigenous Canadian poet E. Pauline Johnson and by Yone Noguchi, a Japanese poet writing in the US. Lindsay Wilhelm's contribution (Chapter 2) on dandyism in Hawai'i illustrates how Anglo-American visions of the dandy traveled across the Pacific during a period of accelerated colonization. Wilhelm also, however, recasts conventional models of influence and exchange by describing how Indigenous conceptions of dandyism and decadence facilitated anticolonial resistance in the Pacific. In this, her work might be a model for transnational criticism that does not privilege the metropole as an aesthetic source or origin. Multiple contributions to the collection similarly emphasize how our sense of literary history might be enriched and complicated if we are not always centering the UK. Sukanya Banerjee's contribution (Chapter 4) on Indian author O. Chandumenon's novel *Indulekha* (1889–90), for example, shows us that realism, to some extent thought to be past its prime in the UK, was performing different kinds of work for colonial writers at the fin de siècle, permitting them to position cultural practices such as matriliny as part of a modern present in India. Banerjee's work helps us to see the political malleability of literary forms and rethink our conventional vision of these forms' historical standing. It is not only the content of these chapters that is so welcome and necessary but their methodologies and orientations, which might operate as models for future approaches to a newly enlarged vision of the late nineteenth century.

The contributions to the volume also model nuanced approaches to the period's accelerated rate of transcultural contact that at once develop our sense of the politics of cosmopolitanism and work against conventional visions of the 1890s as a moment of radicalism and avant-gardism. In discussing mainstream texts on world religions at the fin de siècle, Sebastian Lecourt emphasizes the manner in which popular comparative religious thought anticipated middlebrow religious ecumenicalism in the twentieth century. Neither wholly invested in the aggressive reinscription of imperial hierarchy nor in the wholesale toppling of that hierarchy, these texts enabled forms of liberal tolerance and syncretism that remain part of today's cultural sensibilities. Stefano Evangelista's contribution in Chapter 3 on literary treatments of East Asia in the 1890s identifies the political complexity of these works, their simultaneous enactment of orientalism and cosmopolitanism, their deployment of essentialist attitudes and national stereotypes, their highly critical and self-aware thinking that redirected geopolitical and cultural relations while at the same time deploying essentialist attitudes and national stereotypes. The sensibility of chapters like these, their restraint and refusal to simply affirm or condemn the politics of nineteenth-century literary and cultural practices, attending to multivalence and contradiction, manifests the potential for fresh characterizations of the cultural politics of the 1890s.

If this was a period cosmopolitan in tone, it was, of course, at the same time a particularly jingoistic and anxious period, a moment when an empire at the height of its expansiveness and acquisitiveness was experiencing tensions and generating aggressive responses to those tensions. Zarena Aslami's chapter on race and empire in the 1890s focuses on the work that the category of race performed in service of the empire during this period as well as the duress that the category of the human endured, as those who had been excluded from it demanded recognition. As Aslami argues, the 1890s can be seen as hinge years between two different but related biological notions of the human, as impressible (and thus open to "civilizing" influence) or as essential (and thus forever determined by genetic inheritance), that emerged in response to the shifting realties of imperialism during the late nineteenth century. These variable visions of the human at first held out the possibility of humanness to Asian natives in the British empire and then withheld that promise in ways that in turn engendered fears about refusal to assimilate and modes of anticolonial resistance. Aslami's argument, which builds upon historical interrogations of the category of "the human" in Black studies, operates here as a model of the kind of work we hope to see more of moving forward, work that places nineteenth-century British studies in contact with other fields to create new insights into the history of empire.

The Interdisciplinary 1890s: Religion, Theater, Ecocriticism

These explorations of intersections between nineteenth-century literary studies and other fields and disciplines also speak to this volume's investment in interdisciplinary approaches to the 1890s. While in our current moment we find stark institutional divides in the university between academic subjects, such schisms were scarce when many of these academic disciplines were in the early stages of formation during the fin de siècle. Accordingly, in Chapter 14, Anne Stiles asks us to look beyond clichés about Darwin and the Victorian "crisis of faith" narrative, instead inviting us to think of science and religion as complementary, rather than competing, discourses in the era's literary writing. She makes the bold claim that widespread belief in pseudoscience and the occult in the 1890s complemented, rather than opposed, more traditional forms of religious devotion, and that this aspect of the decade has often been overlooked. She supports this claim by revealing unexpected similarities between the writings of Wilde and those of bestselling popular novelist Marie Corelli. Sebastian Lecourt also emphasizes the religiosity of the 1890s, especially the massive popularity of mainstream texts on comparative religion – a realm often assumed to be beyond the purview of literary studies. He challenges the longstanding assumption that the era's interest in non-Western belief systems was necessarily an avant-garde or subversive move, instead arguing that there existed a popular ecumenicalism that viewed the world's religions as inspirations for secularized versions of self-development. This insight enables us to critique our own era's attempts at universalist spiritual inclusivity, in addition to enhancing our understanding of the period. And although the study of drama has long been within the purview of English departments, Adam Alston brings a distinctly Theater and Performance studies perspective to the analysis of the understudied genre of decadent drama, showing how enduring biases against theatricality within literary studies have prevented us from fully seeing the depth, breadth, and influence of the theater on the Decadent Movement, as well as its transnational reach.

Emily Harrington even claims that the interdisciplinary approach inherent to ecocritical studies, although new to today's literary scholars, was already part of the characteristically fin-de-siècle lyric genre of the nocturne. These poems about the night address relationships between humanity and the natural world, art and the artificial, and in doing so, suggest alternatives to the epoch we now refer to as the Anthropocene. According to her, nocturnes embodied both the era's aestheticism and the new material reality of street-lamps illuminating the city with the power of coal gas, an innovation that thoroughly changed the urban experience of night. This made the nocturne the genre par excellence for depicting interactions between humanity and the environment. In Chapter 7, Ana Parejo Vadillo similarly asks us to return to a genre we think we know – nature poetry by women – and reassess our assumptions about the pastoral, the urban, and the planetary. While such works have often been discussed primarily in terms of the author's femininity, Parejo Vadillo demonstrates how women poets took what we might today call an "intersectional" approach to climate change, addressing the complex entanglements of gender, colonialism, and transnational capitalism.

The notion that fin-de-siècle writing is notably attuned to the conceptual difficulties of the Anthropocene, especially the cognitive challenges of comprehending both the vastness and the intimacy of humanmade climate change, has been articulated in Benjamin Morgan's influential work on "scale" in decadent writing, which has in turn inspired two of our contributors.[21] In Chapters 8 and 9, Elizabeth Carolyn Miller and Dennis Denisoff invite us to view decadent writing not simply as rejecting nature and the natural, as has often been claimed, but rather as an attempt to grapple with the consequences and limitations of human interventions into the environment. Miller looks to Wilde's *Picture of Dorian Gray* (1890, 1891) and "The Decay of Lying" (1891) to be not only queer texts, but also instances of literary microscaling, where magnitude is made comprehensible through miniaturization. These writings helped Victorians make sense of the post-Darwinian vision of nature as indeterminate and non-teleological, shaped by human activity yet beyond human control. For Miller, this was part and parcel of the era's consciousness of itself as an endpoint, a "fin du globe" as well as a "fin de siècle" (to quote Lady Narborough from Wilde's novel) and an expression of the era's growing awareness of humankind's apocalyptic impact on the natural world.[22]

As Denisoff further demonstrates, the human imagination's struggle to grasp the massive changes wrought by environmental destruction was not only explored in decadent writing, but also in works that would later be classified as "weird fiction." Famously defined by H. P. Lovecraft as the "suspension or defeat of those fixed laws of Nature which are our only safeguard against the assaults of chaos and the dæmons of unplumbed space," weird fictions by Arthur Machen and Vernon Lee, as well as visual artworks by Sidney Simes and William T. Horton, took a dark, pessimistic, and ambiguous view of humanity's ability to intervene in destructive processes we ourselves began.[23] Unlike the period's early stirrings of environmentalism, which focused on responsible stewardship of the land for human use, weird fictions offer no easy solutions. Instead, they encourage feelings of awe and deference to the environment and ask us to live with uncertainty, rather than persisting in our futile attempts to assert control over the natural world.

Clarifying the 1890s: Digital Methodologies and Fin-de-Siècle Culture

Holbrook Jackson argued that "no other decade in English history has produced so many distinctive and ambitious publications" as the 1890s, including in his list of notable periodicals the *Yellow Book*, the *Savoy*, the *Parade*, the *Pageant*, the *Evergreen*, the *Chameleon*, the *Rose Leaf*, the *Quarto*, and the *Dome* (41). These journals represent, according to Jackson, "the unique qualities in the literature and art of the decade; they were bone of its bone and flesh of its flesh" (41). Because periodical culture was so central to the avant-gardism of this period, of its bone and flesh, fin-de-siècle studies has benefited enormously from recent work in the digital humanities that has not only inspired the digitization of many of these publications, but also produced scholarship that theorizes how to curate, engage, and teach with digital archives. Key publications such as the *Dome* and *Petit Journal des Refusées* have been made available by the Modernist Journals Project, illuminating "how essential magazines were to the rise and maturation of modernism."[24] *Yellow Nineties 2.0* (previously *The Yellow Nineties Online*) hosts searchable digital editions of eight little magazines of the fin de siècle, such as the *Yellow Book*, the *Savoy*, the *Dial*, and the *Pagan Review*, accompanied by critical introductions, original promotional materials, reviews, biographies of key contributors, and a *Database of Ornament*, which enables analysis of the textual ornaments by which these publications announced their personalities. As Frederick D. King argues, the site, with its wealth of digitized materials along with its reflections on digital pedagogy and the processes of coding, provides a "space for self-reflexive conversation about the printed past and the digital future of media circulation."[25] This work has enlarged our sense of cultural production in the 1890s as well as the potential impacts of large-scale digitization projects on the practice of literary history.

One of the largest and most visible projects currently transforming studies of fin-de-siècle culture is the digitization, transcription, and encoding of the thirty volumes of diaries kept by "Michael Field" (Katharine Bradley and Edith Cooper), two of the most significant poets of the fin de siècle. Marion Thain initiated this work as part of the *Victorian Lives and Letters Consortium*, and Carolyn Dever is now hosting the project at Dartmouth University (in partnership with King's College, London, and the Mark Samuels Lasner Collection at the University of Delaware). The enormity of this project has required a highly innovative approach, involving crowd-sourcing and collaboration across multiple institutions, and fostered thoughtful reflection about the "possibilities the digital environment offers for representing and analysing" life-writing.[26] Participants in the project determine how to represent shifts in voice in a diary written by two people as well as the strange materiality of such an artifact, which often includes letters, newspaper clippings, or dried flowers, as well its emphasis on travel and networks. As Marion Thain has argued, "this diary offers a fascinating experimental field for developing advanced text-encoding strategies and for thinking about how we might use the technology to read in new ways" (240).

Knowing that study of the 1890s has enabled such generative work within digital humanities, we also wished to discuss digital methodologies and to do so in a way that looked forward to futures for the field, acknowledging both the affordances of this work as well its challenges and limitations. Drawing on Caroline Levine's arguments about form, Lorraine Janzen Kooistra establishes in Chapter 15 of this volume the extent to which the remediation of little magazines in the *Yellow Nineties 2.0* (Y90s) magazine rack elucidates their formal elements (whole, hierarchy, rhythm, and network) as well as their position within media history as a technology in transition. Kooistra emphasizes how the manner in which fin-de-siecle magazines are staged on Y90s enables analysis that pushes back against earlier tendencies to extract individual contributions from the volumes in which they appeared and to instead examine these contributions in relation to whole issues or titles or in relationship to a title's design or as part of a network of readers and makers. This is work that invites further work, that indicates how sites like the Y90s have created the possibility for a richer, clarified perception of the period that will require thinking holistically and attending to connections. In Chapter 16, Rebecca

N. Mitchell emphasizes how certain elements of the complexity of 1890s visual culture are elided when we rely on existing digitized resources, which have tended to privilege the decadent productions of the period. At the same time, she welcomes emerging digital protocols that might render other artifacts and collections more accessible and make evident the links between objects and collections. While proposals for this work have gestured toward highly appealing futures for research, these horizons are delimited by practical barriers that inhibit the creation and sharing of metadata. Mitchell's sensitivity regarding the difficulty of this work represents a mode of digital humanities thinking that weds tech optimism with more grounded experience in the realities of implementation. Together these two chapters indicate how our sense of the 1890s might be sharpened by digital methodologies as well as how those methodologies themselves continue to be rethought and reshaped with increasing attentiveness to their possibilities and their limits. These chapters cooperate in foregrounding how digital methodologies might lead us into more immersive contact with the specific pleasures of this period, the particular kinds of beauty and design with which it was so concerned, while also insisting upon how arduous the performance of this work might be.

Conclusion

In his introduction to Martin Secker's *The Eighteen-Nineties: A Period Anthology in Prose and Verse* (1948), John Betjeman instructs the reader, before transporting themselves back to the end of the previous century, to "draw the curtain, kindle a joss-stick in a dark corner, settle down on a sofa by the fire, light an Egyptian cigarette and sip a brandy and soda."[27] *Nineteenth-Century Literature in Transition: The 1890s* certainly does not exclude that method of appreciation and all of its decadent connections, but the work in this collection might also ask you to reflect upon the taste for that cigarette and the colonial economic connections to which it speaks as well as the transnational interplay between joss-stick and brandy in this scenario. And it might, in turn, ask you to enter into a different, less dreamy mode of apprehending the 1890s, to think about the violence and anti-Blackness of the decade against the allure of exoticism as well as the anticolonial thinking enacted by women poets. Pondering the strident environmentalism of some fin-de-siècle writers might require a slightly less supine position. Encountering Indian realisms and Hawaiian dandyisms could populate the reader's imaginings of nations abroad with people rather than simply commodities designed for the consumption of a reclining aesthete. Engaging with modes of radicalism that gazed outward at world religions or the natural world or demanded socialist agitation might require that the curtain be opened, that the reader redirect that inward turn Betjeman affirms as a marker of the period to the broader political concerns of both the 1890s and of our present moment. All of this is to us, however, a source of excitement and optimism about how study of the fin de siècle continues to inspire scholarly innovation driven by an attitude of "experiment and adventure" similar to the ethos that Holbrook Jackson located in his "decade of a thousand movements."

Notes

1 Holbrook Jackson, *The Eighteen Nineties: A Review of Art and Ideas at the Close of the Nineteenth Century* (London: Grant Richards, 1913), 355–56.

2 Holbrook Jackson, *The Eighteen Nineties: A Review of Art and Ideas at the Close of the Nineteenth Century* (London: Jonathan Cape, 1927), 12.

3 This statement occurs on p. 12 of the first edition of the text. The remainder of citations from Holbrook Jackson's *The Eighteen Nineties* will be to the 1913 first edition.

4 Bernard Muddiman, *The Men of the Nineties* (London: Henry Danielson, 1920), 2–3, 132.

5 Osbert Burdett, *The Beardsley Period: An Essay in Perspective* (London: John Lane, The Bodley Head, 1925), 7.

6 W. G. Blaikie-Murdoch, *The Renaissance of the Nineties* (London: De La More Press, 1911), 73.

7 See, for example, Laura Marcus, Michèle Mendelssohn, and Kirsten E. Shepherd-Barr, eds., *Late Victorian into Modern* (New York: Oxford University Press, 2016); and Bénédicte Coste, Catherine Delyfer, and Christine Reynier, eds., *Reconnecting Aestheticism and Modernism: Continuities, Revisions, Speculations* (New York: Routledge, 2017).

8 Vernon Lee, "Deterioration of the Soul," *Fortnightly Review* 59 (1896): 928–43 (938).

9 Elaine Showalter, *Sexual Anarchy: Gender and Culture at the* Fin de Siècle (New York: Viking, 1990).

10 See Linda Dowling, "The Decadent and the New Woman in the 1890s," *Nineteenth Century Literature* 33, no. 4 (1979): 434–53.

11 See Ann Ardis, *New Women, New Novels* (New Brunswick: Rutgers, 1990); Richard Dellamora, *Masculine Desire: The Sexual Politics of Victorian Aestheticism* (Chapel Hill, NC: University of North Carolina Press, 1990); Lyn Pykett, *The "Improper" Feminine: The Women's Sensation Novel and New Woman Fiction* (London: Routledge, 1992); Ellis Hanson, *Decadence and Catholicism* (Cambridge, MA: Harvard University Press, 1994); Joseph

Bristow, *Effeminate England: Homoerotic Writing after 1885* (New York: Columbia University Press, 1995); Kathy Alexis Psomiades, *Body's Beauty: Femininity and Representation in British Aestheticism* (Stanford, CA: Stanford University Press, 1997); Sally Ledger, *The New Woman: Fiction and Feminism at the Fin de Siècle* (Manchester: Manchester University Press, 1997); Kathy Alexis Psomiades and Talia Schaffer, eds., *Women and British Aestheticism* (Charlottesville, VA: University of Virginia Press, 1999); Ann Heilmann, *New Woman Fiction: Women Writing First-Wave Feminism* (London: Palgrave Macmillan, 2000); Talia Schaffer, *The Forgotten Female Aesthetes: Literary Culture in Late-Victorian England* (Charlottesville, VA: University of Virginia Press, 2000); Margaret Stetz, *British Women's Comic Fiction, 1890–1990* (Burlington: Ashgate, 2001), especially the first chapter; Jill Ehnenn, *Women's Literary Collaboration and Late Victorian Culture* (Burlington: Ashgate, 2008); Richard Kaye, "Sexual Identity at the Fin de Siècle" in *The Cambridge Companion to the Fin de Siècle*, ed. Gail Marshall (New York: Cambridge University Press, 2008), 53–72.

12 See Alan Sinfield, *The Wilde Century: Effeminacy, Oscar Wilde, and the Queer Moment* (New York: Columbia University Press, 1994).

13 Stefano Evangelista, "Decadence and Aestheticism," in *The Routledge Companion to Victorian Literature,* eds. Dennis Denisoff and Talia Schaffer (New York: Routledge, 2019), 106–15 (111).

14 See Stephen Arata, *Fictions of Loss at the Victorian Fin de Siècle: Identity and Empire* (New York: Cambridge University Press, 1996).

15 See Matthew Potolsky, *A Decadent Republic of Letters: Taste, Politics, and Cosmopolitan Community from Baudelaire to Beardsley* (Philadelphia, PA: University of Pennsylvania Press, 2013).

16 Leela Gandhi, *Affective Communities: Anticolonial Thought, Fin-de-Siècle Radicalism, and the Politics of Friendship* (Durham, NC: Duke University Press, 2006), 12.

17 Ross Forman, "Empire," in *The Cambridge Companion to the Fin de Siècle*, ed. Gail Marshall (New York: Cambridge University Press, 2007), 91–112 (94).

18 Tanya Agathocleous and Jason Rudy, "Recombined: Anticolonial Form at the Turn of the Century," *Cusp* 1, no. 1 (2022): 105–16 (105).

19 Caroline Levine, "From Nation to Network," *Victorian Studies* 55, 4 (2013): 647–66.

20 Ronjaunee Chatterjee, Alicia Mireles Christoff, and Amy R. Wong, "Undisciplining Victorian Studies," *Los Angeles Review of Books*, July 10, 2020. An expanded version of this article can be found in *Victorian Studies* 63, no. 3 (2020): 369–91.

21 See Benjamin Morgan, "Fin du Globe: On Decadent Planets," *Victorian Studies* 58, no. 4 (Summer 2016); "Scale, Resonance, Presence," *Victorian Studies* 59, no. 1 (2016): 609–35; and "Scale as Form: Thomas Hardy's Rocks and Stars," in *Anthropocene Reading: Literary History in Geological Times*, eds. Tobias Menely and Jesse Oak Taylor (University Park, PA: Penn State University Press, 2017), 132–49.

22 Oscar Wilde, *The Picture of Dorian Gray*, ed. Norman Page (Peterborough: Broadview, 1998), 209.

23 H. P. Lovecraft, *Supernatural Horror in Literature* (1927), revised and expanded 1933–34 (New York: Dover, 1973), 15.

24 https://modjourn.org/about.

25 Frederick D. King, "The Decadent Archive and the Long History of New Media," *Victorian Periodicals Review* 49, no. 4 (2016): 643–63 (643).

26 Marion Thain, "Perspective: Digitizing the Diary – Experiments in Queer Encoding (A Retrospective and a Prospective)," *Journal of Victorian Culture* 12, no. 2 (2016): 226–41 (232).

27 John Betjeman, introduction to *The Eighteen-Nineties: A Period Anthology in Prose and Verse*, ed. Martin Secker (London: The Richards Press, 1948), xi–xvi (xii).

CHAPTER I

Race and Empire in the 1890s

Zarena Aslami

Raymond Williams famously deemed the period from 1880 to 1914 the "interregnum," an interval between, on the one hand, the high literary art of the Romanticists and mid-Victorians and, on the other, the modernist visionaries who could speak to mid-twentieth-century readers like himself.[1] For more recent literary scholars of the realist novel, the 1890s in particular have been cast as the scene of breakdown, when the stability and coherence of the liberal subject is no longer taken for granted or even wished for and when writers paid more attention to the artful, the unconscious, and the irrational rather than self-consciously attempting to represent the real.[2] Literary critics have also identified the late nineteenth century as witnessing the emergence of the Imperial Gothic (Patrick Brantlinger's term for a literary style that fuses the conventions of the adventure story with the Gothic), heightened fears of reverse colonization (a popular narrative structure that, as Stephen Arata influentially explains, features both the fear that the civilized world is on the verge of being conquered by its colonies and guilt around its own violence against those it has conquered),[3] and sexual anarchy (Elaine Showalter's phrase, borrowed from the late nineteenth-century English novelist George Gissing, to describe the 1880s and 1890s, when, she writes, it seemed to contemporaries that sexual and gender norms were collapsing).[4]

Rather than contest these accounts, I suggest we might back up to think more broadly about a category that supersedes yet implicates the processes that these scholars describe: that is, the ongoing violent construction and instantiation of the category of the human. This category has received special attention by Black studies scholars because it is founded not exactly on the exclusion of Blackness but rather on what Zakiyyah Iman Jackson,[5] drawing on Hortense Spillers' notion of *flesh*,[6] calls its *plasticity*: the capacity of Blackness in the Western humanist imagination to be made to produce the meaning of "the human," in part by being continually and ongoingly cast outside of it.[7] In other words, we might consider the political, psychological, national, racial, class, gender, and sexual anxieties of the 1890s in terms of the duress that the Enlightenment category of the human underwent as those whose exclusion from it, including workers, women, and the colonized, demanded inclusion and recognition. During these years, there was increased demand on the part of colonized natives, freed Black people, women, and the working classes – the nonpersons, as Imani Perry terms them in her critique of patriarchy – for participation in what Perry identifies as the pillars of Western humanism: legal person-hood, property ownership, and sovereignty.[8] Taken together, these anxi-eties expose the fragilities, inconsistencies, disavowals, and sheer wishfulness of the edifices upon which British racial superiority was built. Critical to this context is the nineteenth-century biological notion of the human. This conception casts the human body as an organism that inherits physical characteristics, but which is also affected by environment and thus, as Kyla Schuller argues, contains the potential for transforma-tion, cultivation, and impressibility.[9] As Edward Beasley argues, after 1870, "there was an increasingly pan-Western consensus in favour of fixed, heritable, and intellectually unequal skin-colour-based racial groups."[10] By the late nineteenth century, anthropologists would be seeking to discover the "original types in this mixed world," using measurements, which, as Beasley notes, led to "greater frustration," since "such measurements refused to clump into races" (Beasley, *Victorian Reinvention,* 21). The eighteenth- and earlier nineteenth-century biocentric, racist notion of the impressible body would eventually become subsumed in the twentieth century by the biocentric, racist notion of the rigid body determined by genetic inheritance, an ideology that can be tracked directly to European-instigated genocides, such as the Herero and Namaqua genocide (1904–08) and the Holocaust (1941–45).

We can think of the 1890s, then, as the hinge years between these two related but different biological notions of the human (impressible versus essential) and as a racially-epistemologically tumultuous time, one that the title of my chapter might be obscuring. The "and" in "Race and Empire" implies that race might be added to empire and thus perhaps subtracted as well. However, as Ania Loomba and Sylvia Wynter show, practices of racialization are not only inextricable from the exercises of empire but are also in fact foundational to them.[11] Wynter explains that, since the sixteenth century, as European states competed for global markets and wealth, massacring Indigenous peoples and enslaving Africans, under the disapproving censure of the Pope, they sought ways to represent their inhumane and brutal acts as godly as opposed to sinful. The modern notion of race emerged to do this impossible ideological work. Through official "overrepresentations" of what Wynter terms the "genre" of the human as Man1 and Man2 (defined, respectively, by the physical sciences of the Enlightenment and then by the biological sciences of the nineteenth century), race became over the modern period "the non-supernatural but no less extrahuman ground ... of the answer that the secularizing West would now give to the Heideggerian question as to the who, and the what we are" (Wynter, "Unsettling," 264). Thus, rather than isolate "race" as a distinct category amidst the constellation of social anxieties of the period, I extend this argument to suggest that, in fact, it underpins the destabilizing elements of the fin-de-siècle social world. Here, I draw upon Black studies and postcolonial theory to try to reframe our understanding of the period as an age of anxieties and to consider the implications of our field's use of the phrase "race and empire." In other words, by expanding our theoretical framework to consider late nineteenth-century manifestations of anti-Blackness, I argue that we can enrich our mapping of the ways that "race" as a category both propped up and disordered the British empire, thereby expanding on earlier critical interpretations of the workings of empire and difference in fin-de-siècle narratives.

To help me write toward this reframing, I turn to Arthur Conan Doyle's "The Story of the Brown Hand," which was published in a series of ghost stories called "Round the Fire" that he wrote for the *Strand Magazine* in May 1899.[12] This short tale about the ghost of an Afghan hillman haunting a British surgeon upon his return from Mumbai ("Bombay") to Wiltshire might be read within the Imperial Gothic tradition or as a generic reverse colonization narrative. However, I suggest that we can also read it as a tale that exposes how the brownness of Asians took shape through biocentric terms against the period's longstanding anti-Blackness in ways that are historically specific, different from but related to (and ongoing in) the present. As Katherine McKittrick explains, "A biocentric knowledge system and conception of the human ... refers to the lawlike order of knowledge that posits a Darwinian narrative of the human – that we are purely biological and bio-evolutionary beings – as universal."[13] McKittrick uses the term biocentricity to refer to the contradictory set of European systems of thought that posit humans as biological creatures whose range of possibilities is circumscribed by a biologistic account, whether hardwired or conditioned by the environment.

Conan Doyle's story draws attention to brownness, highlighting it in the title, fetishizing brownness primarily through a detached body part, an aesthetic choice that works to contain or limit claims to the ultimate cultivability and thus humanness of "Asiatics" under the British empire. A strategic promise, found in texts such as Thomas Babington Macaulay's "Minute on Education" (1835) and John Stuart Mill's *Considerations on Representative Government* (1861), this assertion of potential to become civilized also postulates that the savage character of "Hindoos" is due to environmental and cultural factors, and is not essential, and thus these subjects of empire are capable of attaining civilization *eventually*. This promise puts into place a ceaseless deferral of equality and autonomy that enables continued, limitless subjugation in the present. We can thus frame the foregrounding of color and bodily fragmentation or nonintegrity ("the Brown Hand") in the title as a British imperialist reconstitution of brown Asian natives as subhuman. In a period stretching from the 1850s, emblematized by the Indian Mutiny of 1857, equality, independence, and sovereignty were being demanded by Indian nationalists and neighboring nations, such as Afghanistan, after the Second Anglo-Afghan War (1878–80) and during the reign of the authoritarian Abdur Rahman, as well as by other nationalists and insurgents in Jamaica, Ireland, Egypt, and Bunyoro.[14] As Antoinette Burton explains,

> In the 1850s and after, colonial subjects in a variety of discrete places took to the streets and the fields in outrage over a variety of grievances, transforming their initial protests into radical, if short-lived, anti-state challenges that aimed to break the link between economic exploitation and political hegemony. In the process, they threw the very presumption of empire's political legitimacy into doubt, revealing the defensive positions imperial policy makers were forced to adopt as they sought to routinize imperial political order on the ground and to carry on with government as usual. (Burton, *Trouble with Empire,* 147)

The potentiality of Asian natives, which operates as their perpetual subhumanness, is also animated by its proximate relation to anti-Blackness. Anti-Blackness enables the projection of this strategic promise of a future humanness onto "Asiatics." It is thus my contention that where Asiaticness, or brownness, is being theorized, anti-Blackness as a set of discourses, practices, and affects is present, inflating, vivifying, and providing context for this brown potentiality or subhumanness attributed to "Asiatics." This is another instance of the plasticity of Blackness as Jackson puts it.

Conan Doyle's story theorizes not only how notions of race and racial difference, and, in particular, the singularity of white bodies and the exchangeability of brown ones, were central to 1890s notions of British selfhood, property, and sovereignty, but also how they destabilized these relations as much as they were used to shore them up. While seeking to thrill and scare, as a good ghost story should, it also contains the seeds of something even more horrifying to late-Victorian sensibilities than being haunted by the ghost of an imperial subject in the recesses of the English countryside. The thrill emerges from the specter of the transformable, racialized body becoming the rigid, racialized body that cannot be controlled physically (by force) or ideologically (being seduced or coerced into aspiring toward inclusion into Enlightenment humanity). This body that could be homogenized, collapsed, and made exchangeable, coded as *less-than*, also harbors the imagined ability to affiliate with others. The Orientalist logic of brown Asian exchangeability may, in fact, become the logic of brown Asian collectivity and refusal in the hands, so to speak, of the othered. Scholars have been foregrounding the voices of Black Victorians and Victorians of color as a necessary revision of the field, an ongoing project that requires more archival access and labor.[15] My choice of a canonical author may thus seem retrograde. However, thinking about race requires not only pluralizing the field of authors, as Ronjaunee Chatterjee, Alicia Mireles Christoff, and Amy R. Wong, the editors of the special issue of "Undisciplining Victorian Studies" put it in their introduction, but also coming to the practice of interpretation in new ways.[16]

As already mentioned, the 1890s are often characterized as an anxious age. Most historical accounts note that this anxiety directly stems from Britain's competition with other European powers for global hegemony. Britain's entwined monopolies on empire and industrial manufacturing, which had expanded exponentially over the nineteenth century, were now glaringly challenged both by the rising powers of the United States, Japan, Germany, and Italy and by colonial insurgencies and demands for sovereignty across the empire. Domestically, Britain was wracked by economic depressions, labor strikes, and the media specters of the New Woman and the New Man, each cast as perversions of traditional gender and sexual identities and as blurring a strict gender binary, that critical marker of civilization, according to imperialist discourse. The rise of mass culture enabled jingoism to bring the working classes into an imperial project articulated through racial and patriarchal logics. By using sensational language and visual images, mass media abstracted and unified whiteness across class position over and against resistant colonized natives abroad as well as against sexual and gender dissidents at home. We are now familiar with the story of how these historical processes led to existential crises for fin-de-siècle Victorians, casting doubt on the privileged racial status of British national identity and eroding national confidence in its imperial mission. These anxieties found expression in the scientific, social, and educational "expert" sociobiological discourse of degeneration: the argument that the English as a race were weakening, devolving to a less civilized state that would lead to their eventually being overtaken and dominated by the races they had long deemed inferior to themselves.[17]

The discourse of degeneration that emerged at the end of the nineteenth century was made possible by a century-long process in which biological notions of racial difference consolidated and the British state increasingly used the concept of the biological to control both domestic and imperialized populations in the name of security.[18] While earlier in the Victorian period, politicians, philosophers, and entrepreneurs had touted the virtues and rationality of free trade, the "liberating" of global markets, to justify imperial expansion, by the 1890s, as Lauren Goodlad argues, the rationale had shifted to a racial-moral logic.[19] Victorians were on the other side of mid-century pseudosciences of race and a broadening acceptance of eugenicist ideas, inspired in part by Francis Galton and his 1883 book *Inquiries into Human Faculty and Development*, in which he advocated for selective breeding among humans. The scientific racism of European writers publishing in the 1850s and 1860s, such as the British anthropologist John Beddoe and evolutionists such as the French writer Arthur du Gobineau and the German scientist Carl Vogt, went further than eighteenth-century natural history in their claims toward the empirical differences among people.[20] In this period, a racial-moral logic drawing upon scientific rationality – such as empirical evidence and quantitative data (skull measurements, phrenology, craniology, etc.) – explicitly propounded the biological difference and superiority of white Europeans. This racial-moral logic fully superseded the economic logic of the earlier Victorian period as rationale for imperial expansion. By the 1890s, scientific racism, with its evolutionary Darwinian principles of heredity, natural selection, and environmental causality, was widespread, but on the verge of being transformed into what would become, as Schuller argues, the hallmark of twentieth-century race science: the theory of genetics and biological determinism.

Thus, as Schuller critically points out, when we disparage the nineteenth century as essentialist, we are in fact misreading it. Nineteenth-century conceptions of race did indeed justify, as Wynter puts it, "African enslavement, Latin American conquest, and Asian subjugation," an ongoing brutal process of European self-making dating back to the fifteenth century (Wynter, *Unsettling*, 263). But they did not do so through rationales of essential identity. Rather, in the nineteenth century, imperial violence was justified as the right of the superior race, understood as superior through a complicated brew of heredity and environmental causality, not biological essentialism. As McKittrick writes, all these biological and differential notions of the human fall under the term biocentric, but are not the same. She explains, "A biocentric knowledge system assumes that, as a species, we have evolved differentially according to our ethnic-racial differences. The result is a kind of Malthusian spatial-racial fallout. Race functions to naturalize this conception of the human" (McKittrick, *Dear Science,* 126). McKittrick clarifies how biocentricity can refer to a range of different scientistic ideologies, all of which serve to fuel and sustain it as a knowledge system: "We must keep in mind that biocentricity is not the same as scientific racism or biological determinism. Scientific racism and biological determinism are ideologies that *animate* a pervasive biocentric belief system" (McKittrick, *Dear Science,* 126).

The last year of the 1890s witnessed the publications of key works lamenting the physical and biological exhaustion of the British empire, even while extolling its power and legitimacy, if only practiced in the *right* way: Rudyard Kipling's poem "The White Man's Burden" (1899), a plea to the United States to take up the imperial mission that Britain was no longer able to maintain; Joseph Conrad's novel *Heart of Darkness* (1899), which dramatizes the brutalities of imperialism by focusing not on the violence of European imperialism on nonwhite people continents away, but rather on the devolution of white subjects who lose their sense of humanity by virtue of their proximity with those deemed subhuman; and Mrs. Ernest Ames' children's book *An ABC for Baby Patriots* (1899), a primer for British children that explicitly teaches pride in empire and the necessity to make it expand ("E is our Empire / Where sun never sets; / The larger we make it / The bigger it gets").[21] These literary works testify both to the widespread popularity of the idea of white superiority, along with the moral imperative to imperialize, and the idea of the precarity of whiteness, the belief it has peaked and is now declining and in need of pedagogical and prescriptive redress.

Enter Conan Doyle's "The Story of the Brown Hand." Published in a series of ghost stories called "Round the Fire," this formally tight and concise narrative, featuring the occult and the paranormal, highlights the triumph of scientific and rational methods for solving the problem of haunting. Dr. Hardacre, whom we learn is a neurologist with an interest in the supernatural, tells the story of the Afghan hillman who haunts a British surgeon, Sir Dominick, every night, searching his collection of jarred specimens for the hand the latter had amputated in Peshawar.

Dr. Hardacre will eventually procure the amputated hand of a Lascar, a South Asian sailor, who suffered from a horrible industrial accident in England, and, thinking it will satisfy the ghost, will drop it in a jar. When the Afghan ghost happens upon it, it apparently fits the bill, and he never returns to haunt Sir Dominick again.

Interlaced through it all is the formulation that all brown bodies are physically exchangeable. The formal tightness of this story, solved by positing the exchangeability of brown bodies and body parts, relies on this formula. The formula does not describe a natural relation that exists in the universe, but instead projects Western European humanist fantasies about the imperial project onto Central and South Asians who have been caught up in it. They are cast as consenting to imperial domination in exchange for the benefits of civilization, but, in the case of the Afghan hillman, who loses his right hand twice, by his alleged consent (first to an amputation and later to the doctor's promise to preserve it, a promise he does not keep), and of the Lascar, who loses both hands twice, not by consent (first, in an industrial accident that leaves him disabled and, second, in the hospital, where the director gives his amputated hands to his friend Dr. Hardacre without consulting him), the benefits are hard to discern. A postcolonial reading allows us to understand the modes of domination that operate in the story, including the homogenization of all of those positioned as coming from the East. However, a Black studies reading might allow us to ask other kinds of questions that move beyond domination and that attend to the possibility of alternative readings and modes of "brown" agency.

If the return of the repressed is a possible interpretation, the repressed being the violence that the British empire wrought on nonwhite subjects in its quest for wealth and power, then what about another repressed content? "The Story of the Brown Hand" theorizes how the concept of race at once enables the British empire to reproduce itself and grow and yet also weakens and threatens it. Specifically, the story contains a counternarrative of racial alliance that exceeds the tightness of its formal closure. By featuring the encounter between British medicine and Afghan spiritual ontology in India, the story is especially pertinent here because Afghanness was conceived as peripheral to empire. Marginal in multiple ways, it becomes an especially malleable site for meaning-making.[22]

The story foregrounds the question of property and patriarchal inheritance. Dr. Hardacre begins the narrative by referencing what "everyone" knows: that he became the heir to the fortune of Sir Dominick Holden, a fortune which transformed him from a "hard-working and impecunious medical man to a well-to-do landed proprietor" (Conan Doyle, "Brown Hand," 499). That our narrator was the sixth in line to this fortune makes his uncle's decision seem "arbitrary and whimsical" (499). The story thus exists as an explanation of this mysterious act of property transfer: Why would Sir Dominick be so moved to bestow his fortune and his manor estate, Rodenhurst, on such a distant relation? The agent of the narrator's transformation from penniless to wealthy turns out to be the eternally restless ghost of an Afghan who has been haunting Sir Dominick for four years, following him from Mumbai ("Bombay") to Wiltshire, seeking what Sir Dominick had taken from him in Peshawar ("Peshawur"). Sir Dominick, "the famous Indian surgeon," was at first in the Indian army and then in private practice in Mumbai ("Bombay"), founding the Oriental Hospital and only returning to England as an old man because of the onset of nervous symptoms. Eagerly pushed out by his colleagues, bound together more by the principles of competitive capitalism and professional advancement than by fellowship, Sir Dominick returns to his native county of Wiltshire. With money from his private practice in India, presumably, he is able to purchase a large estate and he proceeds to invite each of his potential heirs to visit him. In addition to being a neurologist, Dr. Hardacre happens to be a member of the Psychical Research Society and to have an interest in the abnormal in psychical experiences. The story casts the supernatural into the realm of the real and the scientific, collapsing the antimony between Western science and so-called Eastern mysticism. The question of who is, in fact, superstitious and who rational, who the beneficiary of imperialism and who the burdened, is upended, only to be righted again at the conclusion by the rational reassertion of racism.

Just as the carefully constructed binaries between East/West and irrational/rational collapse in the scientific approach to the supernormal, the English countryside starts to look less familiar and nostalgic. As Dr. Hardacre approaches the estate Rodenhurst, he describes the "weird nature of the scenery" (499) as one that mixes the ancient past with the present. The English countryside, often positioned as the symbolic backbone of Englishness, appears ancient, prehistoric, and mysterious:

> The road wound through the valleys, formed by a succession of grassy hills, and the summit of each was cut and carved into the most elaborate fortifications, some circular and some square, but all on a scale which has defied the winds and the rains of many centuries. Some call them Roman and some British, but their true origin and the reasons for this particular tract of country being so interlaced with entrenchments have never been finally made clear. (500)

The manor house itself is dilapidated and in disrepair, despite the wealth of his uncle. Most strikingly, it almost appears as a building to which a siege has been laid: "Two broken and weather-stained pillars, each surmounted by a mutilated heraldic emblem, flanked the entrance to a neglected drive" (500). The ruins of colonial conflict and the bedraggling of the symbols of British empire, announcing its demise, seems to have traveled into the English countryside.

When Sir Dominick learns that Dr. Hardacre has an interest in the supernatural, he and his wife exchange knowing glances. He shows Dr. Hardacre his laboratory and collection of samples for his study of Pathology: "bloated organs, gaping cysts, distorted bones, odious parasites – a singular exhibition of the products of India" (502). He explains that these specimens are all that remains of a much larger collection that had been destroyed when his house burned down in Mumbai in 1892. Sir Dominick offers no explanation for how he procured these body parts, but we learn tangentially, through his story of the ghost, that most likely they had all been procured as the spoils of his surgical procedures on local natives. He invites the narrator to sleep in his laboratory. While disturbed by the sight of what he calls so much suffering, Dr. Hardacre manages to fall asleep, only to be woken several hours later by a sound. He discerns the shape of a man examining each of the jars. The man is described by his stature and what he wears: "It was a man, short and squat, dressed in some sort of dark grey gown, which hung straight from his shoulders to his feet" (504). He is also marked by his skin color and style of hair: "The moon shone upon the side of his face, and I saw that it was chocolate-brown in colour, with a ball of black hair like a woman's at the back of his head" (504). Eventually, the man shows his frustration and departs. In fact, he vanishes. In a story where Afghans, Indians, and Lascars are all exchangeable, the fact that the man vanishes is the one reason that the narrator does not think that he is simply Sir Dominick's Indian servant, described earlier as "a stealthy, quick-eyed Oriental waiter" (501). In the morning, Sir Dominick asks, "'Did you see him?'" The narrator replies, "An Indian with one hand?'" (504). Sir Dominick returns, "Precisely."

However, as Sir Dominick tells the story, we learn that he is not an Indian with one hand, but an Afghan with one hand. Sir Dominick explains that, ten years ago, he had been asked to go to Peshawar to "look at the hand of a native who was passing through with an Afghan caravan" (505). "Native" might refer to Indian, except we next learn that "the fellow came from some mountain tribe living away at the back of beyond somewhere on the other side of Kaffiristan. He talked a bastard Pushtoo

[Pashto], and it was all I could do to understand him." Speaking Pashto and living beyond Kafiristan, now Nuristan, a contested region conquered by Abdur Rahman in 1896, this man, by turns called "native" and "Indian," is, in fact, from Afghanistan. Sir Dominick later refers to him as a "hillman," but then as "my Indian patient." The British typically referred to the Pashtuns living in the mountains as hillmen, but as Shah Mahmoud Hanifi explains, the colonial record is confusing and unapologetically reproduces the confusion of previous documents.[23]

The term "Indian" floats freely throughout the text. For example, the narrator first refers to his rich relation as "the famous Indian surgeon" (Conan Doyle, "Brown Hand," 499). Upon meeting Sir Dominick, the narrator describes him as having a "Red Indian nose." As John Kuo Wei Tchen and Dylan Yeats, citing Shankar Raman and Jonathan Gil Harris, argue, from the early modern period, Europeans applied the term "Indian" so extensively that it became almost meaningless:

> From the translation of a river in what is now Pakistan, the Indus River, the European use of India emerged and then applied to boundaries of the European known world: India, Indonesia, the West Indies, and even to Indiana. Indians appeared everywhere. . . . The term became so all-purpose it was also used to label Ethiopians, and, as late as the eighteenth century, Polynesian peoples and the Maori in New Zealand. All explanatory power outside of the naming practice's own inadequacy is lost.[24]

The drama of "The Story of the Brown Hand" emerges from the exchangeability of different groups of people with different languages, religions, and histories, who are conflated and made to signify brownness. "Indian" here has the power to designate non-Indians such as Afghans, as well as British people who operated in India.

The logic of exchangeability dominates and governs the story on multiple levels. Sir Dominick describes how the native "was suffering from a soft sarcomatous swelling of one of the metacarpal joints" (Conan Doyle, "Brown Hand," 505). The process by which Sir Dominick gains the man's consent casts the notion of consent, and thus native consent, to imperial domination understood as the exchange of sovereignty for the benefits of Western civilization, into question. Sir Dominick tells the narrator, "I made him realize that it was only by losing his hand that he could hope to save his life" (505). Here, a hand is exchanged for a life. Then the procedure itself is exchanged for the hand. When the man asks how he can pay him, Sir Dominick tells him he will take the hand: "After much persuasion he consented to the operation, and he asked me, when it was over, what fee I demanded. The poor fellow was almost a beggar, so that the idea of a fee was absurd, but I answered in jest that my fee should be his hand, and that I proposed to add it to my pathological collection" (505). Sir Dominick narrates his surprise at the native's objection to this proposal: "he explained that according to his religion it was an all-important matter that the body should be reunited after death, and so make a perfect dwelling for the spirit" (505). Sir Dominick dismisses this belief as superstitious and similar to the ancient practice of mummification in Egypt. Sir Dominick offers to keep the hand preserved and safe in his collection. The Afghan agrees but reminds him, "'I shall want it back when I am dead,'" a comment that causes Sir Dominick to laugh at the time, but it is precisely what will cause his suffering later in life. Sir Dominick concludes the story within the story: "I returned to my practice [in Mumbai], and he no doubt in the course of time was able to continue his journey to Afghanistan" (505). Two years later (four years from the present of the story), he recounts to Dr. Hardacre, he first saw his patient in the night, "holding up his stump and looking reproachfully at me" (505). Every night, he shakes Sir Dominick's shoulder, examines each of the jars in the laboratory, then vanishes in despair. By the time the narrator meets Sir Dominick, this nightly performance has been happening for four years, first in Mumbai, every night of the ship voyage to England, and now in his mansion in Wiltshire, slowly wearing the surgeon down, leading to his diminished and emaciated appearance and no doubt to the nervous conditions that had caused him to return to England.

Sir Dominick's story prompts the narrator to draw upon his extensive research and concoct a plan. He returns to London, then goes to Shadwell Seamen's Hospital, where the house-surgeon is an old friend, from whom he asks a favor. The friend retorts, "A brown man's hand! … What in the world do you want that for?" (506). Dr. Hardacre replies, "'Never mind. I'll tell you some day. I know that your wards are full of Indians'" (506). The house-surgeon then asks his assistant, "What became of the hands of the Lascar which we took off yesterday? I mean the fellow from the East India Dock who got caught in the steam winch" (506). The hand is still available, and he gives it to Dr. Hardacre, who returns with it to Wiltshire and places it in a jar in the collection. The Afghan ghost visits in the night, finds the hand, and is excited, only to smash the jar on the floor. It takes Dr. Hardacre a day to realize that he had brought a left hand, when the ghost is missing his right. (Right and left hands are not exchangeable, at least not to the person who has lost the hand.) He races back to the hospital by train, fearful that the right hand of the Lascar had been destroyed, but it has not. He takes the Lascar's amputated right hand

and tries the experiment again. Prevented from sleeping in the laboratory by his anxious host, Dr. Hardacre awakens the next morning to an elated and younger-looking Sir Dominick, who recounts how the ghost came, found the hand, bowed, raised his arms in the air, with both hands intact, and disappeared. Dr. Hardacre concludes this account with, "So that is the curious experience which won me the affection and the gratitude of my celebrated uncle, the famous Indian surgeon. His anticipations were realized, and never again was he disturbed by the visits of the restless hillman in search of his lost member" (508). Upon his death, Sir Dominick leaves his wealth to him, "over the heads of five exasperated cousins" (508). Hardacre is "changed in a single day from a hardworking country doctor into the head of an important Wiltshire family. I at least have reason to bless the memory of the man with the brown hand, and the day when I was fortunate enough to relieve Rodenhurst of his unwelcome presence" (508).

The medium of exchange in all of these relationships remains brown body parts. This, I argue, indexes the deeper panic of the story, a panic that persists in current instantiations of anti-Blackness, US discourses of Islamophobia, and the War on Terror. Underneath the formally neat resolution of Sir Dominick's problem – Dr. Hardacre's clever appeasement of the Afghan ghost seeking his hand by proffering a Lascar hand as substitute – lies a trace of consciousness that the British formulation of brown exchangeability can be flipped on its head and enable brown collectivity, brown resistance, and the brown undoing of empire.[25] However, I must note explicitly that brown exchangeability operates differently from the plasticity of Blackness, as Jackson and others have analyzed it. Brown exchangeability enables British fortunes not through enslavement and captivity and the capacity to make an abstract notion of brownness produce meaning, but through movement and migration that facilitates wealth, property, and inheritance. And, in fact, as Ren Ellis Neyra has argued, if I make arguments about brownness, I must be wary of positing relations with Blackness for that claim of relation can be, as she puts it, "extract[ive]."[26]

In the repressed historical consciousness of "The Story of the Brown Hand," the costs to the brown Asians caught up in the British empire include earthly disability and eternal restlessness. The benefits to the British include wholeness, wealth, property ownership, and patriarchal reproduction. A postcolonial reading might stop here, critiquing the collateral damages of Orientalism, imperialism, global capitalism, and the white savior complex, whether embodied by Sir Dominick or

Dr. Hardacre. But maybe something else is going on. Maybe this brown ghost is appeased not because he is duped and thinks he has his own hand back. Maybe there is a connection going on between the two of them. Does the unconscious of the story fear the possibility expressed by the fictional Afghan hillman knowing full well that this is not his hand but accepting it for other reasons than the ones that the characters presume, namely that he does think that it is in fact his own missing hand? Could there be a supernatural intimacy, a corporeally expressed relationality between this dead Afghan and handless Lascar, both in fact mutilated (to echo the narrator's description of Sir Dominick's heraldic emblem) by empire? What are the possibilities of radical Asian affiliation lightly and perhaps faintly hinted at in the story, suppressed by the explicit representation of the Afghan and Lascar as passive subjects of history?

The resonance of the amputated hands with images of so-called Muslim brutality (the cutting off of hands to punish thieves, for instance) is not lost here, either. These brown hands have been severed not by barbaric Muslim extremists, but by British surgeons to save the lives of their patients, but the equivalence of these acts resounds in the macabre quality of the story. These nameless brown men are migrants caught in Euro-imperialist global trade: the Afghan hillman following the paths of commerce, now blocked and rerouted by the British, most notoriously with the 1893 imposition of the Durand Line, interfering in Central Asian trade routes and borders, and the Lascar, hired by a ship and, as Rozina Visram argues, discriminated against in England, forced to work his passage back to India under any conditions set by the ship's owners and disallowed through legislation from settling in England.[27] The suppressed histories of British interference in South and Central Asian history lie just beneath the surface of this ghost story and its formally clean ending, enabling the satisfactory ending, but also, if we read carefully, undoing it.

I will conclude by listing a set of questions that haunted me as I started writing this chapter. These questions may, in turn, seem to undo what ought to be the conclusion of this chapter. Should it even exist? In the context of an edited volume devoted to revising conventional Victorian studies accounts of the 1890s, does a "race and empire" chapter reproduce the very marginalization or even erasure that it claims to redress? Does it obscure how modern notions of race and racial difference form the epistemological, ontological, and cosmological grounds on which the other topics in this collection cohere? Does it radically reduce the complex, intensely contradictory, malleable, and at times macabre contest between Blackness, Indigeneity, and brownness as the British empire surged across North America, Asia, Africa, Australia, Oceania, and the Caribbean from the sixteenth through the twentieth centuries and, arguably, beyond?

Similarly, I asked myself, by cordoning off empire into its own chapter, are we ejecting, outsourcing even, a deep understanding of how the symbolic and material forces of British imperialism shaped and impacted the spaces, ideologies, and formations of identity for British imperialists, the non-British subjects they encountered, and for British subjects in the nation? In the 1970s and 1980s, Edward Said and Gayatri Spivak argued for how the central concepts of British national identity, such as civilization, freedom, liberal individuality, and modernity, required a fantasy of "the East" as uncivilized, unfree, and unmodern to cohere and reproduce.[28] Moreover, they showed how such a fantasy justified British and other Western European countries' violence against nonwhite peoples. Meanwhile, more recently, Elaine Freedgood and Lisa Lowe have argued that transcontinental imperial processes, such as resource extraction and the brutal traffic in humans through African slavery and Asian indentured servitude, supported British bourgeois and upper-class material lifestyles and class-wide ideological worldviews, while enriching Western European nations.[29] By setting empire off in its own chapter, are we implicitly arguing that it is a detachable structure that can be analyzed separately and thus, perhaps, addressed and settled or, even, worse, ignored in discussions of other topics? Does the self-actualization of whiteness then become the default of the other discussions? Can the 1890s be deboned of empire?[30]

How did I learn to stop worrying and love the race and empire chapter, at least, enough to write it? First of all, I think we have to maintain this chapter's obsolescence as a horizon of optimism for Victorian studies. Future edited volumes, special issues, anthology sections, conference panels, and course syllabuses may not need to address "race and empire" separately. In this future, these topics would not be cordoned off, compartmentalized, packaged, and explicitly attended to by one scholar, one journal issue, one anthology section, one conference panel, one course among a group. Instead, in this future, scholars might methodologically by default be giving space in their inquiries to the material and metaphysical effects of race and empire on the very conditions of possibility of inquiry in the first place. And, in fact, this edited volume includes critical works by Banerjee, Harrington, Lecourt, Wilhelm, Evangelista, etc. that are pointing the way forward to a more transnational approach to Victorian studies that does not isolate the treatment of racialized difference or empire to the race and empire chapter. A central precept that we can learn from ethnic studies, Indigenous studies, and Black studies, is a consideration of the historical forces that lead to the university and specifically, in my case, the US university, one that occupies Indigenous land in a country where, as Eve Tuck and K. Wayne Yang have argued, Indigenous peoples were systematically killed, enslaved, or forced to assimilate, thus erasing their language and culture, and where the land with which they had a reciprocal caregiving relation was privatized into property and then turned economically productive largely through black chattel slavery.[31] Mexicans, Chinese laborers, and, later, other Asian immigrants to the US have been subjected to overlapping but also different modes of domination, with some Latin and Asian Americans, sometimes, often solely by virtue of economic class, being allowed to inhabit a precarious proximate whiteness, always defined over and against Blackness.

In the meantime, though, I decided, after my questions subsided, we still need the space afforded by a chapter titled "race and empire." The space allows us to focus on these questions while leaving spaces for considerations of other human activities across time, the ones that grab our attention from our historical vantage point, for whatever reasons, and remind us that empire was neither totalizing nor inevitable. But, more importantly, the ongoing processes of racialization and imperialism, and the ways they disappear into common sense, their histories erased through collective national amnesia in the US, require us to continue exposing and isolating them for analyses. Perhaps, we might argue for the future obsolescence of the "race and empire" chapter and all of its other disciplinary manifestations. However, as so many critiques of race and empire, in particular of settler colonialism, point out, for this to be the case, these processes – of racialization, attended by racialized violence, and of empire, attended by the death of Indigenous peoples, now perhaps conducted as what Lauren Berlant termed slow death, and also the processes of continued occupation of stolen lands, as well as imperial operations abroad, such as in Afghanistan and Haiti – would themselves need to have ended and been redressed. While these processes continue to structure our present and current future, we continue to need the academic structures, even the distinct disciplines, that create the tools to analyze them and continuously seek to illuminate and expose them. An alternative future in which the "race and empire" chapter is obsolete is also a world in which everything is different, very much including academic labor. In other words, to talk about race and empire in the

1890s now involves attending to the historical specificity of this decade, while also attending to how those historical developments continue to be experienced in the present. The British empire may have formally ended with the handover ceremony of Hong Kong to China in 1997, but its impact and its processes are ongoing.

Notes

1 Raymond Williams, *Culture and Society, 1780–1950* (New York: Columbia University Press, 1983), 161.

2 Refer to Irene Tucker, *A Probable State: The Novel, the Contract, and the Jews* (Chicago, IL: University of Chicago Press, 2000); Terry Eagleton, "The Flight to the Real," in *Cultural Politics at the Fin de Siècle*, eds. Sally Ledger and Scott McCracken (New York: Cambridge University Press, 1995), 11–21.

3 Patrick Brantlinger, *Rule of Darkness: British Literature and Imperialism, 1830–1914* (Ithaca, NY: Cornell University Press, 1988); Stephen Arata, "The Occidental Tourist: *Dracula* and the Anxiety of Reverse Colonization," *Victorian Studies* 33, 4 (1990), 621–45.

4 Elaine Showalter, *Sexual Anarchy: Gender and Culture at the Fin-de-Siécle* (New York: Viking, 1990).

5 Zakiyyah Iman Jackson, *Becoming Human: Matter and Meaning in an Antiblack World* (New York: New York University Press, 2020).

6 Hortense Spillers, "Mama's Baby, Papa's Maybe: An American Grammar Book," *Diacritics* 17, no. 2 (1987): 64–81.

7 Jackson argues, "Plasticity is a mode of transmogrification whereby the fleshy being of blackness is experimented with as if it were infinitely malleable lexical and biological matter, such that blackness is produced as sub/super/human at once, a form where form shall not hold: potentially "everything and nothing" at the register of ontology" (3).

8 Refer to Imani Perry Vexy, *Thing: On Gender and Liberation* (Durham, NC: Duke University Press, 2018), 23–24.

9 Kyla Schuller, *The Biopolitics of Feeling: Race, Sex, and Science in the Nineteenth Century* (Durham, NC: Duke University Press, 2018).

10 Edward Beasley, *The Victorian Reinvention of Race: New Racisms and the Problem of Grouping in the Human Sciences* (New York: Routledge, 2010), 20.

11 Ania Loomba, *Colonialism/Postcolonialism* (New York: Routledge, 2005); Sylvia Wynter, "Unsettling the Coloniality of Being/Power/Truth/Freedom: Towards the Human, After Man, Its Overrepresentation – An Argument," *CR: The New Centennial Review* 3, no. 3 (2003): 257–337.

12 A. Conan Doyle, "The Story of the Brown Hand," *Strand Magazine: An Illustrated Monthly*, 17, no. 101 (1899): 499–508. *ProQuest*, http://ezproxy .msu.edu/login?url=https://www.proquest.com/historical-periodicals/round-fire/docview/4161454/se-2?accountid=12598.

13 Katherine McKittrick, *Dear Science and Other Stories* (Durham, NC: Duke University Press, 2021), 126.

14 The British conducted a second costly and ambivalently concluded war in Afghanistan, the Second Anglo-Afghan War (1878–80), to install a king to their liking and a war against a sovereign king in South Africa, the Anglo-Zulu War (1879). The 1890s themselves were bookended by the Second International (an organization of socialist and labor parties, which formed in Paris in 1890 and marked a growing critique of the capitalist organization of European society) and, on the other end, both the Second Boer War (1899–1902) and the First Pan-African Conference (London, 1900). For more on insurgency during this period, refer to Antoinette Burton, *The Trouble with Empire: Challenges to Modern British Imperialism* (New York: Oxford University Press, 2015), 145–215.

15 I am inspired here by the recent work of Manu Chander on thinking about brownness as a category of collectivity and Amardeep Singh's thoughtful consideration of how to nuance the concept so as not to be extractive of Black Studies.

16 Ronjaunee Chatterjee, Alicia Mireles Christoff, and Amy R. Wong, "Introduction: Undisciplining Victorian Studies," *Victorian Studies* 62, no. 3 (2020): 369–91.

17 Max Nordau, *Degeneration* (New York: Appleton, 1895).

18 Refer to Kyla Schuller.

19 Lauren M. E. Goodlad, *The Victorian Geopolitical Aesthetic: Realism, Sovereignty, and Transnational Experience* (New York: Oxford University Press, 2015), 6.

20 This imperial racial-moral logic goes back much further, of course, with roots in the eighteenth century. The rise of natural history and the classification system developed by scientists such as Carl Linnaeus, a Swedish botanist and physician, was not only applied to plants and animals, but also to people. Linnaeus arranged people into taxonomies articulated on scales of least civilized, and thus most inferior, to most civilized, and thus most superior. Like many European scientists and philosophers, he calibrated these scales to geography, placing Western Europe as the pinnacle of racial progress. Refer to Mary Louise Pratt, "Science, Planetary Consciousness, Interiors," in *Imperial Eyes: Travel Writing and Transculturation* (New York: Routledge, 1992), ch. 2.

21 Mrs. Ernest Ames, "An ABC, for Baby Patriots," in *Empire Writing: An Anthology of Colonial Literature, 1870–1918*, ed. Elleke Boehmer (New York: Oxford University Press, 2009), 277–80 (278).

22 Refer to Zarena Aslami, "Victorian Afghanistan, the Iron Amir, and the Poetics of Marginal Sovereignty," *Victorian Studies* 62, no. 1 (2019): 35–60.

23 As Shah Mahmoud Hanifi writes, "However, through all the intended and unintended distortion it appears reasonably clear that the British first encountered Pathan as the term to distinguish Afghans by the criterion of using

Pashto in writing and/or speech in addition to or instead of Persian" (21). Afghanistan as a nation was created by the British in the late nineteenth century and upheld by Amir Abdur Rahman, who attempted to centralize and consolidate his control over the region as it was carved out by the British (Durand Line of 1893).

Hanifi points out, "It is important to reckon with the historicity and diversity subsumed within each of those three terms, and even basic historical and semantic dissection draws attention to rich bodies of cultural and historical data for future researchers. Here and in general terms it is therefore neither accurate nor productive to impose neat and clear divisions among Afghans, Pashtuns, and Pathans in Kabul, Peshawar, and Qandahar, at least because of the ongoing movement of representatives of these communities between the three market settings. Market constraints and opportunities motivate individuals to consciously self-identify, however loosely, with more than one category. In other words, market environments tend to favor complex and multiple identities" (22). Shah Mahmoud Hanifi, *Connecting Histories in Afghanistan: Market Relations and State Formation on a Colonial Frontier* (Stanford, CA: Stanford University Press, 2008).

24 John Kuo Wei Tchen and Dylan Yeats, *Yellow Peril! An Archive of Anti-Asian Fear* (New York: Verso, 2014), 26.

25 For more on the potential of brown collectivity, refer to Joseph M. Pierce and Manu Samriti Chander, "Cousin Theory: Brown Kinship and the Nineteenth-Century Domestic Novel," *Victorian Studies* 62, no. 3 (2020): 474–85.

26 Instead, drawing on Axelle Karera's reflections on the ethics of nonrelationality, Neyra writes, "However, this nonblack writer does not view relation as a given and writes with the suspended assumption that the sign of blackness must necessarily move toward commonality with nonblack signs and positions – on the levels of poetics, sociality, or aesthetics," a move to which I aspire, as well, in this chapter. Ren Ellis Neyra, "*The Question of Ethics in the Semiotics of Brownness*," SX SALON (2020), http://smallaxe.net/sxsalon/dis cussions/question-ethics-semiotics-brownness. For this important intervention, I am grateful to Amardeep Singh, who refers to Neyra to make a similar point in his Modern Language Association conference presentation on the emergent field of Critical Brownness Studies. Amardeep Singh, "Thoughts on Brownness Studies," Modern Language Association Conference, January 2021, Virtual Conference Presentation (printed on his blog at http://www .electrostani.com/2021/01/thoughts-on-brownness-studies-for-mla.html).

27 Rozina Visram, *Asians in Britain: 400 Years of History*, Kindle ed. (London: Pluto Press, 2002). Refer especially to Visram's ch. 3, "A Community in the Making, 1830s–1914."

28 Gayatri Chakravorty Spivak, "Three Women's Texts and a Critique of Imperialism," *Critical Inquiry* 12, no. 1 (1985): 243–61; Edward W. Said, *Orientalism* (New York: Vintage Books, 1994).

29 Elaine Freedgood, *The Ideas in Things: Fugitive Meaning in the Victorian Novel* (Chicago, IL: University of Chicago Press, 2006); Lisa Lowe, *The Intimacies of Four Continents* (Durham, NC: Duke University Press, 2015).

30 These questions have also been addressed at length and with care by Chatterjee, Christoff, and Wong.

31 Eve Tuck and K. Wayne Yang, "Decolonization Is Not a Metaphor," *Decolonization: Indigeneity, Education & Society* 1, no. 1 (2012): 1–40.

CHAPTER 2

Island Dandies, Transpacific Decadence, and the Politics of Style

Lindsay Wilhelm

In May 1903, the Hawaiian-language newspaper *Ka Nupepa Kuokoa* announced the death of pioneering hula master and musician ʻIoane ʻŪkēkē. ʻŪkēkē, along with his troupe, had been a fixture at the famously lively court of David Kalākaua, who presided over a revival of Kanaka Maoli (Native Hawaiian) dance and music in the 1870s and 1880s.[1] But more noteworthy for the obituary writer was ʻŪkēkē's extravagant personal wardrobe, which had since passed into local legend: in his heyday, the obituary reads, "Ioane was seen in the streets in his velvet coat, beaver hat, monocle and cane; the foreigners called him 'dandy.'"[2] Notices in other newspapers similarly memorialized the natty outfits and elegant carriage of the so-called Hawaiian Beau Brummell, often known as "Dandy" ʻŪkēkē or simply "the Dandy."[3]

His idiosyncratic celebrity aside, ʻŪkēkē is emblematic of a peculiar construction of dandyish masculinity that emerges in transpacific writing from the last decades of the nineteenth century. In this chapter, I explore how Anglo-American conceptions of the dandy crossed and recrossed the Pacific in a period of accelerating colonization in the region, intersecting along the way with Indigenous ideals of courtly masculinity. To that end, I draw on an array of fiction and nonfiction writing by authors from Hawaiʻi, the US, and Britain, including Kalākaua – a folklorist as well as king – the American travel writer Charles Warren Stoddard, Robert Louis Stevenson, and Lydia Liliʻuokalani, Hawaiʻi's last monarch and author of the stirring memoir *Hawaii's Story by Hawaii's Queen* (1898).

My purpose in marshaling these diverse materials is twofold. First, and in the spirit of the entire volume, this chapter challenges the centering of Britishness within Victorian studies. Scholars such as Caroline Levine, Ronjaunee Chatterjee, Amy Wong, and Alicia Christoff have recently called upon us to rethink the field's investment in what Levine calls the "logic of autochthony"; Hawaiʻi, with its historical ties to Britain as well as its position at the crossroads of the Pacific, is in many ways an ideal locus for inquiries that might "reorient" literary studies, to quote Levine again, "around the network rather than the nation."[4] Secondly, in relinquishing the nation as the framing of my analysis, I also consciously push back against the impulse to map these literary sources onto neat lineages of influence – a formulation that can, in effect, relegate writers of color to the relatively passive postures of appropriation or rejection. What I hope to reveal is a more unsettled dynamics of exchange, in which literary figurations of the Hawaiian dandy acquire and shed cultural valences according to the needs and commitments of their authors.

Such an approach seems particularly necessary when it comes to our understanding of the 1890s. As Regenia Gagnier has suggested in her recent essay on feminism and global decadence, we can conceive of decadence not only as a set of shared tropes, circulated among exclusive cliques of Rhymers' Club members and *Yellow Book* contributors, but also an immanent response to the conditions of political, economic, and technological modernity. Dandyism, too – if I may oversimplify Susan Sontag's formulation of the "old style" dandy – is a posture of aristocratic "detachment" from the modern.[5] Seen in this light, decadence is a kind of borderless and transhistorical sensibility that erupts in multiple places at once, in "dialectical relations" with ongoing processes of capitalist globalization and neoliberal nation-building.[6] This conception of decadence allows us to recognize, in turn, its peculiar salience for Hawai'i in the 1890s, when a century of insidious colonial incursion boiled over into armed political conflict. In his protean capacities as an object of queer cross-cultural desire, a lesson in racial degeneration, and a vehicle for countercolonial resistance, the island dandy becomes a potent symbol for his era's deeply conflicted relationship to the modern.

Transpacific Dandyism before 1890

Despite its geographic isolation, the Kingdom of Hawai'i – which lasted from 1795 until Lili'uokalani's forced abdication in 1893 – was a nexus for global cultural exchange, with a richly eclectic national culture, an unusually high literacy rate, and a correspondingly robust periodical market. Over 100 distinct Hawaiian-language newspaper titles appeared between 1834 and 1940, resulting in an astonishingly vast print archive that runs, according to some estimates, into the millions of pages. As Hawaiian studies scholars remind us, this massive archive is only sporadically utilized. Noelani Arista notes that histories of Hawai'i tend to default to English-language sources in the (mistaken) assumption of "primary-source scarcity"; M. Puakea Nogelmeier likewise points out a scholarly over-reliance on the small fraction of Hawaiian-language journalism available in English translation.[7] While my own engagement with these sources is limited by my scanty reading knowledge of Hawaiian, I would draw our attention to this archive, which – if approached with the Indigenously grounded critical praxis that Arista and others lay out – could immensely expand the resources available to researchers of the global nineteenth century.

This is doubly the case because many of these Hawaiian newspapers devoted significant column inches to serialized translations of foreign-language literature. As Noenoe K. Silva and Bryan Kuwada observe in their respective surveys, medieval romances and folktales were especially popular, but nineteenth-century Hawaiian readers also had ready access to more recent fiction, including Walter Scott's *Ivanhoe* (1819), Alexandre Dumas's *The Count of Monte Cristo* (1846), and Jules Verne's *20,000 Leagues Under the Sea* (1870).[8] Given the complexities of translation and the sheer volume of material, it is undoubtedly futile to pinpoint any specific text as the pathway by which Anglo-American ideas of dandyism passed into Hawaiian popular culture.[9] We might more safely posit that this abundance of translated texts, compounded by the sartorial flair of Hawai'i's monarchs (more in the section "Indigenous Dandyism") and the steady influx of foreigners after the mid-nineteenth century, fostered widespread interest in imported fashion. A biographical novel about Mary Stuart, serialized in *Kuokoa* in the 1860s, discusses the cut of her velvet gowns in some detail; from the 1870s onward, advertisements for shops selling silk parasols and other luxury textiles for women and men proliferate in the newspaper's back pages.[10]

Certainly, visitors often commented on the aesthetic attractions of Native Hawaiians and Polynesians more generally. Much of this fascination was trained on the sinuous limbs of women dancers – a cliché that persists in the modern image of the grass-skirted "hula girl" – but travel writing from this period is also replete with instances of queer-coded masculine beauty.[11] As Natasha Hurley observes, Herman Melville's best-selling adventure tale *Typee* (1846), set in Nuku Hiva, features distinctly erotic descriptions of Indigenous men, one of whom the narrator likens to a "Polynesian Apollo."[12] Drawing on Melville's Arcadian visions, Charles Warren Stoddard's memoir *South-Seas Idyls* (1873) candidly recalls his affairs with younger Hawaiian men in terms associated with classical antiquity. He first spots a youth named Joe, for instance, at a "riotous sort of festival" redolent of a moonlit Bacchanal: the boy's physique is so "fresh and joyous," he writes, "that I began to realize how the old Greeks could worship mere physical beauty and forget its higher forms."[13] In a tone by turns affectionate and ironic, Stoddard goes on to recount "how he got me into all sorts of trouble" (Stoddard, *South-Seas Idyls,* 115), including an incident in which Joe spends the author's meager store of cash on a new suit of clothes that renders him "gorgeous beyond description" (117). Throughout Stoddard's account, Joe's beauty is dependent on not only the statuesque proportions of his unclad body, but also his ability to display himself to advantage in both Western and Hawaiian garb.

Stoddard links this Indigenous aesthetics more closely to dandyism in his later memoir *Hawaiian Life,* originally serialized as "Lazy Letters from Low Latitudes" in *Overland Monthly* in 1883–84 and expanded for volume publication in 1894. One of these letters makes special mention of 'Ūkēkē, identified here only as "the dandy." While Stoddard claims that 'Ūkēkē is the "only indigenous dude" (using "dude" in its original denotation, as a slangy synonym for dandy), his surrounding account of urban Honolulu anticipates the metropolitan café societies of the 1890s. On concert nights, Emma Square transforms into what he calls a "playground for the indifferent children of the earth": "pretty girls," "gay riding parties," and "a proper proportion of young gentlemen loungers" who "stroll about in tennis suits" and "distribute their compliments with judicious impartiality."[14] Like the racially liminal Joe, the "highly decorative youths" gathered in this "marvelous green half-acre" both transgress and travesty normative boundaries, especially those demarcating race and class. Lulled by the "easy familiarity of social life in the tropics," the "British admiral . . . meet[s] his crew on the dead level," while the "*gamin* . . . return[s] the royal salute with some pomposity."

For Stoddard, Hawaiian dandies also traverse simplistic distinctions between nature and culture. Elsewhere in his memoirs, he recounts a whirlwind relationship with the lovely Kána-aná, whose own "honest" gaze licenses Stoddard's rather salacious cataloging of the boy's "round, full, rather girlish face" and "ripe and expressive lips." But despite Kána-aná's association with innocent sensuality, the first thing Stoddard notices is his outfit: a "straw hat, bound with wreaths of fern and *maile,*" and a "snow-white garment" that clashes with the lush jungle surrounding him (Stoddard, *South-Seas Idyls,* 27–28). Kána-aná's self-presentation is simultaneously spontaneous and artful, paradoxical in a way that Stoddard exploits to humorous and poignant effect. Through their very ornamentality, "indigenous dude[s]" such as 'Ūkēkē, Joe, and Kána-aná disrupt the writer's fantasies of an Edenic, primordial queerness. The Hawaiian dandy's body becomes the juncture at which primitivism – one of the "organizing categories of colonial discourse," as Rod Edmond explains – runs up against the effusive antinatural energy that Rhonda K. Garelick and Jack Halberstam associate with late nineteenth-century gay aesthetes.[15]

The politics underlying this tension are correspondingly complex. On the one hand, the unabashed homoeroticism of Stoddard's writing complicates the dynamics of what film scholar E. Ann Kaplan terms the "imperial gaze": a mode of looking that centralizes the white Western subject at the expense of the gazed-upon Other. While this gaze often serves as leverage for colonial domination, Kaplan argues that its power cuts both ways, so that "white subjectivities ... can also be destabilized when exposed to the gaze of the Other."[16] Joseph Boone, in his study of homoeroticism and Orientalism, similarly stresses the "never completely coherent aspects" of the image of the "beautiful boy," a topos of queer sex tourism that – like any other Orientalist stereotype – both serves and calls into question Orientalist myth.[17] This destabilization is clearly at work in Stoddard's memoirs, in a manner inextricable from his queering of cross-cultural encounter. In his recollection of Kána-aná, for instance, Stoddard plays against the advantages of age, race, and nationality by casting himself in the feminizing role of seduced ingenue: "at the mercy" of the boy's candid and assertive sexual curiosity, the much older Stoddard feels himself "flatter[ed] ... into submission against [his] will" (Stoddard, *South-Seas Idyls,* 28). That the "highly decorative youths" he "observes" in the square are also engaged in their own observations – 'Ūkēkē, though nearly blind by 1890, "looks in upon us with undimmed eye-glass" – has the effect of muddling the expected directionality of objectification. For Stoddard, the Hawaiian dandy is both a performer of erotic gender indeterminacy and a consummate gazer himself. As such, the dandy's regard grants Stoddard the dual specular pleasures of looking and being looked at, of mastering the other and being mastered by him.

On the other hand, however, Stoddard's tacit characterization of the Hawaiian dandy as decadent airs more nakedly colonialist narratives of racial degeneration, which Patrick Brantlinger groups under the umbrella of "extinction discourse."[18] The dandyish proteges of *South-Seas Idyls,* for example, come to uniformly tragic ends: Stoddard abandons Kána-aná when he begins to recognize "symptoms of imbecility" in the halcyon indolence of their domestic life, and Joe eventually contracts leprosy, which disfigures him so completely as to "kill the memory of his former beauty" (39, 124). In "Lazy Letters," Stoddard describes the now disabled 'Ūkēkē as being "on his last legs," his decrepitude a mute warning to the

bright young things flitting about around him (311). Despite his willingness to engage with them in (albeit brief) relationships of reciprocated
vulnerability, Stoddard structures the lives of these Hawaiian men around
trajectories of stasis and decline, in part to shore up the arc of his own
"prodigal" reckoning (Stoddard, *South-Seas Idyls,* 41). The dandy, to quote
Sontag once again, stands in "extremely sentimental" relation to the past:
in Stoddard's memoirs, this sentimentality expresses itself in proleptic
regret for a way of life that he presumes is passing away (280). His persona
as the wistful chronicler of a bygone era – a persona he reasserts in the even
more nostalgic 1894 edition of *Hawaiian Life* – reduces the Hawaiian
dandy to an avatar for his supposedly doomed people, victims of "the
inevitable climax" of extinction (238).

The Dandy as Degenerate

To many non-Hawaiian writers, Indigenous extinction was tied to the
purported hedonism of a culture that, in Stoddard's words, threatens to
turn tourists and natives alike into "silken Sybarites" (Stoddard, "Lazy
Letters," 312). In this context, the dandy's unapologetic extravagance
makes him something of a poster child for racial decline. Several of
'Ūkēkē's English-language obituaries drew on this elegiac strain, extracting
moral significance from the ignoble circumstances of his death. In a
retrospective on his career, the *Pacific Commercial Advertiser* reminds its
readers that 'Ūkēkē had spent much of the 1890s busking to survive: the
obituary pointedly juxtaposes anecdotes about "the 'Dandy' of old" with a
sketch of the "decrepit, tattered, blind old man, who squatted on Fort
street pavements, playing a jewsharp and extending his hat for alms." The
next day, the *Advertiser* ran an archival photograph of the "Dandy in His
Prime" alongside a caption noting how he "died last week in blindness and
poverty"[19] (Figure 2.1). Underlying these retrospectives is the insinuation
that 'Ūkēkē's impoverishment and disability were the unavoidable, if
regrettable, consequences of his youthful profligacy.

   Among the most enduring of these dandies-turned-cautionary-tales was
the lawyer, editor, and translator William Ragsdale, who makes both
explicit and veiled appearances in late nineteenth-century accounts of the
islands. The mixed-race scion of minor Hawaiian nobility, Ragsdale rose to
prominence as the official interpreter to the House of Commons, where he
developed a reputation as a charismatic public speaker and irreverent wit.[20]
In a letter from 1866, Mark Twain recounts watching Ragsdale translate
legislative proceedings with "a readiness and facility of language that are

"DANDY" IN HIS PRIME.

An Old Photograph of the Hawaiian Beau Brummel who died last week in blindness and poverty.

Figure 2.1 "Dandy in His Prime," *Pacific Commercial Advertiser*, May 5, 1903.

remarkable": an amused Twain also alludes to "a spice of deviltry in the fellow's nature," evident in his habit of inserting a choice word that, "without departing from the spirit of the member's remarks, . . . will make the gravest speech utterly ridiculous."[21] How Twain, who spoke no Hawaiian, detected the nuances of Ragsdale's satirical voice is unclear, but in any case, the writer found Ragsdale so compelling that he later outlined an unfinished novel based on his life.[22]

Part and parcel of Ragsdale's renown as a "rascal" – as Twain designated him – was his studied self-presentation. In her popular travelogue *The Hawaiian Archipelago* (1875), Isabella Bird describes Ragsdale as both "a leading spirit among the natives" and a dandy in the European style: "His conversation was eloquent and poetic, though rather stilted," she writes, "and he has a good deal of French mannerism . . . He has appeared in three different suits, with light kid gloves to match, all equally elegant, in two days."[23] Julius Palmer, a Boston-born journalist who served as Lili'uokalani's secretary after her abdication, similarly recalls the arresting presence of this "island genius" in his 1894 memoir *Memories of Hawaii*. "Bill Ragsdale!" Palmer enthuses, "Shall I ever forget him?" In a subsequent character sketch, Palmer describes how his "own heart thrilled with pride" at the spectacle of Ragsdale on the dais, "attired as usual in a spotless suit of white cashmere that would do honor to any window in the Somerset Club next July." Like Twain, Palmer also delightedly relates Ragsdale's rakish irresponsibility: the stylishness of his cashmere ensemble is made more impressive by the fact that, as Palmer informs us, the interpreter "had just been sent to the chain-gang with his head broken by a drunken brawl."[24]

For Bird and Palmer, Ragsdale's fame as an *enfant terrible* was cemented by his sudden diagnosis of leprosy in 1873. As I have pointed out elsewhere, Bird acknowledges the pathos of his early demise even as she intimates his culpability in his own infection.[25] Late in *The Hawaiian Archipelago*, she watches the stricken dandy, "carefully dressed as usual," deliver his final farewell to a crowd of mourners gathered on the beach before departing for the remote settlement of Kalaupapa. Bird, unmoved by this scene, declares him "certainly the most 'notorious' man in Hilo," then proceeds to elaborate on his ambivalent brilliance: "He has a remarkable gift of eloquence, and his manner, though theatrical, is considered perfect by his native admirers. His moral character, however, has been very low, which makes the outburst of feeling at his fate the more remarkable" (364). While the syntactical logic of "however" suggests a contrast between two distinct aspects of Ragsdale's personality, Bird's indictment of his "moral character" is closely tied to her faint praise for his "gift of eloquence." As Edmond explains, "during the 1870s and 80s leprosy in Hawaii was increasingly moralized as a just punishment" for sexual license and other vices (Edmond, *Representing the South Pacific*, 196). That leprosy is an affliction of the skin, in which internal disorder manifests in easily recognizable lesions, makes the disease especially fitting penance for what Bird represents as Ragsdale's dandyish superficiality. The fact that Ragsdale "might have escaped suspicion for some time" also lends Bird's telling an air of menace: had Ragsdale chosen not to report his diagnosis, his sense of style and talent for the "theatrical," coupled with his status as a "half-white," might have otherwise equipped him to evade detection (Bird, *Hawaiian Archipelago,* 365). At the same time that leprosy promises to disclose his indiscretions on his skin, its latency also remakes his dandyism into a public health risk. It is with some relief, consequently, that Bird sees Ragsdale safely ensconced on the whaleboat that carries him "towards his living grave" (366).

Palmer, a lifelong supporter of Hawaiian sovereignty, handles Ragsdale's story with more sympathy and tact: while "a weaker man would have concealed [the] commencement" of his illness, Palmer's Ragsdale instead surrenders himself to the authorities and "[throws] the whole force of his passionate soul into a farewell address" before bravely embarking on his exile. But even in the midst of his tribute, Palmer nonetheless bemoans what he describes as Ragsdale's incapacity to "conform to the laws of good society," at least when it comes to "certain matters of conduct and morals"; Palmer further claims that Ragsdale shares these vague, unspecified failings "in common with his people" (Palmer, *Memories of Hawaii,* 4, 20). While he stops short of directly attributing Ragsdale's leprosy (and subsequent death in 1877) to his purportedly wild conduct, Palmer imbues him with the trappings of a tragic hero, brought low by a hereditary predisposition to debauchery.

As Palmer's memoirs suggest, Ragsdale's story not only continued to intrigue readers well into the 1890s, but also gained symbolic weight in conjunction with fin-de-siècle discourses surrounding decadence and degeneration. Robert Louis Stevenson and his wife, Fanny Van de Grift Stevenson, repurposed aspects of Ragsdale's biography in their own fiction from this period, which seeks to capture what Robert elsewhere calls the "shadow of mortality" hovering over the Pacific.[26] Chris J. Thomas has recently argued that Stevenson aspired toward an "authenticity" he found lacking in other Anglo-American travel accounts; Ragsdale's meteoric rise and fall, which the Stevensons likely learned about while living in Hawai'i in the 1880s, furnished source material for their conscious deconstruction of paradisical myths about the islands.[27] Fanny's short story "The Half-White," published in *Scribner's Magazine* in 1891, recreates almost exactly the details of the interpreter's early self-diagnosis: like Ragsdale, the Catholic priest Father Canonhurst discovers that he has leprosy when he burns himself on a kerosene lamp and finds that his skin is insensate to pain.[28] While the leper in question is neither a dandy nor a Native Hawaiian, Stevenson's focal character, the languid and listless poet Laurence, candidly admits that he has come to Hawai'i on an aesthete's quest to "[lay] in a rich store of impressions and experiences" (Stevenson, "The Half-White," 282). Canonhurst's tortured confession of his "carnal" love for the titular "half-white" (288) – a half-Hawaiian woman named Lulani, who is also Laurence's beloved – finally jolts the young "lotus-eater" out of his decadent "affectations" (282). Dispersed across all three characters in this love triangle, Ragsdale's example serves to disclose what Fanny presents as the sordid human drama beneath the frothy veneer of island life.

Robert's fairy tale "The Bottle Imp," published in periodical form in 1891 and reprinted in his 1893 collection *Island Nights' Entertainments*, draws more directly from the Ragsdale mythos. The protagonist of the tale, a Hawaiian sailor named Keawe, comes into possession of a mysterious bottle that grants its owner unlimited wishes, but at the cost of his soul: anyone who dies while in possession of the bottle is damned to hell, and one can only sell it at a price lower than what one paid for it. Keawe, aware of the danger, uses the bottle and swiftly passes it along to a new owner before meeting and wooing the beautiful Kokua. On the cusp of their wedding, however, he contracts leprosy and must avail himself of the bottle's power once more in order to cure himself.[29] I have argued previously for reading "The Bottle Imp" as a well-meaning fable about the perils of an aesthetic life, and I would reiterate here how Keawe is clearly modeled on Ragsdale. Besides echoing the (unsubstantiated) rumor that Ragsdale was newly engaged when he fell ill, Stevenson invests his protagonist with Ragsdale's panache and distinctly epicurean tastes (Tayman, *The Colony*, 101). Keawe spends much of his magically obtained wealth on fine things, including a snappy white suit – pictured in the story's original illustrations – and a beautiful house adorned "with all manner of furniture," "pictures ... in golden frames," "weapons of price from all quarters of the world," and other "elegant" and useless "knick-knacks" (167–68). To be sure, the story's fantastic element allows Stevenson to give Keawe a happy conclusion, in which Kokua cleverly uses her knowledge of currency to rescue her husband from eternal damnation. But on a structural level, Keawe's redemption is premised on the excision of his dandyish proclivities: he is struck down in the midst of his luxury, and the successful resolution of the plot depends on his acceptance of Kokua as a resourceful and educated helpmeet rather than merely "the brightest thing in [the house's] three storeys" (194). By the end of the tale, the pair have settled into a comfortable domesticity that stands in tacit repudiation of Keawe's frivolous, and implicitly queer, bachelor life as an effete collector.

Granted, Stevenson offers a kinder portrait of Ragsdale than Bird does – a difference we can attribute in part to Stevenson's affinity for Polynesian culture (he and Fanny lived in Samoa until his death in 1894), his fluency in several of its languages, and his heartfelt support for Indigenous self-determination. But Keawe's dandyism acquires a didactic edge when placed alongside other representations of similar Hawaiian figures. For British and American writers entrenched in late nineteenth-century Western discourses of decadence and racial decline, dandies such as 'Ūkēkē and Ragsdale are freighted with subversive – sometimes thrilling but more often threatening – cultural signification. To varying degrees, these representations perpetuated an understanding of Indigenous precarity that, however well-intentioned, also paved the way for colonialist intervention in the Pacific. These constructions of dandyism were, furthermore, not endemic to Hawai'i: after all, when searching for a moniker for 'Ūkēkē, the press landed on the eminently British touchstone of Beau Brummell. For the remainder of this chapter, I explore evocations of dandyism in several writings by Hawaiian authors, with an eye toward unearthing approaches to style that both overlapped with and cut across transplanted figurations of the dandy.

Indigenous Dandyism

In her analysis of Black dandyism, Monica L. Miller explains how the dandy "can, at once, subvert and fulfill normative categories of identity at different times and places as a gesture of self-articulation"; in this capacity, he necessarily embodies "a critique against the hierarchies that order society."[30] As Miller reminds us, the social critique inhering in the dandy's "pointed redeployment of clothing, gesture, and wit" is particularly powerful when leveled by people of color (Miller, *Slaves to Fashion*, 5). Consider 'Ūkēkē, who proliferated his own image through studio photographs of himself both alone and with members of his troupe (Figure 2.2). These portraits reveal a man whose command of Western style seems calculated to overturn primitivist stereotypes: in them, the hula master is invariably outfitted in the elaborate suits he designed himself, and he often sports his signature monocle and cane. His posture, from his crossed leg to the tilt of his top hat, projects a self-conscious, mincing delicacy that

Figure 2.2   Detail from Hawaii album, Miscellaneous Items in High Demand collection, Prints & Photographs Division, Library of Congress, LC-DIG-ds-09909.

amplifies the resplendence of his dress. He strikes gestural poses – puffing from an unlit cigar (as pictured) or holding his monocle up to one eye – that both emulate and caricature European class pretension. Importantly, 'Ūkēkē also trains his gaze directly at the camera, as if daring the observer to reconcile, if they can, his manifest glamour with reductive fantasies of "going native."

The political stakes of this oppositional dandyism emerge with striking clarity in the life and work of David Kalākaua, who served as Hawai'i's monarch from his election to the throne in 1874 until his death in 1891. Scholarly and well-traveled, Kalākaua reinvigorated the Kingdom's extant program of international diplomacy, which developed, under his management, into a network of consulates spread across six continents; in 1881, he circumnavigated the globe with the goal of cementing existing alliances, securing immigration agreements, and observing the inner workings of other governments.[31] Due partly to his diplomatic commitments and partly to the circumstances of his ascension, Kalākaua's assertions of authority at home and abroad depended to an unusual degree on his proficiency in the outward forms of European aristocratic life. Clothing, bearing, and address were thus integral to the monarch's self-presentation. Many of the letters he sent during his world tour touch on official decorations and matters of fashion – one missive from London, for example, conveys detailed instructions for alterations to his party's uniforms, down to the specific embroidery motifs – and he continued to invest immense expense and thought into state rituals and regalia throughout his reign.[32]

Kalākaua's dandyish merger of courtly formality with avant-garde sensibility largely defined his reputation. In 1894, a few years after Kalākaua's death, Stoddard described the late monarch as both a romantic figure – "such a king one reads of in nursery tales" – and a free-thinking, aphoristic bon vivant who "even affected Bohemianism to a degree."[33] The sparkling urbanity of his deportment and conversation also made Kalākaua something of a celebrity in the global press, which fawned over his ability to speak French "as well as a Parisian," his "strikingly low, mellow, and musical voice," and his keen interest in statecraft and technology.[34] Several more hostile write-ups articulated these qualities in a recognizably aesthetic idiom. The *New York Times*, for instance, reported that his "elegant figure . . . is dressed by a fashionable English tailor," and observed that "the rose and sprig of jessamine in his buttonhole give him a foppish air"; the *Hampshire Telegraph*, noting that Kalākaua had attended a staging of F. C. Burnand's new satire *The Colonel* (1881), archly charged its readers to "just fancy the King of the Sandwich Islands 'doing' an aesthetic play!"[35] Even positive coverage fired off racially charged quips about the incongruity of Kalākaua's refinement, which outlets such as the *Telegraph* bolstered with unsourced claims about cannibalism.

In *The Legends and Myths of Hawaii* (1888), Kalākaua pushes back against this skepticism by establishing a precedent for his dandyism in precontact Hawaiian culture. A compendium of folklore and historical record, *Legends and Myths* presents an ideal of Indigenous masculinity in which dress, etiquette, and a certain flamboyant confidence form important components. "The Sacred Spearpoint," for example, follows the pleasure-seeking prince Kaululāʻau, whose adventures begin when he is exiled from Maui for his "rollicking spirit of mischief and merriment." Although the story initially sets up what appears to be an instructive contrast with his more "austere and circumspect" cousin, Kaululāʻau is ultimately rewarded not only for his cleverness and verve, but also for his ability to utilize the performative trappings of kingship. At the climax of the story, when the young prince is mistaken for a common warrior and detained by a malicious priest, Kaululāʻau sneaks back onto his canoe in order to "hurriedly invest himself with the regalia of rank, including helmet, feather mantle, and spear"; outfitted with the accoutrement of aliʻi, or royalty, he outmaneuvers his jailors and pays a formal visit to the local chief, who recognizes Kaululāʻau as a peer and soon sets the matter to rights (interestingly, the spear in this scenario functions as pure symbol, and the issue is resolved peaceably).[36] The prince's strategic reliance on stylistic finesse and nimble diplomacy, rather than brute force, recurs throughout the collection. In Kalākaua's telling, the protagonists of these tales are almost invariably "dignified, correct and courtly," and they bear out these qualities both in what they wear – "mantle[s] of finely-woven and decorated cloth," wreaths of "brilliant feathers," ornaments of bone and shell – and in their blithe, festive generosity (126).

Like ʻŪkēkē, then, Kalākaua capitalizes on the capacity for dress to disarm the expectations of white observers, but *Legends and Myths* moreover insists on the broader geopolitical efficacy of Kaululāʻau's (and, by extension, Kalākaua's) sartorial heroics. As Lorenz Gonschor argues, Kalākaua's foreign policy departed "from earlier approaches of cultural Westernization as a strategy of similitude to one of advocating modernity but emphasizing cultural distinctiveness."[37] The model of leadership he presents in *Legends and Myths* evinces, accordingly, a cultural and temporal hybridity, drawing together Native Hawaiian modes of governance, the "courtly" practices of European royalty, and the insurgent epicureanism of the fin de siècle. In this context, the attention to dress and manner that the *New York Times* deemed "foppish," and which Stoddard attributed to an affected "Bohemianism," emerges as a viable apparatus of soft state power. Far from a mere personal freak, dandyism furnishes the means by which Kalākaua bodies forth the balance between Indigenous tradition and cosmopolitan modernity that he attempts to strike also in his governance.

Establishing this balance became especially critical after 1887, when a group of aggrieved foreign elites coerced Kalākaua into signing a new constitution that stripped him of most of his executive authority. While their motivations were manifold, the proponents of what came to be known as the Bayonet Constitution – the opening salvo in a conflict that culminated in the overthrow of the Hawaiian monarchy six years later – publicly justified their objections by painting the king as a spendthrift hedonist.[38] His sister and successor, Lydia Liliʻuokalani, addresses these charges of "reckless extravagance" in her 1898 memoir *Hawaii's Story by Hawaii's Queen*, written partly in a bid for American support for her restoration.[39] Tellingly, she defends Kalākaua not by denying his prioritization of "merrymaking," but rather by contesting his critics' utilitarian calculus. She reasons that "festivities" such as his coronation, in which the grounds of the newly built ʻIolani Palace "were given up to pleasure," serve to "awaken in the people a national pride." On this basis, she declares Kalākaua's expenditures "quite justified," and she dismisses his detractors as "men who 'carry the bag'" and are thus "not always the best judges of royal obligations" (Liliʻuokalani, *Hawaii's Story,* 104–05). As Jonathan Kay Kamakawiwoʻole Osorio points out, her assessment emphasizes "class distinctions" between the conspirators – political actors whose primary concern is the national budget – and aliʻi such as herself and her brother, whom she exempts from such considerations by virtue of their royal blood (Osorio, *Dismembering Lāhui,* 203).

For Liliʻuokalani, these competing imperatives bear on issues far weightier than the cost of Kalākaua's coronation. Her memoir presents both the dispute over her brother's legacy and the Kingdom's struggle for autonomy as several fronts in a much grander "revolution" in social relations (Liliʻuokalani, *Hawaii's Story,* 169). Liliʻuokalani broaches the effects of this momentous shift in the very first pages of her narrative, which offer a retrospective on her father's experiences as a minor aliʻi on Oʻahu. She asserts that her father's fiefdom, and Indigenous Hawaiian society more generally, operated on principles of mutuality, fostered by the kind of open-handed extravagance for which Kalākaua had been pilloried. By caring for his retainers without stint, aliʻi such as her father maintained their power without the need for formalized economic arrangements such as mortgages or rent (she goes on to blame the "homeless condition of the Hawaiians at the present day" squarely on the introduction of these financial innovations [3]). Liliʻuokalani detects echoes of similar changes in the estate surrounding Clivedon House in Buckinghamshire, which she visited in 1887. Only a hundred years prior, she reflects, "the element of sport and the thirst for pleasure" formed the basis of the manor's social life, "and yet, with all their gayety, [the lords and mistresses] were able to provide for the sustenance and happiness" of their tenants. By contrast, the vacant, "desolate" Clivedon of the late nineteenth century attests to the paucity of a world increasingly structured around capital accumulation: "Now the lord of the manor rises early, and hurries away to the city, where important matters at the bank, or the shipping-office, or the lawyer's desk, are waiting for him" (169). Like Hawai'i, the English countryside bears the ghostly traces of a happier, more genial way of life no longer sustainable under capitalism.

It is against the backdrop of this joyless pragmatism that the dandy makes his unexpected, but surprisingly appropriate, reentrance into the memoir. After narrating her sobering tour of Clivedon, Lili'uokalani recounts how she and her party then steamed down the Thames to admire the "many pretty pictures of modern life" along its "picturesque" banks. She recollects with special fondness "the presence of two entertaining young men of leisure," who joined the party at the last minute and "contributed much to our pleasure and information" (170). Although she cannot recall their names, her description of these strangers hearkens back to her earlier recollections of both Kalākaua and their late younger brother Leleiohoku, with his marked "taste for the social pleasures, and . . . the gay and festive element of life" (52). Without identifying any of these figures as dandies per se, Lili'uokalani links her brothers, the young men of leisure, and the old lords of Clivedon through their shared penchant for styles of affect and conduct devalued in a contemporary society "intent on . . . business." The purposeless fun of Lili'uokalani's "delightful day" on the Thames – in the very city that she recognizes as the "grand center" of global commerce – evokes the dandy's gleeful contempt for the modern regime of workaday productivity (169–70).

These defiantly joyful episodes dwindle in the last third of *Hawaii's Story*, which relates the harrowing circumstances of Lili'uokalani's imprisonment and abdication. But the memoir's preceding celebration of the "gay and festive element of life" throws into starker relief its concluding protest against the Western "race for conquest," in which the deposed queen warns that the US will "degenerate" into "a colonizer and a land-grabber" if it takes the fatal step of annexing Hawai'i (372). Against the threat of violent dispossession, driven by "enterprising people" bent on "mak[ing] money for themselves" (362), the pursuit of pleasure in that which furthers no profit motive – dress and ornament, coronation feasts, a trip down the Thames – acquires all the might of political rebellion. Like Kalākaua, Lili'uokalani underscores the Janus-like ambivalence of the dandy (or the "man of leisure"), who embraces fin-de-siècle heterodoxy while also channeling precapitalist, precolonial modes of social relation. Divested of the moral stigma inhering in Anglo-American discourses of decadence, their representations of dandyism offer us an alternative perspective on the 1890s: one in which the dandy's style enacts, on a small scale, nuanced modes of Indigenous persistence at the turn of the century.

This perspective bears out, I hope, the value of defining decadence more broadly, in ways that surface latent connections between apparently far-flung cultural phenomena. Turning to the disciplinary questions that structure this volume, I would reiterate how the Hawaiian dandy in particular – situated at the intersections of past and present, globalism and Indigeneity – affords modes of literary and historical analysis beyond the paradigm of influence. I admit that I tend to cleave to just this model of study; in comparing texts, my first instinct is to search for traces of verifiable contact and transmission. Anyone expecting such concrete connections will likely find this chapter's claims rather gauzy. But what we might lose in rigor, we gain in comprehension: by expanding our scope outward, we catch glimpses of a decadence that transcends national borders, crystallized in a decade that saw itself as the end of one age and the herald of a new one.

Notes

1 Christopher B. Balme, *Pacific Performances: Theatricality and Cross-Cultural Encounters in the South Seas* (Basingstoke: Palgrave Macmillan, 2007), 111–12.

2 "Ua Nalohia Kona Leo Uhene," *Nupepa Kuokoa* (Honolulu, HI), May 8, 1903.

3 "Dandy in His Prime," *Honolulu Advertiser*, May 5, 1903.

4 Caroline Levine, "From Nation to Network," *Victorian Studies* 55, no. 4 (Summer 2013): 647–49; Ronjaunee Chatterjee, Alicia Mireles Christoff, and Amy R., Wong, "Undisciplining Victorian Studies," *Los Angeles Review of Books*, July 10, 2020.

5 Susan Sontag, "Notes on Camp," in *Against Interpretation and Other Essays* (New York: Picador, 2001), 288.

6 Regenia Gagnier, "From Barbarism to Decadence without the Intervening Civilization; or, Living in the Aftermath of Anticipated Futures," *Feminist Modernist Studies* 4 (2021): 166–81 (167).

7 Noelani Arista,"Ka Waihona Palapala Mānaleo: Research in a Time of Plenty. Colonialism and the Hawaiian-Language Archives," in *Indigenous Textual Cultures*, eds. Tony Ballantyne, Lachy Paterson, and Angela Wanhalla (Durham, NC: Duke University Press, 2020), 33; M. Puakea Nogelmeier, *Mai Pa'a I Ka Leo: Historical Voice in Hawaiian Print Materials, Looking Forward and Listening Back* (Honolulu, HI: Bishop Museum Press, Awaiulu Press, 2010), xiii.

8 Bryan Kuwada, "How Blue *Is* His Beard? An Examination of the 1862 Hawaiian-Language Translation of 'Bluebeard'," *Marvels & Tales: Journal of Fairy-Tale Studies* 23, no. 1 (2009): 17–39 (19–21); Noenoe K. Silva, *The Power of the Steel-Tipped Pen: Reconstructing Native Hawaiian Intellectual History* (Durham, NC: Duke University Press, 2017), 108.

9 See Kuwada, "How Blue *Is* His Beard?", and Cristina Bacchilega and Noelani Arista, "The *Arabian Nights* in a Nineteenth-century Hawaiian Newspaper: Reflections on the Politics of Translation," *Fabula* 45 (2004): 189–206.

10 "Ke Kaao Moolelo no Mary Stuart (Mere Situata), Ka Moiwahine Nani O Sekotia," *Nupepa Kuokoa* (Honolulu, HI), March 19, 1864. Craig Howes, who has surveyed much of this material, identifies the source text for this translation as G. W. M. Reynolds's novel *Mary Stuart, Queen of Scots* (1859).

11 Adria Imada, *Aloha America: Hula Circuits through the U. S. Empire* (Durham, NC: Duke University Press, 2012), 4.

12 Natasha Hurley, *Circulating Queerness: Before the Gay and Lesbian Novel* (Minneapolis: University of Minnesota Press, 2018), 66–67; Herman Melville, *Typee: A Peep at Polynesian Life*, ed. John Bryant (London: Penguin, 1996), 135.

13 Charles Warren Stoddard, *South-Seas Idyls* (Boston, MA: James R. Osgood and Company, 1873), 114.

14 Charles Warren Stoddard, "Lazy Letters from Low Latitudes," *Overland Monthly* 3 (March 1884): 307–15 (311).

15 Rod Edmond, *Representing the South Pacific: Colonial Discourse from Cook to Gauguin* (Cambridge: Cambridge University Press, 1997), 96; Rhonda K. Garelick, *Rising Star: Dandyism, Gender, and Performance in the Fin de Siecle* (Princeton, NJ: Princeton University Press, 1998), 5; Jack Halberstam, *Wild Things: The Disorder of Desire* (Durham, NC: Duke University Press, 2020), 18.

16 E. Ann Kaplan, *Looking at the Other: Feminism, Film, and the Imperial Gaze* (New York: Routledge, 1997), xix.

17 Joseph Boone, *The Homoerotics of Orientalism* (New York: Columbia University Press, 2014), 52.

18 Patrick Brantlinger, *Dark Vanishings: Discourse on the Extinction of Primitive Races, 1800–1930* (Ithaca, NY, and London: Cornell University Press, 2003), 1.

19 "Hawaiian Beau Brummel Dead," *Pacific Commercial Advertiser* (Honolulu, HI), May 4, 1903; "Dandy in His Prime," *Honolulu Advertiser*, May 5, 1903.

20 John Tayman, *The Colony: The Harrowing True Story of the Exiles of Molokai* (New York: Scribner, 2010), 343.

21 Mark Twain, Letter from May 23, 1866, in *Mark Twain's Letters from Hawaii*, ed. A. Grove Day (Honolulu, HI: University of Hawai'i Press, 1975), 111.

22 Mark Twain, Letter to W. D. Howells from January 7, 1884, in *Mark Twain's Letters*, vol. 2, ed. Albert Bigelow Paine (New York and London: Harper &

Brothers, 1917), 440; Stephen H. Sumida, "Reevaluating Mark Twain's Novel of Hawaii," *American Literature* 61 (December 1989): 586–609.

23 Isabella Bird, *The Hawaiian Archipelago: Six Months among the Palm Groves, Coral Reefs, & Volcanoes* (London: John Murray, 1875), 50–51.

24 Julius A. Palmer, *Memories of Hawaii and Hawaiian Correspondence* (Boston, MA: Lee and Shepard, 1894), 4.

25 Lindsay Wilhelm, "Bright Sunshine, Dark Shadows: Decadent Beauty and Victorian Views of Hawai'i," *Nineteenth-Century Literature* 75 (March 2021): 495–526.

26 Robert Louis Stevenson, *In the South Seas* (New York: Charles Scribner's Sons, 1896), 31.

27 Chris J. Thomas, *Pacific Possessions: The Pursuit of Authenticity in Nineteenth-Century Oceanian Travel Accounts* (Tuscaloosa, AL: The University of Alabama Press, 2021), 110.

28 Fanny Van de Grift Stevenson, "The Half-White," *Scribner's Magazine* 9 (March 1891): 282–88; Tayman, *The Colony*, 101.

29 Robert Louis Stevenson, "The Bottle Imp," in *Island Nights' Entertainments* (London: Cassell & Company, 1893), 155–222.

30 Monica L. Miller, *Slaves to Fashion: Black Dandyism and the Styling of Black Diasporic Identity* (Durham, NC: Duke University Press, 2009), 5, 10.

31 Nicholas B. Miller, "Trading Sovereignty and Labour: The Consular Network of Nineteenth-Century Hawai'i," *International History Review* 42 (2020): 260–77.

32 David Kalākaua to Lydia Lili'uokalani, July 14, 1881, in Richard A. Greer, ed., "The Royal Tourist – Kalakaua's Letters Home from Tokio to London," *Hawaiian Journal of History* 5 (1971), 97; Stacy Kamehiro, *The Arts of Kingship: Hawaiian Art and National Culture of the Kalākaua Era* (Honolulu, HI: University of Hawai'i Press, 2009); Tiffany Lani Ing, *Reclaiming Kalākaua: Nineteenth-Century Perspectives on a Hawaiian Sovereign* (Honolulu, HI: University of Hawai'i Press, 2019); Cindy McCreery, "Orders from Disorder? King Kalākaua's 1881 Global Tour and the Hawaiian Monarchy's Late Nineteenth-Century Deployment of Royal Orders and Decorations," *History Australia* 18 (June 2021): 219–40.

33 Charles Warren Stoddard, *Hawaiian Life: Being Lazy Letters from Low Latitudes* (New York: F. Tennyson Neely, 1894), 115. *Liverpool Mercury*, July 8, 1881; "King Kalakaua's Movements: His Majesty Examines the Edison Electric Light," *New York Times*, September 26, 1881.

34 Douglas V. Askman, "Kalākaua and the British Press: The King's Visit to Europe, 1881," *Hawaiian Journal of History* 52 (2018): 27–55; Askman, "A Royal Traveler: American Press Coverage of King Kalākaua's Trip Around the World," *Hawaiian Journal of History* 51 (2017): 69–90.

35 "Kalakaua's Paris Visit: How He Enjoyed Himself There and What He Says of the Trip," *The New York Times*, August 31, 1881; "London Gossip," *Hampshire Telegraph* July 20, 1881.

36 David Kalākaua, *The Legends and Myths of Hawaii: The Fables and Folklore of a Strange People*, ed. R. M. Daggett (New York: Charles L. Webster & Co., 1888), 210, 223.

37 Lorenz Gonschor, *A Power in the World: The Hawaiian Kingdom in Oceania* (Honolulu, HI: University of Hawai'i Press, 2019), 65.

38 Jonathan Kay Kamakawiwo'ole Osorio, *Dismembering Lāhui: A History of the Hawaiian Nation to 1887* (Honolulu, HI: University of Hawai'i Press, 2002), 1–3, 200–03.

39 Lydia Lili'uokalani, *Hawaii's Story by Hawaii's Queen* (Boston, MA: Lothrop, Lee & Shepard Co., 1898), 104–05.

CHAPTER 3

The 1890s and East Asia: Toward a Critical Cosmopolitanism

Stefano Evangelista

The opening lines of Percival Lowell's *The Soul of the Far East* (1888) rehearse a familiar set of tropes about the encounter with East Asia:

> The boyish belief that on the other side of our globe all things are of necessity upside down is startlingly brought back to the man when he sets foot at Yokohama. If his initial glance does not, to be sure, disclose the natives in the every-day feat of standing calmly on their heads, an attitude which his youthful imagination conceived to be a necessary consequence of their geographical position, it does at least reveal them looking at the world as if from the standpoint of that eccentric posture. For they seem to him to see everything topsy-turvy.[1]

Perhaps the most striking feature of Lowell's opening gambit is the way he presents traveling to this part of the globe as a return to childhood. The arrival in the port of Yokohama – a cosmopolitan center of world trade in nineteenth-century Japan – is like stepping back into the world of Victorian children's fairy tales and picture books. In particular, his gendered language ("boyish," "man") calls to mind the popular genre of boys' adventure stories, which the writer uses as a prism to translate his feelings of wonder and anticipation. The journey into this strange land, which Lowell reenacts in a series of chapters devoted to social customs, the arts, religion, and psychology, will confirm the initial impression that the East presents an inversion of familiar ideas and categories of perception prevalent in the West.

The Soul of the Far East was one of the most influential books about East Asia written in English in the nineteenth century. Its author's profile as an amateur or renaissance man was also exemplary of a time when travel from the West to these regions was still rare and cultural expertise thin on the ground: after being trained as a scientist in America, Lowell encountered East Asia through travel and diplomatic networks. Despite the fact that he wrote with the explicit intent to counteract current prejudices, his channeling of the literature of colonial romance, his way of constructing Asian culture as an object of knowledge, his binarism of East and West, his essentialism, his use of stereotyping, his framing of cultural difference through evolutionary science, the overlaps of his thinking with imperialist mentality – all these display the hallmark of orientalism as defined by Edward Said in his classic 1978 study, *Orientalism*.

Indeed, orientalist attitudes pervade 1890s writings about China and Japan that were produced in the wake of *The Soul of the Far East*. To dismiss this body of work, however, would be to overlook the fact that it also articulates complex responses to travel, cultural exchange, and globalization that are certainly worth interrogating from the new critical perspectives on cosmopolitanism and comparative and world literature that have emerged in recent decades.[2] Within the field of world literature, for instance, Pheng Cheah has called for approaches that prioritize the study of literature as "an active power in the making of worlds, that is, both a site of processes of worlding and an agent that participates and intervenes in these processes."[3] Cheah's object of inquiry is twentieth- and twenty-first-century postcolonial literature. However, his methodological insight can easily be applied to the profoundly different geopolitical context of the turn of the twentieth century: approaching writings about East Asia from this period, we should look out for how they affected the world consciousness of the 1890s and simultaneously contributed to the processes of literary networking that opened English literature to wider exchanges and connections.

In the brief quotation from Lowell's book, the focus on glance, perspective, and point of view introduces the problem of how to relativize one's own position in the world as the real challenge of writing about East Asia. The encounter with its different culture teaches us to see the Other more clearly and sympathetically; simultaneously, it discloses the gaze of the Other as directed at our Self. It is telling that in the opening pages of his book Lowell relies on different optical devices to explain different perceptions of the world. Mirrors and lenses draw attention to the processes of mediation and refraction that inevitably shape cross-cultural dialogues. The stereoscope provides him with the best metaphor for why the West should be eager to get to know this alien point of view: the East Asian "mind-photograph of the world can be placed side by side with ours, and the two pictures combined will yield results beyond what either alone could possibly have afforded. Thus harmonized, they will help us to realize humanity" (Lowell, *Soul of the Far East*, 4). Lowell's dream of "realiz[ing] humanity" expresses a liberal cosmopolitan sentiment shared by many nineteenth-century cultural mediators and world travelers. According to this fundamentally optimistic model inherited from Enlightenment philosophy, national and ethnic divisions would progressively be overcome by means of encounter and dialogue. Like Lowell's, many representations of East Asia fed into this cosmopolitan mentality that saw the world's cultures as operating in a harmonious communal space rather than in relationships of hierarchy and conflict. To paraphrase Lowell, just as the stereoscope combines two separate two-dimensional views into a single three-dimensional image, the different cultures of the East and the West complement each other and, when brought together, form a more balanced and complex understanding of humanity's shared being in the world.

From our present perspective, Lowell's liberal optimism is bound to elicit a skeptical reaction. Our own task in dealing with 1890s writings on East Asia should not be simply to affirm their cosmopolitanism in light of the extensive body of liberal critiques of globalization that has taken shape since the turn of the twenty-first century.[4] Rather, we should use them to interrogate that cosmopolitanism critically as a historically bound, unstable, and contested concept. Borrowing a term developed within the political and social sciences, we should view literary encounters with East Asia as articulating a "critical cosmopolitanism," that is, as employing ideas of world citizenship reflexively in order to critique and transform geopolitical and cultural relations.[5] Studying these works, we should therefore be aware that they contended with different ways of understanding and practicing cosmopolitanism. At the same time, we should put pressure on the very methods they employ to set cultures in dialogue and compare them (the optical illusion of Lowell's stereoscope): we should question their representation of mobility (in geographical terms, but also in relation to social and gender identities) and the limits and failures of the cosmopolitan project in aesthetic, ethical, and political terms.

This chapter focuses on two works from the 1890s that arose from encounters with Japan and China respectively: Lafcadio Hearn's *Kokoro* (1896) and Wo Chang's *Britain Through Chinese Spectacles* (1897). Like Lowell, both these writers used East Asian cultures to widen the cultural, moral, and political horizons of their English-speaking readers. They did so from very different points of view, however: Hearn wrote as a European living in Japan, while Wo Chang challenged current perceptions on China by presenting himself as a Chinese subject commenting on British society. What they had in common was a claim to an intimate first-hand knowledge of their adopted countries and the ability to frame that knowledge in a wider global perspective. Approaching their writings, it is important, first of all, to pay attention to the historical and geopolitical specificities of Western encounters with Japan and China in order to break down the geographical category of East Asia or, as the area used to be called at the time betraying the bias of the Eurocentric world view, "the Far East." Lowell is again exemplary of the then widespread orientalist practice of conflating Japan, China, and Korea, as *The Soul of the Far East* aims to give a synthetic overview of the three countries (although Japan really provides the prism through which Lowell sees the other two).

In studying Hearn and Wo Chang's writings as sites of literary world-ing, we should also bear in mind that, while there was a sizeable and growing body of literature in English about China and Japan, the general lack of linguistic expertise meant that translation of East Asian literatures into English was extremely limited. In his pioneering 1884 anthology put together from over 2000 years of Chinese prose and poetry, the British translator Herbert A. Giles (another diplomat) lamented that "English readers [would] search in vain for any work leading to an acquaintance-ship, however slight, with the general literature of China."[6] Giles prefaced his *Gems of Chinese Literature* with an epigraph from Thomas Carlyle: "What work nobler than transplanting foreign thought?" The implication was that, as Carlyle had enriched English literary culture in the mid-century by introducing German literature, notably Goethe, the time was now ripe for a further expansion of English readers' horizons toward China and the East (Goethe himself was, of course, reading rare nineteenth-century French translations of Chinese novels when he came up with the idea of world literature). The same was true of Japanese literature, which remained terra incognita in the West despite the enormous growth in popularity of Japanese art among literary circles in the second half of the century. It was only in the early decades of the twentieth century that readers of English gained fuller access to classical Chinese and Japanese literature thanks to the work of Arthur Waley and others. They would have to wait even longer for translations of modern writers.[7]

This is to say that, while the networks of trade and travel intensified very rapidly over the course of the nineteenth century, literary networks with East Asia were slower to form. In the 1890s, therefore, there was no temporal alignment between the modern literatures of English-speaking countries and those of East Asia, no direct exchanges of the kind that took place between English writers and, say, their French, German, or Scandinavian counterparts. Yet, the 1890s initiated a series of private literary exchanges that would only visibly bear fruit later on. For instance, the work of the American art historian Ernest Fenollosa, a friend of Hearn who spent a substantial amount of time in Tokyo in the 1890s, directly inspired both the imagist adaptations of Chinese poetry made by Ezra Pound and Amy Lowell – Percival Lowell's sister – and W. B. Yeats's experiments with Japanese Nōh theater.[8] Also when it comes to East Asia, therefore, the 1890s built a bridge toward the literature of modernism.[9]

Self-Conscious Orientalism and Evolutionary Cosmopolitanism in Lafcadio Hearn's *Kokoro*

"Japan, for us, was born yesterday."[10] An article published in the international journal *Le Japon artistique / Artistic Japan* in 1889 captures the impression of freshness and novelty with which people in the West regarded Japan at the end of the nineteenth century. The author, Ernest Hart, reminded readers of how much work still needed to be done in order to spread an informed knowledge of Japanese art. He emphasized the linguistic barrier that separated Japan from Europe and, not unreasonably, claimed that very few in the West would be able to associate the name of any Japanese artist with a specific period or style. Hart certainly had a point. Since Japan's enforced opening to world trade in the mid-century, Japanese art had exploded in popularity. In the 1870s, the love of Japanese things already had its own name, *japonisme* – an epithet coined by the French art historian Philippe Burty and soon naturalized into English to designate the new taste that was having a significant impact not only on modern art but also on literary culture.[11] The exquisitely illustrated *Artistic Japan* (1888–91) marked an important milestone in this process of dissemination and regulation of Japanophilia: edited by the influential art dealer and collector Siegfried Bing, it sought to promote an accurate knowledge of Japanese arts and, at the same time, to rescue *japonisme* from being excessively commercialized and from sliding into a form of generic popular culture. At the opening of the 1890s, therefore, Japan presented itself to the West as caught in a complex temporality: Japan was new ("born yesterday") and old at the same time, so that its ancient arts could be aligned to what counted as extremely modern, modish, or even avant-garde in the West, its traditional aesthetics shading into impressionism and the beginnings of abstraction. The novelty of Japan was likewise compounded with a strange sense of saturation – the feeling captured in Gilbert and Sullivan's operetta *The Mikado* (1885) that the country had already been talked about to an excessive degree.

This is the context in which Lafcadio Hearn began writing about Japan in the mid-1890s. Landing in Yokohama in 1890 after reading his Lowell, Hearn also saw Japan through the lens of orientalist romance. His record of that fateful first day on Japanese soil, later published in *Glimpses of Unfamiliar Japan* (1894), is focused, like Lowell's, on how the embodied experience of Japan unsettles familiar categories of perception. Riding a jinrikisha through the streets of Yokohama where modern Western-style settlements rubbed shoulders with native architecture, the world suddenly presented itself to Hearn on a different scale: familiar colors and sounds were made strange and even the simplest everyday objects aroused a feeling of aesthetic curiosity. The series of overwhelming aesthetic impressions narrated in the essay culminates in a vivid dream in which the *kanji* or Chinese characters that Hearn had admired in rapt amazement during his ramblings came back to him at night in the form of monstrous insects:

> I lie down to sleep, and I dream. I see Chinese texts – multitudinous, weird, mysterious – fleeing by me, all in one direction; ideographs white and dark, upon sign-boards, upon paper screens, upon backs of sandalled men. They seem to live, these ideographs, with conscious life; they are moving their parts, moving with a movement as of insects, monstrously, like *phasmidæ*. I am rolling always through low, narrow, luminous streets in a phantom jinrikisha, whose wheels make no sound.[12]

Hearn's nightmare of the insectiform words taking on a life of their own reveals his anxiety about not understanding Japan. As the attractive day-time spectacle of the city replays itself in such uncanny form, the writer is haunted by the vision of language eluding him as he is unable to make out the meaning of unfamiliar signs – literally, to read Japan. At the same time, the vision of words slipping away from him signifies the struggle to find the right language to describe his new experiences – a perception that recurs frequently in travel writing and is here magnified through the prism of exoticism.

In the extensive corpus of Hearn's writings, the feeling of anxiety of his first Japanese dream often comes back in the form of uncanny images, failures of translation, and the collapse of realist categories of representation. Far from being an element of weakness, however, this all-pervasive self-consciousness adds cultural sensitivity and literary complexity to Hearns's work. The English-language authors who had written about Japan so far were mostly travelers and diplomats, such as Lowell. In recent years these were being supplemented by specialized scholars such as Hearn's friends Fenollosa and the British philologist Basil Hall Chamberlain, who looked at the country through an academic prism. By contrast, Hearn brought to bear his literary background as translator of French literature and writer on local color, which he had built during nearly two decades working for newspapers in the United States. His essays often present Japan through sophisticated textual devices such as intertextual allusion, the use of the supernatural, and multiple narrative frames (the dream in "My First Day in the Orient" is an example of the latter), which emphasize their literariness. His work thus embodies a kind of aesthetic cosmopolitanism, that is, a worlding of the text by means of literary form and technique.

Hearn also collected and translated Japanese folk tales when, as we have seen, translation from Japanese literature into English was otherwise nearly nonexistent. Japanese scholars later paid tribute to Hearn's important contribution to preserving Japanese folklore at a time in which the country was bent on a program of modernization that risked destroying large swaths of its heritage.[13] Looking at Hearn's work of mediation from a European point of view, Vernon Lee compared Hearn's Japanese writings to Madame de Staël's influential treatise *De l'Allemagne* (1810), which earlier in the century introduced French readers to the literature, philosophy, and manners of their German neighbors.[14] De Staël's book had disclosed a new world that her French contemporaries tended to ignore or dismiss, even though it was just across the border. The implication was that what de Staël had done for the culture of the Germanic North, facilitating the spread of romanticism in France and across the European continent, Hearn had now done for the Eastern culture of Japan: he had brought Japan closer to the West and into its imaginative sphere, facilitating a process of connectivity and cosmopolitan mediation that would later have many ramifications in the networks of world literature.

Lee's comparison with de Staël aptly captures the combination of essentialism and idealism that characterizes Hearn's Japanese works. Both these qualities are strongly in evidence in his second Japanese collection, *Kokoro* (1896). *Kokoro* takes its title from the Japanese word for "heart" or "spirit" or "soul," with an implicit nod back to Lowell's *Soul of the Far East*. After six years in Japan, however, Hearn had a deeper and much more personal investment in the country than Lowell. On the title page Hearn reproduced the Japanese character for "kokoro" (心) prominently printed in red and glossed as signifying heart, but also "mind, in the emotional sense; spirit; courage; resolve; sentiment; affection; and inner meaning."[15] The use of the evocative concept of *kokoro* reveals that Hearn's essentializing approach to Japanese culture rested on a depth model that explicitly rejected the superficial accounts that constituted the bulk of the literature of *japonisme*. His emphasis on the heart as a site of meaning and value promised to provide a knowledge of Japan based on the emotions rather than cold objective observation. At the same time, however, the notion of *kokoro*, with its lack of a straightforward English equivalent, also suggests that Japanese culture, and maybe all cultures, are ultimately untranslatable. The book's subtitle, "Hints and Echoes of Japanese Inner Life," amplifies this feeling that an outsider's journey into the heart of a foreign culture may entail no more than clutching at fragments and refractions. *Kokoro* thus relies on romantic notions of essentialism and authenticity but simultaneously deconstructs those ideals by asking readers to reflect critically on acts of mediation and translation.

Hearn's self-consciousness about his strategies of mediation comes through particularly strongly in one of the book's most striking essays, "A Street Singer." Typically for Hearn, the essay starts with an anecdote of Japanese life, as he describes the unexpected arrival at his house of a female itinerant singer. When a crowd spontaneously gathers to hear the woman sing a ballad, Hearn is struck by the contrast between the physical appearance of the singer, who has been disfigured and made blind by smallpox, and the beauty of the sound of her voice, which holds him spellbound even if he cannot understand her words. After the performance, he invites her to tell the story of her life (which he briefly records) and buys from her a copy of the ballad – a sentimental tale about a *shinjū*, or double suicide, of a type that was then widespread in Japanese popular culture. Hearn then translates and includes the full ballad in the essay. From here he turns to a series of abstract speculations about music's ability to convey emotions across different cultures, before closing the essay with a flashback to another encounter that took place twenty-five years earlier: in conclusion we learn that the Japanese street singer brings back to Hearn's mind the voice of another stranger – a girl he once fleetingly heard in a London park wishing "good night" to a passer-by.

Hearn manages to pack all this within the brief space of seven pages, in which he swiftly shuttles backwards and forwards between memoir, aesthetic theory, translation, and even ekphrasis (the copy of the ballad that he purchases comes in an illustrated woodblock print). In the center of the essay is the mesmerizing and affecting figure of the blind singer: at the same time so marginal and fleeting and yet so central to what Hearn sees as the essence of Japan, the street singer is a perfect embodiment of Hearn's notion of *kokoro*. Her performance triggers an immediate emotive connection with the heart of Japan:

And as she sang, those who listened began to weep silently. I did not
distinguish the words; but I felt the sorrow and the sweetness and the
patience of the life of Japan pass with her voice into my heart, – plaintively
seeking for something never there. A tenderness invisible seemed to gather
and quiver about us; and sensations of places and times forgotten came
softly back, mingled with feelings ghostlier, – feelings not of any place or
time in living memory. Then I saw that the singer was blind. (Hearn,
Kokoro, 41–42)

As in that first dream on Asian soil, Hearn is confronted again with his
own inability to decipher the Japanese language, this time as presented
through the medium of song rather than written signs. In this essay the
linguistic gap once more takes on an uncanny register, emphasized by
Hearn's dramatic withholding of the singer's blindness until the end of her
performance. Materializing out of nothing and vanishing into nothing at
the end of the brief sketch, the blind street singer is an uncanny figure: a
stranger who has the power of bringing back familiar memories. Indeed,
she embodies the potential of the uncanny as a channel of communication
between the *kokoro* of Japan and the heart of the foreign observer. The
listener's lack of linguistic understanding turns out to be not only imma-
terial but possibly even an advantage as the epiphany experienced by
Hearn rests on a perfect perception of indeterminacy – a seeming paradox
that is key to his aesthetic cosmopolitanism. In fact, when Hearn does
provide his translation of the ballad, it is to show its relative lack of
remarkable features rather than to fetishize the importance of an accurate
comprehension of the Japanese original.

In "A Street Singer," Hearn seeks a rational explanation for this uncanny
experience of being moved by words that he does not understand and a
melody that does not evoke distinctive cultural associations. In order to do
so he turns to evolutionary science, concluding that the human voice
carries with it, and therefore has the power of reawakening, inherited
memories of basic feelings of sympathy and grief that are common to
the whole of humanity: "In the voice of the singer there were qualities able
to make appeal to something larger than the sum of the experience of one
race, – to something wide as human life, and ancient as the knowledge of
good and evil" (45). Hearn's conclusion shows the influence of Herbert
Spencer's *Principles of Psychology* (1855), a source that he cites several times
in *Kokoro* along with Grant Allen's writings on psychological aesthetics and
color science. What is striking is that Hearn's reading of Japan through the
prism of evolutionary psychology opens up to something more expansive.
Elsewhere in *Kokoro* he borrows the concept of "cosmic emotion" – glossed

by the philosopher W. K. Clifford as "an emotion which is felt in regard to the universe or sum of things, viewed as a cosmos or order"[16] – to articulate a model of ethical cosmopolitanism based on evolutionary science:

> The teaching of Evolution is . . . that each of us is many, yet that all of us are still one with each other and with the cosmos; – that we must know all past humanity not only in ourselves, but likewise in the preciousness and beauty of every fellowlife; – that we can best love ourselves in others; – that we shall best serve ourselves in others; – that forms are but veils and phantoms; – and that to the formless Infinite alone really belong all human emotions, whether of the living or the dead. (Hearn, *Kokoro*, 305–06)

Even more strikingly, Hearn associates this evolutionary cosmopolitan ethics with an eclectic mix of Eastern spirituality and philosophy made up of the Buddhist idea of preexistence (which, we are told, is incorrectly believed to be the "fundamental idea [that] especially differentiates Oriental modes of thinking from our own" [222]), the Asian doctrine of *karma*, and elements of Shinto. Hearn offers this original synthesis as an alternative not only to Western materialism, which he intensely disliked, but also to normative Western ideas of cosmopolitanism inherited from the Greeks by way of the German Enlightenment. The most important reason for studying the inner life of Japan is precisely that it enables readers to discover this path to a different understanding and, as it were, practice of humanity's shared being in the world. This is why Hearn believes that the work of oriental philologists and experts on Asian philosophy and religions was as urgent as that of evolutionary scientists. Both were working in parallel to forge a fundamentally new understanding of the self in relation to the wider humanity. The changes brought about by their work could be seen in the way in which literature too was expanding its aesthetic and ethical horizons, "destroying old tastes, and developing higher feelings. . . . Even in fiction we learn that we have been living in a hemisphere only; that we have been thinking but half-thoughts; that we need a new faith to join past with future over the great parallel of the present, and so to round out our emotional world into a perfect sphere" (248).

Western Cosmopolitanism through Wo Chang's Spectacles

One of the essays in *Kokoro* imagines the reverse journey from the one that its author undertook in 1890. Hearn tells the story of a Japanese man from an ancient samurai family who grows up at the time of the country's opening to the West. Fascinated by the new ideas coming from abroad, the young man learns English, studies European literatures, and even converts to Christianity for a period. He then decides to travel to Europe and America, where he is, however, bitterly disappointed by what he perceives to be the moral shallowness and hypocrisy of Western civilization. Indeed, after observing the West with his own eyes, he turns back to the traditional culture of old Japan that he had initially rejected, embracing it now with an evident feeling of nationalist fervor: the young man vows "to fearlessly oppose further introduction [into Japan] of anything not essential to national self-preservation, or helpful to national self-development" (206). Tellingly entitled "A Conservative," Hearn's story is about the failure of cosmopolitanism as witnessed from the point of view of Japan. It pessimistically portrays global connectivity – at least as conceived in the terms set out by the commercially and militarily powerful West – as leading to incomprehension and entrenched divisions:

> During those years he saw Western civilization as few Japanese ever saw it. ... But he saw with the eyes of the Far East; and the ways of his judgments were not as our ways. For even as the Occident regards the Far East, so does the Far East regard the Occident, – only with this difference: that what each most esteems in itself is least likely to be esteemed by the other. And both are partly right and partly *wrong*; and there never has been, and never can be, perfect mutual comprehension. (197)

In the closing decades of the nineteenth century, figures like Hearn's "conservative" were to be seen more and more frequently in Europe and America. As Japan became more deeply embedded in the networks of world trade, an increasing number of Japanese people traveled abroad to acquire knowledge and learn skills that were not readily available at home, often on government-sponsored schemes. This first generation of geographically mobile intellectuals included some of the most prominent Japanese writers of the early twentieth century: Mori Ōgai, for instance, spent time in Berlin in the 1880s training to be a military doctor and Natsume Sōseki traveled to Britain to study English literature. Back in Japan, they both wrote about their experiences in essays and memoirs.[17] It would take a long time before their impressions of Europe – ambivalent and satirical in the case of Sōseki – made it back to the West in translation.

Just one year after the appearance of *Kokoro*, however, a book published in Britain set out to provide the record of a European country written from the perspective of a "Chinaman" who had gained a first-hand acquaintance with British life and society: Wo Chang's *Britain Through Chinese Spectacles* was a highly self-conscious attempt to reply to British writing about China and to challenge current perceptions of East Asia. Once again, the use of an optical device – the spectacles in this case – drew attention to the defamiliarizing effect of the foreign point of view. While, as we have seen, 1890s readers could still be under the impression that Japan was "born yesterday," the longer history of cultural and economic exchange with China had resulted in a steady trickle of essays, books, and travelogues that produced a greater sense of familiarity.[18] In his preface, however, Wo Chang summarily dismissed this body of writing from the last half century as "worthless" superficial impressions coming "from the pens of the 'globe-trotting' tribe."[19] He lamented English observers' overwhelming ignorance of Chinese language, literature, and philosophy and claimed that the limited coverage of the country's vast and varied geography made the English "as unfit to appreciate the inner life of the [Chinese] people as a blind man would be to comprehend the artistic masterpieces of the National Gallery, or as one who is deaf would be to enjoy the music of a Handel Festival."[20] Wo Chang's evocation of the overlooked "inner life" of the Chinese strikes a chord with Hearn's revisionist project of capturing the Japanese *kokoro*. However, while Hearn's writing is informed by the desire to establish a "mutual comprehension," to go back to his terms in "A Conservative," Wo Chang's is driven by an open sentiment of competition. He decides, as he says, to take for granted "the countless virtues which adorn every department of English life" in order to concentrate on the national "defects."[21] He therefore systematically takes to pieces English social customs, the education and legal systems, the economic structure, and the idea of democracy, providing a relentless deconstruction of Victorian liberalism.

Postcolonial critics have persuasively argued that *Britain Through Chinese Spectacles* should be read as an interrogation of Britain's imperial identity. Ross Forman in particular has drawn attention to the way in which "Wo Chang's account characterizes British society by replicating the discourse of reverse colonization, invoking the vocabulary of savagery and primitivity familiar to British readers both from the Yellow Peril fiction of writers like [M. P.] Shiel and the slum literature of Booth, Harkness and their fellow reformers."[22] Published the same year as Bram Stoker's *Dracula*, *Britain Through Chinese Spectacles* enters a dialogue with this body of literature by shifting the setting of the culture clash between East and West to the very heart of the British empire. From this vantage point, Wo Chang counters the racist discourse generated by British encounters with the Chinese in East Asia exemplified in a wide range of fiction from this period, from Rudyard Kipling's *From Sea to Sea* (1889) to W. Carlton

Dawe's *Kakemonos* (1897), which was published in England that same year. In fact, Dawe's collection provides a very good illustration of the different practices of stereotyping Japan and China prevalent at this point: the stories set in Japan typically center on romantic plots involving a Western man and a vulnerable Japanese woman, following the trope of Pierre Loti's extremely popular *Madame Chrysanthème* (1887);[23] by contrast, those set in China often feature physical confrontations between Western and Chinese men, functioning as displaced narratives of imperial competition, that is, of the political struggle to control East Asian trade routes and territories.[24] The fact that *Kakemonos* was part of John Lane's prestigious Keynote series – a venue associated with literary decadence and with the treatment of controversial social issues – shows that the faraway world of East Asia was increasingly perceived as being highly topical and connected to what English audiences experienced as their own modern condition; but it also shows how widely that modern globalized outlook relied on regressive stereotyping, even within elite culture.

Britain through Chinese Spectacles responds to this negative characterization of the Chinese in fin-de-siècle literature. Wo Chang goes out of his way to give an image of China as a country that was, in fact, highly civilized in the meaning that English readers ascribed to this concept, most notably when it came to literature:

> In China there are more books and more readers than in any part of the world. … We had the printing press five hundred years before it was known in the West, and we have so much reverence for pure literature that we post on the walls of cities, in shops, and by the wayside bills, by tens of thousands with these words on them: "Reverence lettered paper," for every letter and word written with pencil or pen with us is sacred. The letters of our alphabet we call "the eyes of the sages," and "the tracks the sages have left behind them." … We have societies whose one object is to send men through the streets and lanes to gather up all the scraps of lettered paper that may have fallen on the ground, and these are solemnly burned in a furnace made for the purpose. (Chang, *Britain through Chinese Spectacles*, 34)

The care bestowed on the written word in China – an older and bigger literary economy than any in the West, as Wo Chang points out – is contrasted with England, whose neglect for culture Wo Chang bemoans with a morally indignant voice that could occasionally remind readers of John Ruskin or Matthew Arnold. Like these Victorian critics he understands English modernity essentially as a condition of fall. The difference is that he is able to present the cultural conservatism of China as an attractive counternarrative.

In fact, in a parallel with Hearn's aesthetic cosmopolitanism, Wo Chang's careful construction of his voice is a key part of his argument. Nothing is known about the mysterious Wo Chang, who many suspected of being the exotic adopted identity of an English writer. A review in the *Spectator*, for instance, noted that "it has not been uncommon for some long-suffering Englishman to vent his wrath with the national institutions under the guise of a foreign observer."[25] Whether a real Chinese person transplanted to England or an English satirist in disguise, what is beyond doubt is that the author projects a worldly and very widely read persona whose impressive range of quotations goes from the Greek and Latin classics to Max Nordau. As he explains, his ability to be equally at home in Chinese and European cultures is due to his having "had the advantage not only of a sound Chinese education, but also of an extended training in the English language and literature, under a very learned and wise English tutor residing at one of the treaty ports" (Chang, *Britain through Chinese Spectacles*, n. p.).

The urbanity of Wo Chang's tone compounded with his social privilege, his openness to other cultures, and wide knowledge of the world – all these proclaim him as the legitimate representative of a cosmopolitan ideal, which, like much else in England, he shows to have been corrupted by modernity: "globe-trotting," the nineteenth-century neologism that Wo Chang uses to describe British writings about China, associates the global outlook of the West with a debased cosmopolitanism purely based on economic privilege and the pursuit of pleasure – a degraded version of world citizenship reconfigured through the superficial touristic mentality of a rich imperial nation. By staking a claim to an authentic cosmopolitan identity, the author of *Britain Through Chinese Spectacles* therefore disputes cosmopolitanism as a prerogative of the West. Lowell had concluded *The Soul of the Far East* by pointing out the danger to which globalization and increased contact with the West exposed East Asian nations: "Just as surely as morning passes into afternoon, so surely are these races of the Far East, if unchanged, destined to disappear before the advancing nations of the West" (226). By contrast, the cosmopolitan Wo Chang showed that the Chinese were fully able to turn global connectivity to their own advantage, while remaining rooted in their own traditional cultural values.

Conclusion

The *Spectator* reviewer of *Britain through Chinese Spectacles* made fun of the false sense of familiarity that the English felt towards East Asia:

> The great mass of excellent people derive all that they know or want to know on such subjects from works like the *Geisha* or the *Mikado*. China and Japan are all one to them. The present writer once heard an indignant visitor to the Savoy say that he disliked the *Mikado* very much, because he had just come back from Japan, and had seen nothing there at all like it. (Anon, "English at Home," 828)

This humorous anecdote captures the entanglement of worldliness and provincialism that characterizes 1890s attitudes to East Asia: projection mixes with misunderstanding, desire with disillusionment. In order to influence those attitudes, Hearn and Wo Chang wrote critically about Eurocentric models of cosmopolitanism, looking for alternative ways of understanding global connectivity. Producing knowledge about Japan and China that metropolitan readers were keen to acquire, they sometimes deployed essentialist, conservative, or even nationalist attitudes that reveal the contradictions within the liberal ideal that we now mostly associate with cosmopolitanism. It is important that we learn to unravel the conflicted politics and aspirations of these writings, and pay close attention to how they translate cosmopolitanism on the level of aesthetics, in order to appreciate the full complexity of works that can otherwise all too easily be reduced to simple orientalism. As Wo Chang's reviewer hints in his comments on the *Mikado*, a lot remains to be done to go beyond the dizzying surface of the nineteenth-century fascination with "the Orient" in order to discover how encounters with East Asia shaped the critical cosmopolitanism of the literature of the 1890s.

Notes

1 Percival Lowell, *The Soul of the Far East* (Boston and New York: Houghton, Mifflin & Co., 1888), 1.
2 Recent critics of Western representations of China and Japan have found different strategies for going beyond Said's foundational work, while respecting his insights on the cultural politics of orientalism. See Ross Forman, *China and the Victorian Imagination: Empires Entwined* (Cambridge and New York: Cambridge University Press, 2013), 6; Grace E. Lavery, *Quaint, Exquisite: Victorian Aesthetics and the Idea of Japan* (Princeton, NJ: Princeton University Press, 2019), 36–38; and especially Christopher Reed, *Bachelor Japanists: Japanese Aesthetics and Western Masculinities* (New York: Columbia University Press, 2016), 19–26.
3 Pheng Cheah, *What Is a World?: On Postcolonial Literature as World Literature* (Durham, NC: Duke University Press, 2016), 2.
4 Key here is Kwame Anthony Appiah, *Cosmopolitanism: Ethics in a World of Strangers* (London: Allen Lane, 2006). A full survey of recent theories of

cosmopolitanism is beyond the scope of this chapter. For approaches that are particularly attentive to plurality and extra-European perspectives, see Bruce Robbins, Paulo Lemos Horta, and Kwame Anthony Appiah, *Cosmopolitanisms* (New York: NYU Press, 2017). Relevant discussions of cosmopolitanism in relation to 1890s decadence include Regenia Gagnier, *Individualism, Decadence, Globalization: On the Relationship of Part to Whole, 1859–1920* (Basingstoke and New York: Palgrave Macmillan, 2010); and Matthew Potolsky, *The Decadent Republic of Letters: Taste, Politics, and Cosmopolitan Community from Baudelaire to Beardsley* (Philadelphia, PA: University of Pennsylvania Press, 2013).

5 Gerard Delanty, "The Idea of Critical Cosmopolitanism," in *Routledge Handbook of Cosmopolitanism Studies*, ed. Gerard Delanty (Abingdon and New York: Routledge, 2012), 38–46.

6 Herbert A. Giles, *Gems of Chinese Literature* (London: Bernard Quaritch; Shanghai: Kelly & Walsh, 1884), iii.

7 For an overview of translations from East Asian languages, see Peter France, ed. *The Oxford Guide to Literature in English Translation* (Oxford and New York: Oxford University Press, 2000), 222–50. France notes that "translation of Korean literature into English only really began in the 1940s" (249).

8 After Fenollosa's death in 1908, his widow Mary entrusted his papers to Pound, who shared them with Yeats. For an account of this famous episode from a translator's perspective, see Eileen Kato, "W. B. Yeats and the Noh," *Irish Review* 42 (2010): 104–19.

9 For a study of the cross-cultural currents between the modernism of the West and the East, see Patricia Ondec Laurence, *Lily Briscoe's Chinese Eyes: Bloomsbury, Modernism, and China* (Columbia, SC: University of South Carolina Press, 2003).

10 [Ernest Hart], "Ritsuo and his School," *Artistic Japan* 12 (April 1889): 139–47 (140).

11 Burty first defined *japonisme* in a series of articles for *La Renaissance littéraire et artistique* issued from May 1872. In 1875, he published a revised version of that series in the English periodical the *Academy*. It is significant for the disciplinary location of *japonisme* that both periodicals bridged literature and the visual arts.

12 Lafcadio Hearn, *Glimpses of Unfamiliar Japan*, 2 vols. (Boston and New York: Houghton Mifflin, 1894), vol. 1, 28.

13 See Yoko Makino, "Lafcadio Hearn and Yanagita Kunio: Who Initiated Folklore Studies in Japan," in *Lafcadio Hearn in International Perspectives*, ed. Sukehiro Hirakawa (Folkestone: Global Oriental, 2007), 129–38. The names of modern Japanese scholars publishing in English are given using the English convention of first name followed by surname. For Japanese writers, I have followed the standard Japanese practice of giving surname followed by first name.

14 Vernon Lee, "Bismarck Towers," *New Statesman* (February 20, 1915), 481–83 (482).

15 Lafcadio Hearn, *Kokoro: Hints and Echoes of Japanese Inner Life* (Boston and New York: Houghton Mifflin, 1896).

16 W. F. Clifford, "Cosmic Emotion," in *Lectures and Essays*, 2 vols., eds. Leslie Stephen and Frederick Pollock (London: Macmillan, 1879), vol. 2, 253–85 (253).

17 See Karen Brazell, "Mori Ōgai in Germany: A Translation of Fumizukai and Excerpts from Doitsu Nikki," *Monumenta Nipponica* 26, 1/2 (1971): 77–100; Ann-Marie Dunbar, "'Three Leagues away from a Human Colour': Natsume Soseki in late-Victorian London," *Victorian Literature and Culture* 46, no. 1 (2018): 221–36.

18 See Douglas Kerr and Julia Kuehn, eds., *A Century of Travels in China: Critical Essays on Travel Writing from the 1840s to the 1940s* (Hong Kong: Hong Kong University Press, 2007).

19 Wo Chang, *Britain Through Chinese Spectacles: Leaves from the Notebook of Wo Chang* (London: Cotton, 1897), [the Preface is unpaginated].

20 Ibid.

21 Ibid.

22 Ross Forman, "Empire," in *The Cambridge Companion to the Fin de Siècle*, ed. Gail Marshall (Cambridge and New York: Cambridge University Press, 2007), 91–111 (108). See also Michael Hill, "The Historical Roots of Reverse Orientalism and their Recapitulation in Wo Chang's *England through Chinese Spectacles* (1897)," *Asian Journal of Social Science* 38 (2010): 677–96.

23 For the persistence of this master narrative in writings about Japan, see Christopher Reed, *The Chrysantème Papers: The Pink Notebook of Madame Chrysanthème and other Documents of French Japonisme* (Honolulu: University of Hawai'i Press, 2010); and Lavery, *Quaint, Exquisite*, 138–57.

24 W. Carlton Dawe, *Kakemonos: Tales of the Far East* (London and New York: John Lane/Bodley Head, 1897); cf., for instance, the stories "Sayōnara" and "A Night in Canton."

25 [Anon.], "The English at Home," *Spectator* (December 4, 1897): 828–29 (828).

Indulekha, *or The Many Lives of Realism at the Fin de Siècle*

Sukanya Banerjee

Discussions of nineteenth-century realism tend to focus on realism's mid-Victorian incarnation, with the implication that the end of the century witnessed the waning of realism as a narrative mode. The fin de siècle, we are inclined to believe, cleared ground for the advent of modernism, privileging nonmimetic and experimental modes of representation over and against realism, which was relegated to receding obsolescence. But we also know better. We know that realism was never only (or ever) about mimeticism and that the distinction between realism and modernist techniques of representation cannot be sharply drawn chronologically or aesthetically.[1] We also know that although the latter decades of the century marked the publication of important realist novels (by the likes of Thomas Hardy, George Gissing, and George Moore), these were overshadowed only by the easy lure of romance and adventure novels that became immensely popular.[2] The relation between popularity and the literary status or health of a genre is of course a vexed one: the standing of sensation novels in the 1860s serves as a case in point. But if popularity were to function as even a provisional barometer, then it is surely necessary to turn to a realist novel that was immediately successful upon publication and reprinted every year for almost a century after its original date of publication, Indian author O. Chandumenon's *Indulekha* (1889–90).

To turn to *Indulekha*, which engages with a matrilineal (and polyandrous) family structure in late nineteenth-century Malabar, which comprises the present-day state of Kerala located on the southwest coast of India, is not just to add another non-Western text to the nineteenth-century corpus (important as that task remains), but to get to the heart of the fin-de-siècle discussion of realism. It is, in fact, to query the relation between the two terms and consider how the fin de siècle offers a lens for reading the story of realism and its changing map in the final decade of the nineteenth century. If the fin de siècle is associated with sexual and cultural dissidence, it also marks a heightened moment of political change and uncertainty in Britain.[3] Jed Esty looks to the late-Victorian moment as marking a shift from British to American hegemony. For him, this shift triggers what he terms the "realism wars," which is not so much about the merits of one kind of realism over another as a jostling between different modes of representation.[4] In linking the political character of the fin de siècle to its aesthetic production, we must also keep in mind the fact that the fin de siècle registered a nascent nationalist consciousness in colonies such as India. An Indian nationalist sensibility was at that point neither programmatic nor unified, but lent a ballast, nonetheless, to the radical energies (and uncertainties) that we associate with fin-de-siècle Britain. But as far as India is concerned, the fin de siècle marked an interstitial if not ambivalent moment in nation-making, one in which the ideological boundaries between nation and empire remained indeterminate.[5] Significantly enough, the aesthetic configurations of this amorphous moment – such as the realist novel, for instance – tend to get overlooked or are read through a postcolonial lens that posits the nation as a fait accompli.[6] Staying with and in the fin de siècle, therefore, not only offers a granular view of the "realism wars" in Britain but also affords a fuller account of Indian realism as well. Both perspectives inflect each other to remap Victorian realism in ways that reinforce and account for its prominence (popularity!) beyond the mid-century as well as the geoethnic contours of Britain. Or, put another way, reading *Indulekha* renders the fin de siècle a heuristic, not least because the novel questions fundamental assumptions around which conventional Victorian society organized itself in Britain, assumptions that normativized a patrilineal social structure and posited matriliny as primordial (and relegated it to the genre of romance). By depicting bourgeois themes of courtship and marriage through a realist lens but within the matrilineal setting of contemporary Malabar, *Indulekha* delinks matriliny from romance, a generic linkage that otherwise played a significant role in positing patriliny (and British Victorians) at the civilizational apex.[7] In so doing, *Indulekha* not only accounts for realism's many lives at the fin de siècle but also attaches a key geopolitical dimension to the fin de siècle's recasting of sexual and reproductive relations.

Appearing in January 1890, *Indulekha,* written in Malayalam, Chandumenon's native language, was received with remarkable enthusiasm, and the first edition of the novel sold out by March 1890. In the nineteenth century, the Malabar was administered by the Madras Presidency and comprised Mysore, Cochin, and Travancore. Mysore was annexed by the British after their defeat of the native ruler Tipu Sultan during the infamous Siege of Seringapatam, an event that is famously dramatized in the opening pages of Wilkie Collins's *The Moonstone* (1868). *Indulekha*'s plotline is woven around the Nair system of matriliny, which was governed by the *marumakkathayam* law. The Nairs, a Hindu community in the Malabar, followed a gynocentric social system, and a Nair household, the *taravad*, typically comprised a woman, her children, grandchildren, brothers, and descendants in the female line. Nair women did not marry but initiated relationships (*sambandhams*) with men of their choice and were free to dissolve them at will. Children continued to live with the mother as part of the *taravad*, which was managed by her eldest brother, and all residents of the *taravad* were considered coparceners, or joint heirs. Nairs ranked lower than Brahmins in terms of caste status, but Nair women could enter *sambandhams* with Nambuthiris (a Brahmin community in the Malabar). Nambuthiris followed patriliny and primogeniture, and the eldest son married within the Nambuthiri community, thereby keeping the property intact. Younger sons entered into *sambandhams* with Nair women, with the assurance that their children would be looked after by the *taravad* and therefore not stand to inherit Nambuthiri property. Ironically, Nair matriliny sustained Nambuthiri patriarchy.[8]

As a politically powerful and visible community of the Malabar coast, a region that featured as a focal point in the spice trade, the Nairs find mention in Portuguese accounts from the sixteenth century. For Portuguese observers, it was not just the wealth of the Nairs that was noteworthy but also the peculiar laws of succession entailed by a matriarchal line of descent. Alfonso Albuquerque, along with his compatriots, was more than a little taken aback by the fact that the "sons of Malabar kings do not inherit; instead the kingship usually devolves on the sons of their sisters, who are usually the mistresses of Brahmins."[9] The Nairs occasioned comment in the nineteenth century as well. In 1812, Percy Bysshe Shelley wrote in a letter to James Lawrence: "Your *Empire of the Nairs*, which I read this spring, succeeded in making me a perfect convert to its doctrines. I then retained no doubts of the evils of marriage."[10] Lawrence's utopian romance, *The Empire of the Nairs*, was inspired by Nair matriliny, and in an essay prefacing the volume, he reimagined gender relations on the model proffered by his reading of Nair society: "Let every female live perfectly uncontrolled by any man," Lawrence states, adding the rejoinder: "Let the inheritance of her daughters descend in like manner to their offspring."[11] The expansive futurity envisaged in these lines, however, is offset by the fact that, although events in *The Empire of the Nairs* are partly set in the Malabar, the fact of Nair matriliny functions more as a convenient point of reference; its material realities and contingencies have little bearing on the unfolding of the plot. In fact, subtitled "A Romance," Lawrence's work tellingly links matriliny with romance, a linkage that is reinforced in the latter decades of the nineteenth century as well. Offering a richly textured account of a matrilineal Nair family in late nineteenth-century Malabar, on the other hand, *Indulekha* marks Chandumenon's attempt at novelistic realism, thereby breaking the generic mold in which matriliny had been cast.

Indulekha is billed as the first novel in Malayalam. Conscious not only of taking on a relatively new literary form (the novel) but also a new genre (realism) – we are obliquely reminded of the novelty of both through *Indulekha*'s numerous references to classical Sanskrit poetry – Chandumenon is at pains to point out in his preface:

> I have also been asked by some others whether people would enjoy a story that dealt only with the everyday life of our time and did not have anything that would excite wonder or amazement. This is my response to them: Before people here saw and began appreciating oil paintings of the kind done in Europe, they used to take pleasure in images of Narasimhamurthy that were impossible in reality. ... Today many of those people have tired of such depictions and admire oil or water-colour paintings that depict people or animals or other things in their everyday form. ... In the same way, a new taste will emerge with well-written stories about ordinary things and everyday events and replace the taste for the old stories of fantastic happenings.[12]

Drawing a connection between visual and literary representation and thereby recalling the impress of John Ruskin's *Modern Painters* on George Eliot, the premise of statements such as this are not entirely singular (or new) even in the context of nineteenth-century India, for a similar sentiment prefaces Lal Mohan Day's *Bengal Peasant Life* (1870), where Day pledges to provide "a plain and unvarnished tale of a plain peasant," in contrast to the fantastic tales of "kings with ten heads and twenty arms" penned by his predecessors.[13] At one level, the impetus to a mimetic, documentary realism capturing the quotidian can be read as an effect of a radial metropolitan literary legacy. However, such a reading would need to assume, amongst other things, a modular metropolitan realism, which, as Elaine Freedgood has persuasively demonstrated, never quite existed.[14] Moreover, despite its professed realist inclination, *Indulekha*'s realist credentials stand on shaky ground. As Meenakshi Mukherjee notes, "Chandumenon's novel veers toward pre-novel forms of storytelling and away from the realistic mode he so admires."[15] I will return to this latter point in the final section of this chapter, but for now

I want to emphasize that even as the discussion of colonial realisms invites discussions of derivativeness or belated arrivals – of realisms trying to play catch-up – it may be productive to turn the discussion around to pluralize realisms in a transimperial frame, which is to say, to think of Victorian realisms as responding to literary and cultural imperatives that are as myriad as they are entwined. This chapter reads *Indulekha* not so much on account of Chandumenon's foray into realism but due to his decision to narrativize matriliny in a realist mode, given not only the imperiled status of realism in 1890s England but also the fact that matriliny was widely considered the purview of myth or romance, the latter featuring as an ascendant genre in fin-de-siècle Britain. In what follows, I situate the question of *Indulekha*'s genre alongside fin-de-siècle discussions of matriliny in Britain; I then consider *Indulekha* in terms of how the novel's formal and thematic inconsistencies index the work of realism at the fin de siècle broadly conceived, which is to say at the interstices – spatial and temporal – of empire and a nation that is yet to be made.

Romance, Realism, and the Malabar

Indulekha's author, Chandumenon (1847–99), was born into a Nair family near Thallesary in Malabar. Schooled in both English and Malayalam, he followed his father into government service and was appointed head clerk of the Calicut civil court in 1872. Notably, he assisted William Logan, the subcollector at Thallesary, in the latter's compilation of the compendious *Malabar Manual* that not only detailed the lives and customs of the inhabitants of the Malabar but also surveyed the flora, fauna, and crop cycles of the region. It was through his association with Logan that Chandumenon acquired an interest in reading "English novels," which he narrated in translation to his friends and family. Narrating Benjamin Disraeli's *Henrietta Temple* (1837), a novel in which the maternal uncle of one of the central characters plays a significant role, inspired Chandumenon to write a novel of his own, given the salience of maternal uncles in the Nair household. *Indulekha* was immensely popular upon publication, and a second edition appeared within six months of the first. As Chandumenon noted in his preface to the second edition: "Malayalis who had not read in Malayalam any book in the manner of English novels, immediately read and enjoyed this book and praised it."[16] As he informed his audience too, an English translation of the novel by the acting collector of the Malabar, W. Dumergue, was also underway (Chandumenon, "Preface to the Second Edition," 241). Clearly, even as the novel fed into a latent Malayali predilection for the everyday – one evidently untutored by "English novels" – its realist mode also paid bureaucratic dividend. Of course, Chandumenon's involvement with the *Malabar Manual* and his consequent interest in novel-reading signals the consanguinity between the bureaucratic and literary imagination, a significant relationship that I can only gesture toward in this chapter.[17] And that the colonial state should seize upon *Indulekha* as a viable source of information about the Malabar – as a companion piece, perhaps, to the *Malabar Manual* – speaks to the sociological lure of realist depiction, one that allegedly detracts from realism's aesthetic merits. But what I am interested in here are the terms in which Dumergue, the administrator-translator, couches *Indulekha*. Praising Chandumenon for his ingenuity, he notes that "modern Malabar is depicted in his pages and the language of *Indulekha* is the living Malayalam of the present day."[18] Dumergue goes even further to say:

> So far as Europeans are concerned, the value of a book like *Indulekha* can hardly be overestimated. Few amongst us have opportunities of learning the colloquial and idiomatic language of the country, which, so far as I am competent to express an opinion, is far more important for the ends of administration than all the monuments of archaic ingenuity which we read and mark and leave undigested. (Dumergue, "Dumergue's Preface," 245)

Although guided by interests of administrative instrumentality, or because of it, Dumergue is clearly interested in introducing a wider swath of Europeans to an India (or Malabar) in "colloquial" and "idiomatic" frames, in terms, that is, of the contemporary. Such an inclination, of course, runs counter to a European reluctance to do so. While the tendency to depict the East either as anterior (or timeless) can generally be attributed to an Orientalist ensemble of representative technologies that date back to at least the eighteenth century, I am specifically interested in the metropolitan investment in portraying matriliny in terms of primordialism in the latter decades of the nineteenth century: such a portrayal affected the kind of stories that British Victorians told at the fin de siècle because it had everything to do with the story that they were telling about themselves.[19]

The totemic appeal that Nair matriliny held out for Lawrence anticipated the status accorded to matriliny in the Victorian imaginary over the course of the nineteenth century, especially as the newly professionalized discipline of anthropology charted a story of human development that relegated matriliny to a prior state of social organization, a designation that was as much about time (it was marked "primitive") as it was about place:

matrilineal societies provided a point of comparison for adumbrating the
"West." While the notion of matrilineal origins of human society was by
no means an uncontested one – Henry Maine, for one, took exception to
the theory – it was universally couched, nonetheless, in terms of sexual
promiscuity that could – and needed to – be reined in by defined
patrilineal descent guaranteed by monogamous marriage, which, according
to anthropologists such as John McLellan, marked the passage from
barbarism to civilization.[20] Within such a framework, bourgeois monogamy placed British Victorians at the apex of the civilizational hierarchy.
Indeed, stages such as barbarism, primitivism, etc., characterized Lewis
Henry Morgan's treatise on marriage, upon which Friedrich Engels based
his *Origins of the Family, Private Property, and the State* (1884).[21] Yet Marx,
who died before Engels's work was published, was, as his notes on the
topic indicate, less confident about the teleological progress toward private
property, the arc that Engels draws, informed as he (Engels) was by
Morgan's limning of the trajectory from a matrilineal structure to patrimony. Moreover, as commentators have noted, by associating private
property with greed and reading it therefore as a "social mutation,"[22]
Engels fails to note the interceding tensions besetting collective ownership,
a blind spot in Morgan's disquisition that Marx was otherwise alert to in
his unpublished analysis of Morgan's work.[23]

Marx's departure from Engels on the reading of Morgan issues a
rejoinder to the tendency to ahistoricize matrilineal societies or read them
in terms of a unitary, unchanging essence. It was certainly such a tendency
that underwrote Victorian anthropological discourse, which relied on
travelogues and missionary narratives as much as on fiction and popular
myths for evidence.[24] Indeed, if matrilineal societies were narrativized in
the latter decades of the nineteenth century, it was through the genre of
romance, as indeed had been the case with Lawrence's *Empire of the Nairs*
at the beginning of the nineteenth century. That it was so cannot simply
be attributed, however, to an unbroken continuity in representational
choices (although one cannot discount the abiding currency of such
choices) but to what Kathy Psomiades outlines as the increasing sway of
anthropological thinking over the literary imaginary, at least with reference
to the marriage plot.[25] In this schema, the "evolutionary" progress from
"primitive" (polyandrous, matrilineal) marriage to "modern" (monogamous, patrilineal) marriage provided the *ur*-marriage narrative, and matriliny became the stuff of "mythic romance," operating at once as the
"other" of the realist marriage plot and its progenitor (Psomiades,
"Mythic Marriage," 25). But even as the marriage depicted in mythic

romance is placed in a prior chronological time, the genre of mythic romance – where anthropology meets (and inflects) the realist marriage plot – was new and popular in the closing decades of the nineteenth century, not least on account of realism's waning popularity at the fin de siècle. Marked as "feminine," realism was losing ground to the more masculinist, action-packed romance, which, in offering an escape from the confines of the late-Victorian world, shared its appeal with the non-mimeticism of experimental modernism (Esty, "Realism Wars," 322). Psomiades, in fact, places the emergent popularity of the "mythic marriage plot" with some precision (1886–91), noting the fascination (in novels such as Rider Haggard's *She*) with the relationship between a mortal male lover and an otherworldly female goddess commanding authority and lineage (Psomiades, "Mythic Marriage," 27).

Chandumenon's decision to write about matrilineal marriage in the realist mode in 1889–90, therefore, is not without significance. There is no way to tell if this was a deliberate choice designed to fly in the face of current metropolitan trends, or if Chandumenon's familiarity with met-ropolitan literary output was simply dated; he was, after all, taken in by Disraeli's 1837 novel. But literary sleuthing – what Chandumenon may or may not have read at the time that he was writing the novel – seems beside the point, at least in this instance, for it risks obscuring the larger terms of Chandumenon's engagement with *Indulekha*. While he was taken in by English novelists, he was by no means singular in his effort to write in the realist mode. Rather, as evidenced by Lal Mohan Day's prefatory remarks cited earlier in this chapter, the late nineteenth century witnessed an interest in realism in India, which needs to be viewed not only in relation to the changing literary map in fin-de-siècle Britain but also the aesthetic response that a rapidly changing political landscape in late nineteenth-century India generated. By explicitly focusing on the 1890s, the remit of this present volume in any case calls for a specific linkage between aesthetics and history. But the case of 1890s realism provides further warrant – were one needed – for adopting such a focus, for the trajectory of realism as a genre, as already mentioned, is inflected by geopolitical shifts in Britain's imperial standing. What Esty terms "realism wars" – manifested in the waning years of empire in the popularity of romance vis-à-vis realism – is more a tussle or "shifting of gears" between mimetic modes used to describe and exercise limited control and nonmimetic modes to produce expansive authority (Esty, "Realism Wars," 328). Without reducing realism to mimesis, Esty spatializes the difference between realism and romance, which is to say that realism, which is more about description (and control), finds its boundaries within the nation, whereas romance enables projection (and escape) elsewhere and beyond (Esty, "Realism Wars," 328).

Esty's point is generative, and, interestingly, if we were to follow through with it by viewing the analytic from the perspective of writers across the colonial divide, then we are presented with a somewhat different proposition. It is through a realist depiction of the *taravad* – the matrilineal household – that Chandumenon projects a future that can surpass the nation that is yet to be made. And doing so is necessary for Chandumenon, for by the time of his writing of the novel, the fate of Nair matriliny was on hold, caught as it was between the normativizing efforts of the colonial state as well as that of an emergent, self-styled native bourgeoisie, which considered the continuation of the *taravad* system an embarrassment as well as an impediment to individual property rights.[26] The place of a localized practice such as Nair matriliny was also tenuous in the nationalist imaginary as indeed it was in the colonial worldview, with both constituencies accruing credibility in the name of the "modern."[27] Significantly, the Malabar Marriage Commission, appointed in 1891 by the Government of Madras to reform the practice of Nair *sambandhams* and bring them in line with normative marriage practices included, among other Indian members, Chandumenon. But he was one of two members to dissent from the decision to introduce reform and expressed his views in a lengthy note (1891). Therefore, even as Dumergue extolled the benefits that *Indulekha* offered to the administrative cadre in terms of sociological yield, it is worth considering how the novel also evades and exceeds this remit. To be sure, by conceiving of *Indulekha* in the realist mode Chandumenon delivers the *taravad* to a history that is otherwise denied it in the British Victorian imaginary. But doing so also enables him to stylistically present the *taravad* in ways that endow it with a staying power precisely at its moment of ebbing in the colonial and nationalist imaginaries.

In the *Taravad*

However, as a reading of *Indulekha* demonstrates, the novel grapples with its depiction of the *taravad*, and the narrative is noteworthy for its generic jumps and structural inconsistencies. The inconsistency, I suggest, is not only on account of Chandumenon's straddling of distinct literary traditions (Indian classics and British novels) but also of the specific moment – the 1890s – of the novel's publication and reception. The novel centers around the eponymous heroine, Indulekha, who belongs to a wealthy, landowning Nair household. While the narrative deploys conventional methods to describe her physical beauty (through conventions derived from classical Sanskrit literature), such a description is immediately followed by an accounting of her "modern" education:

> She was taught English and trained in the finer details of Sanskrit drama. She received an advanced education in music and acquired skills in playing the piano, the violin, the veena, and other musical instruments. Besides this, she was taught to embroider and paint like the young ladies in Europe. (7)[28]

In what abides as a striking visual memory of the novel, Indulekha is often depicted reading, be it a novel or newspaper. She recites Sanskrit verses with as much ease as she recommends English novels to her lover, Madhavan. While in the world of the novel, Indulekha is exceptional by virtue of her education, it is worth pointing out that to a late nineteenth-century Malayali reading public, a female character with an amalgamated worldview such as Indulekha would have been recognizable even if aspirational, but not improbable or fantastical.[29] Although she has received an English-style education, Indulekha is, as the narrator points out early on, "keenly aware of her Malayali identity" (7).

This authorial comment is clearly important for the novel, for its formal choices are guided by an overriding interest in inhabiting or accommodating dualities. In this, Indulekha and Madhavan make an apt couple, for while Indulekha combines both English and Malayali sensibilities, her cosmopolitanism is offset by Madhavan's more parochial worldview, parochial in the sense that he is completely enamored of "modern" ideas and is unable to think expansively of the *taravad*. Mouthing the precepts of a normative bourgeois sexuality, Madhvan expresses his discomfiture with the apparent casualness of *sambandhams* (the sexual relation that a Nair woman engages in): "The women of this region are not faithful to their husbands like women of other lands. They take and discard husbands as they please, they have other freedoms also," (24) he tells Indulekha. Here and elsewhere in the novel, Madhavan, though not associated with the nationalist cause, is clearly identified with the reformist faction that disapproves of the existence of the *taravad*, associating it with apparent licentiousness and amorality. Indulekha's response to his comment is swift and spirited:

> Really! Remarkable words! Is this your regard for Malayali women? . . . If you think that just because we Nair women are unlike Nambuthiri women, who lead a cloistered life without talking to other people and without being educated; because we do not live like beasts, we are labelled adulterous or not devoted to our husbands, nothing can be more faulty than this. (25)

This feisty exchange is not without its own erotic charge, for Indulekha and Madhavan are very much in love with each other, and the early section of the novel narrates their many meetings (in a scene that is presented entirely without narratorial comment, she is depicted kissing him on the lips [29]). Indulekha is determined to marry Madhavan, who in his accomplishments and education is deemed worthy of her by her family. However, although the two are eminently compatible and the early scenes of the novel focus on their romance, any possibility of a long-term relationship is snuffed out by Panchumenon, Madhavan's granduncle and the overseer of the *taravad* that he is born into. Panchumenon is also Indulekha's maternal grandfather, making Madhavan and Indulekha cousins, twice removed. Panchumenon, irascible and temperamental, forbids the relationship because of his displeasure with Madhavan, who, in yet another sign of his discontentment with the *taravad* system, openly questions Panchumenon's authority as the overseer of the *taravad* in the opening pages of the novel. Therefore, though aware and approving of Indulekha and Madhavan's mutual fondness for each other, Panchumenon arranges a *sambandham* between Indulekha and Surinambuthiri, a rich (Nambuthiri) Brahmin, who is the second son of his family and therefore has license to engage in liaisons with Nair women, a benefit that he has apparently availed himself of quite freely. The novel's plotline is driven by Indulekha's determination to thwart this *sambandham,* in favor of marriage to Madhavan, an endeavor that she is ultimately successful in at the end of the novel.

In her reading of *Indulekha*, Mukherjee comments that despite its investment in realism, *Indulekha* lacks character development, for we do not get a sense of Indulekha's (or anyone's) interiority (Mukherjee, "Epic and Novel," 598). It is certainly true that the characters occupy fixed and stated positions throughout the novel, and their internal desires, doubts, or motivations remain opaque. If it is the case that psychological interiority features as a key element for adjudging aesthetic merit for both realist and nonmimetic styles (Esty, "Realism Wars," 321), then *Indulekha* falters at such a test. We never know for sure what drives Indulekha's resolve nor do we gain insight into her feelings for Madhavan or the untampered modernity that he is made to represent. But in lieu of a disassembled interiority, what we do get is Indulekha's awareness of her position as a Nair woman, an awareness that endows her with a remarkable degree of self-possession and calm resolve. Surinambuthiri, her suitor, is taken aback by the number of times she uses "I" in her exchanges with him: "The 'I' startled the Nambuthiripad [Surinambuthiri]. A Nair lady had never spoken to him like that" (102). Although the sentence singles out Indulekha since no other Nair lady had spoken like that to Surinambuthiri, its phrasing also makes clear that it is precisely Indulekha's Nair identity that sanctions such locution. Nair matriliny therefore stands in as an explanation for character traits that the novel successfully exteriorizes inasmuch as it presents Indulekha as a highly compelling figure navigating a social situation that bears enormous personal consequences.

Significantly, Indulekha succeeds in her efforts to call off the *sambandham* with Surinambuthiri without deploying any ruse or stratagem, the details of which one might have expected to constitute a significant portion of the plot. Rather, she simply stands her ground as a Nair woman assured of her right to choose her partner at will, and this position is not questioned or refuted by Panchumenon or other family members. The plot thereon focuses, quite comedically, on Panchumenon and Surinambuthiri devising ways to save face at the otherwise embarrassing social situation that Indulekha's obdurate resolve produces. What follows is a series of missed encounters and mistaken identities – a veritable comedy of manners in which Indulekha and Madhavan are separated for a while, only to be reunited in marriage at the end of the novel. That the novel lapses into comedy – a stock stylistic choice – at an otherwise consequential moment of Indulekha's life seems both incongruous and generically inconsistent (even gesturing to the prenovelistic mode of storytelling alluded to by Mukherjee). But that it can afford to do so bears testimony to the ideological recourse that Nair matriliny provides Indulekha, even as Panchumenon's adherence to the *taravad*'s customary practices (denoted by his invitation of the *Nambuthiri* to engage in a *sambandham*) is precisely what impedes her potential marriage with Madhavan. The choice of comedy, therefore, under-lines the novel's presentation of the *taravad* both in its limits and its possibilities, producing an ambivalence that I read as a key feature of the novel's realism, a point that I shall return to. But I also want to point out that this ambivalence is complemented by what seems to be the novel's willed misrepresentation of the *taravad* itself.

At one level the misrepresentation echoes the colonial state's misrecog-nition of the customary practices not just of the *taravad* but also of the land relations that it both subtended and was sustained by (Arunima, "Multiple Meanings," 295). With the annexation of Mysore in the late eighteenth century, the colonial state took charge of revenue collection in the Malabar, and in the process readjusted land tenure. Contrary to extant practice, landholders (usually Nambuthiris) were granted permanent, inalienable rights to the land, which was let out to renters (Nairs). The Nairs, who were noncultivators, subleased the land at extraordinarily high

rates to those who cultivated it, and, in the process, enriched themselves at
the cost of the peasant-cultivators as well as the landowners, who were often
cash-poor. Resentful of the Nairs acquiring increasing wealth and authority,
landowners tried to reverse the tide of Nair ascendancy by attempting to limit
the tenure of their tenancy and secure the right to evict them when necessary.
As an educated middle-class, however, Nairs held more sway in influencing
legislation on their behalf, and in October 1885, the Board of Revenue in
Madras rejected official proposals to secure safeguards for the peasants as well
as the landowners' bid to obtain eviction rights against the Nairs.[30]

While Nairs may have benefited from this favorable ruling, the diver-
gence of Nair and Nambuthiri interests in the land also led to Nair male
resentment of Nambuthiri *sambandhams* with Nair women, a factor that
questioned the viability of the *taravad* from within (as exemplified by
Madhavan in the novel). The metaphoric relation between land and the
female body is a critical commonplace and may well provide a lens here for
reading the Nair male desire to curtail Nambuthiri *sambandhams* with
Nair women in the face of fraught land relations. But such a reading
should not forestall an accounting of the interlinked ways in which the
land question weighed heavily on the future of the *taravad* and its relatively
capacious definition of female sexuality. Moreover, the indivisibility of
taravad property became a bone of contention for Nair men increasingly
employed by the colonial state, who wished to bequeath their self-acquired
property to their heirs rather than consign it to the nominal control of the
karanavan (the position that Panchumenon occupies in the novel as the
eldest brother overseeing his sister's *taravad*). Liberating the *taravad* from
the authority of the *karanavan* became an important step, as Praveena
Kodoth puts it, toward "facilitating the possibility of a conjugal family."[31]

But the position of the *karanavan*, too, was misread by the colonial
state, which rewrote him as sole head of the *taravad* whereas earlier women
had comparable standing (Arunima, "Multiple Meanings," 298).
Indulekha also partakes of this misreading, although to different effect.
To be sure, Panchumenon plays a critical role through his approval – or
withholding thereof – of Indulekha's *sambandhams* in ways that belie the
autonomy that Indulekha derives from her Nair status, a discrepancy that
is historically accurate inasmuch as the *taravad* was matrilineal but deeply
patriarchal.[32] But that it is Panchumenon who arrogates control over
Indulekha's sexual choices as her grandfather (albeit the maternal one)
brings him closer to the role of a paterfamilias of his marital family at the
expense of downplaying his position as Madhavan's *karanavan*, the avun-
cular overseer of his sister's (Madhavan's mother's) *taravad*.[33] In terms of

the logic of the *taravad*, Panchumenon's sustained involvement with his marital family seems anomalous. But puzzling as it may be, the anomaly resituates the novel on familiar ground (familiar, that is, to a non-Nair Malayali audience in the Malabar; Chandumenon could perhaps not have anticipated a non-Malayali audience in the rest of India and elsewhere that would read the novel in translation). Presenting Panchumenon as the paterfamilias of his conjugal family makes the novel legible in ways that offset the potentially disorienting effects of the *taravad*. When mapping family relations in the novel, for instance, readers may get a distinct sense of reading "backward," for matriliny in *Indulekha* is not depicted through visible relays of female authority but an implicit organizational structure where men constitute the locus of authority, but only via a proxy owner-ship of and access to land and capital, as brothers and uncles in a household that otherwise belongs to their sister.

The affective charge of this disorientation makes the novel emblematic of the fin de siècle, be it in Britain or Malabar (caught as the latter was between nationalist and colonialist modernities that were conjoined in their patriarchy). But the novel attempts to offset such disorientation by locating Panchu's sister's *taravad* (that he oversees) adjacent to his conjugal household, where his wife resides, along with their adult children and grandchildren (including Indulekha).[34] The novel shuttles between the two domestic spaces, but we are admitted into the interior spaces of Panchu's conjugal home, and Panchu's actions throughout the novel bear more consequence for his marital family. The trajectory of this back-and-forth movement, veering as it does toward Panchu's conjugal home in ways that underline his position as husband, father, and grandfather pre-sages the precarity, if not eventual demise, of the *taravad* in the face of a family structure and lineage oriented around patrilineal conjugal domes-ticity. However, it is also possible to read the novel as positing the latter (the conjugal home), not as superseding the former (the *taravad*) but as superimposed upon it so that the *taravad* is made legible through the lens of normative conjugality. The realist mode and its ideological investments domesticate the *taravad* such that it can be narrativized in ways that Chandumenon can argue for its self-correction.

Writing the Colonial Fin De Siècle

As mentioned, at the Malabar Marriage Commission, Chandumenon was one of two members to strike a note of dissent, noting that proposed changes to the *taravad* would fundamentally alter Nair laws of succession and even identity.³⁵ *Indulekha* seems to offer evidence of the *taravad*'s ability to evolve on its own terms. Not only does Indulekha's characterization offer proof positive of the *taravad*'s salutariness, but that she eventually marries an unrepentant Madhavan – and that, too, with Panchumenon's blessings – ensures that Madhavan's oppositional stance is accommodated within the world of the *taravad*. Moreover, it is Surinambuthiri, the rich Nambuthiri Brahmin, who embodies what could be viewed as the distasteful excesses of the *sambandham* system – apart from being gauche in his tastes and negligent in his stewardship of the lands he owns, he expresses interest, when rebuffed by Indulekha, in initiating a *sambandham* with her mother. Significantly enough, he occupies limited space in the novel and appears in the chapters that read more like comedy. Cast as a comic villain, it is almost as if he belongs to another era. Yet even as the novel "reforms" the *taravad* from within through its choices in character economy and narrative technique, it concludes with Indulekha moving away to marry Madhavan and setting up her conjugal home in the city of Madras, away from the *taravad*. Such an ending offers a teleology of marriage with the conjugal family as the end point. Indeed, the fact that Indulekha stays true to Madhavan over the course of the novel, rejecting other *sambandhams* that she could well have engaged in, speaks to her chastity and faithfulness in ways that may recommend her in terms of bourgeois morality. However, the fact that it is her more expansive position within the *taravad* that enables her to stay the course and build her life with the partner of her choice makes the *taravad* not just prior to but coeval with her conjugal home.

The novel makes a case for the *taravad*, therefore, through conjugal marriage and vice versa. This dynamic injects an ambivalence that formally manifests itself through doubleness: the novel, as mentioned, shuttles between the two spaces. But it is also unable to sustain this doubleness, and there are narrative breakdowns, as when Madhavan, upon being misled into believing that Indulekha has entered into a *sambandham* with Surinambuthiri (through confusion caused by mistaken identities) embarks on a long voyage away from the Malabar and visits different parts of the country – Bombay, Calcutta, Lucknow, etc. The novel at this point is so deeply engrossed with Madhavan's experiences and mishaps across the country that it is almost as if we are reading another story: the *taravad* seems a world away – as indeed it was, given that the rest of the country would have only a dim familiarity with Nair matrilineal practice. What appears as a narrative disjuncture, then, thematizes the gap not only between alternate structures of family and marriage but also between region and a nation in the making. *Indulekha's* realism, therefore, does not serve as an accomplice to nation-making; rather, it critiques it. It offers a glimpse of notions of family and sexuality on the verge of being eclipsed in the name of the modern nation and its impetus to "conformative sexuality" (Kodoth, "Courting Legitimacy," 354). Doing so would have been in keeping with the fin-de-siècle contestation of sexual identities and mores. It certainly recalls the subtitle of Lawrence's work: "The Rights of Woman." This is not to suggest that the *taravad* system was free from patriarchal control, far from it. But, as legal historian Janaki Nair points out, "the system guaranteed women inviolable economic rights and a far degree of freedom in the choice of marriage partners, paving the way for greater equality within the family. Women were not considered a burden to the family" (Nair, *Women and Law,* 163).

It is hard to assess Chandumenon's own position on women's rights or sexual autonomy, given the lack of definitive information on that score. The ambivalence undergirding the novel, can certainly signal his own uncertainty on the question despite – or because – of his proprietary interest in securing the future of the *taravad*. Such uncertainty, if it existed, would only be compounded by the uncertain position that this novel occupies, along with many others, on the historical cusp of the nineteenth and twentieth centuries as well as the ideological gap between colony and nation, a gap that we tend to foreclose too quickly in its amorphousness. The fin de siècle offers an extended moment for considering this gap, and *Indulekha's* ambivalence becomes a key element of its realism, for it captures the precarity and the possibilities of the *taravad* as well as the conditions for doing so in ways that compel a rewriting of what realism can and cannot do in the closing decade of the nineteenth century.[36]

Acknowledgment

My thanks to Dustin Friedman and Kristin Mahoney for their helpful editorial suggestions. Thanks, too, to Joseph Bristow, Neil Hultgren, and Elizabeth Miller for organizing the symposium series, "Victorian Apocalypse: The *Siècle* at its *Fin*," where I presented an early version of this chapter.

Notes

1 While this point has been abundantly made by commentators on realism, such as George Levine, for a more recent rendition of this point with reference to the changing geopolitics of the late nineteenth-early twentieth century, see

Joe Cleary, "Realism After Modernism and the Literary World-System," *Modern Language Quarterly* 73, no. 3 (September 2012): 255–68.

2 Lauren Goodlad, "Introduction: Worlding Realisms Now," *Novel: A Forum on Fiction* 49, no. 2 (2016): 183–201 (194–95).

3 These two movements are not unrelated; see Stephen Arata, *Fictions of Loss in the Victorian Fin De Siècle: Identity and Empire* (Charlottesville, VA: University of Virginia Press, 1996).

4 Jed Esty, "Realism Wars," *Novel: A Forum on Fiction* 49, no. 2 (2016): 316–42 (322).

5 See Sudipta Kaviraj, "The Imaginary Institution of India," in *Subaltern Studies* vol. 7, eds. Partha Chatterjee and Gyandendra Pandey (Delhi: Oxford University Press, 1993), 1–40.

6 This is to say that the teleology of the nation predetermines a reading of nineteenth-century Indian realism, a reading that could otherwise pause further at the irreconcilabilities and disjunctures engendered by the complexities of nation-making. Meenakshi Mukherjee's magisterial *Realism and Reality: The Novel and Society in India* (Delhi: Oxford University Press, 1985), a study to which I remain indebted, takes due note of the nineteenth-century Indian novel's engagement with nation-making but not necessarily of the erasures, incompatibilities, or uncertainties that the novels register on account of it.

7 I use "Victorian" in an expansive sense, not delimiting the referentiality of the term to the geoethnic boundaries of Britain alone; I use the qualification "British Victorian" for that purpose.

8 See G. Arunima, "Multiple meanings: Changing Conceptions of Matrilineal Kinship in Nineteenth and Twentieth Century Malabar," *Indian Economic and Social History Review* 33, no. 3 (1996): 283–307. For a classic study of matrilineal formations, see Kathleen Gough and David M. Schneider, eds. *Matrilineal Kinship* (Berkeley, CA: University of California Press, 1961).

9 Quoted in Donald F. Lach, *Asia in the Making of Europe*, vol. 1, book 1 (Chicago, IL: University of Chicago Press, 1965), 355.

10 Percy Byshhe Shelley, "Letter to James Lawrence," in *The Letters of Percy Byshhe Shelley: Containing Material Never Before Collected*, ed. Roger Ingpen (Sir Isaac Pitman and Sons, 1912), 356.

11 James Lawrence, "Introduction: An Essay on the Nair System of Gallantry and Inheritance," in *The Empire of the Nairs; Or the Rights of Women, An Utopian Romance* vol. I, 2nd ed. (London: T. Hookham Jun., and E. T. Hookham, 1813), i–xliii (xxvii).

12 O. Chandumenon, "Preface to the First Edition of *Indulekha*," in *Indulekha by O. Chandumenon*, trans. and ed. Anitha Devasia (Delhi: Oxford University Press, 2005), 240–41.

13 Quoted in Satya P. Mohanty, "The Epistemic Work of Literary Realism: Two Novels from Colonial India," in *A History of the Indian Novel in English*, ed. Ulka Anjaria (Cambridge: Cambridge University Press, 2015), 45–58 (50).

14 Elaine Freedgood, *Worlds Enough: The Invention of Realism in the Victorian Novel* (Princeton, NJ: Princeton University Press, 2019).

15 Meenakshi Mukherjee, "Epic and Novel in India," in *The Novel: Vol. I. History, Geography, and Culture,* ed. Franco Moretti (Princeton, NJ: Princeton University Press, 2006), 596–631 (598).

16 Chandumenon, "Preface to the Second Edition of *Indulekha*," in Devasia, *Indulekha*, 241.

17 I take up this relation more fully in "Writing Bureaucracy, Bureaucratic Writing: Charles Dickens, *Little Dorrit*, and Mid-Victorian Liberalism," *Nineteenth-Century Literature* 75, 2 (2020): 133–58.

18 W. Dumergue, "Dumergue's Preface," in Devasia, *Indulekha*, 245.

19 These representative strategies of course date back even earlier than the eighteenth century, but I mention that as a marker by way of referring to the specific strategies that Said refers to in *Orientalism*.

20 John McLellan, *Primitive Marriage: An Enquiry into the Form of Capture in Marriage Ceremonies* (Edinburgh: Adam and Charles Black, 1865).

21 Engels took much of the data *for Origins of the Family* from American anthropologist Lewis Henry Morgan's *Ancient Society* (1877).

22 Irving Goldman, "Evolution and Anthropology," *Victorian Studies* 3, no. 1 (1959): 55–75 (62).

23 Carolyn Fluehr-Lobann, Bettina Aptheker, Jules De Raedt et al., "A Marxist Reappraisal of the Matriarchate," *Current Anthropology* 20, no. 2 (1979): 341–59 (34, 348).

24 See Kathy Alexis Psomiades, "The Marriage Plot in Theory," *Novel: A Forum on Fiction* 43, no. 1 (2010): 53–59.

25 Kathy Alexis Psomiades, "Mythic Marriage: Haggard, Frazer, Hardy and the Anthropology of Myth," in *Replotting Marriage in Nineteenth-Century British Literature,* eds. Jill Galvan and Elsie Michie (Columbus, OH: Ohio State University Press, 2018), 55–75.

26 Janaki Nair, *Women and Law in Colonial India* (New Delhi: Kali for Women, 1996), 154.

27 As Mytheli Sreenivas notes, "Indian nationalism figured its hegemonies over national culture through a process of displacement and erasure of alternative national visions." *Wives, Widows, and Concubines: The Conjugal Ideal in Colonial India* (Bloomington, IN: Indiana University Press, 2008), 71. In what is indicative of the various scales along which national identity is conceived of, in the context of Nair matriliny, it is Nair self-identity that stands in for an "alternative national vision," as is evident in Chandumenon's note of dissent.

28 All references to the novel are to the edition edited and translated by Devasia and will be parenthetically cited in the text.

29 See J. Devika, "Negotiating Women's Social Space: Public Debates on Gender in Early Modern Kerala, India," *Inter-Asia Cultural Studies* 7, no. 1 (2006): 43–61.

30 K. N. Panikkar, "Agrarian Legislation and Social Classes: A Case Study of Malabar," *Economic and Political Weekly* 13, no. 21 (27 May 1978): 880–88 (883).

31 Praveena Kodoth, "Courting Legitimacy or Delegitimizing Custom? Sexuality, Sambandham, and Marriage Law in Late Nineteenth-Century Malabar," *Modern Asian Studies* 35, no. 2 (2002): 349–84 (362).

32 As mentioned, Nair matriliny feeds into Nambuthiri patriarchy. The difference between descent and authority is one along which matriliny and matriarchy split: the two are not necessarily coincident.

33 For a discussion of the colonial state's reading of the *karanavan* as paterfamilias, see Arunima, "Multiple Meanings," 297.

34 Panchumenon's anomalous position in his conjugal home is precipitated by the fact that his eldest son, Indulekha's maternal uncle had died, which is why he decides to take over the running of the household. This thematic detail offers fictional sleight of hand for the novel to juxtapose conjugal domesticity with that of the *taravad*.

35 O. Chandumenon, "Chandumenon's Memorandum to the Marriage Commission," in Devasia, *Indulekha*, 249.

36 Taking from Georg Lukács's deliberations on realism in *Studies in European Realism* (1964), Ulka Anjaria makes a similar point about the twentieth-century Indian novel, arguing that "incommensurabilities and gaps [should not be] seen as detriments to realism but as constitutive of a more capacious realism." Ulka Anjara, *Realism in the Twentieth-Century Indian Novel: Colonial Difference and Literary Form* (Cambridge: Cambridge University Press, 2012), 11. In my reading, such an understanding of realism is critical for studying Indian literary texts written in the ideologically and historically transitional moment between the late nineteenth-early twentieth century.

CHAPTER 5

Reading World Religions in the 1890s

Sebastian Lecourt

In the Preface to Volume 1 of his massive 50-volume *Sacred Books of the East* (*SBOTE*) series, published by Oxford University Press between 1879 and 1910, the Oxford Sanskritist F. Max Müller informed readers that they might be disappointed by the series' contents:

> Readers who have been led to believe that the Vedas of the ancient Brahmans, the Avesta of the Zoroastrians, the Tripitaka of the Buddhists, the Kings of Confucius, or the Koran of Mohammed are books full of primeval wisdom and religious enthusiasm, or at least of sound and simple moral teaching, will be disappointed on consulting these volumes. Looking at many of the books that have lately been published on the religions of the ancient world, I do not wonder that such a belief should have been raised; but I have long felt that it was high time to dispel such illusions, and to place the study of the ancient religions of the world on a more real and sound, on a more truly historical basis.[1]

Do not read these books, Müller warned, if you simply crave mystical wisdom or "fragrant" Oriental flowers. For, in fact, a serious perusal of Asian scriptures reveals them to be full of "brambles and thorns" too: incomprehensible rituals, morally problematic commands, obtuse presci-entific cosmologies (Müller, "Preface," x). Alongside "so much that is fresh, natural, simple, beautiful, and true," Müller cautioned, "the Sacred Books of the East . . . contain so much that is not only unmeaning, artificial, and silly, but even hideous and repellent" (xxii).

In sounding this cautionary note, Müller was casting shade on an increasingly lucrative market for popular works on "world religions." He himself was the closest thing that existed to an official academic authority on the subject that existed in Britain in 1879. A Prussian national and student of the great French Indologist Eugène Burnouf, Müller had first moved to England in the 1840s to edit the massive *Rig Veda* text possessed by the East India Company. His multivolume edition of that text (1849–74) and his subsequent English translation (1869) made Sanskrit a respectable subject in British academia, while his *Introduction to the Science of Religion* (1873) legitimated the notion that non-Western religions were worth studying. Thanks in large part to Müller's efforts, by the dawn of the 1880s there was an active conversation among British philologists, anthropologists, theologians, and philosophers about religion as a cross-cultural phenomenon.[2]

Müller's *SBOTE* were supposed to represent the culmination of this work: a series of well-vetted English translations with correct scholarly apparatus that would make the major texts of Indian, Persian, and Chinese religion accessible to general readers. At the same time, Müller was dismayed to find that such readers could increasingly turn to volumes like the American transcendentalist and freethinker Moncure Conway's *The Sacred Anthology* (1874), a collection of excerpts from world scriptures, or the British poet Edwin Arnold's *The Light of Asia* (1879), a Tennysonian epic about the life of the Buddha. These texts – both massive bestsellers by the time the *SBOTE* debuted – had no scholarly pretensions but instead promised readers nuggets of universal wisdom that could beautify their everyday lives. Müller reacted to them defensively because he saw them as cheapening the academic and political respectability of what he called the science of religion. "The time has come," he wrote in his Preface, "when the study of the ancient religions of mankind must be approached in a different, in a less enthusiastic, and more discriminating, in fact, in a more scholarlike spirit" (x, xi–xii). Such a spirit was important to Müller because, he felt, it would allow the classification of religion to aid the cause of empire. In his *Introduction to the Science of Religion* (1870), Müller had suggested that the proper motto of his discipline was "*Divide et impera* ... 'Classify and conquer.'"[3] In his 1874 address to the International Congress of Orientalists, meanwhile, Müller wrote that by annexing India to Europe's "empire of learning" philology had also bequeathed to the West its proper civilizational inheritance: "We live indeed in a new world; the barrier between the West and the East, that seemed insurmountable, has vanished. The East is ours, we are its heirs, and claim by right our share in its inheritance."[4] Volumes like Conway's and Arnold's compromised that goal by entertaining nonscholarly readers' spiritual curiosity or aesthetic fantasies.

This chapter offers a brief overview of the sort of popular publications on world religions that frustrated Müller but racked up remarkable sales during the 1880s and 1890s. What English language books were available to ordinary readers intrigued by Buddhism or Hinduism or Islam? What fascinations did they encourage, and what fantasies did they feed? On one level, I will argue, examining these texts promises to open up our political narrative about the history of religious studies. In recent years, influential monographs like Tomoko Masuzawa's *The Invention of World Religions* (2005) have, in good Saidian fashion, portrayed Victorian comparative religion as an expression of colonialist power-knowledge. By sketching a world map populated by different religions whose messages metropolitan readers could compare, they argue, scholars like Müller were projecting a cultural hierarchy with Protestant Christian modernity at the top.[5] Such a claim certainly fits some of Müller's assertions; but if we shift our attention toward popular publications, we can see how the study of comparative religion fed a wider set of cultural and political desires.[6] Middle-class aesthetes, radical Dissenters, occult dabblers – all of them found paths to chart across the new map of world religions. Meanwhile, popular Orientalist translations were often crucially important to colonial readers who lacked fluency in Sanskrit or classical Persian. In particular, I will argue, popular Orientalism enabled forms of creative syncretism during the period – attempts to build new systems of universal values by cross-fertilizing religious traditions. As Tanya Agathocleous and others have recently shown, late-Victorian syncretism is an intellectual project that is harder to distance ourselves from than classical imperialism, insofar as it tried to imagine a universal framework of human values that could unsettle the primacy of the West without becoming merely relativistic. In this sense, paying attention to such thinking can help us both paint a richer vision of late-Victorian thought and turn a critical eye on our own universalisms.[7]

In regard to our specific understanding of the 1890s, examining popular comparative religion can complicate our preoccupation with the transgressive, avant-garde, or protomodernist aspects of the fin de siècle. Scholars of the period have devoted much commentary to outré spiritual organizations like the Theosophical Society, the Hermetic Society, and the Hermetic Order of the Golden Dawn, which advertised themselves as stewards of an ancient wisdom tradition open only to initiates. Such groups play into our dominant narrative of the "Naughty Nineties" as a contrarian decade and are especially attractive to literary scholars because they seem to preview how modernism used Eastern religions to challenge middlebrow taste.[8] A broader survey of religious publishing in the period, however, shows how non-Western religions appealed to a more mainstream sensibility too – a kind of middlebrow ecumenicalism that saw the different religions of the world as humanistic influences for self-cultivation. In this way Victorian comparative religion lay the groundwork not only for modernism but for popular religious liberalism in the twentieth century as well.

To begin, it is worth noting that the *SBOTE* were themselves not as removed from a commercial logic as Müller himself would have had it. The series was published on a subscription model, with the hope being that the profits from the first twenty-four volumes would pay for the remaining twenty-six. Although few individuals seem to have purchased a full subscription, particular volumes sold well enough for the funding scheme to succeed.[9] N. J. Girardot compares the *SBOTE* to those two other giant, "bureaucratized" Oxford publications – the revised Authorized Version of the Bible and James Murray's Oxford English Dictionary (229–30). Müller's translation of the *Upanishads* and Georg Bühler's translation of the *Dharmashastra* led the series off in 1879; subsequent volumes included James Darmesteter's *Zend-Avesta* (1880), E. H. Palmer's *Qur'an* (1880), and T. W. Rhys Davids's collection of seven *Buddhist Suttas* (1881). The final translation – of Mahayana Buddhist scriptures – appeared in 1894, while the last actual volume, an index to the whole, would not be released until 1910 (Girardot, "Müller's *Sacred Books*," 226–27).

Along similar lines, Müller's goals for the series were divided between a kind of disinterested, scholarly logic and a more populist vision. His Preface, as we have seen, makes much of the need to confront what seemed strange, vexing, or distasteful about Eastern religions. However, with his German Pietist upbringing and Romantic linguistic training, Müller also felt that the goal of studying world religions was ultimately to suss out a universal feeling for the divine that all traditions shared.[10] For instance, elsewhere in the Preface Müller ventures that these volumes do not merely represent Orientalist curiosities but might instead point the reader toward transcultural truths:

> If some of those who read and mark these translations learn how to discover some such precious grains in the sacred books of other nations, though hidden under heaps of rubbish, our labour will not have been in vain, for there is no lesson which at the present time seems more important than to learn that in every religion there are such precious grains; that we must draw in every religion a broad distinction between what is essential and what is not, between the eternal and the temporary, between the divine and the human; and that though the non-essential may fill many volumes, the essential can often be comprehended in a few words, but words on which "hang all the law and the prophets." (Müller, "Preface," xxxviii)

The final quote here is Jesus speaking in Matthew 22, claiming to distill the message of the Mosaic Law into two simple commandments: "Thou shalt love the Lord thy God" and "Thou shalt love thy neighbor as thyself"

(22:37, 39). Müller repurposes the phrase to suggest a logic of syncretism that exceeds the scholarly exactitude that he had otherwise advertised for the *SBOTE*. As against his claim that the series will disinterestedly anatomize the religions of the East, this passage suggests that the payoff of such collecting will be a distillation and synthesis into some more purely realized future religion.

This kind of enthusiastic sorting and sifting was precisely what many of the more popular genres of comparative religion offered unabashedly. There were, for example, what Alexander Bubb calls Oriental miscellanies – collections of excerpts from various Eastern texts, often adapted into English from French and German translations (Bubb, "Asian Classic Literature," 123). Perhaps the most influential was Louisa Costello's bestselling *Rose Garden of Persia* (1845), which offered nonscholarly readers a tour of sixteen classical Persian poets in translations adapted from French and German and set among elaborate arabesque margins. It was Costello, Bubb shows, who created the market for the best-remembered Victorian collection of Persian poetry, Edward Fitzgerald's *Rubaiyat of Omar Khayyam* (1857), as well as countless other anthologies of gorgeous Eastern words that were cramming bookshelves by the fin de siècle: William Rounseville Alger's *Poetry of the East* (1856), B. Freeman-Mitford's *Tales of Old Japan* (1871), W. A. Clouston's *Arabian Poetry for English Readers* (1881), Charles Mills's *Pebbles, Pearls and Gems of the Orient* (1882), Herbert Giles's *Gems of Chinese Literature* (1884), and Edward S. Holden's *Flowers from Persian Gardens* (1902) (Bubb, "Asian Classic Literature," 124). These volumes offered their readers bewitching collectibles – small, precious, exotic objects that were also fungible and fully compatible with the English drawing room.

Some of these volumes went further and promised not only a miscellany of delightful trinkets, but also some broader vision of what different religions shared. Such ecumenical digests, as Bubb names then, were often edited by Unitarian clergymen and, behind their quaint titles, hid a genuine spiritual agenda (124). Alger's *Poetry of the East*, for instance, is less concerned with documenting the literary or historical origins of its selections than with telegraphing their perennial message. Although Alger's introduction, which comprises nearly a third of the volume, goes into great historical detail, most of his selections are left unattributed and instead given moralistic titles that foreground their spiritual significance: "Speaking the Truth," "The Power of Words," "The Vanity of Rank," "The Soul's Triumph Over Nature," "Vice Neutralizing Virtue." Similarly, and necessarily, Alger's index is organized topically rather than by author or title: "Emulous Love," "End and Means," "Enjoyment or Improvement."[11] Mills's volume, too, features short chapters that gather unattributed passages from different traditions under moral-topical titles such as Humility, Fate, Freedom, or Domestic Devotion. In his Introduction, Mills describes his book as aiming to "select and present, in a body together, from the literatures of the ages, the choicest gems of thought and expression . . . scattered along the different centuries of human history."[12] He finds precedent in the ancient traditions themselves, quoting a Tibetan proverb that, "Though there be . . . an immense number of forests, few are the lands that have growth of sandal-wood; so, though there are many wise men, the golden sayings are very rare" (viii).

By far the most widely read ecumenical digest was Moncure Conway's *Sacred Anthology* (1874). Conway introduces his book as having a specific religious mission – that of illuminating "the converging testimonies of ages and races" on the faith that "the utterance . . . which many peoples utter . . . is the voice of God."[13] He figures this process through a metallurgic metaphor that recalls the "jewels" and "gems" of the Oriental miscellanies, but with stronger implications of distillation and even transformation. "The purpose of the work," he writes, is "to separate the more universal and enduring treasures contained in ancient scriptures, from the rust of superstition and the ore of ritual" (5). Like Mills, Conway groups his selections into thematic chapters with titles such as Worship, Superstition, Knowledge, Love and Friendship, Nature, Character, and Action. Each individual selection carries a thematic label ("Prohibitions," "Four Virtuous Inclinations," "The Eightfold Path") and a cultural tag ("Parsi. Mainyo-i-khan. 6th cent."). Selections from the Old and New Testaments abound, which can make the volume feel like an extended defamiliarization of the Bible. Conway removes Bible verses from their familiar contexts and recontextualizes them amid parallel texts from other traditions, the result being that the biblical passages feel nondogmatic and cosmopolitan, while the Eastern ones feel almost biblical.

A similar set of syncretic possibilities animated another emerging fin-de-siècle publishing genre: the classics series.[14] Where the adjective "classic" had long been reserved for the civilizations of ancient Greece and Rome, the Victorians would transform it into the name of a generic phase of civilization that all cultures supposedly passed through.[15] They would also make it a marketing category, a label under which publishers could gather together works old and new, foreign and domestic, at an affordable price for the nonspecialist reader. One especially influential series was the Temple Classics, inaugurated by the publisher J. M. Dent in 1896 with

Shakespearean scholar Israel Gollancz as its editor.[16] In 1906 it would be absorbed into Dent's new Everyman's Library, but continued as a separate imprint until the 1950s. Although initial volumes focused on English poets like Wordsworth and Swift, 1899 saw the series debut verse translations of the great Hindu epics *Ramayana* and *Mahabharata* by the Bengali man of letters Romesh Chunder Dutt.[17] An even more ambitious set of Asian religious classics would arrive in 1904, when Allen Upward's Orient Press and the larger house of John Murray unveiled their *Wisdom of the East* series. Printed in distinct square volumes, the series promised "by means of the best Oriental literature – its wisdom, philosophy, poetry, and ideals – to bring together West and East in a spirit of mutual sympathy, goodwill, and understanding."[18] The series would ultimately encompass several dozen volumes, including Upward's *Sayings of Confucius* (1904), Lionel Giles's *Sayings of Lao Tzu* (1904), S. A. Kapadia's *Teachings of Zoroaster* (1905), and E. J. Thomas's *Buddhist Scriptures* (1913).

Accompanying these new collections of world scriptures was a proliferation of world religions guidebooks. These books often argued explicitly what was mostly implied by the anthologies and series: that, by comparing and contrasting different world religions, one could arrive at a larger assessment of which human values were universal and which were merely local or particular. For instance, some guidebooks saw liberal clergymen use the comparison between different religions to reflect upon the relative progress that different cultures had made toward a certain notion of civilization. In *The Distinctive Messages of the Old Religions* (1892), for example, the Scottish minister George Matheson argued that the greatness of Christianity lay not in its privileged access to divine truth but rather in its "many-sided" "reconciliation" of the better aspirations of the human soul as expressed by various world religions.[19] Each chapter is named after, and unpacks, the "Message" of a certain historical faith or people. The message of both Vedic Hinduism and Buddhism is the soul's desire to unite with the divine; the message of Zoroastrianism is that the world is a battlefield between good and evil; the message of Judaism is that true power resides with the humble and the marginal (Matheson, *Distinctive Messages,* 329–39). The goal of Christianity, in turn, is not to abolish these different historic faiths but rather to serve as a "meeting place" where "Indian and Greek, Roman and Teuton, Buddhist and Parsee, Egyptian and Chinaman, can meet . . . hand in hand" (329, 341). In a similar spirit, Alan Menzies's *History of Religion* (1895) refuses to divide religions among "the true one, Christianity, and the false ones, all the rest"; instead, Menzies (a professor of Biblical Criticism at St. Andrews) shows how each religion reflects a human grasping toward the "absolute and unconditioned," a definition of religion that he derives from both Müller and from Herbert Spencer.[20] Insofar as religion reflects this kind of aspiration, it may also function as an index to a people's level of civilization. "Religion and civilization advance together" because "the religion of an age shows what at that time constituted the object of man's aspiration and endeavor" (Menzies, *History of Religion*, 14). In short, Menzies, like Matheson, has replaced a theological discourse on true versus false religion with a discourse on universal values. For instance, Menzies argues that the key distinction in religious history is not between "true and false," or "natural and revealed," but rather "between tribal and national" – between religions that codify a set of culturally or ethnically specific values and those that attempt to theorize a more universal and pluralistic set of values (78–79). Although both proclaim Christianity to be the highest religion, they do so by making religion itself a byword for a secularist ethos to which Christianity itself can seem largely marginal.

Menzies and Matheson were both ministers in the Church of Scotland, and their projection of a humanistic teleology onto world religions very much reflects an Edinburgh Enlightenment faith in the progress of civilization. Writers from quirkier corners of the dissenting world, however, could use East–West comparison to purge Christianity of both its imperialism and its "popery" and reorient itself toward the global south. For example, Joseph Edkins's *The Early Spread of Religious Ideas, Especially in the Far East* (1893), which appeared in the Religious Tract Society's "By-Paths of Bible Knowledge" series, drew upon the history of Chinese religion to mount a critique of the "medieval" priestcraft that he felt had long since corrupted Christianity in the West. Edkins was an evangelical missionary who spent most of his career in China producing Chinese-language primers in Western science and conducting philological research. The result was a profound attraction to Chinese religion that he leveraged against what he liked least about modern Christianity: its institutions, its ritualism, and its ethnocentrism. His argument in *Early Spread* was that there was a primordial revelation made to Noah, Enoch, and other "primitive patriarchs" – "the duty of prayer ... a divinely taught moral law, and ... the doctrine of a future life" – that was best outlined in the Old Testament but that also, thanks to geographical isolation, had been preserved remarkably intact in China:[21] "Though bedimmed, that light was, however, not obliterated, and it is the duty of the Christian investigator, in seeking to recover primaeval religious teaching, not only to decipher cuneiform tablets, but to study with a purpose the classical books of all Eastern countries" (Edkins, *Early Spread*, 11–12).

An even more pointed version of the same claim may be found in Robert Cust's *Essay on the Common Features Which Appear in All Forms of Religious Belief* (1895). Cust was a graduate of Fort William College, the government school in Calcutta where William Jones and the original British Orientalists had taught.[22] In his *Essay*, he argues that, although Christian missionaries have been dismissive of Asian religions, understanding them is, in fact, crucial to the evangelical project of purifying Christianity itself. Looking at Asian religions, we see all of the decadences that have corrupted Christianity since the age of Constantine: "Priestcraft, witchcraft, exorcism," and extravagant church décor; ceremonial cleanliness or uncleanliness; fasting celibacy, asceticism, eremitism.[23] Yet we also come to realize that the Bible is not alone in pronouncing divine truth – for "Búddha, Kong-Fu-Tsee, Zoroaster, the Hindu Sages, received a supernatural elevation of their moral and intellectual faculties: in fact, they were favoured through the fog around their generation to recognize the existence of Moral Truth, and to see God" (Cust, *Common Features*, 4–5). It is a measure of imperial Britain's depravity that it cannot recognize this fact. "Who are we," he asks, "the most drunken Nation in Europe, to throw dirt upon the Mahometan, and the ancient conceptions of India and China, whom the Lord of the world has permitted to exist for three thousand years?" (21). For a corrective, Cust suggests, Western Christians can look to the Buddha, who saw through the false promises of ritualism and asceticism and instead "determined to practice moderate asceticism ... [a] subduing of the Passions, Precepts of the eight-fold Noble Path leading to the supreme God" (71). But Cust's ultimate hope is that the colonial churches will eventually take Christianity out of the bloodied hands of Europe entirely:

> I doubt not, that the nascent Churches of Asia, Africa, and Oceania, will assert their right to sweep away the accretions of ignorant, arrogant, mediaeval, European Christianity, and go back to the words and examples of the Master, who lived and died amidst Asiatics in Asia. New forms of Christianity may appear from an Asiatic matrix, and free themselves from the effete ligaments of mediaeval Europe. (180)

Here, a puritanical fantasy of Christianity shedding its medieval accretions becomes a kind of postcolonial fantasy of Christianity being saved from the Europeans who have stewarded it so badly over the past 1500 years.

Perhaps no figure from the fin de siècle epitomized the cosmopolitan possibilities of popular world religions publishing like the poet and journalist Edwin Arnold. No relation to Matthew, Edwin studied at the Universities of London and Oxford before securing a teaching position at a British government college near Bombay (now Mumbai).[24] Upon returning to England in 1860, he took a post with the *Daily Telegraph*, which gave him the financial stability to publish a series of Sanskrit, Arabic, and Persian translations aimed at a mass readership. These included the first English version of the *Gita Govinda*, which Arnold titled *The Indian Song of Songs* (1875); a set of freestanding episodes from the *Mahabharata* called *Indian Idylls* (1883); *Pearls of the Faith* (1883), a collection of ninety-nine poetic excerpts based on the form of the ninety-nine-bead Muslim "rosary"; and a widely read translation of the *Bhagavad Gita, The Song Celestial* (1885) (Wright, *Interpreter*, 59, 66–67, 120). By far Arnold's most popular work, however, was a verse life of the Buddha entitled *The Light of Asia* (1879). The poem gathers material from a range of more scholarly translations into an eight-book *Bildungsroman* in sonorous blank verse (86).[25] Buddhism, in Arnold's portrayal, is a kind of Protestantism-*sans*-Christianity – a minimalist, ethical religion grounded in personal experience rather than in supernatural faith (93–94). His Buddha is (in Brooks Wright's words) a "witness for religious liberalism" who preaches that "Within yourselves deliverance must be sought; / Each man his prison makes" (71).[26]

Today Arnold is often dismissed as an appropriator of Eastern religions for Western tastes. The interesting thing, though, is that Arnold's work also played a key role in the formation of South Asian nationalisms. Most famously, the young law student Mohandas K. Gandhi first became intrigued by the political possibilities of Hinduism when two of his Theosophist friends gave him a copy of Arnold's *Song Celestial* in London in 1889. They were seeking Indian insight into the poem's terminology, and when Gandhi confessed himself quite ignorant on these matters, the three men undertook a comparative study of Arnold's *Song Celestial* alongside *The Light of Asia* and the New Testament.[27] Meanwhile Arnold himself sent a copy of *Light* to the King of Siam, the only independent Buddhist monarch in the region, who in turn thanked him for having helped the Buddha "speak beautifully in the most widespread language of the world" (Wright, *Interpreter*, 108). By the mid-1880s Arnold was regularly receiving invitations to address Buddhist audiences in India, Burma, and elsewhere (111). In 1885, Arnold visited Ceylon, where he was welcomed as a hero by Weligama Sri Sumangala, leader of the Buddhist revival movement on the island (115–16). Arnold's poem would have a special impact upon the thinking of a young Sinhalese named Don David Heravitharama, a rising star in anticolonial politics.[28] Specifically Arnold's portrayal of the Buddha as a *Bildung*-hero played a key role in helping Heravitharama reimagine the Buddhist monk as an activist figure on the evangelical model.[29] He took for himself the name Anagarika Dharmapala – "Anagarika" being a traditional Sinhalese word meaning "homeless" that he adapted as an epithet for an individual straddling the roles of religious renouncer and social reformer.[30] In his preaching, Dharmapala would portray Nirvana not as "a postmortem existence" but as "a realization in perfect consciousness in this earthly body, purified both physically and mentally," that inspired worldly activism.[31]

The transimperial resonance of Arnold's work was indicative of the growing power of ecumenical networks linking Europe, America, and Asia at the fin de siècle. As Leela Gandhi has shown, the communication networks of empire increasingly allowed Western intellectuals and Asian reformers to exchange ideas and create syncretic institutions.[32] Perhaps the most famous example was the great Parliament of Religions held at the Chicago World's Columbian Exposition in 1893. The brainchild of the lawyer Charles Carroll Bonney and the Presbyterian minister John Henry Barrows, the Parliament assembled two hundred representatives of Hinduism, Jainism, Taoism, Sikhism, Confucianism, Greek Orthodoxy, Roman Catholicism, and Shinto in Chicago's Jackson Park.[33] Edwin Arnold was invited to serve on the Advisory Council alongside Max Müller and other academic luminaries.[34] Meanwhile Anagarika Dharmapala delivered an address entitled "The World's Debt to Buddhism" that began with a quote from *The Light of Asia* and went on to promote Buddhism as a "Religion of Humanity" that recognized human evolution, rejected "distinction of caste and race" (Barrows, *World's Parliament*, 2:873), promoted "freedom of thought and opinion" (876–77), and, of course, endorsed temperance (878).

Although the Parliament was hailed as an epochal event, today it can seem like the last gasp of a naive universalism that died in the fires of World Wars I and II.[35] If we keep our attention fixed upon popular publishing however, we can see a broader continuity between the Parliament and the longer history of liberal culture in the twentieth century. For, in fact, the sorts of popular world religions texts that topped bestseller lists in the 1880s and 1890s would remain publishing staples through the 1950s and 1960s. As Matthew Hedstrom has recently shown, the first half of the twentieth century represented a period when "liberal approaches to religion" that were "intellectually engaged, psychologically oriented, and focused on personal experience" became central to main-stream culture in the Anglo-American world.[36] The driving factor, he argues, were the religious imprints of major publishing houses like Macmillan's and Harper's, events like Religious Book Week in the 1920s, as well as institutions like the American Library Association's Religious Books Roundtable. All of these things "popularized and democratized a cosmopolitan spiritual outlook that had previously been the privileged domain of a cultural elite" (Hedstrom, *Rise,* 10).

One reason we seldom remember this high tide of twentieth-century religious liberalism is that it would be eclipsed by fundamentalist revivals in America and the postcolonial world starting in the 1980s. But another reason, David Hollinger argues, is that it planted the seeds of its own demise. "What has come to be called liberalism in politics and in the debates over social and cultural issues," Hollinger writes, in many ways owes its purchase "to the success of the Protestant liberalizers in pushing their constituents in those directions."[37] The culture of religious ecumenicalism fostered in the mainline Protestant churches – and increasingly within liberal Catholic and Jewish circles too – created a climate of mainstream opinion friendly to the liberal reforms of the 1940s–1960s. At the same time, the crises and divisions within the white middle class during the 1960s pushed many young Boomers out of the mainline churches and into some kind of secularist or post-Christian orientation. These children, Hollinger and Hedstrom show, were at once heirs to the old mainline Protestant ecumenicalism, but also those who forgot that this attitude had anything to do with religion (Hollinger, *Cloven Tongues,* xii). From the Victorianist point of view, it is also worth noting that they were very much the heirs of the popular world religions publishing of the 1890s. Just as reprints of Victorian translations can be found in used bookstores and on the web, so does the kind of secular ecumenicalism epitomized by *The Light of Asia* still live on in a culture that has forgotten that poem. This is what the 1890s have left us too: not just antibourgeois subversion, but a transformed bourgeois culture itself.

Notes

1 F. Max Müller, "Preface to the Sacred Books of the East," in *The Upanishads*; *SBOTE*, vol. 1 (Oxford: Clarendon Press, 1879), ix–lv (ix–x).
2 Arie L. Molendijk, *Friedrich Max Müller and the Sacred Books of the East* (New York: Oxford University Press, 2016), 14–20. For a survey of the field as it looked right around the turn of the century, see Louis Henry Jordan, *Comparative Religion: Its Genesis and Growth* (Edinburgh: T & T Clarke, 1905).

3 F. Max Müller, *Introduction to the Science of Religion* (1870; New York: Scribners, 1872), 41.

4 F. Max Müller, "Address [to the Aryan Section] by Professor Max Müller, President," in *Transactions of the Second Session of the International Congress of Orientalists. Held in London in September, 1874*, ed. Robert K. Douglas (London: Trübner, 1876), 177–204 (183).

5 Tomoko Masuzawa, *The Invention of World Religions* (Chicago, IL: University of Chicago Press, 2005); David Chidester, *Empire of Religion: Imperialism and Comparative Religion* (Chicago, IL: University of Chicago Press, 2014); Peter Van der Veer, *Imperial* Encounters*: Religion and Modernity in India and Britain* (Princeton, NJ: Princeton University Press, 2001).

6 Here I'm taking my cue from recent work by Alexander Bubb and other book historians, who have recentered the topic of Orientalism around publishing rather than ideology. See "Asian Classic Literature and the English General Reader, 1845–1916," in *The Edinburgh History of Reading*, eds. J. Rose and M. Hammond (Edinburgh: Edinburgh University Press, 2020), 116–36; "The Race for Hafiz: Scholarly and Popular Translations at the Fin de Siècle," *Comparative Critical Studies* 17, no. 2 (June 2020): 225–44.

7 See "Syncretism: From East and West to the Darker Nations," the fourth chapter in Agathocleous's *Disaffected: Emotion, Sedition, and Colonial Law in the Anglosphere* (Ithaca, NY: Cornell University Press, 2021); as well as Winter Jade Werner and Mimi Winnick, "How to See Global Religion: Comparativism, Connectivity, and 'Undisciplining' Victorian Literary Studies," *MLQ* 83, no. 4 (December 2022): 499–520.

8. See Alex Owen, *The Place of Enchantment: British Occultism and the Culture of the Modern* (Chicago, IL: University of Chicago Press, 2007); as well as the essays collected by Nicola Bowen, Carolyn Burdett, and Pamela Thurschwell in *The Victorian Supernatural* (Cambridge: Cambridge University Press, 2004). For the fascist affinities of modernism, see Vincent Pecora, *Secularization and Cultural Criticism* (Chicago, IL: University of Chicago Press, 2006), 101–30.

9 N. J. Girardot, "Max Müller's *Sacred Books* and the Nineteenth-Century Production of the Comparative Science of Religion," *History of Religions* 41, no. 3 (Nov. 2002): 213–50 (226).

10 For my own account of Müller's intellectual project, see *Cultivating Belief: Victorian Anthropology, Secular Aesthetics, and the Liberal Imagination* (New York: Oxford University Press, 2018), 33–67.

11 William Rounseville Alger, *Poetry of the East* (Boston, MA: Whittemore, Niles, and Hall, 1856).

12 Charles D. B. Mills, *Pebbles, Pearls, and Gems of the Orient* (Boston, MA: George H. Ellis, 1882), vi.

13 Moncure Conway, *The Sacred Anthology: A Book of Ethnical Scriptures*, (3rd ed. London: Trübner, 1874), v.

14 For approaches to the series as a publishing format, see the essays collected in John Spiers, ed., *The Culture of the Publisher's Series; Authors, Publishers, and the Shaping of Taste,* vol. 1 (New York: Palgrave, 2011); and John Spiers, ed., *Nationalisms and the National Canon,* vol. 2 (New York: Palgrave, 2011); Lise Jaillant, *Cheap Modernism: Expanding Markets, Publishers' Series, and the Avant-Garde* (Edinburgh: Edinburgh University Press, 2017); and the encyclopedic website, "A Series of Series" (https://sites.owu.edu/seriesofseries).

15 See Phiroze Vasunia, *The Classics and Colonial India* (New York: Oxford University Press, 2013), 12–16.

16 On the Temple Classics and subsequent Everyman's Library, see Terry I. Seymour, "Great Books for the Millions: J. M. Dent's Everyman's Library," in *Nationalisms and the National Canon,* vol. 2, ed. John Spiers (New York: Palgrave, 2011), 166–72.

17 See Sebastian Lecourt, "'Greek to Me': Two Versions of Modern Epic in Victorian Bengal," *ELH* 88, no. 4 (Winter 2021): 935–67.

18 See https://seriesofseries.owu.edu/wisdom-of-the-east-series.

19 George Matheson, *The Distinctive Messages of the Old Religions* (Edinburgh and London: Blackwood, 1892), 341, 328.

20 Alan Menzies, *History of Religion: A Sketch of Primitive Religious Beliefs and Practices, and of the Origin and Character of the Great Systems* (New York: Scribner, 1895), 9.

21 Joseph Edkins, *The Early Spread of Religious Ideas, Especially in the Far East* (New York: Fleming H. Revell, 1893), 11.

22 See Gerald H. Anderson, ed., *A Biographical Dictionary of Christian Missions* (Grand Rapids, MI: Eerdmans, 1999), 162–63.

23 Robert Needham Cust, *Essay on the Common Features Which Appear in All Forms of Religious Belief* (London: Luzac and Co., 1895), 63, 68, 69.

24 Brooks Wright, *Interpreter of Buddhism to the West: Sir Edwin Arnold* (New York: Bookman, 1957), 15, 27.

25 For my own extended take on the poem and its global reception, see "'Idylls of the Buddh': Buddhist Modernism and Victorian Poetics in Colonial Ceylon," *PMLA* 131, no. 3 (May 2016): 668–85.

26 Edwin Arnold, *The Light of Asia; or, the Great Renunciation* (1879; Boston: Roberts, 1889), 213.

27 Eric J. Sharpe, *The Universal Gita: Western Images of the* Bhagavad Gītā (La Salle: Open Court, 1985), 115–16; Richard H. Davis, *The Bhagavad Gita: A Biography* (Princeton, NJ: Princeton University Press, 2015), 137.

28 Heravitharama is the subject of two recent biographies: Steven Kemper's *Rescued from the Nation: Anagarika Dharmapala and the Buddhist World* (Chicago, IL: University of Chicago Press, 2015); and Sarath Amunugama's *The Lion's Roar: Anagarika Dharmapala and the Making of Modern Buddhism* (Oxford: Oxford University Press, 2019).

29 H. L. Seneviratne, *The Work of Kings: The New Buddhism in Sri Lanka* (Chicago, IL: University of Chicago Press, 1999), 25–27.

30 Richard Gombrich and Gananath Obeyesekere, *Buddhism Transformed: Religious Change in Sri Lanka* (Princeton, NJ: Princeton University Press, 1988), 205.

31 George Bond, *The Buddhist Revival in Sri Lanka: Religious Tradition, Reinterpretation, and Response* (Columbia, SC: University of South Carolina Press, 1988), 57–58.

32 Leela Gandhi, *Affective Communities: Anticolonial Thought, Fin-de-Siècle Radicalism, and the Politics of Friendship* (Durham, NC: Duke University Press, 2006).

33 Eric J. Ziolkowski, "Waking Up from Akbar's Dream: The Literary Prefiguration of Chicago's 1893 World's Parliament of Religions," *Journal of Religion* 73, no. 1 (1993): 42–60 (43–44).

34 See John Henry Barrows, *The World's Parliament of Religions*, 2 vols. (Chicago, IL: The Parliament Publishing Company, 1893), 1:40, 45.

35 For assessments of this kind, see Richard Hughes Seager, "Pluralism and the American Mainstream: The View from the World's Parliament of Religions," *Harvard Theological Review* 82 (1989): 301–24 (311); see also, Martin E. Marty, *Modern American Religion*, vol. 1 of (Chicago, IL: University of Chicago Press, 1986), 17–31.

36 Matthew S. Hedstrom, *The Rise of Liberal Religion: Book Culture and American Spirituality in the Twentieth Century* (New York: Oxford University Press, 2013), 4.

37 David A. Hollinger, *After Cloven Tongues of Fire: Protestant Liberalism in Modern American History* (Princeton, NJ: Princeton University Press, 2013), xii.

CHAPTER 6

Night Lights: The 1890s Nocturne

Emily Harrington

The fin-de-siècle nocturne was from the start a transnational, transmedia genre. In a series of paintings entitled "Nocturne" in the 1870s, John McNeil Whistler, an American artist working in London, took his inspiration from Japanese art and his title from the music of Frédéric Chopin. Whistler aimed to focus his art on form over content, drawing attention to color, shape, and line. By 1890, the trend he had started in the 1870s was widely emulated and his libel suit against John Ruskin for accusing him of "flinging a pot of paint in the public's face" in his *Nocturne in Black and Gold: The Falling Rocket* had made him into a celebrity.[1] Hélène Valance asserts that the heyday of the nocturne in American art was 1890–1910, but the genre also became important and popular among poets writing in English in the 1880s and 1890s. A longstanding view of the aestheticism of the 1890s sees Whistler's influence among the poets. In 1957, Robert Peters identified how Oscar Wilde, Arthur Symons, and W. E. Henley took industrialized urban scenes, often by the Thames, and transformed them into "silhouettes of magical beauty."[2] Poets were inspired by Whistler, who was inspired by Japan; the poets, like Whistler were inspired by French poetry and music. Though their nocturnes were often set in London, Symons and A. Mary F. Robinson also set their nocturnes in Venice. The genre proclaimed its cosmopolitanism.

One does not need to be a 1950s-era critic to see the resemblance between Oscar Wilde's 1881 "Impression du Matin" and Whistler's *Nocturne in Black and Gold*, in which spots of yellow paint speckle a black, blue, and gray background. A standard reading of Wilde's poem notices how it articulates the same kind of formal primacy and moral neutrality that Whistler championed. However, reading the poem in light of recent work in ecocriticism, it is impossible to ignore that those aesthetic effects are a product of burning fossil fuels. The poem points to the similarities between the exploitation of the earth and of its people:

> The Thames nocturne of blue and gold
>   Changed to a Harmony in gray:
>   A barge with ocher-colored hay
> Dropt from the wharf: and chill and cold
>
> The yellow fog came creeping down
>   The bridges, till the houses' walls
>   Seemed changed to shadows, and S. Paul's
> Loomed like a bubble o'er the town.
>   . . .
> But one pale woman all alone,
>   The daylight kissing her wan hair,
>   Loitered beneath the gas lamps' flare,
> With lips of flame and heart of stone.[3]

The woman at the end of the poem, presumably a sex worker, is likened to a piece of coal; her heart, like a lump of coal, is a stone, with a flame on her lips akin to the "gas lamps' flare" beneath which she stands. In this volume, Elizabeth Miller describes the yellow fogs as aestheticizing "the climate of industrial pollution," yet Wilde recognizes in the sex worker and the gas lamp, both made of stone and flaming, the source of his aesthetics. The fog, the blurring, the muted colors, the noise, the altered vision, and particularly in British nocturnes, the possibility for sexual exploitation, are the familiar tropes of this genre.

In the 1890s, across the globe, the nocturne poem epitomizes the aestheticism of the era, in its synesthesia and its privileging of artistic form. These short, nonnarrative poems about the night take a variety of forms, from predictable stanzas to stanzas with shifting line lengths and feet to prose poems. Though poets of the 1890s used poetic form in a variety of ingenious ways, it was not overall a particularly formally innovative era. In their introduction to their volume entitled *Decadent Poetics*, Jason David Hall and Alex Murray "successfully fail" to find a "unified, stable definition of decadent poetics."[4] In her chapter of that volume, Meredith Martin concludes that there is not necessarily a "decadent meter," and that any critical wish to associate decadent poems' prosody with rebelliousness obscures the "transnational circulation of poetic forms," which is not "inherently transgressive" but which does define the fin de siècle.[5] Here, I find a widespread transnational circulation not of a form, but of a genre: the nocturne. Rachael Scarborough King defines genre as "a cluster of textual characteristics and conventions, which could include form but also cover a range of features such as topic, theme, medium, historical context, authorship, and intended or actual audience."[6] She also argues that genre, more so than form, helps us understand the breadth of literary history and change between periods, because it indicates correspondences between texts rather than patterns within a text. However, I turn to the genre of the nocturne in order to understand literary history in depth, in the focus of a decade, across a wide geographical stretch of the English-speaking world. Meredith Martin and Catherine Maxwell have both asserted that decadent and aestheticist poetics are more recognizable by their themes and topics, than by formal characteristics. I take them seriously as a feature of genre, if not of a form, arguing that late nineteenth-century nocturnes are distinct because their poets write in an environment where coal gas lamps light up the nights in cities more brightly than had ever been possible. I argue that approaching the nocturne as a genre illuminates how the transnational and ecocritical approaches that are new to scholars now were already embedded in the nocturne genre of the 1890s, which was highly conscious, even anxious, about the relationships between the human and the natural, the aesthetic and the artificial.

A history of the genre shows how unique it was in the 1890s. Erik Martiny traces a history of the nocturne's evolution from poems that feared evil in the medieval period, to the "exquisite numinous experiences," "solitary melancholics," and "amorous playgrounds" of the Renaissance, to the graveyard poems of the eighteenth century, to the way that Romantic era poetry plays with all of these modes, adding Keats's privileging of hearing over sight in "Ode to a Nightingale," and Whitman's identification of night as offering new insights with altered vision.[7] Martiny, characterizing a genre even in 2012 with reference to nary a woman poet, looks to James Thomson, Matthew Arnold, and Gerard Manley Hopkins to describe the late-Victorian nocturne as full of "soul-destroying negativity" (Martiny, "Nox Consilium," 392). The progression Martiny identifies certainly fits with King's argument that attention to genre "can reveal the shifting dynamics of literary history" (King, "The Scale of Genre," 267). But by leaving out the 1890s, Martiny's approach misses the fundamental global and environmental concerns at the heart of that decade, the very reasons that the nocturne was an exemplary genre of the time. A focus on the nocturnes of the 1890s reveals a genre at the convergence of aesthetic and technological development. The 1890s nocturne centralizes the new relationship between the artificial and the natural, between art, nature, aesthetics, and illumination both literal and figurative.

Though poets have always written poems about the night, the 1890s nocturne both embodied the aestheticist spirit often associated with the era and represented a nighttime that was radically transformed in cities, from the mid-nineteenth century on, by lamps fueled with gas made from coal. The genre embodies how poets across the English-speaking world conveyed wishes and anxieties about their increasingly industrialized, urbanized, and globalized environments. The vogue for nocturnes in music, art, and poetry happened at the same time that fossil fuels came to be in widespread use in cities for lighting. Whereas prior to the nineteenth century, animal oil and wood were the primary substances combusted for nighttime lighting, by 1860, coal gas – available only in cities because it needed to be piped from the power plant that produced it – was used throughout cities to illuminate both public and private spaces. In the 1890s, mantles using rare earth minerals became available so that lamps were able to burn much more brightly. The 1890s also saw the increasing use of electric lights, especially in large public places such as factories and department stores.[8] By the 1890s, coal gas had fundamentally changed the look and experience of night in the city, which may account for the predominance of so many nighttime poems. This transformation of night might explain the temporal confusion in John Davidson's "Nocturne," in which "Broad lightnings stream silently down / On the silent city beneath... / And I have a vision of noon,"[9] or in Laurence Binyon's second section of *London Visions*, "Summer Night," in which "With pendent dazzling moons, that cast a noon-day white, / The full streets beckon."[10] It is no accident that the title for Jesse Oak Taylor's book *The Sky of Our Manufacture*, about the literal air of the nineteenth century, came from 1890s poet Alice Meynell.

I focus not only on how British poets saw night skies that were both smoky and bright as simultaneously menacing and beautiful, but also on how Canadian poets adopted the nocturne fashion, and how E. Pauline Johnson (Tekahionwake), an Indigenous Canadian poet, used the genre to imagine a more harmonious ideal connection between the human, the natural, and the divine; I also discuss how Yone Noguchi, a Japanese poet who launched his career writing poetry in English in San Francisco in the 1890s, capitalized on an American naturalist tradition and the inherent, implicit Japonisme of the nocturne genre. Noguchi and Johnson both play into European stereotypes that people and writers of color offer a premodern mystique; yet both also resist that stereotype by fully engaging with the artistic and poetic trends of the 1890s in their nocturnes and offering alternative visions of modernity. Concentrating on genre allows a study of literature that is not circumscribed by national boundaries and that brings topical, as opposed to geographical, coherence into greater focus. The nocturne has long been a staple of 1890s art and poetry, but this genre is exemplary not just for its foggy aesthetic but because it is transnational and centrally concerned with the interface of the human-made and the natural.

Symons, *London Nights*

Nowhere in *London Nights* does Arthur Symons, long one of the most visible poets of the 1890s, use the term "nocturne," but this collection evinces elements of the genre already present in Whistler's and Wilde's nocturnes. Joseph Bristow asserts that Symons's attempts to "redefine the locations, the forms, and the language in which his art might make sense of modern culture at the century's end" have often been dismissed as designed merely to "titillate his audience."[11] As Bristow notes, John Lane, who along with his ex-partner, Elkin Mathews, published most of the poets I refer to in this chapter, found *London Nights* too outré for his own shop, and so Symons brought it out with the more adventurous Leonard Smithers (Bristow, "Introduction," 2). It is the sexual exploitation in the foreground of the work that incited both outrage and dismissal, but it is its link with the environmental exploitation in the background that interests me here. Against the backdrop of shadows and light of gas lamps, with muted cloudy colors reminiscent of Whistler, Symons's volume takes the wan-faced, flame-lipped woman with the heart of stone in Wilde's "Impression du Matin" and animates her in numerous variations, project-ing the male speakers' desire to be desired onto music hall dancers. Symons brings out nighttime's potential for sex, implying that the urban setting presents a rotating cast of women, who both embody and are embodied by the other features of the night: in the gas lamps, fog, darkness, and shadows, the play of color and light become a kind of erotic tease. Most of the poems are permeated by artificial light, coming from gas lamps outdoors, in theaters, and in gloomy bedrooms. In these scenes, the light merges with rain, with bodies, with walls, with air, so that all elements are clearly part of a human-made vision of a human-made world. In this way, Symons's nocturnes are what Jesse Oak Taylor would call "abnatural," the prefix signaling a withdrawal from nature, both in taking from it and moving away from it. Gas lamps draw from nature and also change the very nature of the night and its inhabitants.[12] The women in Symons's poems are as abnatural as the gas lamps, presented as objects, as resources to be exploited.

Fragmentary body parts – faces, lips, hair – in "On the Stage" become more explicitly fake in the indoor nocturne of the theater:

> Lights, in a multi-coloured mist,
> From indigo to amethyst,
> A whirling mist of multi-coloured light;
> And after, wigs and tights,
> Then faces, then a glimpse of profiles, then
> Eyes, and a mist again;
> And rouge, and always tights, and wigs, and tights.[13]

The artificial lights swirl into the coverings of bodies, artificial hair, faces separated from bodies, makeup separated from faces. Symons breaks the theatrical illusion by drawing attention to all the methods of creating the spectacle, rhyming tights with lights. This representation would seem like the standard decadent separation of part from whole (Murray and Hall, "Introduction," 3), but the speaker tells us, "You see a dance of phantoms" while he sees "A girl, who smiles at me." He would seem to perceive a whole person, but the girl he sees is clearly only a projection of his own desires; all her expressions, her "memories and messages," are "for me," he tells us. The artificial, the poem suggests, is all of human (and perhaps especially male) perception and desire, not just the hair that makes the wig or the pigments of the rouge meant as an imitation and amplification of the natural, but even other people's interior states are manufactured by us, in our own minds and in our poems. Likewise, he shows poetic meter to be as manufactured as the light from gas lamps. Although iambs were considered to be "natural" to the English language and exemplary of the nation, they are as amenable to "and wigs, and tights" as to any lofty expressions of Shakespeare or Milton. Poetic technology for Symons is as artificial as wigs or gas lamps.

Among the scandalous representations that must have prompted John Lane to refuse to publish the book was this dingy postcoital bedroom scene, in which mutual understanding is as distant as physical intimacy is present. More explicitly here, he links the fuel for the light with the stink of disconnection:

> The little bedroom papered red,
>   The gas's faint malodorous light,
> And one beside me in the bed,
>   Who chatters, chatters, half the night.
> (Symons, *London Nights,* 45)

This scene is described in an incomplete sentence, the only action the bedmate's chattering in a relative clause, suggesting stasis. The poetry here is even more like the technology of modern life, the sibilant, unstressed, possessive syllable of "gas's" mimicking the flow of the noxious fuel, both dim and smelly. Its sibilant flow creates a dim syllable as well as a faint light. The gas lamp becomes a marker of the dissipation of urban life. The lack of prosodic innovation of the 1890s that critics like Martin point to, noting that the newness of the decade was in poets' willingness to take on taboo subjects, as Symons does here, emerges as Symons's own complaint, the regular tetrameters in this poem even more restricted than other stanzaic forms in the collection. That other signifier of modern life, the clock, has a "tick" as "tyrannic" as the tetrameters. Both are inescapable; the tetrameters tick on like the clock, though they seem as exhausted as the man and as the light produced by the gas. Like Wilde's "Impression du Matin," Symons's *London Nights* associates the coal gas not just with the night but with women, with sex, and even with poetic language: objects for exploitation, taken from nature and transformed into something human-made for human use. Symons notes, as Elizabeth Miller shows extensively in *Ecologies of Extraction: The Literature of the Long Exhaustion*, that there is something utterly exhausting about that process of transformation and use, both of the earth and of women's bodies. The ecocritical focus of Miller and Taylor call attention to the central role of the gas lamps that illuminated the seamy nights of decadent poetry. Symons's poems suggest that he owes his avant-garde aesthetic to fossil fuels, to the strange light they created and to the way they illuminated both figuratively and literally the nighttime sexual practices on the urban and poetic fringe.

Mathilde Blind, "Manchester by Night," and the Exploitation of the Working Class

Mathilde Blind's "Manchester by Night" starts with some standard nocturne conventions, romanticizing a polluted sky, suggesting that night turns what is ugly into something mysterious and beautiful. In using the sonnet form for this instance of the nocturne genre, Blind calls attention to the duality of the beautiful and the ugly that nocturnes tend to obscure in urban settings in particular, where clouds and smoke become indistinguishable. Blind also reverses the sonnet's tendency to describe a problem in the octave and to offer a solution, or at least a resolution, in the sestet. By describing a gauzy, maternal Night in the octet and the crushed, hungry labor force of the factories in the sestet, Blind suggests that the aestheticization of industrialization and urbanization is no resolution at all:

O'er this huge town, rife with intestine wars,
Whence as from monstrous sacrificial shrines
Pillars of smoke climb heavenward, Night inclines
Black brows majestical with glimmering stars.
Her dewy silence soothes life's angry jars:
And like a mother's wan white face, who pines
Above her children's turbulent ways, so shines
The moon athwart the narrow cloudy bars.

Now toiling multitudes that hustling crush
Each other in the fateful strife for breath,
And, hounded on by diverse hungers, rush
Across the prostrate ones that groan beneath,
Are swathed within the universal hush,
As life exchanges semblances with death.[14]

The poem begins with conflict, presumably between labor and management. Taylor reminds us that whereas the smoke over London came from homes and was largely a result of a rapidly increasing population, the smoke in industrial cities like Manchester came from industry (Taylor, *The Sky of Our Manufacture*, 2). In calling the smokestacks of factories "monstrous sacrificial shrines," Blind recognizes both the devotion to capitalist greed they signify and the human toll of the labor that makes them function, but in comes Night, nocturne-style, to obscure all that. Blind plays with scale, the conflict at the heart of the city starting out as a war, ending as a children's squabble. That stalwart of the nocturne, the aestheticist darling, the moon, is here a maternal figure, whose wan white face is both placid and disturbed, "pining" but not really interfering. Just as the metaphors for urban conflict wind down to the familiar, the domestic, and the comfortable, the irregular pentameter lines of this sonnet move from the barely scannable in the first line, with an unusual pyrrhic, followed by spondee and a trochee, to only a few spondaic substitutions, to a fully regular line of five iambs by the end of the octet. The night sky has subdued the production of industrial smoke prosodically and figuratively.

The "Now" that begins the sestet signals a new moment, when the factory workers are released from a long day, so long that they finish after nightfall. While the octet follows nocturne conventions in its focus on what the air *looks* like, the sestet emphasizes what it is like to *breathe* it, as the workers struggle against the crowd just to take in the smoke-filled air. The "intestine wars" of the first line now appear as a rapacious competition over scarce resources among the working class. The quiet of night, Blind clarifies, is not the quiet of sleep, rest, dreams, and blurred outlines in the sky, but the hush of death. Blind's nocturne of Manchester critiques the genre by showing how it shields the monstrosity of industry that deprives people of their lives, both by working them to death and polluting their air. In her 1893 collection, Blind follows this poem with two poems entitled "The Red Sunsets, 1883," in which soot "begrimed" workers emerge from the factories to a brief aesthetic experience of an "Apocalyptic glow" in a life that is otherwise "starved of nature's beauty by Man's grudging hand" (Mathilde Blind, *Songs and Sonnets*, 104). It's not clear that Blind understood that red glow to be a direct product of the pollution produced by the factories, but she did understand the role that industrialization played in reserving aesthetic experience for the privileged few; she understood aesthetics to be denied to and dependent on, in myriad ways, the working class. Patricia Murphy reads this poem as bemoaning a human failure to connect with nature, while James Diedrick points out that it was likely not selected for an anthology of sonnets because it was too radical.[15] But by situating this poem as an example of the genre of the nocturne, rather than simply of Blind's politics, I read this poem as making explicit what was unavoidable in the genre in the era after gas lamps: the aesthetic effects of those remarkably lit nights came at the expense of tremendous human suffering.

Canadian Nocturnes: E. Pauline Johnson's Divine Night Vision

Canadian poets, too, took up the 1890s nocturne trend. Here I mention briefly two 1890s Canadian poets – S. Frances Harrison and Charles G. D. Roberts – to demonstrate how widespread the conventions of the nocturne were, but I will focus largely on E. Pauline Johnson, the daughter of a Mohawk Indian father and a white mother, who both deploys and departs from those conventions, and writes from an Indigenous cosmopolitan perspective. Her work should be understood as part of a broader turn to the nocturne by Canadian poets, which includes the work of poet and composer S. Frances Harrison (Seranus) who was already satirizing the French aestheticist life 1891 in "Vie de Boheme! Or The Nocturne in G." In comic tetrameters, Harrison represents an artist's urban flat with a broken chandelier, a dead mouse, and a sleeping-in model, and then exhorts the artist to paint the tragic subject of his own heart:

> If you want to and can with this in your ears,
>   The sad soul of Chopin on violin strings!
> Ah! Paint me the picture the most full of tears,
>   Tear your own heart out and pluck off your wings.[16]

Harrison seems to want to take down the association of France, Chopin, music and art, and all the sometimes-ridiculous earnestness of aesthetes. That she could poke fun in this way suggests how well-known and understood the association of nocturnes with aestheticism was from Paris to London to Toronto. It is as though she cleanses the scene from Symons's poems with parody. A leading and prolific Canadian poet of the turn of the century, Charles G. D. Roberts also took up the nocturne in his 1898 collection *New York Nocturnes*, one year after he moved to that city. Though D. M. R. Bentley asserts that he "drank deep of the *symboliste* spring,"[17] Roberts's nocturnes would not fall into the decadent category the way that Symons's urban nocturnes so clearly do. For Roberts, women are not an embodiment of the degraded urban night, but a relief from it: "Faint with the city's fume and stress / I came at night to Her."[18] When the speaker of these poems is not waiting for his beloved at a railway station, he is seeking respite with her:

> O city night of noises and alarms,
>   Your lights may flare, your cables clang and rush,
> But in the sanctuary of my love's arms
>   Your blinding tumult dies into a hush.
>   (Roberts, *New York Nocturnes*, 34)

The city remains threatening here, especially at night. Roberts compares street lamps to spies that reveal "the folly day would fain forget." Some things, he suggests, are better left unrevealed, unilluminated. Such lamps, altering "natural" temporality, coexist uneasily with the honeysuckle in the small urban garden that offers a natural respite. Roberts's apostrophe to the city suggests his engagement with the noise and potential sin of the city night, even as he insists on the comfort of his love. Roberts's and Harrison's nocturnes deploy some standard nocturne tropes of the urban night – the unpleasant smell of coal gas, the noise and light, the pushing of sexual boundaries – they are similar to British nocturnes. The need for respite that Roberts identifies creates an opening for the startlingly original poems of E. Pauline Johnson (Tekahionwake), who provides a vision of night in which one can enjoy but not exhaust the landscape.

Johnson was a sometime part of the "Confederation" of Canadian poets born in the 1860s, of which Roberts was a leading figure. Much more widely known now among scholars of Victorian poetry than Roberts, Johnson visited London in 1894, where she gained publication for *The White Wampum* with John Lane, publisher to the aestheticist elite of London (the same publisher who rejected Symons's *London Nights*). While there, she also performed privately, reciting her poetry. During these performances, she would wear Indigenous clothes, a composite from multiple traditions, and then change into a European evening gown.[19] For Kate Flint, these dual costumes signified an unstable identity, while also pointing to her mixed parentage. Flint suggests that British audiences expected from Native American visitors "an atavistic reminder of a premodern phase in human development ... a foil to modernity ... [not] participants in modernity's developing forms" (Flint, "Transatlantic Modernity," 183). I want to suggest, along with Carole Gerson, that Johnson originated a poetry that was at once Indigenous, aestheticist, and feminist. Noting Johnson's "prowess" as a canoeist alongside her descriptions of a man's clothes draping open over his musculature while in a canoe, Gerson finds an eroticism in Johnson's wilderness poetry that aligns her with the figures in Elaine Showalter's *Daughters of Decadence* (Gerson, "Rereading Pauline Johnson," 55).

Calling for more attention to the aesthetic quality, and indeed modernism of Johnson's poetry, Glenn Willmott insists on the aestheticism of Johnson's work in his close reading of "Shadow River: Muskoka," which is a nocturne poem describing rowing a canoe at night.[20] This poem draws on the familiar visual tropes of "undertone," shadows, and shading, linking this aesthetic to the act of canoeing: "But all the shade / Is marred or made, / If I but dip my paddle blade." The manipulation of light comes not from a paintbrush nor from burning coal gas in a lamp, but, strikingly, from a canoe paddle. Johnson's misty, dreamy aesthetic, so familiar in British poets, exults in without exploiting the environment or the people in it. In writing aestheticist poems, she was not simply putting on a poetic evening gown, instead of the Indigenous garb of a poem like "The Cry of the Indian Wife." A "wampum," a string of beads, is a perfect description for a collection of poems; this title suggests that in poems such as "Shadow River: Muskoka" as well as "Nocturne," she adapts aestheticist tropes to an Indigenous context, showing how her indigeneity participates in developing modern forms.

Johnson's fantastically original "Nocturne" brings together the urban and the divine, while also suggesting that the solipsism that is often associated with fin-de-siècle aestheticism – apparent in the way that Symons's speakers seem to think that women think, and feel, and act for him primarily – need not define visions of nocturnal beauty and light, of "A sky of grey and gold." Her first stanza calls upon a standard nocturne vision, and then offers another that is powerfully different:

> Night of Mid-June, in heavy vapours dying,
> Like priestly hands thy holy touch is lying
> Upon the world's wide brow;
> God-like and grand all nature is commanding

> The "peace that passes human understanding;"
> I, also feel it now.[21]

The first line echoes two staples of nocturnes, the fog of course, and the month of June when sunsets are late and nights are short. Yet the second line introduces the divine, a topic rare among 1890s poems about night, the simile of "priestly hands" echoing and elevating the erotic content common to nocturnes. Whereas British nocturnes, as I have shown, are a genre of the Anthropocene, linking the exploitation of people with the use of nature's resources to make an unnatural night, this nocturne makes the human, the poetic "I," incidental. The human here is not creating, and not imagining, and not establishing its perceptions as the only knowable truth – on the contrary, Johnson's allusion to Philippians 4:7 reminds us that humans are incapable of understanding some things. A conventional reading would presume the "I" to be apostrophizing the Night all along, but the last line of this stanza reveals the "I" to be only "also," peripheral rather than central. The next stanza goes on to say more explicitly that a single person's desires simply do not matter so much: "What matters it tonight, if one life treasure/ I covet, is not mine!" Though "Nocturne" seems to deploy the gauzy European aesthetic, its emphasis on broadening beyond the self, and on the aesthetic as existing beyond human perception, fits with the broad-minded empathy of "A Cry from an Indian Wife" in which the Indigenous speaker imagines what European wives and mothers must feel, even as she acknowledges they do not do the same for her. Johnson's "Nocturne" opens and closes by explicitly downplaying the importance of the desires of an individual self. The ideal of possession – of "my desire" and coveted treasure – cannot "measure / The gifts of Heaven's decree." The end of the poem reiterates that the night can "hush my longing" (Johnson, *White Wampum*, 86).

In the middle of the poem, the city Johnson envisions offers not an opportunity for nocturnal pursuits of individual desires, but divine visions. Accordingly, the light of her city comes not from gas lamps, but from the setting sun, in an image that could be either a real skyline reflecting the sun's glare as it sets, or some kind of heavenly vision:

> Like to a scene I watched one day in wonder:–
> A city, great and powerful, lay under
> A sky of grey and gold;
> The sun outbreaking in his farewell hour,
> Was scattering afar a yellow shower
> Of light, that aureoled

> With brief hot touch so marvellous and shining,
> A hundred steeples on the sky out-lining,
> Like network threads of fire;
> Above them all, with halo far outspreading,
> I saw a golden cross in glory heading
> A consecrated spire.
>
> I only saw its gleaming form uplifting,
> Against the clouds of grey to seaward drifting,
> And yet I surely know beneath the seen, a great unseen is resting,
> For while the cross that pinnacle is cresting,
> An Altar lies below.
>
> (Johnson, *White Wampun*, 85–86)

"Network threads of fire" is perhaps a prescient phrase to describe an electrical grid that was not yet widespread in 1895, but here Johnson describes a city skyline that seems entirely made of churches – the steeples being the key features. The tropes of the poem echo previous nocturne poems, and Johnson's prosody brilliantly creates a poetic analog to visual blurriness. The poem's longer, pentameter lines all conclude with feminine endings, catalectic rather than trochaic ones, most with present participle or present continuous "-ing" ending. These falling syllables create a prosodic blurring akin to the misty, cloudy skies seen so often in 1890s nocturne poetry, and familiar from Whistler's paintings. Yet the divine brightness, the transformation of the city sky to the heavenly sky, the insistence on subsuming individual desire to something larger all transform the British 1890s nocturne into a spiritual aesthetic experience. In adopting the tropes of poets such as Wilde, Symons, Davidson, and Blind, Johnson writes into the aestheticist arena to modify it. Her alternate vision of aestheticist tropes marvels at an intense point of contact between the natural, the human, and the divine. Johnson's performances in which she dressed in an Indigenous costume, a composite gleaned from various tribes, or in a European evening gown seem to suggest that she could occupy both Indigenous and European or settler-Canadian cultural identities and spaces. However, in *The White Wampum*, poems such as "Nocturne" sit alongside poems with explicitly Indigenous themes and stories, such as "The Cry of the Indian Wife." To say that "Nocturne" is not Indigenous is to deny the possibility of a cosmopolitan, modern Indigenous poetry, one inevitably transformed by settler colonialism, but fully in the present, engaging with European culture from a vantage point that is not assimilated either. Non-European nocturne poets could echo some part of the misty nighttime aesthetic that British poets were known for, but cleansed of gas lamps and pollution, an aesthetic vision renaturalized and deindustrialized. Johnson offers an alternative nocturne that both revels in beauty and takes exploitation out of the equation.

Yone Noguchi: Modern Poetics, Ancient Nature

The work of Yone Noguchi, a Japanese poet who came to San Francisco in the 1890s when he was only nineteen and wrote in English, provided a convenient occasion for American, and later, British critics to separate the 1890s nocturne aesthetic from urban pollution and to situate it in an Orientalist context that at least one editor conflated with the premodern. In Noguchi's first book of prose poems, written in a Whitmanesque style, a solitary figure confronts a landscape absent of urbanization and industrialization, while still questioning the boundaries between nature and the human. Noguchi was taken under the wing of Joaquin Miller, the same American poet who dressed as a miner in E. Pauline Johnson's private performances in London in 1895 (Flint, "Transatlantic Modernity," 189). Like Johnson, Noguchi had to navigate cultural stereotypes while also making his own way as a young poet. If the 1890s nocturne genre originated with Whistler in an idea of a Japanese aesthetic of form over content, then Yone Noguchi's poetry fulfilled that idea of Japan for audiences on the other side of the globe from London, and later for audiences in London and for American transplants, such as Ezra Pound, who noted in a 1911 letter to Noguchi that his books "lie with my own in Mathews' shop."[22] Gelett Burgess, the poet, critic, and editor who introduced Noguchi's first book *Seen and Unseen, or Monologues of a Homeless Snail* (1897), emphasized Noguchi's book as at once foreign, antimodern, and aestheticist. Burgess's introduction insists on reading this young poet, barely in his twenties, as a voice from an ancient past:

> *I would have you think of him as I know him, a youth of twenty years, exiled and alone*, separated from the mother, far away, abandoned by his native land and Time, *a recluse and a dreamer, in love with sadness, waiting for the time to come to do his part in recalling the ancient glory of the great poets and philosophers of his land; watching, calm-eyed and serious, the writers of this new world, to see if the old words can live in the Western civilization; and if the sheeted memories of the Past may be re-embodied in our English tongue.*[23]

Burgess incorporates words and phrases from Noguchi's poems into his introduction, indicating them by putting them in nonitalic font. On Burgess's account, Noguchi seems like both an orphaned child and an aged hermit, rather than a member of the burgeoning literary community of San Francisco in the 1890s. His role is to bring back an ancient Japanese glory, to test it in and fit it to "Western civilization" and to the English language. Burgess's metallurgic metaphor, saying that Noguchi takes the "crude metal" of English and mints it into "golden coin," positions him as a preindustrial alchemist. Noguchi not only represents the "ancient glory of the poets and philosophers of his land," he also, in Burgess's account, represents a West so old it is not just preindustrial, but prehistoric as well. Burgess pulls out a phrase to signify the iron age: "*For his is the voice of the Occident speaking from the* iron bodied yore-time." This insistence on older and older eras of human history presents Noguchi as an antimodern ideal.

At the same time, Burgess suggests that Noguchi out-aesthetes the aestheticists: "*Yet it were but partly true to call this symbolism. It is too vague, too subtly suggestive for that. Such moods and nuances of feeling as these are not translatable into the logical and definite processes of Occidental thought.*" Vagueness and subtle suggestion are Symons's calling cards in his essay "The Decadent Movement in Literature," and yet Noguchi, Burgess suggests, writes a poetry even too vague for the vagueness of symbolism. Mood and nuance, standard terms for 1890s poetry, Burgess suggests come in a form that is untranslatable into "*the logical and definite processes of Occidental thought.*" Although it might seem as though one original inspiration for fin-de-siècle aestheticism – Japonisme – had returned in a better way that outdid the aestheticists at their own game, Burgess is quick to say that Noguchi's poems are "not distinctively Japanese in sentiment or in art" but nonetheless have "*their intangible delicacy,*" akin to Ho-ku or haiku poetry. Noguchi's culture of origin is important to, though not definitive of, his aestheticism, Burgess suggests, offering a rationale linked to the vagueness he admires in the poetry. Although Noguchi does include of a number of night-themed poems in this collection, Burgess is the one who calls them nocturnes, while commenting on their "*sincerity and simplicity*" he calls them "*nocturnes set to the music of an unfamiliar tongue.*" The uncomfortable dual-cultural provenance of the poetry, Burgess suggests, allows Noguchi's poems to both align with and outdo European and American poetry of the latter half of the nineteenth century. Grace Lavery notes that Noguchi finds nineteenth-century British mainstream poets "quite Oriental," especially Dante Gabriel Rossetti, whose "The Blessed Damozel" Lavery argues is a model for Noguchi's haiku. Situated as "ancient" by Burgess, Noguchi might even seem almost like a source as well as an inheritor of Victorian verse culture. Lavery also notes that in addition to a rather credible charge of plagiarism from Edgar Allen Poe, Noguchi was accused of having been invented by Burgess. Though Noguchi and his poems were decidedly real, his idea of originality, Lavery argues, meant "a new way of inhabiting an existing literary tradition."[24] Burgess's introduction shapes his reception to figure him as a source of Victorian literature – with his ancient aesthetic that a tepid West might not even be able to comprehend – as well as an inheritor of it. Though Noguchi is, as Lavery argues, post-Victorian, his aesthetic is ancient because it is Oriental, according to Burgess.

Positioned as representative of the aesthetic source of the Victorians who served as a source for him, and geographically distanced from them, Noguchi can bypass what he called "old smoky London"[25] in his own nocturnes. Noguchi deindustrializes the nocturne by situating his verses in a landscape at once both Orientalized (and therefore old) and Californian (and therefore new). The surreal quality of the verses smooths over these contradictions. Burgess asserts that Noguchi's verses seem strange because Western "logic" occludes the subtlety of Noguchi's greater understanding of the natural world. Noguchi's nocturnes in *Seen and Unseen*, unlike Symons's and Blind's urban visions, consider what it is like to grope in the darkness in the wilderness. Though images of nature are everywhere in Noguchi's first volume, the writing is too surreal, too densely figurative to be considered naturalistic. Take the curious subtitle, "monologue of a homeless snail," which isn't referred to until well into the collection, poem XXX: "Alas, my soul hides, closing its eyes, – hides in the mobile body-cabin, praying the darkness to be a sympathetic friend" (Noguchi, *Seen & Unseen*, Poem XXX). Although elsewhere a cabin seems to be just a cabin, here it is a figure for a body, the snail a figure for a visibly dual soul and body. The darkness, like other natural objects and abstractions in the collection is personified and alive. Like many nocturne poets, Noguchi envisions "A Night in June," with a synesthesia familiar to aestheticists and a fully Romantic and perhaps antimodern refusal of anything human made:

> The sad, tears-wrapping cricket songs moisten, as if by rain at evening, the
>   western fire-skirt—the dying glories of the Sun.
> At night, the sleeper-scorning cricket speaks, overflowing the shy
>   breathless garden, smiting my soul.
> A heavy-colored darkness swallows up the blushing-cheeked, shuddering roses.
>   (Noguchi, *Seen & Unseen*, Poem XLII)

Despite the absence of a human-built world, everything here is human: the crying, singing cricket, the horizon that wears a skirt, the garden that would breathe, even again, the darkness itself. Rather than being eliminated or mitigated by streetlamps, fog, and mist, darkness is a force in Noguchi's poem, which fits his title. It can be seen only as an absence, but it is felt in various ways, as a friend or as an engulfing adversary.

"The Night-Lyre Echoes" figures stars as lanterns, returning a source of artificial light to a natural one. Yet the fragmentary surrealism offers no holistic picture of a natural setting:

> Resting on my pillow, the strings of the night-lyre echo in my ears, the storm reveling in the wall-less chamber of heaven, under the dim lanterns of the stars.
>
> Alas, the lantern-fires, burning up my forgotten love-sheets, bid the mist-wreathed phantoms laugh me to scorn.
>
> Enclosed by stillness, ghosts live there alone.
>
> What welcome fate, then for me!
>
> Even my friend the broken-hearted banana tree at my cabin door sleeps like a strange idol.
>
> "O storm, for my sake, make my friend chant his sadness again, again!"
>
> O smileless silence of midnight–Now the barking of a dog, far away, ripples lonelily along the waves of tears.
>
> The untimely chatter of a flying meadow lark drops away into the unknown West.
>
> Ah, what about my own sweet love! (Noguchi, *Seen & Unseen*. Poem XLVII)

Noguchi's poems make the whole world unfamiliar, and even unknowable. The night appears often because it perfectly figures the feeling of clarity stripped away. In reading this poem, the bark of a dog seems recognizable, yet how it can ripple along a wave of tears requires more imagination. Are the love-sheets sheets of the poet's paper or the sheets of his bed? How do they get burnt by the stars? The paradox of "wall-less chamber" reveals the intentionally contradictory logic of this poem and others. The paradoxes, the fragmentariness, the presumably recognizable world made unfamiliar, the everyday objects – pillows, sheets, lanterns, stars, trees – scrambled and reordered, all offer a modernist method and aesthetic. But while the human-generated brightness of the gaslit night in the British poems delights, horrifies, and exploits, Noguchi's poems, like Johnson's, also blur the boundaries between the human, the human-made, and nature. They place their questions – Who creates the night sky? Who determines how we think about its lights? – outside of industrial time.

Noguchi also raises questions about place, alluding to plants from various climates, from banana trees to redwoods. Where is the "unknown West" if we do not know where here is? These moves make it easy for Burgess to lean into the ancient and the antimodern. Noguchi concurred, claiming an authentic connection between himself and Nature in his 1915 autobiography, saying that his first book conveys "How I read the heart of Nature."[26] California is represented as a place of natural, even pre-modern expansiveness, in comparison with "old smoky London," where he went in 1904 to shore up his literary reputation in the place that was still "the arbiter of literary taste" (Marx, *Yone Noguchi*, 118).

Conclusion

The poets I have discussed are connected both by genre and by literary and publishing networks – John Lane, Joaquin Miller, Symons himself, all form professional nodes amongst this transnational group. Although Noguchi and Johnson traveled to London because it was the literary center of the 1890s, the recovery of their work and other transnational approaches demonstrate that scholars of the decade no longer need to take London as *their* center. The study of genre allows this very kind of geographical decentralization, and the nocturne in particular calls attention to the ways in which poets across the globe described the changes in the air and the sky of the night that came in the wake of industrialization, the burning of fossil fuels, and the use of gas lamps in particular. English poets like Wilde, Symons, and Blind portrayed the exploitation both sexual and environmental of bright night lights. Portraying a less smoky world, Noguchi and Johnson at once fulfill expectations of antimodernity from a foreign or Indigenous poet, while also laying claim to modern, avant-garde aesthetics, fashioning them anew for themselves. Noguchi and Johnson both decenter the human and offer nocturnes that are neither pre-nor post-industrial, but of their own moment and anti-industrial. By reading their work alongside Wilde, Symons, and Blind, we see what was always true of the nocturne: it is a global and an environmentally focused genre.

Notes

1 Hélène Valance and Jane Marie Todd, *Nocturne: Night in American Art, 1890–1917* (New Haven, CT: Yale University Press, 2018), 3–12.
2 Robert L. Peters, "Whistler and the English Poets of the 1890's," *Modern Language Quarterly* 18, no. 3 (1957): 251–61 (258).

3 Oscar Wilde, *Poems* (New York: G. Munro's Sons, 1895), 77.

4 Alex Murray and Jason David Hall, "Introduction: Decadent Poetics," in *Decadent Poetics: Literature and Form at the British Fin de Siècle*, eds. Jason David Hall and Alex Murray (London: Palgrave Macmillan UK, 2013), 1–25 (14).

5 Meredith Martin, "Did a Decadent Metre Exist at the Fin de Siècle?" in *Decadent Poetics: Literature and Form at the British Fin de Siècle,* ed. Jason David Hall and Alex Murray (London: Palgrave Macmillan UK, 2013), 46–64.

6 Rachael Scarborough King, "The Scale of Genre," *New Literary History* 52, no. 2 (2021): 261–84 (262).

7 Erik Martiny, "Nox Consilium and the Dark Night of the Soul: The Nocturne," in *A Companion to Poetic Genre*, ed. Erik Martiny (Hoboken, NJ: Wiley-Blackwell, 2012), 390–403 (391–92).

8 David DiLaura, "A Brief History of Lighting," *Optics and Photonics News* 19, no. 9 (2008): 22–28 (22).

9 John Davidson, *In a Music-Hall, and Other Poems* (London: Ward and Downey, 1891), 30.

10 Laurence Binyon, *First Book of London Visions*, The Shilling Garland; No. 1 (London: E. Mathews, 1896), 9.

11 Joseph Bristow, "Introduction," in *The Fin-de-Siècle Poem: English Literary Culture and the 1890s*, ed. Joseph Bristow (Athens, OH: Ohio University Press, 2005), 1–46 (5).

12 Jesse Oak Taylor, *The Sky of Our Manufacture: The London Fog in British Fiction from Dickens to Woolf* (Charlottesville, VA: University of Virginia Press, 2016), 5. Taylor suggests that it was widely known that gas came from the accumulated solar energy of the past, from the matter of dead plants and animals (127).

13 Arthur Symons, *London Nights* (London: L. C. Smithers, 1895), 15.

14 Mathilde Blind, *Songs and Sonnets* (London: Chatto & Windus, 1893), 103.

15 Patricia Murphy, *Reconceiving Nature: Ecofeminism in Late Victorian Women's Poetry* (Columbia, MO: University of Missouri Press, 2019), 88; James Diedrick, *Mathilde Blind: Late-Victorian Culture and the Woman of Letters* (Charlottesville, United States: University of Virginia Press, 2017), 170.

16 S. Frances Harrison, *Pine, Rose and Fleur de Lis* (Toronto: Hart, 1891), 112.

17 D. M. R. Bentley, *The Confederation Group of Canadian Poets, 1880–1897* (Toronto: University of Toronto Press, 2004), 22.

18 Charles George Douglas Roberts, *New York Nocturnes: And Other Poems* (Boston; New York; and London: Lamson, Wolffe and Company, 1898), 5.

19 Carole Gerson, "Rereading Pauline Johnson," *Journal of Canadian Studies/ Revue d'Etudes Canadiennes* 46, no. 2 (2012, Spring): 45–61 (48); Kate Flint, "Transatlantic Modernity and Native Performance," in *The Cambridge History of Native American Literature,* ed. Melanie Benson Taylor (Cambridge: Cambridge University Press, 2020), 182–96.

20 Glenn Willmott, "Paddled by Pauline," *Canadian Poetry* 46, no. 46 (2000): 46–68.

21 E. Pauline Johnson, *The White Wampum.* (London: John Lane, 1895), 85.

22 Anita Patterson, "Global America Revisited: Ezra Pound, Yone Noguchi, and Modernist Japonisme," *Nanzan Review of American Studies* 33 (2011): 53–69 (56).

23 Yone Noguchi, *Seen & Unseen, or, Monologues of a Homeless Snail* (San Francisco, CA: Gelett Burgess & Porter Garnett, 1897), pages are unnumbered; italics in original.

24 Grace E. Lavery, *Quaint, Exquisite: Victorian Aesthetics and the Idea of Japan* (Princeton, NJ: Princeton University Press, 2019), 85–86.

25 Edward Marx, *Yone Noguchi: The Stream of Fate: Vol. I. The Western Sea.* (Botchan Books, 2019), 118.

26 Yone Noguchi, *The Story of Yone Noguchi* (Philadelphia, PA: G. W. Jacobs & Co., 1915), 19–20.

CHAPTER 7

The Green 1890s:
World Ecology in Women's Poetry

Ana Parejo Vadillo

I know that you will help.

A. Mary F. Robinson

Women poets of the 1890s were extremely prolific in nature poetry. But their poetics, perhaps because traditionally framed within discourses of femininity, have been left out of important discussions relating to environmental politics and ecological theories. Fabienne Moine's *Women Poets in the Victorian Era: Cultural Practices and Nature Poetry* (2015) and Patricia Murphy's *Reconceiving Nature: Eco-Feminism in Late Victorian Women's Poetry* (2019) have recently made compelling arguments about what Murphy calls – too tamely – the "nascent" ecofeminism of their poetics.[1] These two groundbreaking books are particularly strong in their gendering and eroticizing of nature. However, what the present chapter wants to trace is how women poets at the fin de siècle thought politically of the environmental issues of their day. Considering the dramatic changes to their habitats, what world ecology did their poetry reveal?

Our existential environmental crisis has refocalized the literatures of the fin de siècle, revealing resonances between their period and ours, and shedding light in the process on forgotten or suppressed writers, or writers that did not quite fit into well-known canonical narratives of literary periods. An example of how such an approach can redefine a field is Dennis Denisoff's *Decadent Ecology in British Literature and Art, 1860–1910* (2022). Through its engagement with environmentalism and pagan spiritualities, Denisoff has recovered a wealth of turn-of-the-century material, uncovering in the process, as he summarizes, "the pervasive influence of decadence and paganism on modern understandings of nature and the environment, queer and feminist politics, national identities, and changing social hierarchies."[2] His book not only reveals a more porous relationship between humans, nonhumans, and ecological systems, but it also gives way to a more profound and radical vision of 1890s politics than previously acknowledged. Another important book in this respect is Elizabeth Miller's *Extraction Ecologies and the Literature of the Long Exhaustion* (2021), which, though not on the 1890s per se, skillfully examines how mining and extraction transformed British novelistic styles from the 1830s to 1930s. The literature of extraction Miller presents here portrays Britain as an empire thoroughly dependent on mining. Her nuanced study of narrative shows how literature dealt with and reflected upon the emergence of a new relationship between humans and the materials of the Earth based on aggressive extraction.[3]

As this process of recovery goes on, what is emerging is that the period had its own green agenda: the Green 1890s, as I propose here. The 1890s may still be defined by its love of masks and artificiality, and yet a stunning number of works by women poets of the fin de siècle revisited nature in far more political ways than has been recognized. As I show here, their work was concerned with the fact that the natural world was being affected by human agency and by humanity's political decisions. Defamiliarizing ourselves with the poetics of the 1890s as we know it might therefore steer us into a new familiarity with their world.

In taking this step back, important realignments of form and content emerge which suggest a new landscape of the period and its poetries. For example, the pastoral in women's poetry emerges as a form that rebels against global agrilogistics. Urban aestheticism and decadence mean not just excitement at the freedoms offered by modern cities but fighting for green spaces and coping with pollution aesthetically and politically. Their pervasive emphasis on the plant world unveils a potent critique of the politics of eco-imperialism as plants become symbols of nationhood and independence from the British empire. As Gayatri Spivak tells us in "Planetarity," "to learn to read is to learn to dis-figure the undecidable figure into a responsible literality, again and again. It is my belief that initiation into cultural explanation is a species of such a training in reading."[4] As I understand Spivak, "Planetarity" is a praxis that enables the production of a plural planet that speaks of its own radical alterities and to which we aspire as readers and planet citizens. My analysis aims to capture how 1890s poetics were led by the alterity of women's approach to ecology. In establishing the breadth of ecological criticism rooted in their poetics, the chapter reconsiders their poetry as an archive of structural and paradigmatic thinking about the rural, the urban, and the planet that challenges current conceptions of aestheticist and decadent poetry.

To learn to read the work of women poets of the 1890s, even to reread them, is this chapter's task. With a backward gaze, then, and using the lens of our current environmental emergency, this chapter's goal is to study their poetics in light of the destruction of the biosphere in their own time. This method is after all the very definition of the decadent style in poetry. In doing this, the chapter reveals a world of affinities, an arcade of knowledges and activist practices in women's poetry of the 1890s. As shall be seen, for example, an important outcome of this methodology is that it highlights how they critiqued gendered and colonial capitalist ideologies that made nature, in the words of Mathilde Blind, "the produce of their age and nation."[5] Blind's use of the word "produce" is noteworthy. In *Capitalism in the Web of Life,* Jason W. Moore speaks of "'capitalism as a world-ecology,' joining the accumulation of capital, the pursuit of power, and the co-production of nature in dialectical unity."[6] The poets discussed in this chapter understood that to restore the natural world back to itself required the dissection of national politics and global economics that generated environmental damage.

To appreciate the political intent of their poetics with regards to the environmental issues of their time, the chapter is divided into three sections that focus on three points of contestation. The first discusses the poetics of ecological disaster in the countryside. It moves then to a discussion of a poetics of soot and recycling in urban poetry. I end with a discussion of plant thinking in a transnational, anti-colonial context. While all the poets discussed here are of the 1890s, to understand the origins of their ecological thinking and the continuation of their politics into the twentieth century, the essay necessarily spills beyond the boundaries of the 1890s.

Dark Ecologies in the Countryside

Since Raymond Williams, the dialectics of countryside versus city has dominated the approach of critics to England's social habitats, often with a focus on male writers.[7] But how do writings about the countryside reflect the concern of women poets with the environment? In this first section, I examine three approaches to the English countryside: Christina Rossetti's *Goblin Market* (1862), the much lesser-known A. Mary F. Robinson's *The New Arcadia* (1884), and finally Mathilde Blind's *The Heather on Fire: A Tale of the Highland Clearances* (1886). Far from offering a primitivist romanticization of the rural, these three poets offer dark readings of the countryside, which they see as profoundly damaged by globalization and industrial agriculture. I start with Rossetti not only because she was recognized among her peers as *the* leading woman poet of the fin de siècle, but because her *Goblin Market*, reissued in 1893, would become the blueprint of much ecological thinking in the 1890s. Rossetti, and later Robinson and Blind, established the groundwork for rethinking the fantastical and the pastoral as genres that critique industrial agrilogistics.

Goblin Market is a better title than "Global Market," yet Rossetti's poem is an allegory about the agricultural logistics that started to become prevalent at the end of the nineteenth century. Though the collection was published at the peak of Pre-Raphelitism, its tale of addiction and its effect on the decaying body of Laura, one of the sisters at the heart of the poem, made Rossetti one of the leading figures of 1890s poetics, particularly for women. The book has since been reproduced, republished, and illustrated by major leading artists, from the original illustrations by her brother, Dante Gabriel Rossetti, to color illustrations by Kinuko Craft for *Playboy* magazine.[8] Yet Laurence Housman's illustrations for the 1893 edition capitalized more than the original illustrations by Dante Gabriel Rossetti the most profound and disturbing aspect of the story: how global capitalism and agrilogistics were affecting the planet and human life, with the goblins greedily occupying and harvesting the trees, whose fruits would later be sold in the market (Figures 7.1–7.5).[9] We know that Rossetti did not like "his" goblins, which she deemed too ugly.[10] She had a point: the poem suggests that their power lies in the allure of beauty.

Rossetti experimented with irregular meters to produce the song-like rhythm that continues to mesmerize readers, who can almost hear the goblins tempting buyers with their wares.

> Apples and quinces,
> Lemons and oranges,
> Plump unpecked cherries,
> Melons and raspberries,
> Bloom-down-cheeked peaches,
> Swart-headed mulberries,
> Wild free-born cranberries,
> Crab-apples, dewberries,
> Pine-apples, blackberries,
> Apricots, strawberries;
> (Rossetti, Goblin Market, 9–10)

John Ruskin famously described Rossetti's "irregular measures" as "the calamity of modern poetry."[11] His phrase might be better placed to reflect on the trade the poem decries. Her irregular measures (as irregular were the all-season products) created the lusciousness of the fruits to reflect the wild

Figure 7.1 Laurence Housman, "The Goblins Selling their Wares in the Market," illustration for Christina Rossetti's *Goblin Market* (Macmillan & Co, 1893), 3.

Figure 7.2 Laurence Housman, "The Goblins Harvesting Crops," illustration for Christina Rossetti's *Goblin Market* (Macmillan & Co, 1893), 8.

Figure 7.3   Laurence Housman, "The Goblins Handling the Harvest," illustration for
Christina Rossetti's *Goblin Market* (Macmillan & Co, 1893), 9.

exuberance of the trade. Only a global market could make such a display of fruits possible, with the goblins being the agents of a system that both produce in large scale and commercialize at a local level their global produce. Fruits from Southern Europe and the Global East are on sale together with English summer fruits. Laura and her sister, Lizzie, suffer the effects of their trades, both in their bodies and in their lives. As Laura tells Lizzie as she worries about the provenance of the goblin men's wares, "We must not look at goblin men, / We must not buy their fruits: / Who knows upon what soil they fed / their hungry thirsty roots?" (14–19). Rossetti might have reservations about industrial agriculture and the sustainability of a global trade, but the intricate line verses connote the exploitation of the labor force too.

Despite her own admonition, Laura falls for the goblin men, and having no money, she accepts their offer (their fruits in exchange for her body), paying for the fruits with a lock of her golden hair. She gets poisoned by the trade as her body enters a high stage of addiction and decay, which presages barrenness and ultimately death. Lizzie tells her of Jeanie, who "ate their fruits and wore their flowers." She died, and "to this day no grass will grow / Where she lies low: / I planted daisies there a year ago / that never blow" (35–36). Jeanie becomes an example of how an exploitative global agriculture brings barrenness and endangers the habitat. Body and soul are now body and soil. Indeed, Laura's "tree of life drooped from the root" (49). The more she needs the goblin fruits, the more she distances herself from their own domestic economy and communal life: "She no more swept the house, / Tended the fowls or cows, / Fetched honey, kneaded cakes of wheat, / Brought water from the brook: / But sat down listless in the chimney-nook / and would not eat" (56).

Lizzie is determined to save her sister, which also means saving nature and their own ecosystem from exploitation. Rossetti uses Lizzie's encounter with the goblins to suggest that global capitalism both reaps the earth of its fruits through a global market and rapes nature too, and Rossetti does indeed present capitalism in gendered terms, whereby a gendered nature is prostituted and raped through exploitation. Unlike Laura, Lizzie takes a silver coin to pay the goblins, offering a monetary value for their wares. The goblins aspire to have Lizzie bound by a symbolic communion to their world and, enraged, they forcefully try to make her eat. Violence toward Lizzie allegorically voices the violence perpetrated by agriculture on an industrial global scale to the land, which is exploited to perform according to capitalist wishes. Tortured by the goblins, she resists eating "Like a fruit-crowned orange-tree / White with blossoms honey-sweet / Sore beset by wasp and bee" (73). She saves her sister, and therefore their very own environment, by refusing their wares. Lizzie, in other words, represents the very body of activism shielding the habitat. Lizzie's activism ensures a renewal of the soil. Both become mothers and their gynocentric community, founded on care, survives and flourishes. The goblins remain a cautionary tale of a futurity that may still become too real if one falls for their trade.

While Rossetti worked with allegories to admonish her readers of the barrenness perpetrated on the land by global trade, A. Mary F. Robinson's *The New Arcadia* worked in a naturalist mode to highlight the modern condition of England's countryside.[12] As Robinson explained in 1902, "I have never been able to write about what was not known to me and near. Tim Black, the Scapegoat, and most of the personages of the New Arcadia, lived in a common in Surrey near my garden gates: all of them are drawn from human models."[13] In this provocative book, much disliked by her contemporaries, who did not believe Robinson, the poet of dreams, could ever have witnessed such living conditions, Robinson suggests that the crisis facing rural England is of the same magnitude as that of cities, and that it has consequences for humans, nonhumans, and the environment. The collection starts with a poem entitled "Prologue" that immediately presents the countryside and its rivers as highly polluted: "Not only in great cities dwells great crime; / Not where they clash ashore, and break and moan, / Are waters deadliest." Robinson used in the "Prologue" the rhyme royal. Also called the "Troilus stanza," Chaucer used it famously in *Troilus and Criseyde*, to tell his readers of the tragic ending awaiting both lovers. In similar ways, Robinson's choice of form foretells what is to come in her Arcadia. The ferocious critique displayed in "Prologue" indicts the actions of men, who both destroy environments and fetishize the natural world:

> They cover it up with leaves, they make a show,
> Of Maypole garlands over, but there shall be
> A wind to scatter their gauds, and a wind to blow
> And purify the hidden dreaded thing
> Festering underneath; and so I sing.
> . . .
> Lend me your souls, and do not stand aloof,
> Saying what happy lives these peasants win,
> Praising the plushy lichens on the roof.
> Leave off your praising, brothers, and come in.
> See, round the hearth, squat Ignorance, Fever, Sin.
> See on the straw the starving baby cries;
> The mother thanks her God another dies.
>
> (Robinson, "Prologue," 4, 7)

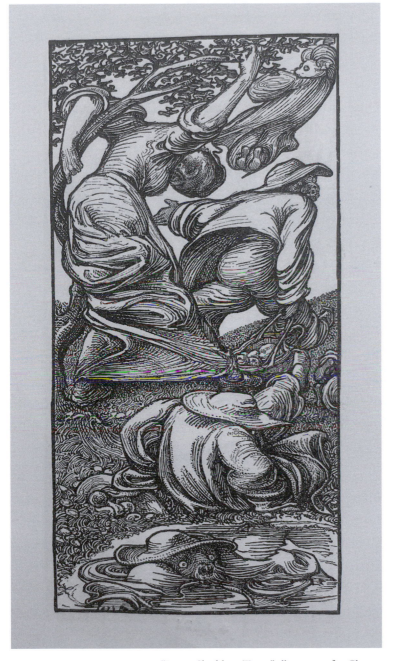

Figure 7.4   Laurence Housman, "Lizzie Shielding Trees," illustration for Christina Rossetti's *Goblin Market* (Macmillan & Co, 1893), 52.

Figure 7.5   Laurence Housman, "Goblins Abandoning the Land," illustration for
Christina Rossetti's *Goblin Market* (Macmillan & Co, 1893), 53.

Against a more idyllic vision of Arcadia as a pastoral world in which humans live in harmony with nature, Robinson presents the New Arcadia as a living hell.

The collection is Emile Zola on steroids. The poems in this superb but harrowing book expose the hardships of rural life: poverty, hunger, displacement, brutality, alienation, loneliness, abandonment. As Emily Harrington notes, Robinson presents here "a discordant song, one that attempts to awaken readers by denying them the poetic pleasure they expect."[14] The countryside brings out the savagery of men: violence (against humans and animals), hatred, misogyny, abuse, subjugation. In Robinson's "Man and Wife," an old couple decide to stay living in utter destitution instead of being separated in the workhouse (19–21). Craving for love and needing money, the abandoned country girl in "The Scape-Goat" becomes a prostitute (25–26). A mother murders her daughter with lead in "Cottar's Girl" (59–65). "The Wise Woman" is vilified as a witch (69–75). In the Darwinian "Men and Monkeys" (79–81), a lowbrow monkey pitifully admires the beauty of nature (and the poem makes clear both that monkeys are abused by men and that men in modern times have retreated to a pre-evolutionary age). There's no dialectical difference à la Raymond Williams between country and city in this book. Robinson voices England's dark ecology as a loop, the other side of which is the city. Both are ecologically damaged. The volume ends with an "Epilogue" in which Robinson reinforces the vision of England's modernity, of this New Arcadia, as a regressive futurity brought about by capitalism. The New Arcadia is the capitalist's hunting ground.

> The stunted lives from hunger never free,
>> The crowded towns, the moors where never hoe
>> Stirs in the fallow soil, where live and grow
> The grouse and pheasant where the man should be,
> The shiftless, hopeless, long, brute misery
>> That gathers like a cloud, racked to and fro
>> With lightning discontent – I cannot show,
> I cannot say the dreadful things I see.
>
> And worse I see, more spectral, deathlier far;
>> Class set from class, each in its separate groove;
>> Straight on to death I watch them stiffly move,
> None sees the end, but each his separate star;
> Too wrapt, should any fall, to reach a hand;
> Nor, should one cry, would any understand.
>
> (Robinson, "Epilogue," 97)

Robinson foresees a spectral future that has already taken place. Capitalism depletes nature and produces a class divide, strengthened by a voracious individualism in which humans no longer care for each other.

My final example in this section is *The Heather on Fire: A Tale of the Highland Clearances*, by German-born cosmopolitan poet Mathilde Blind.[15] The book offers an anticolonial, antinationalistic, and anticapitalist reading of the countryside in Scotland. Blind's mother and stepfather had participated in the socialist uprising of the Revolutions of 1848 and, as a child, Blind followed her mother in her exile to Britain. *The Heather on Fire* is the work of an activist writer who is attuned to the emotional, political, and financial consequences of capitalism and exile. As James Diedrick notes, Blind published the volume with the intent of persuading politicians to change the law on the Highland Clearances, which she had visited in 1884.[16] In 1883, Gladstone had set up a commission to enquire into the conditions of the crofters (Scottish agricultural workers who lived as tenants in the land). He had also introduced a bill in Parliament in 1885 to grant security of tenure and fair rents, which was passed through in 1886, the year of publication of Blind's tale. As Blind puts it in the Preface: "the ferocity shown by some of the factors and ground-officers employed by the landlords in evicting their inoffensive tenantry can only be matched by the brutal excesses of victorious troops on a foreign soil" (1). She made a point of sending Gladstone a copy of the poem.

The book is a call to arms against the ecological and human "atrocities" (Blind's term) perpetrated by rich landowners in the Highlands and Western Isles of Scotland. To introduce a much more profitable capitalist system of production, rich landlords phased out crofting (the traditional system in Scotland defined by small-scale food production) by violently evicting from the land tenants (or crofters) who, for generations, had been caring for the land. Most of the crofters (who lost everything in the process) were forced into mass migrations overseas (Australia, Canada, and United States). The British government was complicit – it sent the army, stationed the police, and allowed outsiders to acquire land in the Highlands. As Blind puts it: "industrious peasantry, full of poetic instincts and ardent patriotism" was "ruthlessly expelled [from] their native land to make way for sporting grounds rented by merchant princes and American millionaires" (Blind, *Heather on Fire*, 3). (As a side note, Blind's vision turned out to be true, with coastal areas in Scotland today owned by Donald Trump for the creation of golf courses.) In the poem, Blind presents the strong connections between national, colonial, and transnational policies that bind up land and oceanic communities and ecologies.

Her multidirectional approach shows how all the political forces interacted and were responsible for the destruction of Scotland's ecosystem.

Blind rejected English poetic forms to write this book, choosing instead the duan, a type of heroic song used in Scottish Gaelic and Irish Gaelic literature. The poem was thus deliberately written in an anticolonial poetic form. Blind set her historical poem in the 1830s to record one of the most brutal moments of the clearances. The book follows the lives of two young lovers, Michael and Mary, who just subsist by living off sea and land, the women looking after the croft while the men spend winters at sea fishing. Blind presents the preindustrial croft as respectful of the environment. Her vision can be framed in relation to the ecocritical concept of "dwelling" or to use Tom Ingold's terminology "dwelling perspective," which suggests that "the landscape is constituted as an enduring record of – and testimony to – the lives and works of past generations who have dwelt within it."[17] Blind describes how the land echoes "the swift pulsation of the heart of time":

XVI

A lone, green place, with no live thing around,
No barks, or bleats, or lowings, save the sound
Of running waters, that, with many a fall
And fluid splash, meandered musical;
Running through months, years, ages, on and on,
Monotonously beneath moon or sun,
With fugitive, ever-recurring chime
Echoing the swift pulsation of the heart of time.

(Blind, *Heather on Fire*, 13)

The crofters' communion with nature might seem idyllic, but their lives and livelihoods are owned by landlords and kings. The poem presents feudalism as a precursor of capitalism. A large part of the poem is devoted to stories of men who were foot soldiers in the King's army and made possible the liberation of Spain in the Napoleonic colonial wars. But on their return, human losses were never rewarded financially by those for whom they fought. Severely crippled from battle, they are an extra burden on children and wives, who must work the land to pay the landlord. Blind's critique could not be more ferocious. Children in the croft are so poor that they are bare footed. The population has "weathered the same tale of centuries" (27), but in "these latter days men's lives are cheap; / and hard-worked Highlanders pay worse than lowland sheep" (55). Land and people are owned by the capitalist:

XLVI

To him belonged the glens with all their grain;
To him the pastures spreading in the plain;
To him the hills whence falling waters gleam;
To him the salmon swimming in the stream;
To him the forests desolately drear,
With all their antlered herds on fleet-foot deer;
To him the league-long rolling moorland bare,
With all the feathered fowl that wing the autumn air.

XLVII

For him the hind's interminable toil;
For him he ploughed and sowed and broke the soil,
For him the golden harvests would he reap,
For him would tend the flocks of woolly sheep,
For him would thin the iron-hearted woods,
For him track dear in snow-blocked solitudes;
For him the back was bent, and hard the hand,
For was he not his lord, and lord of all that land?

(28)

The poem ends with a harrowing description of the clearance. The cottages were set on fire and many died trying to escape from the flames. Rocks, trees, animals caught fire; "Wives, mothers, children – howling, weeping, swearing" (66). The crofters are thrown out with nothing and ushered into ships that will take them overseas. The land has been "cleared" for large-scale sheep farming. Blind's political message cannot be sharper: colonialism and capitalism have destroyed the environment and the symbiotic relationship between humans and the land.

In this section we have seen how three poets perceived the destruction of the natural world in the countryside. This work has been necessary in order to establish the traditions of thinking about the destruction of the natural world that women writers in the 1890s would draw upon as they theorized their perception of the accelerated degeneration of the environment at the fin de siècle. Rossetti uses the sisters Laura and Lizzie, as allegories of both life and soil. Her tale rejects global agriculture, proposing instead local communities of care. Robinson's hyperrealism admonishes against a regressive future that has already destroyed whole rural communities: degeneration is the product of industrial agriculture. Capitalism is not only experienced by those living in cities but has permanently damaged the very humanity of rural England. Blind's book shows how capitalism is bound with imperial and colonial policies. All three write against the exploitation of humans and the environment by capitalism. Their intention was political. Robinson writes thus in the Prologue to engage her readers into activism (and the links to Rossetti's *Goblin Market* are clear):

> For I do not sing to enchant you or beguile;
> I sing to make you think enchantment vile,
> I sing to wring your hearts and make you know
> What shame there is in the world, what wrongs, what woe;
>
> Because your deaf ears, only, are to blame,
> Not your deaf hearts. Look now, and if you see
> Men as they are, contended in their shame,
> I know that you will help.
>
> (Robinson, "Prologue," 10–11)

Botanizing the Asphalt

An important way in which decadent women poets tackled the world's ecological crisis was by botanizing the asphalt. William Sharp (who also wrote as Fiona McLeod) remembers a conversation between Christina Rossetti and a friend about the poetic advantages of living in the countryside. Rossetti made her position very clear. "I am," she said, "not only as confirmed a Londoner as was Charles Lamb, but really doubt if it would be good for me, now, to sojourn often or long in the country." "But," the lady insisted, "let me ask, do not you yourself find your best inspiration in the country?" Rossetti's answer could not have been more emphatic: "Oh dear, no!" "My knowledge of what is called nature is that of the town sparrow which makes an excursion occasionally from its home in Regent's Park or Kensington Gardens." "I am fairly sure," Rossetti added, "that I am in the place that suits me best."[18] Mythologized by her contemporaries as the "singing bird" of 30 Torrington Square, in Bloomsbury, London, where she lived from 1873 to 1894, Rossetti's writings expressed what Emma Mason has called "an ecological love command," "a spiritual but also cosmic community that extends to all aspects of creation, the seen – plants, animals, minerals, and fungi – and the unseen – the dead, angels and spirits."[19] But, as this conversation shows, Rossetti's fascination with nature was critically urbane.

She was not alone. Poets like Amy Levy and Alice Meynell often wrote
of their preference for the city despite pollution. Pollution and nature are
intertwined in their writings, to great aesthetic effect, as they mobilized the
natural world around the urban and polluted. In *Dark Ecology,* Timothy
Morton writes of the need to accept the damage caused by the
Anthropocene, calling it *ecognosis,* literally ecological awareness.[20]
Describing our ecological moment as a loop, he proposes that we imagine
a future past the Anthropocene in which we coexist with nature and the
waste of the past as recycled by nature. One finds writers of the 1890s
already reflecting provocatively and proleptically about humans in derelict
and ruinous urban habitats. H. G. Wells's *The Time Machine* (1895), or
the deliciously titled *Ceres' Runaway* (1909) by Alice Meynell are two
examples. Denisoff hits the nail on the head when he points out that one
of the reasons "why the eco-morphological aspect of British decadence has,
to date, not garnered greater scholarly attention" is because "from the start
of the cultural phenomenon, decadence has been associated with the
urban, the cultural, the artificial, and, not infrequently, with the insincere"
(Denisoff, *Decadent Ecology,* 4). In this section, I show, however, that what
has also been occluded is how ecological thinking was part of the way in
which writers botanized the decadent city. A closer attention to environmental politics in decadent writing reveals the cohabitation of an environmental consciousness and the already polluted. Their writings connote a
paradigmatic shift in urban poetics toward a politics of recycling and
sustainability even if their aesthetics present us with what Vernon Lee
calls, albeit in another context, *Beauty and Ugliness.*[21]

Amy Levy rejected the idealism of the pastoral in her last book of
poems, *A London Plane-Tree and Other Verse* (1889). As Susan Bernstein
notes, renewal and sustainability are central to this book, in which the
ecological and the urban are bedfellows.[22] London, the collection suggests,
is made up not only of people, industries, and buildings; it is also a site for
cultivation of plants and books. Using London's most iconic tree, the
plane tree, her collection makes a conscious intervention in rethinking the
urban in ecological terms. Hers is a poetry that plants trees. The first poem
of the collection, also entitled "A London Plane-Tree," starts with the
word "green": "Green is the plane-tree in the square, / The other trees are
brown; / They droop and pine for country air; / The plane-tree loves the
town" (17). While other trees long for the countryside, the poem continues, the plane tree finds solace and joy in the city, which it helps heal.
Its "bud and blow" recuperate the air, producing oxygen and cleaning the
atmosphere:

> Here from my garret-pane, I mark
>   The plane-tree bud and blow.
> Shed her recuperative bark,
>   And spread her shade below.
>
> Among her branches, in and out,
>   The city breezes play;
> The dun fog wraps her round about
>   Above, the smoke curls grey.
>
> Others the country take for choice,
>   And hold the town in scorn;
> But she has listed to the voice
>   On city breezes born.
>   (17)

The plane tree may be common, even un-treelike in its preference for city life, but for Levy "she" is the heroine of the modern world, for she cares for and improves the city's biosphere.

Levy was a forward thinker. Though plane trees were relatively recent additions to the city, Levy's home was surrounded by them. She lived at 5 Endsleigh Gardens, and all the squares around her home, namely Gordon Square, Tavistock Square, Russell Square, and Torrington Square (Levy was Christina Rossetti's neighbor), were planted with plane trees.[23] These are the very same trees that today inhabit Bloomsbury. In his history of city trees, Henry Lawrence notes that they were cultivated to combat air pollution. The Platanus x. acerifolia

> gained acceptance steady during the second half of the nineteenth century. By the end of the nineteenth century it was on the way to becoming the most widely planted of all city trees. Resistance to pests and to most air pollution was its greatest virtue, for by then the air was so thick in some cities that many species of trees could not survive.[24]

Resistance and resilience are key to the collection. Speaking as a Russian Jewish immigrant and refugee, Michael Marder reflects on what it means to be unrooted in the world, for both plants and people.[25] Having lived since childhood in permanent uprootedness, and linking nationalistic politics to the destruction of the biosphere, Marder writes that nations also colonize and violate other nations by eradicating their autochthonous flora (he cites as an example Israel's uprooting of olive trees in Palestine, but we could also add how the woods of dispossessed landowners in eighteenth-century Ireland were cut by new English proprietors).[26] Nationalistic ideologies recognize that identity is linked to the vegetal world that surrounds us. Colonizing the land and deracinating humans are two sides of the same ideology. Yet, no matter one's geographical location, "plants provide us with a peculiar shelter where the traditional distinction between interiority and exteriority no longer applies" (Marder, *Through Vegetal Being*, 120). It is helpful to follow Marder's ideas in relation to Levy, who as a Jewish lesbian woman, often felt uprooted within English decadent circles. In feminizing the tree, Levy presents the city dweller in symbiotic relationship with the plant world. Nature shelters humans in urban environments, protecting them. They root humans, Levy appears to say.

Rooted but supple to motion, the tree moves its branches to the rhythm of wind and smoke. Perhaps what is most radical about Levy's vision is that traditional ideas about segregation between interiority and exteriority, the natural and the polluted, humans and the natural world, are not applicable anymore. Marder notes that "for too long, our psychic and physical dwelling places have been constructed in such a way as to separate us from the threatening outside world, until we cut ourselves off almost completely and lost touch with it" (120). Speaking from his own experience, Marder writes of the suffering he experienced by being uprooted: "Those of us who have been expelled from our social environments, communities, or countries, however, sensed on our very skin an additional separation from the dwelling." That is why, he suggests, humans seek "refuge in the plant world," which for him is not "a mere substitute for the loss of human dwelling." One finds "refuge in the absolute exposure – of and to plants, the elements, or a new sort of energy, following the model of vegetal growth" (120 and passim). Levy's feminization suggests a similar idea, for the tree alerts the reader of the emotional synergy that connects them. For Levy, the London plane tree is emotionally and politically her refuge. Trees in London are, by extension, refuges for London dwellers.

In her exploration of Levy's recycling poetics, Susan Bernstein proposes that the book itself is a form of recycling and she links interestingly Levy's tree poetics with the ecology of the book: paper is the product of trees. She also makes a connection between the plane tree's lyrical recycling of pollution and the fact that, soon after finishing the book, Levy committed suicide by charcoal asphyxiation. Nonetheless, for Bernstein the tree remains a positive figure, one in which recycling resists and wins out. Levy's poetic form, I think, helps us to think further about the links between the poet and the feminized tree. She wrote this poem in ballad form (a medieval verse, with a melodic tone, often used in musical settings), to choreograph what I see as a dance-off with death. Today we know that trees' capacity to renew polluted air has reached its capacity. Levy appears to forewarn humans of the city's suicidal cohabitation with pollution. In Levy's London, humans, plant world, and pollution coexist dangerously and symbiotically.

A landscape and city poet, Alice Meynell's nature poetry permeates her whole oeuvre. In a radical rewriting of male Romantic poets, she assuredly identifies her authorship (and her poetry) with nature. As a Catholic poet, her nature also consistently expresses the mind of God. In these two strands, her nature is Edenic, Christian, feminist, intimate, and allegorical. Yet her analysis of modern agriculture is surprising. In the poem "The Threshing Machine" she mourns the death of a foregone England.[27] As expected in a nature poet, she presents modern agrilogistics as inhumane and out of sync with the biosphere. Yet, and this separates her from the poets discussed in the first section of this chapter, she finds herself not rejecting industrial agriculture altogether. The poem implicitly highlights the inherent contradictions of modern agriculture: it saves human time and the body's energy, but this comes at a great cost, for it disregards nature's own time:

> No "fan is in his hand" for these
> Young villagers beneath the trees,
>> Watching the wheels. But I recall
>> The rhythm of rods that rise and fall,
> Purging the harvest, over-seas.
>
> No fan, no flail, no threshing-floor!
> And all their symbols evermore
>> Forgone in England now – the sign,
>> The visible pledge, the threat divine,
> The chaff dispersed, the wheat in store.
>
> The unbreathing engine marks no tune,
> Steady at sunrise, steady at noon,
>> Inhuman, perfect, saving time,
>> And saving measure, and saving rhyme –
> And did our Ruskin speak too soon?
>
> "No noble strength on earth" he sees
> "Save Hercules' arm"; his grave decrees
>> Curse wheel and seam. As the wheels ran
>> I saw the other strength of man,
> I knew the brain of Hercules.
>> (Meynell, "The Threshing Machine," 119)

In *Unto This Last* (1860), Ruskin had denounced industrial capitalism and the destruction of the natural environment that it brought with it. He founded the Guild of St George to promote preindustrial values in agriculture. Meynell's approach to farm machinery is certainly somewhat similar. But, while she agrees with Ruskin in its unnaturalness, the poem's last lines suggest an uncomfortable truth: human intelligence eases hard labor.

The aim of much of Meynell's writing was to reclaim and protect nature in urban environments. As Murphy writes, nature in her writing is "a vibrant entity on its own terms and is not to be marginalized as a vehicle for human interests" (Murphy, *Reconceiving Nature*, 129). In essays and poems she attacks how plant life in cities is under strict municipal control. For example, she criticizes in "Grass" (1896) how in London's modern suburbs "public servants – men with spades and a cart" cut the grass and then "carry it away to some parochial dustheaps."[28] It is a worldwide problem. She condemns in "Ceres' Runaway" (1909) how the Municipality of Rome is also "hot in chase of a wild crop."[29] But the natural world always fights back: "Impartial to the antique, the mediæval, the Renaissance early and late, the newer modern, this wild summer finds its account in travertine and tufa, reticulated work, brick, stucco and stone." The air "has lodged in a little fertile dust the wild grass, wild wheat, wild oats!" she writes in exhilaration (11). Her writing speaks against the Municipal bodies that restrain and violate nature's natural growth. She wants Ceres to run away wildly in antique and modern cities. She argues for sustainable cities, as in the poem "A Dead Harvest: In Kensington Gardens" (1902), where she complains that the crop in Kensington Gardens is not used for recycling purposes, but instead fires the pyres of London, further enhancing the city's pollution.[30]

A writer known for the impenetrability of her poetry, her writings on urban environmentalism fudge the natural and the concrete; the past in the present and the present in the future; the political and the aesthetical; the national and the transnational; clear air and smoke. She writes to bring ecognosis in her readers and motivate them into environmental action. Most of her essays were first published in the "Wares of Autolycus" column in the London daily evening paper the *Pall Mall Gazette,* to which she was a regular contributor between 1895 and 1898. Londoners would be reading here her discerning account of how nature suffers at the hands of pollution. But, uniquely, Meynell's writings on nature and pollution do two interconnected things: they criticize industrial modernity yet recognize its powerful (and "beautiful") aesthetics. A good example of this is the poem "A Dead Harvest (In Kensington Gardens)" in which Meynell decries the dead crop produced in parks. It suggests that nature in the city does not always get repurposed. Instead, it smoulders the pyre and contributes to pollution:

> Along the graceless grass of town
> They rake the rows of red and brown, -
> Dead leaves, unlike the rows of hay
> Delicate, touched with gold and grey,
> Raked long ago and far away.
>
> . . .
>
> A futile crop! For it the fire
> Smoulders, and, for a stack, a pyre.
> So the town's lives on the breeze,
> Even as the shedding of the trees;
> Bosom nor barn is filled with these.
>
> (Meynell, "A Dead Harvest," 31–32)

Provocatively, Meynell sees pollution as the creative force behind impressionism in Britain. The environmental work that combines these two strands is the unique *Impressions of London* (1898), a collection of illustrated essays in which a critique of pollution is bound up with her experiments with impressionism.[31]

Figure 7.6   William Hyde, "An Impression," *London Impressions* (1898).

Meynell was the new Baudelaire, the writer of the polluted city. In *London Impressions* she castigates humans for polluting the world, yet some of the most vivid writing in this book comes when she muses about what pollution does poetically. In "The Effect of London" she argues that "it is no wonder if the painters of London are somewhat eager for the help of the smoke" (6). Smoke helps urban artists, who face the mammoth challenge of painting the city's infinite mass of detail. Painters may produce beauty, but we must be cautious in our appreciation. As she puts it in "The Climate of Smoke": "Only by acknowledging the climate of London to be more than half an artificial climate, and by treating our own handi-work – the sky of our manufacture – with a relative contempt, are we excused for thinking the effects in any sense beautiful" (9). The illustra-tions of this book, photogravures by William Hyde, emphasize the cloud of pollution that engulfs the city (Figure 7.6). She calls this polluting cloud "handsome grime." Smoke diffuses and unites ideas, people, plants, air, buildings. As *the* modern subject for modern art, London offers to artists a unique visual effect: an ungraspable mass of details smudged by air pollution. Pollution is the charcoal of modern art.

Meynell also discusses the pictorial effect of electric and gas-lamp lighting in London. But just like smoke, light pollution tortures nature in the city in multiple ways. In "The Trees," she argues that trees are oppressed by the tyranny of electric lighting in London. We saw how for Levy nature disrupts the boundaries of interior and exterior, that the plane tree paradoxically cleans the environment in its dance with death. Meynell does not discuss such heroism; instead, she voices the torture suffered by trees in cities. Trees in squares "do taste of darkness," but "the single trees that have their roots under grey pavements, and that breathe in the little accidental standing-places of the wayside, the railed-in corners left by the chance-medley of London streets – these have the strange fate to be in perpetual light" (12).

Meynell does not let industry, governments, and humans get away with it. In "The Smouldering City," London is smothered by pollution. "The fire in London never escapes," Meynell writes. "The thousand thousand little chambers" are lighted for man's sake. "Man," she continues, "will-ingly pays the wages of such a wildness in servitude, and spends mines and forests to keep the mobile creature close within his gates." She quotes the proverb "there is no smoke without a fire" to emphasize very literally the ecological damage caused by man's addition to industry. She suggests that this has resulted in a surprising change in the city's architecture, a change that has transformed its color and ornamentation. Instead of choosing the classical white or stucco, London architects have turned to the "kindling reds of her various bricks." Linking fire to the color of the city, she tells us, "it is as when you touch the red of a deep cheek and find it cool" (29). The last sentence of the essay "The London Sunday" could not make her point more clearly: "It helps the summer to put out many fires, and helps the live wind to sift the darkness from the sunlight" (3). Smoke engulfs the city and has infested the river Thames, whose waters "could hardly quench so great a multitude of imprisoned flames." Because ships and boats run with coal, they have contaminated its waters. Meynell summarizes: "With its cold ashes and its cold grime, with the burden of its chill refuse, all the remote roads and byways of the town seem to be utterly choked and filled" (30). She hammers the point home: London is insatiable. Linking the level of pollution to the Great Fire of London, Meynell admits that "London is not destroyed again, but it has become the place of immeasurable destruction" (31).

Eco-Activism and Legacies of Eco-Imperialism

In this last section, I discussed how Levy and Meynell encouraged political activism by focusing on urban pollution. Arguing for a "green" city, Levy's melancholic account of the London plane tree as a refuge for modern afflictions envisioned the possibility of regeneration by making equally visible the powerful specter of death by carbon suffocation. Meynell, on the other hand, exposed the aesthetic lure of smoke as a surface ornamentation in life and art in order to critique the coal and electric industries that let pollution run lawlessly free, while nature was terrorized and municipally chastised.

I would like to conclude this chapter by focusing on the legacy of eco-imperialism. Writing against colonialism, Irish poet and activist Katharine Tynan and Indian poet and politician Sarojini Naidu centered specifically on the revival of neglected autochthonous plants as symbols of national identity. Acknowledging the damage caused by eco-imperialism in their respective countries, there is in their poetry a liberation through flora from colonial policies and a reappropriation of flora for political purposes. Formally speaking, their poetics upcycled the English language and its "imperial forms," which they reoccupied with their own poetic traditions (Celtic, Persian, Urdu, etc.).

While better known during her lifetime than our own, Katharine Tynan was in the 1880s and 1890s a leading figure in both the Irish Literary Revival and London's transnational decadent circles. She supported

Charles Stewart Parnell, leader of the Irish Party. Within the Irish literary community, she worked within feminist nationalist networks as she became a close ally of writers such as Jane Barlow, Nora Hopper, Hannah Lynch, Rosa Mulholland, and Dora Sigerson. Her political poetry had a strong influence on W. B. Yeats's writings. They were engaged, though in the end she turned down Yeats's offer of marriage.[32] She was an admirer of Amy Levy. Alice Meynell was her closest friend and, during Tynan's periods in London (particularly between 1893 and 1911), she was an assiduous member of Meynell's cenacle of Catholic poets (which included Francis Thompson and T. S. Eliot). Tynan also had strong connections with the Rossetti family, and dedicated her second book of poems, *Shamrocks* (1887), to Christina Rossetti and her brother William Michael Rossetti (who was a Republican).[33] She was an extremely prolific writer, publishing more than sixteen books of poems (most on her Irish activism and Catholicism) and nearly 150 novels, most of them on feminist New Woman themes that also focused on Ireland. In great need of money, she wrote consciously for the many, not for the few.

Shamrocks is, as its title indicates, the work of an Irish eco-activist (Figure 7.7). As Meynell put it: "I do think *Shamrocks* a good title – *very* good for Ireland."[34] Like all her poetry before the First World War (e.g., *Ballads and Lyrics* [1891], *Cuckoo Songs* [1894], *The Wind in the Trees* [1898], and *Irish Poems* [1912]), *Shamrocks* worked across three main themes: cultural ecology in a revivalist form, feminism, and Catholic poetics.[35] As Anna Pilz and Andrew Tierney have shown, much of the environmental work of the Irish Literary Revival was directed toward the reforestation of trees in Ireland. One of the direct effects of colonization had been the destruction of Ireland's native woodland. Emily Taylor, for example, had decried in 1837: "Our trees, who shall restore them! Tradition says, that these mountains were once clothed with oaks and pines, but the English burnt our forests, as they destroyed those in Wales, because they furnished shelter for the rebels, as the Irish were called" (quoted in Pilz and Tierney, "Trees, Big House," 67). This deforestation was superseded by an eco-colonization of certain areas of Ireland. The native landscape was anglicized in big house estates, where the English landscape tradition became the dominant mode. It is for this reason that the Irish revival movement centered on the need to cultivate a native landscape. As Pilz and Tierney write: "The Irish discourse surrounding trees and reforestation of the late nineteenth and early twentieth centuries has its roots in Irish colonial history, and that discourse emerged potently in literary texts that looked to the Irish landscape for narrative and meaning."[36]

This also extended to poetry. In her work, Tynan revived her country's landscape, poeticizing it as profoundly Irish. In poems such as "In the May" (122) and "The Irish Hills" (135), Tynan's forestry imagery is environmentally political. A high point in the book, and the poem that most visibly articulates Tynan's activism and Irishness, is the patriotic "Shamrock Song":

> Oh, the red rose may be fair,
> And the lily statelier;
> But my shamrock, one in three,
> Takes the very heart of me!
>
> (162)

Politically and aesthetically, the poem was the heart of the book, and for this reason, its cover was decorated with the shamrock. Tynan would inspire other Irish women poets, who would also use the shamrock to identify their works with a national literature for Ireland. Iconic book covers are Jane Barlow's *Irish Idylls* (1892) (Figure 7.8) and the superbly decadent Nora Hopper's *Ballads in Prose* (1894) (Figure 7.9). Books are made of paper; they are the offspring of trees. And these books represent the revival of the Irish landscape as a political reinscription of the national. Their covers aligned their eco-poetics with demands for liberty and independence.

While Tynan's "Shamrock Song" may not seem to critique England (the rose) or France (the lily), the poem argues for choice and self-determination.[37] By placing the shamrock alongside two national flowers, Tynan proposes that Ireland is their equal as a nation. Significantly, the poem links the rose and the lily with decay and death, suggesting that empires also decay and die. By contrast the shamrock is a symbol of Irelands' regeneration and reforestation:

> But when Summer died last year
> Rose and lily died with her;
> Shamrock stayeth every day,
> Be the winds or gold or grey.
>
> Irish hills, as grey as the dove,
> Know the little plant I love;
> Warm and fair it mantles them,
> Stretching down from throat to hem.

As in her book cover, the shamrock covers the body of Ireland; it is an all-season plant that preserves the country as ecologically alive and distinct.

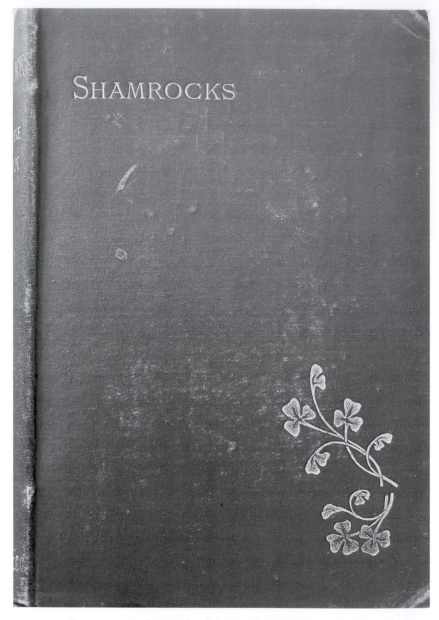

Figure 7.7   Book cover for Katharine Tynan's *Shamrocks* (1887).

Figure 7.8   Book cover for Jane Barlow's *Irish Idylls* (1898).

Figure 7.9　Book cover for Nora Hopper's *Ballads in Prose* (1894).

Shamrocks' politics were the outcome of Tynan's early involvement in Irish politics during the 1880s. One of the founding members of the Ladies' Land League, Tynan defined the movement as "the expression of the Nationalistic spirit in Ireland."[38] Its foundation was suggested by Michael Davitt to continue the political work carried out by the Irish National Land League, a pressure group to win reduction of rent at a time of famine, whose leaders had all been arrested. Tynan wanted to call it the Women's Land League, but she was told it was too democratic (Tynan, *Twenty-Five Years*, 75). Led by Anna Parnell (sister of Charles Stewart Parnell), the Ladies' Land League mirrored the New York Ladies' Land League, whose aim was to raise funds for the Irish cause, and which was led by another sister of Parnell, Fanny.[39] Tynan would explore the work the Ladies' Land League carried out in Ireland in the Catholic ballad "The Charity of the Countess Kathleen." The poem was published in *Ballads and Lyrics* (1891), a book dedicated to Rosa Mulholland.[40] The lyric is an allegory of the women's defense of Irish tenants' rights against landowners. It is based on the Irish folk legend of the Countess Kathleen, who sold her soul to the devil during the Irish famine. She gave this money to tenants who, by this action, were saved from starvation and damnation:

> Black fell potato blight
>   On the kindly fruit;
> Evil demons came by night,
>   Withered flower and root.
> And the corn-ears never filled,
>   And the sun drew dark;
> All the floods of heaven were spilled,
>   And we had no ark. (45)
> . . .
>
> There are come in the town
>   Merchantmen twain;
> Dark are they, of renown,
>   Have sailed many a main.
> With gold fillets on their hair,
>   And gold in their hands,
> They buy a merchandise most rare,
>   The rarest in all lands.
>
>   (46)

Tynan reclaimed autochthonous flora and used Celtic mythology to show how eco-colonialism destroyed landscapes and brought about hunger. Mike Davis's *Late Victorian Holocausts* (2000) and Upamanyu Pablo Mukherjee's *Natural Disasters and Victorian Empire* (2013) have compellingly argued that natural disasters (famines and fevers in particular) were not natural catastrophes per se, but the direct result of colonialism's ferocious capitalism that depleted peoples of the product of their land and labor, thus undermining their capacity for action.[41] In a point of fact, Davis speaks of "climates of hunger" instead of "natural disasters" (Davis, *Late Victorian Holocausts*, 239–78). Davis's and Mukherjee's analyses enlighten Tynan's poem on the Irish famine. For Tynan, the tenants' situation is the result of a catastrophic colonial policy (those "merchant men" with "gold in their hands"). Writing in ballad form, Tynan tied the poem with the Celtic folklore's oral traditions to great effect. Moreover, the poem connected with, and upcycled for the Irish cause, two other key works: the mordant fairy-like sounds of Andrew Lang's Old French ballade "Ballade of Worldly Wealth" (1880), a critique of global capitalism, and Rossetti's attack on global agrilogistics in *Goblin Market*.

In her poetry, Sarojini Naidu would also recover India's autochthonous flora to offset the damage made by British imperialism. As an active politician who led India to independence from British rule, one of Naidu's main strategies was to recover the precolonial and preindustrial landscape of India, its plant world as well as village life. In "Ode to H.H. The Nizam of Hyderabad," for example, she speaks of how "ancient forests hoard and hold / the legends of their centuried sleep."[42] Primarily, Naidu's aim was always to appraise India as an aesthetic ancient cosmopolitan nation built for tomorrow. She did this in two ways. First, as an Indian poet writing in English, she upcycled English to decolonize it. Secondly, as a symbolist, her poems became pregnant with the potential for a utopian landscape.

The key to her eco-activism was her strategy of upcycling English, robbing it from its national context to convert it into an Anglophone world language.[43] She extracted from it, and decolonized it from, its English imagery, and reconditioned it with an antique and symbolic landscape from India's past that envisioned India's future, cutting out India's colonial present. She transformed English into an Anglophone language, without an imperial identity politics, with which to transmit the idea of an already cosmopolitan India to influence a global audience ("In brotherhood of diverse creeds, / And harmony of diverse race" as she put it in "Ode to H.H. The Nizam of Hyderabad" [59]). Aesthetically and politically, her poetry was deeply embedded into the many Indian cultures and languages of present and past, including Sanskrit and metrical and stanzaic forms of Urdu-Persian literature, for example. Though, as she acknowledged in a 1906 letter to Toru Dutt's father, "it needs a scholar, and a true lover of that ancient literature, one who lives close to the meaning and reality of all that antique world of speech and silence to judge whether a modern like me – a little [?] spoilt by unessential [sic] western things – has caught the genuine note" (Naidu, *Selected Letters*, 50).

Formally and philosophically, Naidu was a symbolist, and she used the landscape of India as her imagery. This symbolism has been derided by critics such as Makarand Paranjape, for whom "the India of her poems is . . . an exotic place" (Paranjape, "Introduction," 15). She was not always successful in her strategy, which often eliminated from view the damage caused not only by colonialism but by feudalism too. She has been for this reason often interpreted too literally. But in refusing an aesthetic of realism, Naidu aimed to transcend eco-colonialism to pursue a reenchantment with the Indian landscape through a reactivation of its mythic quality. It also enabled a rereading of the landscape with an intrinsic eco-critical view by giving her symbols the capacity to illuminate what had been lost, to imagine a new future. Naidu was thinking in a manner best expressed by Spivak's concept of planetarity, that is, configured symbolically the radical otherness of the landscape of India by showing how India's many cultures and collectives lived with the landscape before colonialism permanently changed the relations between nature, humans, and nonhumans.

The Golden Threshold was published in 1905 and contains poems written in England (1896–98), as well as in India between 1898 and 1905. The book symbolizes the union of two poetic identities: the rising star in decadent symbolist circles in London that included Mathilde Blind, Edmund Gosse, and Arthur Symons, and the proclaimed national poet of India after her return to the country. The collection is for this reason a liminal book about crossing thresholds: a transnational book in its creation that was aesthetically orientated toward resisting an imagery of colonized India; a revivalist book of an antique India for the creation of a tomorrow's India; an atemporal book about Indian life and a book that made India the country of decadence; politically green but aesthetically gold; rural and mystic.[44]

The collection focuses on the Indian countryside, particularly the section called "Folk Songs." In the fascinating "Village-Song" a female speaker rejects marriage and motherhood because she has heard the voice of nature. She leaves village life and goes to the wild forest to become a poet:

> Mother mine, to the wild forest I am going,
> Where upon the champa boughs the champa buds are blowing;
> To the köil-haunted river-isles where lotus lilies glisten,
> The voices of the fairy-folk are calling me: O listen!
>
> (37)

Whilst the speaker here is not Naidu, the poem does highlight her call to poetry as political: the renaissance of the champa boughs and buds announce the renaissance of India, where the national flower, the lotus lily, glistens. The call of the Indian forest represents her laced identity as a decadent and national poet.

It is this renaissance that *The Golden Threshold* proposes. Mahesh Rangarajan has argued that the colonial era in India was a watershed in India's environmental history, which, in large scales, caused deforestation to build railways, facilitated the control of wild animals, and created canal-irrigated land.[45] Naidu never addressed these major areas directly, but they emerge in her symbology. A case in point is the poem "Snake-Charmer," a critique of colonialism and Indian patriarchy (33–34). With "the magic of [his] flute-call," the snake-charmer tries to tame the snake under the veil of providing food. Their relationship is sexual, with the male snake-charmer "mellifluous[ly]" trying to woo the female snake into the seclusion of a basket. But the snake never shows up; one imagines she remains distrustful of the charmer's allure, or perhaps the destruction of the ecosystem has decimated them. Or "Corn-grinders," in which a mouse, a deer, and a bride all suffer the consequences (presumably) of colonialism: their lovers are killed by farmers and hunters though we are not told why the spouse-to-be dies (35–36). The poem gets its meaning from the Vedanta philosophy of transmigration or rebirth: the possibility that the same soul is experiencing the same traumas. But it also speaks of the universality of pain felt by sentient beings, which Naidu sees as vulnerable and defenseless in India's patriarchal social system. In all these poems, symbolism is what allows one to cross the golden threshold between poetics and politics, the destruction of the Indian ecosystem and the political battle for India's independence.

In poem after poem, the otherness of the Indian landscape occupies the space of poetry in English. "In Praise of Henna" is a case in point (39). Naidu transforms the henna into the heart of the art of India and its traditions, highlighting how it brings together art, humans, and nature. In a world of coal-tar synthetic dyes devised for the textile industry, the poem "praises" the Henna tree, whose leaves, when ground, produce a natural pigment used by women in India since antiquity to paint hands and feet, particularly during the Mehndi pre-wedding ceremony. Another fascinating poem in this respect is "In the Forest," perhaps Naidu's most outspoken poem, in which the Indian forest becomes the place from which to fight back:

Here, O my heart, let us burn the dear dreams that are dead,
Here in this wood let us fashion a funeral pyre
Of fallen white petals and leaves that are mellow and red,
Here let us burn them in noon's flaming torches of fire.

We are weary, my heart, we are weary, so long we have borne
The heavy loved burden of dreams that are dead, let us rest,
Let us scatter their ashes away, for a while let us mourn;
We will rest, O my heart, till the shadows are gray in the west.

But soon we must rise, O my heart, we must wander again
Into the war of the world and the strife of the throng;
Let us rise, O my heart, let us gather the dreams that remain,
We will conquer the sorrow of life with the sorrow of song.

(63–64)

Gaining strength from the forest, she grounds India's political battle in its
autochthonous ecology.

Conclusion

In a 1909 essay entitled "Tithonus," Meynell would disparage against
using wax liquified with petroleum on the Portland stone of St. Paul's
cathedral for restoration purposes. "Posterity," she adds, "is not compelled
to keep our pictures or our books in existence, nor to read nor to look at
them; but it is more or less obliged to have a stone building in view for an
age or two." (Meynell, "Tithonus," 81). "This is not a matter of art-
criticism," she writes, but an "ethical question hitherto unstudied" (85)
Art must be environmentally sustainable. The irony of using petroleum to
save a monument that would be so badly damaged across time by pollution
is not lost to us, and neither was it to Alice Meynell who, as we have seen,
saw how pollution radically altered London's architecture. And yet, though
the essay was anchored on the ethics of restoring St. Paul's with petroleum,
Meynell's point is about her generation's responsibility toward the future.
She asks: "Will this victory over our sons' sons be the last resolute tyranny
prepared by one age for the coercion, constraint, and defeat of the future?"
(81). "Tithonus" is a meditation on how the present forces itself – often
violently – upon the future, whether posterity likes it or not, hence her call
for an ethical approach to environmental politics.

The 1890s were perhaps aesthetically yellow, but they were politically
green. I began this chapter arguing for a rereading of women's 1890s

poetry in light of their own environmental moment fundamentally because, to repurpose Meynell's phrase, it has remained largely unstudied. My analysis demonstrates that women's aestheticist and decadent poetry looks radically different when focusing on the environmental politics of their time. It has also uncovered that some of the most advanced ecological thinking of the period was produced by women poets. They experimented with genres such as the pastoral, realist, and symbolist poetry and turned them into portable structures capable of producing potent critiques of environmental politics at all levels: rural, metropolitan, national, and transnational. They worked with meters to produce nuanced political readings of environmental imperialism. Pollution became in their hands the material of impressionism, with their urban poetics depicting wind and smoke as bedfellows of an environmentally damaged modern world. Their anticolonial, feminist thought is the foliage of their poetics. My analysis also fundamentally shows that the landscape of women's poetry of the 1890s looks different too: poets forgotten by past and modern scholarship become central to understand the period, its poetries, and its politics.

Ecology was clearly for Meynell a question of ethics, the responsibility of one's generation toward the future. The writings of women poets of the 1890s speak to us of our own concerns with the natural world and warn us of our own responsibility to the future. These women and their poetry urge us to act ethically when planet-thinking the world.

Notes

1 Fabienne Moine, *Women Poets in the Victorian Era: Cultural Practices and Nature Poetry* (Surrey: Ashgate, 2015); and Patricia Murphy, *Reconceiving Nature: Eco-Feminism in Late Victorian Women's Poetry* (Columbia, MO: University of Missouri Press, 2019).

2 Dennis Denisoff, *Decadent Ecology in British Literature and Art, 1860–1910: Decay, Desire, and the Pagan Revival* (Cambridge: Cambridge University Press, 2022).

3 Elizabeth Miller, *Extraction Ecologies and the Literature of the Long Exhaustion* (Princeton, NJ: Princeton University Press, 2021), 3.

4 Gayatri Spivak, *Death of a Discipline* (New York: Columbia University Press, 2003), 71–102 (72).

5 Mathilde Blind, *Shelley's View of Nature Contrasted with Darwin's* (London: Privately Printed, 1886), 9.

6 Jason W. Moore, *Capitalism in the Web of Life: Ecology and the Accumulation of Capital* (London: Verso, 1915), 3.

7 Raymond Williams, *The Country and the City* (London: Chatto & Windus, 1973); Raymond Williams, Gerald MacLean, and Donna Landry, eds., *The Country and The City Revisited: England and the Politics of Culture, 1550–1850* (New York: Cambridge University Press, 1999). Useful are Gemma Goodman and Charlotte Mathieson, *Gender and Space in Rural Britain* (London: Chatto & Windus, 2014); and Margaret Thomas-Evans and Whitney Womack Smith, eds., *Representing Rural Women* (London: Lexington Books, 2019). The latter has sections on the New Woman, but none includes research on women's poetry.

8 Kinuko Craft, "Lizzie's Temptation," from *Goblin Market* by Christina Rossetti, in *Playboy* (Sept. 1973):115–19.

9 Christina Rossetti, *Goblin Market*, illustrated by Laurence Housman (London: Macmillan & Co, 1893). All quotations from *Goblin Market* are from this text.

10 Laurence Housman, *Unexpected Years* (London: Jonathan Cape, 1937), 118.

11 John Ruskin to Dante Gabriel Rossetti, January 24, 1861, in *Letters of Dante Gabriel Rossetti*, vol. 2, eds. Oswald Doughty and John Robert Wahl (Oxford: The Clarendon Press, 1965), 391.

12 A. Mary F. Robinson, *The New Arcadia and Other Poems* (London: Ellis & White, 1884).

13 A. Mary F. Robinson (Madame Duclaux), *The Collected Poems. Lyrical and Narrative of Mary Robinson* (London: T. Fisher Unwin, 1902), x.

14 Emily Harrington, *Second Person Singular. Late Victorian Women Poets and the Bonds of Verse* (Charlottesville and London: University of Virginia Press, 2014), 102.

15 Mathilde Blind, *The Heather on Fire: A Tale of the Highland Clearances* (London: Walter Scott, 1886).

16 See James Diedrick, *Mathilde Blind. Late-Victorian Culture and the Woman of Letters* (Charlottesville, VA: University of Virginia Press, 2017), 201–02.

17 Tim Ingold, *The Perception of the Environment* (London: Routledge, 2000), 189.

18 William Sharp, *Papers Critical and Reminiscent. Selected and Arranged by Mrs William Sharp* (New York: Duffield & Company, 1912), 70.

19 Emma Mason, *Christina Rossetti. Poetry, Ecology, Faith* (Oxford: Oxford University Press, 2018), 24.

20 Timothy Morton, *Dark Ecology: For a Logic of Future Coexistence* (New York: Columbia University Press, 2016), 159.

21 Vernon Lee and Clementina Anstruther-Thomson, *Beauty and Ugliness and Other Studies in Psychological Aesthetics* (London: John Lane, 1912).

22 Susan David Bernstein, "Recycling Poetics: Amy Levy's London Plane Trees," *Nineteenth-Century Studies* 24 (2010): 101–22.

23 For Levy's London, see my Ana Parejo Vadillo, *Women Poets and Urban Aestheticism: Passengers of Modernity* (Houndsmill: Palgrave Macmillan, 2005), 38–73.

24 Henry W. Lawrence, *City Trees: Historical Geography from the Renaissance through the Nineteenth Century* (Charlottesville, VA: University of Virginia Press, 2006), 273.

25 Luce Irigaray and Michael Marder, *Through Vegetal Being [Two Philosophical Perspectives]* (New York: Columbia University Press, 2016). See in particular his chapter "Seeking Refuge in the Vegetable World" (117–21).

26 See Anna Pilz and Andrew Tierney, "Trees, Big House Culture, and the Irish Literary Revival," *New Hibernia Review* 19, no. 2 (2015): 65–82 (73).

27 Alice Meynell, *The Poems of Alice Meynell. Complete ed.* (New York: Charles Scribner's Sons, 1923), 119.

28 Alice Meynell, "Grass," in *The Colour of Life and Other Essays on Things Seen and Heard* (London: John Lane, 1896), 61. See also Linda H. Peterson, "Writing Nature at the *Fin de Siècle*: Grant Allen, Alice Meynell, and the Split Legacy of Gilbert White," *Victorian Review* 36, no. 2 (Fall 2010): 80–91.

29 Alice Meynell, *Ceres' Runaway & Other Essays* (London: Burns & Oates, 1909), 9.

30 Alice Meynell, "A Dead Harvest," in *Later Poems* (London: John Lane, The Bodley Head, 1902), 31–32.

31 Alice Meynell, *London Impressions. Etchings and Pictures in Photogravure by William Hyde and essays by Alice Meynell* (London: Archibald Constable, 1898).

32 For more on Tynan's life see Katharine Tynan, *Twenty-Five* Years: *Reminiscences* (Smith, Elder & Co., 1913); Katharine Tynan, *The Years of the Shadow* (London: Constable & Company, 1916); Katharine Tynan, *The Middle Years* (London: Constable & Company Ltd, 1916); and Katharine Tynan, *Memories* (London: Eveleigh Nash & Grayson, 1924).

33 Katharine Tynan, *Shamrocks* (London: Kegan Paul, 1887).

34 Damian Atkinson, *The Selected Letters of Alice Meynell: Poet and Essayist.* (Newcastle upon Tyne: Cambridge Scholars, 2013), 31. (Italics in the original).

35 For a nuanced analysis of Tynan's difficult position after the fall of Parnell and her "exile" in London see Whitney Standlee, "'A World of Difference': London and Ireland in the Works of Katharine Tynan," in *Irish Writing London: Vol. I. Revival to the Second World War*, ed. Tom Herron (London: Bloomsbury, 2013), 70–83.

36 See Pilz and Tierney on the complex history of reforestation in nineteenth-century Ireland as influenced by English colonialism.

37 See Octavian Blewitt, *The Rose and the Lily: How They Became the Emblems of England and France: A Fairy Tale* (London: Chatto & Windus, 1877).

38 Katharine Tynan, *Twenty-Five Years: Reminiscences* (New York: Devin-Adair Company, 1913), 81.

39 Diana Urquhart, "'The Ladies' Land League have [sic] a crust to share with you': The rhetoric of the Ladies' Land League's British campaign, 1881–2," in *Irish Women, War and Letters, 1880–1922*, eds. T. O'Toole and G. McIntosh

(Dublin: UCD Press, 2016), 11–24. See also, Tina O'Toole, *The Irish New Woman* (Houndsmill: Palgrave Macmillan, 2013).

40 Katharine Tynan, *Ballads and Lyrics* (London: Kegan Paul, Trench, Trübner, 1891), 45–50.

41 Mike Davis, *Late Victorian Holocausts* (London: Verso, 2000); Upamanyu Pablo Mukherjee, *Natural Disasters and Victorian Empire* (London: Palgrave Macmillan, 2013).

42 Sarojini Naidu, "Ode to H.H. The Nizam of Hyderabad. Presented at the Ramzan Durbar," in *The Golden Threshold,* with an Introduction by Arthur Symons (London: Heinemann, 1905), 60. This poem is an example of the complex position of Naidu in India at the turn of the century as seen from a postcolonial perspective. She presented it to Mir Mhbub Ali Khan (1866–1911), the Nizam of Hyderabad, a charismatic ruler. The poem was translated into Urdu by a well-known poet, Naidu writes, though today his identity remains unknown. Naidu writes that "it is something quite novel in the annals of Indian tradition for a woman to present a poem to a sovereign in full durbar. It savours almost of the forbidden." See Sarojini Naidu, *Selected Letters 1890s–1940s,* ed. Makarand Paranjape (New Delhi: Kali for Women, 1996), 41. Paranjape, however, notes that Naidu "always remained loyal to the Nizam" because her husband was his employee. He further notes that "it gave her the comfort to retreat into a dream world, to deny the onslaught of modernity and capitalism." See Sarojini Naidu, *Selected Poetry and Prose,* ed. Makarand Paranjape (New Delhi: Harper Collins, 1991), 15–16. The poem feels antique but it was written thus on purpose. In my view, Paranjape misses its feminist and nationalist tone through which she invokes India's cosmo-politan past and its landscape to offset the forces of colonialism, whose fight she will lead. The poem in true decadent style invokes and emulates the poetry of Persian poet Abul-Qâsem Ferdowsi Tusi (940–1010 BCE), particularly his *Shahnameh* (which translates as *Book of Kings*).

43 See Akshya Saxena, *Vernacular English. Reading the Anglophone in Postcolonial India* (Princeton, NJ: Princeton University Press, 2022). Saxena argues that English in India is a vernacular language. She proposes moving away from the term global English, which conforms to colonial power, and suggests using instead the term Anglophone, because it speaks of world cultures.

44 See my own Ana Parejo Vadillo, "Decadent Women Poets: Translingual Thresholds," *Feminist Modernist Studies* 4, no. 2 (2021): 146–65.

45 Mahesh Rangarajan, "Environment and Ecology Under British Rule," in *India and the British Empire,* eds. Douglas M. Peers and Nandini Gooptu (Oxford: Oxford University Press, 2012), 212–31.

CHAPTER 8

"Only Nature Is a Thing Unreal": The Anthropocene 1890s

Elizabeth Carolyn Miller

To most students of the period, the 1890's in England . . . are less a chronological designation than a state of mind. For some, the decade conjures yellow visions of Decadence, of putrescence in life and art, with its loss of the "complete view" of man in nature, perhaps best symbolized by fetid hothouses where monstrous orchids, seemingly artificial, are cultivated as a challenge to nature and an assertion of man's cunning.

> Preface to Karl Beckson's *Aesthetes and Decadents of the 1890's* (1966)[1]

Nature is so indifferent, so unappreciative. Whenever I am walking in the park here, I always feel that I am no more to her than . . . the burdock that blooms in the ditch.

> Oscar Wilde, "The Decay of Lying" (1889; 1891)[2]

Years before the term Anthropocene was coined, Karl Beckson's classic 1966 anthology on the literature of the 1890s opened with this chapter's first epigraph, foreshadowing several descriptive tropes of the anthropogenic age: the alienation of "man" from "nature," the key figure of the greenhouse or hothouse, and the object of nature (here, an orchid) that seems newly monstrous and unnatural.[3] The menace of "man's cunning" against nature is now measured in parts per million, but in the 1890s it was already being measured in *fleurs du mal*.[4] Arthur Symons's 1895 poem "Violet," for example, praises the "sweet white wildwood violet" found growing amid the orchids "under hot-house glass" where "the flowers forget / How the sun shines."[5] This stray hothouse violet has taken on "the orchid's coloring," growing "in this spice-laden atmosphere, / Where only nature is a thing unreal." Far superior to Wilde's "burdock that blooms in the ditch," this fantastic hothouse violet is, for Symons's speaker, the "artificial flower of my ideal." Theodore Wratislaw's 1896 poem "Hothouse Flowers" offers a less sophisticated take on the same decadent trope: "I hate the flower of wood or common field," the

170

speaker says, and "the cultured garden's banal yield," but "I love those flowers reared by man's careful art."[6]

Beckson reads "the exotic flowers that grow in decadent literature" and the hothouses in which they grow as "central images of the decadents' disdain of nature" (Beckson, "Introduction," xxvii).[7] The decadent hothouse flower trope can be traced back to Charles Baudelaire and J. K. Huysmans, and both Elizabeth Hope Chang and Dennis Denisoff have held it up for extended ecocritical analysis – Chang emphasizing the temporal and geographical estrangements produced by the greenhouse garden, and Denisoff calling attention to the many decadent writers (hothouse trope notwithstanding) who actually "relied heavily on nature and nature worship for conceptualizing and articulating their nonnormative tastes and social values."[8] Such work usefully updates and revises the "disdain of nature" hypothesis articulated by Beckson and other early critics of decadence – going back to Max Nordau, who also described the decadents' "aversion to nature" in his diatribe *Degeneration* (1892–93, English trans. 1895).[9] But I want to begin this chapter by instead reading the prevalence of decadent hothouses and hothouse flowers as paradigmatic of the greenhouse gas effect and thus as projections of the power of human anthropogenic agency over seemingly impervious natural domains such as climate and the atmosphere.[10] In this way the decadent greenhouse will provide a point of departure for this chapter's broader investigation of the Anthropocene imaginaries of the fin de siècle and their reorientation of the literary and cultural imagination toward new understandings of time and the human place in the natural world.

When we revisit this period with a perspective informed by ecocriticism and the climate change humanities, the 1890s emerge as a microperiod of concentrated meaning – a hothouse of the Anthropocene – with the era's texts and authors providing an intensely distilled account of the arrival of anthropogenic nature. For this reason, I will suggest, the 1890s have a special significance in the literary history of the Anthropocene, not only due to the themes of the era's literature but also the methods through which we have studied it. The fin-de-siècle has traditionally been understood to be the era when artifice triumphed over nature, but reexamining the period today, we can instead see how literature and art of the period reckoned with the idea of an indeterminate nature without design, purpose, or end, profoundly shaped by human forces and yet beyond human reckoning and control. The concentrated finitude of the era reflects its own grasp of the finitudes and vicissitudes of the natural world.

At the same time, writers of this era also grappled with the tangle of meanings gathered together under the sign of "natural." Symons's description of the hothouse flower, in the poem quoted above, denaturalizes nature itself by declaring "only nature is a thing unreal." This suggests the complex registers of meaning and reference in which the hothouse image intervenes, for the term "natural" has multiple, overlapping implications: it can denote "ordinary; conforming to a usual or normal character," or "formed by nature; not subject to human intervention, not artificial," or "occurring in, or part of, the environment."[11] "Natural" overlaps with "normative," in other words, while also problematically referring to an order of being separate from the human, and this complex of meanings constitutes a terminological (and epistemological) obstacle in our understanding of decadent nature as well as anthropogenic nature.

In his important article "Fin du Globe: On Decadent Planets," Benjamin Morgan argues that "although decadence is often associated with a rejection of nature in favor of artifice, it is better understood as a mode of ecological thought that undermines the distinction between the natural and the made."[12] Such a distinction between the natural and the made is an example of the kind of binary thinking that has traditionally separated "Nature" from "Society" in Western epistemology, "the Cartesian order ... in which Society and Nature interact rather than interpenetrate" as Jason Moore describes it, a dualism that Moore identifies at the core of "the violence of modernity," "drip[ping] with blood and dirt."[13] The nature/society binary has long obscured the reality of human interdependence with the world around us as well as the profound human impacts on Earth's creatures and systems.[14] But decadent literature, as Morgan says, called into question the conception of nature as "not subject to human intervention," and the enclosed atmosphere of the greenhouse or hothouse, an image that appeared frequently across the work of decadent writers, put forth a microcosm of this human-shaped environment.[15] Even further, as Jesse Oak Taylor and Heidi C. M. Scott have both discussed, nineteenth-century glasshouses "provided the basis for conceiving of Earth's atmosphere in terms of the greenhouse effect," modeling a "condition in which nature exists" not apart from the human but "apart from itself," which is to say, in a state of profound alteration and disruption.[16]

Disruption was the order of the day in the 1890s. Oscar Wilde's April 1895 arrest in London was perhaps the defining event of the decadent era and a historical watershed in the legal history of non-normative sexuality; and though it may seem completely unrelated, it was just one year later, in

April 1896, that Svante Arrhenius published his watershed article "On the Influence of Carbonic Acid in the Air upon the Temperature of the Ground" in the *London, Edinburgh, and Dublin Philosophical Magazine and Journal of Science*. Arrhenius's publication was the first to attempt to calculate what we now call the greenhouse gas effect (although it did not use the words "greenhouse," "hothouse," or "glasshouse"). The article asked, "Is the mean temperature of the ground in any way influenced by the presence of heat-absorbing gases in the atmosphere?"[17] In posing this question, Arrhenius was far more concerned with the long history of global temperature change and the origins of the Ice Age than with the climate impacts of "the industrial development of our time" (271), which he saw as minimal, but nevertheless his work provided an empirical basis for the idea that an "effect on the earth's temperature" would result from a "variation of the aërial carbonic acid [CO_2]" (263).[18] If the hothouse is, as Taylor has put it, "the quintessential habitat of the Anthropocene" (23), the prominence of this image and trope within decadent literature and the near-simultaneous calculation of the greenhouse gas effect within scientific literature suggest, together, that this period has a special significance for the literary history of the Anthropocene, or at least that the Anthropocene has a special significance for understanding this period. In this chapter, I aim to tease out the environmental and ecological inheritance of the decadent 1890s while simultaneously teasing apart the complex conceptual contestation between rival assaults on the category of the "natural" within this era, assaults that can be roughly grouped around Wilde's 1895 denaturalizing of heterosexuality and Arrhenius's 1896 denaturalizing of the atmosphere. This conglomeration of seemingly unrelated events made the 1890s, as I will argue, a period of intensely concentrated disruptions of the very idea of "the natural," accompanied by observations on the rise of anthropogenic nature in the industrial era.

The Anthropocene 1890s

We are now living, as the Anthropocene Working Group has proposed, in a new geological age characterized by the transformation of Earth systems through anthropogenic activities.[19] As we survey the path of modernity's storm and anticipate its future permutations, stratigraphers and cultural historians debate when, exactly, the Anthropocene began: the birth of the steam engine in the British Industrial Revolution has been one contender; the nuclear era and the post–World War II Great Acceleration another. Some recent critics have suggested that its origins are traceable less to a particular technological regime than to a means of organizing social, labor, and natural relations, such as capitalism, colonialism, or the plantation system.[20] To my knowledge, the 1890s have never been hazarded as a starting point for the Anthropocene, and it is not my intention to suggest that they should be; in an ideational sense, however, the decade warrants a reconsideration from the standpoint of anthropogenic climate change, and the prevalence of literary and figurative greenhouses at the very moment when the greenhouse gas effect was first being calculated is but one indication that this is the case.

Regardless of which origin story one settles on, the Anthropocene thesis has already forced a widespread reconsideration of periodization within the humanities, asking us to think at wider scales and to connect the past to the present in new ways.[21] World ecology, world systems theory, the Anthropocene, the planetary: there is no shortage of new ways to think big. What are the implications of such magnitudinous approaches for scholarly work on the diminutive period of the 1890s, especially in literary criticism? Viewed now in the context of climate history, slow violence, and ecological crises such as climate change that play out over the longue durée, it may be difficult to sustain the idea that the 1890s are as exceptional as they have seemed.[22] The decade makes for an unusual period of literary history precisely because of its brevity. In these ten years that shook the world (so the story goes), Victorianism died, modernism was born, and everything changed – everything, it would seem, except the weather. Lord Henry's flip remark in *The Picture of Dorian Gray* (1890, 1891), "I don't desire to change anything in England except the weather," takes its humor from the supposed imperviousness of the weather to human intervention, but in the era of global warming, the line invites new questions about the ecological significance of the fin de siècle and the particular environmental imagination which grew from this era – an imagination cultivated from within the weather-altering capacities of the greenhouse.[23]

Considering, for example, that Lord Henry's family's money comes at least in part from the coal industry, his line about changing the weather takes on a new air. For it was understood by the 1890s that the burning of coal actually *does have* the capacity to change the weather, if not the climate (since climate change was not fully theorized at the time, as discussed earlier in this chapter with reference to Arrhenius's work).[24] More importantly, as Wilde's novel suggests, the fossil economy was also imagined to have an unprecedented capacity to free individuals from the constraints of environmental materiality. In a novel full of leisured, languid characters,

Lord Fermor, who is Lord Henry's uncle, has perfected "the great aristo-cratic art of doing absolutely nothing" by paying "some attention to the management of his collieries in the Midland counties, excusing himself from this taint of industry on the ground that the one advantage of having coal was that it enabled a gentleman to afford the decency of burning wood on his own hearth" (Wilde, *Dorian,* 71). Fossil capital is equated here with a complete freedom from the burdens of labor and with a total access to consumer choice, such that one may opt to heat his home with wood despite literally owning a coal mine. Such incredible magnitude of personal freedom is evident also in Lord Henry's expressed desire to change the weather, and in his famous declaration that "what our century wants" is "a new hedonism" (63).

Dorian Gray's new hedonism is an Anthropocene hedonism, not a classical hedonism, for it translates not just to the pursuit of sexual and sensual pleasure, but also to a denial of natural limits that manifests, most obviously, in the phenomenal acquisitiveness of title character Dorian Gray. Dipesh Chakrabarty has argued that the "mansion of modern freedoms stands on an ever-expanding base of fossil-fuel use," and I would suggest that the pointed inclusion of Lord Fermor's collieries in *Dorian Gray* is a nod to the economic roots of the freewheeling consump-tion enjoyed by the novel's characters.[25] Dorian's collections of gemstones, textiles, and ecclesiastical vestments, among other beautiful objects, form the primary subject of chapter 11, where they are cataloged and described at length. If Dorian's sins are famously left to readers' imaginations, his purchases are lengthily documented in great detail in a chapter that describes, as Potolsky puts it, "his descent into decadence" (Potolsky, *Decadent Republic,* 17). "Pleasure is Nature's test, her sign of approval," Lord Henry remarks (Wilde, *Dorian,* 114), but importantly, pleasure in this novel extends well beyond the realm of the bodily into the realm of consumption, property, and object ownership, exemplifying, perhaps, Benjamin Morgan's useful framing of decadence as "an expression of the over-refined individual thriving at the expense of the whole" (Morgan, "Fin du Globe," 621).

Dorian Gray is a monument in the history of gay literature and was even quoted and discussed in the context of Wilde's trial, but today we must wrestle with the connection the novel sometimes draws between a release from sexual puritanism and a release from finite nature.[26] To overcon-sume, the novel at times seems to suggest, is to overcome "tedious ... middle-class virtue" (Wilde, *Dorian,* 144). At the same time, however, the novel also presents such excessive acquisitiveness as a drug, not unlike the opium which Dorian will also come to imbibe: "these treasures, and everything that [Dorian] collected in his lovely house, were to be to him means of forgetfulness, modes by which he could escape" (172). What is more, *Dorian Gray's* deeper, more philosophical materialism continually relocates us back *within* the bounds and affordances of nature, even despite the supernatural plot and the characters' immoderate consumption.[27] Dorian is apt, for example, to trace "the thoughts and passions of men to some pearly cell in the brain or some white nerve in the body" and to link "the absolute dependence of the spirit on certain physical conditions" (166). Lord Henry, too, wonders "whether we could ever make psychology so absolute a science that each little spring of life would be revealed to us" (97). Such formulations of the metaphysics of morality and desire suggest a liveliness, a "spring of life," within the material world, a vision of environmental materiality that is vital rather than inert, contravening the logics of objectification and accumulation. In this sense *Dorian Gray* captures a paradox of the Anthropocene, where the agency of the natural world becomes manifest precisely in the wake of its abject commodification.[28]

This paradox is also central to another novel of the 1890s, H. G. Wells's *The War of the Worlds* (1898), which opens with a vision of humanity lulled into a false sense of overmastering agency over an inert universe: "With infinite complacency men went to and fro over this globe about their little affairs, serene in their assurance of their empire over matter." Under these conditions, "no one gave a thought to the older world of space" – until space asserts itself in the form of a Martian attack.[29] Ultimately, however, once the Martians are defeated, the narrator comes to feel that the invasion was "not without its ultimate benefit" since it "robbed us of that serene confidence in the future which is the most fruitful source of decadence" (Wells, *War of the Worlds,* 179). *The War of the Worlds* was written and published in the 1890s, at the height of the decadent movement, but it is set in the early twentieth century. To describe "the great disillusionment" of human agency that came with the Martian invasion, and the consequent end of the decadent stage, Wells found it necessary to look to the near future. Wells's temporal imagination, spilling into the twentieth century, raises the question again of how to situate the 1890s within the Anthropocene framework and whether the period's scope is too short to afford any special anthropogenic significance, given how crucial temporal duration must be to any form of environmental consciousness. To convincingly depict catastrophic change, Wells felt the need to move beyond his own decade, and after all, a ten-year period barely registers within the vast scale of geological history. Yet this point is popularly understood today at least in part thanks to another work published by Wells in the 1890s, *The Time Machine* (1895), a novel that resolutely stays fixed to one place (southwest suburban London) while imaginatively voyaging forward to the year 802,701 CE and beyond – till the end of the Earth.

In different ways, in other words, these 1890s novels by Wells and Wilde are all grappling with similar questions around environmental agency and temporal duration, suggesting the centrality of this decade to the Anthropocene as an idea. The example of *The Time Machine* reminds us that literature is not fixed to its moment but is an essentially durational art, one that grows from existing literature, archives its own moment, and persists into the future every time it is read, sometimes even imagining the future within its pages. Dorian Gray's portrait within Wilde's novel is a figure for this durational capacity, since – contrary to the nature of most portraits – it records its subject's gradual degradation and degeneration over time and experience even while his body persists, intact and unmarked by the years' ravages. As the greenhouse concentrates light and atmosphere, the portrait concentrates years, referencing the temporal frames through which we read art, literature, and literary movements.[30] Though initially the painting memorializes just one modeling session at the beginning of the novel, it comes to convey an arc of change across the whole of Dorian's lifetime; similarly, the arts of the fin de siècle convey a longer history and future of change and decline. In a discussion of M. P. Shiel's decadent novel *The Purple Cloud* (1901), Morgan has suggested that "cultural production[s] of the fin-de-siècle Decadent Movement can help us understand the promise as well as the limitations of a widely held view that criticism oriented by climate change requires expanded scales of analysis that are cognizant of planetary space and deep time" (Morgan, "Fin du Globe," 610). In a novel like *Dorian Gray*, we can see the virtue of contracted as well as expanded scales of analysis, and we can see how decadence shadowed forth the end of the world from the rather delimited experience of the end of the century. To the extent that the painting of Dorian is a metacommentary on the role of art in a decadent society, Wilde seems to suggest that art's compactness imbues it with the capacity to miniaturize problems otherwise too large to grasp.

Hothouse Periodization: Micro-scaling and the Concentration of Meaning

We might say, then, that Dorian Gray's portrait, and the Decadent Movement more generally, are case studies for microscaling as a literary-environmental method: an interpretive mode where the small elucidates the big, where the foreshortened or delimited renders the wide-angle view. The fin de siècle and its decadent imaginary appear capable of perceiving fin du globe precisely from the narrow circumstance of a century's end: the greenhouse gas effect captured in the green carnation. This figure and method of magnification, I want to suggest, has long been an underlying, underdiscussed principle in our approaches to the 1890s and our dominant ways of understanding the period. Take the career of Wilde, the writer who often serves to embody the 1890s as the spirit of the age. His career was tragically shortened by imprisonment with hard labor under the charge of "gross indecency," and by his premature death following his release, but Wilde's artificially limited oeuvre has proved remarkably expansive. He should have written more novels, but he wrote only one – a circumstance that inspired a recent internet list to declare, "You Only Need To Strike Gold Once. Wilde only completed one novel – but *The Picture of Dorian Gray* is one of the best ever."[31] In part because of its singularity, *Dorian Gray* has been understood to magnify the story of its age in all its distorted temporalities. Comparing Wilde's lifetime, 1854–1900, with those of his close contemporaries George Bernard Shaw (1856–1950) or H. G. Wells (1866–1946), we can see why: Wilde's early death, which stopped him at the doorstep of the twentieth century, invites the peculiar interpretive formation that I have called microscaling, where magnitude is grasped through miniaturization.

The fin de siècle, too, was a period defined by its end, and its power was amplified by its limit. In this way, the 1890s eerily resemble the Anthropocene imaginary, which rests, above all, on the idea of "this world that will have been," as Rob Nixon has recently phrased it.[32] As several critics have discussed, the dominant trope of Anthropocene discourse is that of "an alien geologist from the future" who "detects in the strata of the ground evidence of the presence of humans long after we have gone extinct."[33] Who will remain to read such evidence in the Earth? "Nature is always behind the age," as Vivian says in "The Decay of Lying, "and in some ways, authors of the 1890s seem to have voiced the pre-posthumous Anthropocene condition long before the accumulation of greenhouse gases in the atmosphere led to widespread recognition of the dominant form of environmental catastrophe in the industrial age (Wilde, "Decay," 1078).

Vivian's claim that "Nature is always behind the age" is a precursor for his more famous assertion in "The Decay of Lying" that "Nature, no less than Life, is an imitation of Art" (1086). In leading up to this point, Vivian's interlocutor Cyril prompts him to define his terms, and Vivian significantly presents his intervention as encompassing "nature" in both the "normative" and "environmental" senses. In other words, he claims that his point holds whether "we take Nature to mean natural simple instinct as opposed to self-conscious culture" or whether "we regard Nature as the collection of phenomena external to man" (1078). This is important because it suggests that Wilde's dialogue, in its famous declaration that nature imitates art, is taking on the entire constellation of meanings gathered under the sign of "nature." His discussion of nature does not, perhaps cannot, separate the natural world from its etymological connection to normativity and its etymological opposition to culture and art. This helps explain Wilde's essay's apparent hostility to nature and its dismissive tone, evident from the opening lines when Cyril enjoins Vivian, "Let us go and lie on the grass and smoke cigarettes and enjoy Nature," to which Vivian responds, "Enjoy nature! I am glad to say that I have entirely lost that faculty. ... My own experience is that the more we study Art, the less we care for Nature. ... Art is our spirited protest, our gallant attempt to teach Nature her proper place" (1071). Keeping in mind the multiple meanings of "nature" at play in the dialogue, Vivian's riposte may be directed as much against normative sociality as against the "hard and lumpy and damp" grass on which Cyril foolishly expects him to lie. Elsewhere in the dialogue, however, when the natural world enters the conversation as polluted rather than pastoral, Vivian's performative ecophobia bears much more directly on the atmospheric questions with which this chapter began.

In explaining to Cyril how "Nature" can be viewed as "an imitation of Art," and how "Nature follows the landscape painter," Vivian takes the Impressionists as his central example in a description that presents decadent intimations of an anthropogenic nature in a rhetorical posture of something akin to, or anticipating, climate denial:

> Where, if not from the Impressionists, do we get those wonderful brown fogs that come creeping down our streets, blurring the gas-lamps and changing the houses into monstrous shadows? ... The extraordinary change that has taken place in the climate of London during the last ten years is entirely due to a particular school of Art. ... For what is Nature? Nature is no great mother who has borne us. She is our creation. It is in our brain that she quickens to life. Things are because we see them, and what we see, and how we see it, depends on the Arts that have influenced us. ... There may have been fogs for centuries in London. I dare say there were. But ... they did not exist til Art had invented them. (1086)

The passage hovers between a startling recognition of the false binarism of Nature/Society ("Nature is no great mother who has borne us. She is our creation") and an equally startling overprivileging of the individual impression and individual experience as a source of knowledge ("Things are because we see them"). From our perspective today, where climate change has been rendered conceivable through a constellation of data points that dwarfs the miniscule empirical capacity of any lone seer, impressionism's fixation on rendering the glancing, individual consciousness may feel like a reaction against new methodologies in the sciences and social sciences, already in the late nineteenth century, which were proving the informational insufficiency of the individual gaze. As Katharine Anderson explains, the new Victorian science of meteorology "called attention to the new scale of scientific activities, which required coordination and centralization that put the work beyond any one individual's abilities and resources." Because meteorology required "the collective organization of science working in official or semi-official bodies," it was a focus for debate about data and technocratic authority.[34] Wilde's dialogue emerges instead from the Walter Pater tradition where "experience ... is ringed round for each one of us by that thick wall of personality through which no real voice has ever pierced ... each mind keeping as a solitary prisoner its own dream of the world."[35] But the rival example of meteorology reminds us that the privileging of individual perspective in Pater and Impressionism was a romantic response to the individual's attenuated authority and diminished capacity for making truth-claims in the era of statistical knowledge.

As is so often the case in Wilde's writings, however, one can hardly take Vivian's statements about Impressionism straight, followed as they are by a satirical chaser: "It must be admitted, fogs are carried to excess. They have become the mere mannerism of a clique, and the exaggerated realism of their method gives dull people bronchitis" (Wilde, "Decay of Lying," 1086). Wilde's reference to bronchitis is a reminder that the health effects of London's smog had worsened significantly in the 1890s, leaving little doubt that the city's climate had indeed changed. While London *had* had fogs for centuries, as Vivian says, these fogs had become much worse in the context of the coal-powered Victorian era, hitting a dangerous nadir in the 1890s.[36] In his poetry, Wilde, like many writers of his day, described that fog in terms that could be said to aestheticize the climate of industrial pollution: "like a yellow silken scarf / The thick fog hangs along the quay," he wrote in "Symphony in Yellow," and his poem "Impression du Matin" reads like an accompaniment to Monet's Houses of Parliament series: "The Thames nocturne of blue and gold / Changed to a Harmony in grey: / ... The yellow fog came creeping down / The bridges, till the houses' walls / Seemed changed to shadows."[37] Perhaps the yellow of the yellow nineties was not merely an allusion to the covers of unseemly French fiction, but also to this foul yellow fog.

Socialist writer and advocate of gay rights Edward Carpenter wrote just one year after "The Decay of Lying," in his 1890 article "The Smoke-Plague and Its Remedy," that the death rate in London increased significantly whenever the city was overtaken by a dense fog such as that described in Wilde's poems. Carpenter saw in this increasingly common effluvium the sign of an anthropogenic nature: "There is a common impression that the climate of England is not so fair as it used to be in the good old times. What if there be a truth in this – that the climate is worse ... and that we have made it so? After a careful study of the midland districts of England ... I feel now next to no doubt that the continued cloud ... is largely due to the continual presence of a thin film of smoke from our manufacturing centres."[38] Both Carpenter and Wilde confronted the industrialized nature of the Victorian era as gay men, in the context of a cultural and linguistic community where the double meanings of "natural" could seem to align the values of nonhuman phenomenal reality with a categorical heteronormativity. Wilde responded to this knot of conceptual confusion with a performative ecophobia that ultimately undermined the Nature/Society binary and reenvisioned nature as an anthropogenic creation, but Carpenter went in the other direction. Like Walt Whitman before him, Carpenter presented homosexual love as "natural" in all senses of the word: as he wrote in his 1906 volume *Days with Walt Whitman*, Whitman's work "upset all former and formal moralities, and exposed himself to the fiercest opposition; but some day ... it will be seen that 'Leaves of Grass' is, perhaps of all books ever written, the most natural."[39] If Carpenter naturalized queerness, Wilde queered nature.

Conclusion: Fin du Globe

The Anthropocene has warped our chronologies, lengthening temporal perspectives and asking us to view the present from the perspective of the future. "I wish it were *fin du globe*," Dorian famously remarks in *Dorian Gray* (Wilde, *Dorian,* 209): a man born too soon.[40] Wilde's novel offers a synopsis of such chronological distortion. Indeed, Wilde's entire oeuvre, tragically shortened though it is, is full of similar figures of chronological disruption. Salome, the lead figure in Wilde's 1891 play of the same name and perhaps the most ostentatiously decadent of all his characters, is a teenage girl in the space of transition from child to adult who draws the unwelcome sexual attention of her uncle/stepfather, Herod. At the climax of the play, she dances the dance of the seven veils under a moon that "has become red as blood," a figure for menstruation, before calling for the head of Iokanaan (John the Baptist) and kissing his severed head because "I was chaste, and [he] didst fill my veins with fire."[41] The play's stylized narrative of the most perverse menarche of all time interweaves the moon and the female cycle to involve the natural world more forcefully in the deformed temporalities of Wilde's decadent characters. Killed by order of Herod at the end of the play, Salome's life is cut short at the very onset of sexual maturity and well before the process of adult decay sets in – a female Dorian, more explicitly linked to unnatural nature through the play's obsessive lunar imagery. Nature in *Salome* is anything but natural, in other words, and Salome's short life and violent death contain within them a big, Biblical epic of the human interpenetration with the natural world.

The socialist journal the *New Age* said in the opening column of its January 25, 1908, issue that a "serious symptom of decadence" is "the incapacity for long views."[42] Speaking specifically of Britain's ruling Labour government, the editor diagnoses "a hectic flush of haste in all the present Cabinet's work, as if they felt the hand of death" (242). Decadence means, in this passage, the sense of impending death that generates, para-doxically, a speeding up, a rushed feeling of haste that inhibits the "long view." Ultimately, this is the legacy of the decadent 1890s for the Anthropocene: the era's keen sense that civilization is in decline, that the downward trend has begun – a rushed, hectic slide. This affective-temporal mood was palpable across the domains of literature, politics, and art at the end of the nineteenth century, where fin du globe was everywhere evident in fin de siècle. Within Wilde's career, we might read his major work of prison writing, *De Profundis*, as especially emblematic of this concentrated concep-tual space: here the constrained space of imprisonment and the abbreviated temporal horizon of the sentence lend themselves, paradoxically, to consid-erations of great depth and scope ("de profundis" means "from the depths"). As Wilde wrote to Lord Alfred Douglas in this long, painful letter, "Of course I discern in all our relations, not Destiny merely, but Doom: Doom that walks always swiftly, because she goes to the shedding of blood."[43]

Notes

1 Karl Beckson, "Introduction" to *Aesthetes and Decadents of the 1890's* (New York: Vintage, 1966), xii–xxii (xii).
2 Oscar Wilde, "The Decay of Lying" (1889; 1891), in *The Complete Works of Oscar Wilde*, 5th ed. (Glasgow: HarperCollins, 2003), 1071–92 (1071).

3 The Anthropocene is the proposed term for a new geologic epoch characterized by indelible human impacts on Earth systems, including but not limited to anthropogenic climate change. Although used informally before its publication, the term "Anthropocene" is usually dated to Paul J. Crutzen and Eugene F. Stoermer, "The 'Anthropocene,'" *Global Change Newsletter* 41 (2000): 17–18.

4 For a daily measurement of atmospheric CO_2 levels in parts per million at Mauna Loa Observatory, Hawaii, see https://climate.nasa.gov/vital-signs/carbon-dioxide.

5 Arthur Symons, "Violet: I. Prelude" (1895), in *Poems*, vol. I (New York: John Lane, 1902): 85.

6 Theodore Wratislaw, "Hothouse Flowers," from *Orchids* (London: Leonard Smithers), 23.

7 Matthew Potolsky offers a helpful historical orientation regarding the emergence of decadence: "As a literary movement with a name and a manifesto, decadence dates to 1886, when Anatole Baju published the first issue of his flagship journal *Le Décadent*"; Matthew Potolsky *The Decadent Republic of Letters: Taste, Politics, and Cosmopolitan Community from Baudelaire to Beardsley* (Philadelphia, PA: University of Pennsylvania Press, 2013), 3. As useful as the designator "decadent" is, it is a term, as Kristin Mahoney explains, that should be used advisedly given its history of negative connotations. *Literature and the Politics of Post-Victorian Decadence* (Cambridge: Cambridge University Press, 2015), 4.

8 See Elizabeth Hope Chang, *Novel Cultivations: Plants in British Literature of the Global Nineteenth Century* (Charlottesville, VA: University of Virginia Press, 2019), ch 2; see also Dennis Denisoff, "The Dissipating Nature of Decadent Paganism from Pater to Yeats," *Modernism/modernity* 15, no. 3 (2008): 431–46 (432).

9 Max Nordau, *Degeneration* (New York: Appleton, 1895), 317.

10 "Greenhouse gas effect" is the term that describes how heat-trapping gases such as carbon dioxide and methane produce global warming when released into the atmosphere.

11 "natural, adj. and adv." OED Online. June 2021. Oxford University Press, https://www.oed.com/view/Entry/125333?isAdvanced=false&result=3&rskey=ho7Cao& (accessed July 7, 2021).

12 Benjamin Morgan, "Fin du Globe: On Decadent Planets," *Victorian Studies* 58, no. 4 (Summer 2016): 609–35 (611).

13 Jason W. Moore, *Capitalism in the Web of Life: Ecology and the Accumulation of Capital* (New York: Verso, 2015), 180, 4.

14 See also John Bellamy Foster: "To be sure, the human relation to nature is less direct than that of other species since it is mediated by society, and society is the immediate human environment. But society has nature as its environment." John Bellamy Foster, *Marx's Ecology: Materialism and Nature* (New York: Monthly Review Press, 2000), 241.

15 See also Dennis Denisoff's *Decadent Ecology in British Literature and Art, 1860–1910* (Cambridge: Cambridge University Press, 2021), which

understands decadent ecology as "disruptive interfusions among the natural, cultural, spiritual, and imaginative, as well as the individual and the collective" (32).

16 Jesse Oak Taylor, *The Sky of Our Manufacture: The London Fog in British Fiction from Dickens to Woolf* (Charlottesville, VA: University of Virginia Press, 2016), 18, 23. See also Heidi C. M. Scott, *Chaos and Cosmos: Literary Roots of Modern Ecology in the British Nineteenth Century* (University Park, PA: Pennsylvania State University Press, 2014). Scott notes that the term "greenhouse effect" was coined in 1937, but that scientific experiments and theories leading to this coinage, and reliant on the greenhouse concept, were conducted much earlier by scientists such as Joseph Fourier and John Tyndall.

17 Svante Arrhenius, "On the Influence of Carbonic Acid in the Air upon the Temperature of the Ground," *Philosophical Magazine and Journal of Science* (April 1896): 237–96 (237).

18 On nineteenth-century Ice Age science and its role in Victorian scientific and literary culture, see Michael Thomas Gaffney, "The Birth of the Ice Age: On Narrative and Climate History in the Nineteenth Century," *Nineteenth Century Contexts* 42, no. 2 (2021): 1–14.

19 For recent work on the Anthropocene from the perspective of literary studies, see Jeremy Davies, *The Birth of the Anthropocene* (Berkeley, CA: University of California Press, 2016); and Tobias Menely and Jesse Oak Taylor, eds. *Anthropocene Reading: Literary History in Geologic Times* (University Park, PA: Pennsylvania State University Press, 2017).

20 On the Capitalocene as an alternative framing to the Anthropocene, see Andreas Malm, *Fossil Capital: The Rise of Steam Power and the Roots of Global Warming* (New York: Verso, 2016); or Moore, *Capitalism in the Web of Life*. Kathryn Yusoff, drawing on the work of Sylvia Wynter and other critical race theorists, argues instead for identifying the origin of the Anthropocene with colonial genocide in the Americas and the beginning of the Atlantic slave trade in the sixteenth century, since this is the point at which "Blackness becomes characterized through its ledger of matter" (35); Kathryn Yusoff, *A Billion Black Anthropocenes or None* (Minneapolis, MN: University of Minnesota Press, 2018). On the Plantationocene as a frame that centers exploited labor as well as large-scale agriculture and monocultural land use, see Donna Haraway, *Staying with the Trouble: Making Kin in the Chthulucene* (Durham, NC: Duke University Press, 2016).

21 On scaling and periodization in the Anthropocene humanities, see, for example, Dipesh Chakrabarty, "The Climate of History: Four Theses," *Critical Inquiry* 35 (Winter 2009): 197–222; and "The Planet: An Emergent Humanist Category," *Critical Inquiry* 46 (Autumn 2019): 1–31. For work in Victorian studies on this topic, see Benjamin Morgan, "After the Arctic Sublime," *New Literary History* 47, no. 1 (2016): 1–26; and "Scale as Form: Thomas Hardy's Rocks and Stars," in *Anthropocene Reading: Literary*

History in Geologic Times, eds. Tobias Menely and Jesse Oak Taylor (University Park, PA: Pennsylvania State University Press, 2017): 132–49.

22 I take the concept of "slow violence" from Rob Nixon, *Slow Violence and the Environmentalism of the Poor* (Cambridge, MA: Harvard University Press, 2011). For conceptions of "slow causality" as they came to be grasped within the Victorian scientific and cultural sphere, see Tina Young Choi and Barbara Leckie, "Slow Causality: The Function of Narrative in an Age of Climate Change," *Victorian Studies* 60, no. 4 (Summer 2018): 565–87.

23 Oscar Wilde, *The Picture of Dorian Gray* (1891), ed. Norman Page (Peterborough: Broadview, 1998), 79.

24 As Peter Brimblecombe explains, it was understood by the late Victorian period that "high levels of pollution . . . aid the formation of fog," and that because of smoke pollution the fogs "were thicker, more frequent and of a different colour from those of the past"; Peter Brimblecombe, *The Big Smoke: A History of Air Pollution in London since Medieval Times* (London: Methuen, 1987), 109.

25 Chakrabarty, "The Climate of History" 208.

26 Attorney Edward Carson, after reading in court a passage from the novel where Basil Hallward confesses his adoration for Dorian, asked Wilde on the stand, "Do you mean to say that that passage describes the natural feeling of one man towards another?" Testimony of Oscar Wilde on Cross Examination, April 3, 1895. Douglas O. Linder, Famous Trials, https://famous-trials.com/wilde/346-literarypart (accessed July 8, 2021). On materialism and ecological thinking, see John Bellamy Foster, *Marx's Ecology: Materialism and Nature* (New York: Monthly Review Press, 2000).

27 On materialism and aestheticism, see Benjamin Morgan, *The Outward Mind: Materialist Aesthetics in Victorian Science and Literature* (Chicago, IL: University of Chicago Press, 2017).

28 As Bruno Latour puts it, in the era of global warming we see nature unexpectedly take on the role of active subject after having been evacuated of agency, objectified and turned into a "zombie atmosphere"; Bruno Latour, "Agency at the Time of the Anthropocene," *New Literary History* 45, no. 1 (Summer 2014): 1–18 (12, 13). For another version of this argument, see Sylvia Wynter's discussion of "the West's epochal historical rupture," with the advent of colonialism and capitalism, in its thinking about the natural world: the "de-supernaturalization of the physical cosmos"; Sylvia Wynter, "On How We Mistook the Map for the Territory, and Re-Imprisoned Ourselves in Our Unbearable Wrongness of Being, of Désêtre: Black Studies toward the Human Project," in *Not Only the Master's Tools: African-American Studies in Theory and Practice*, eds. Lewis R. Gordon and Jane Anna Gordon (Boulder, CO: Paradigm, 2006), 107–72 (159). See also Amitav Ghosh, *The Nutmeg's Curse: Parables for a Planet in Crisis* (Chicago, IL: University of Chicago Press, 2021), for more on the politics of animacy.

29 H. G. Wells, *The War of the Worlds* (London: Penguin, 2005), 7.

30 At the beginning of the novel, Dorian seems to be "little more than a lad, though he is really over twenty" (51). Soon the timescales of art and life are reversed and Dorian is frozen in time while his portrait ages without him. This eventuality is explained through the metaphor of the seasons: "when winter came upon [the portrait], he would still be standing where spring trembles on the verge of summer" (141). Lord Henry believes that "the lad was premature" and that "he was gathering his harvest while it was yet spring" (96). In other words, the passage of time in the novel is marked always by discrepancies among Dorian, the painting, and the natural world.

31 Danielle De Wolfe, "16 Things We Can Learn from Oscar Wilde" (July 2, 2014), https://www.shortlist.com/news/16-things-we-can-learn-from-oscar-wilde.

32 Rob Nixon, "All Tomorrow's Warnings," *Public Books*, https://www.publicbooks.org/all-tomorrows-warnings (accessed August 17, 2020).

33 Nils Bubandt, "Haunted Geologies: Spirits, Stones, and the Necropolitics of the Anthropocene," in *Arts of Living on a Damaged Planet,* eds. Anna Tsing, Heather Swanson, Elaine Gan, and Nils Bubandt (Minneapolis, MN: University of Minnesota Press, 2017), 121–41 (G135).

34 Katharine Anderson, *Predicting the Weather: Victorians and the Science of Meteorology* (Chicago, IL: University of Chicago Press, 2005), 2, 10.

35 Walter Pater, *The Renaissance: Studies in Art and Poetry* (Berkeley, CA: University of California Press, 1980), 187–88.

36 Meteorological records indicate that "fog frequency appears to have reached a peak in the 1890s," (Brimblecombe, *The Big Smoke*, 111).

37 Oscar Wilde, *Complete Poetry*, ed. Isobel Murray (Oxford: Oxford University Press, 1997), 142, 129. For a reading of Victorian poetry in the context of a dawning Victorian recognition of the power of nonhuman agencies and compromised anthropogenic mastery, see Devin Garofalo, "Victorian Lyric in the Anthropocene," *Victorian Literature and Culture* 47, no. 4 (2019): 753–83.

38 Edward Carpenter, "The Smoke-Plague and Its Remedy," *Macmillan's* 62 (1890): 204–13 (207).

39 Edward Carpenter, *Days with Walt Whitman* (New York: Macmillan, 1906), 59–60.

40 Morgan notes that in manuscript, Wilde had originally used the phrase "fin du monde" before revising it to "fin du globe" – a suggestive revision ("Fin du Globe" 619).

41 Oscar Wilde, *Salome*, in *The Major Works*, ed. Isobel Murray (Oxford: Oxford University Press, 1989), 300–29 (322, 328).

42 A. R. Orage, ed., "Notes of the Week," *New Age* 2, no. 13 (January 25, 1908): 241–43 (242).

43 Oscar Wilde, *De Profundis*, in *The Complete Works of Oscar Wilde* 5th ed. (Glasgow: HarperCollins, 2003), 980–1059 (995).

CHAPTER 9

Weird Ecologies and the Limits of Environmentalism

Dennis Denisoff

In 1906, on his publisher's request, Arthur Machen gathered together some of his most successful writings and published them as *The House of Souls*: "A Fragment of Life" (written 1899; published 1904), "The White People" (written late 1890s; published 1904), *The Great God Pan* (1894), "The Inmost Light" (1894), "The Three Impostors" (1895), and "The Red Hand" (1895). Despite the author's notoriety for evoking overwhelmingly weird and often gruesome scenarios, it does not appear that any of these works inspired the subject of Sidney Simes's cover image for the first edition of the collection (Figure 9.1). It depicts a naked figure with humanoid body, legs, and arms and insectoid head, wings, and antennae. Sitting in a field of fungi that have begun to colonize the creature's thighs, the curious being has its arms raised skyward as if performing some mysterious ritual. One of the fungi, meanwhile, has begun to manifest a distinctly animal-like form. It is not any particular subject but rather the weird spirit of Machen's works that Simes most effectively captures in this illustration. A surreal synthesis of human, animal, plant, and occult, the image evokes the disturbing transspeciesism found in many weird works by Machen and other authors and artists of the 1890s. Equally important to a sense of the weird, Simes presents an act of otherworldly veneration in which humans are not distinct from the vegetal or the nonhuman animal. As Simes's art implies, the weird offered an insightful, alternative perspective to the dominant environmentalist view of the 1890s, which saw humans as the inherent stewards of the natural world and nature (a problematically blurry concept) as a passive resource for human use and consumption.

In the context of art and literature, the term "weird" does not refer to a genre, but rather to a sense of anxiety or terror regarding an ecological force seemingly acting on indeterminate motivations with little or no concern for people. While there are many works that are utterly driven by their evocation of the weird, the sense can also be found in works more readily recognized as the gothic, decadence, horror, adventure, science fiction, and

Figure 9.1   Sidney Simes, untitled cover image for Arthur Machen's *The House of Souls* (1906). Courtesy of Special Collections, McFarlin Library, University of Tulsa.

even realism. The eco-weird does not reflect an earnest concern regarding the welfare of organic ecologies, nor an outright ecophobia, so much as an implicitly deferential awe. H. P. Lovecraft, renowned master of the weird, states in *Supernatural Horror in Literature* (1927) that weird fiction contains "a certain atmosphere of breathless and unexplainable dread of outer, unknown forces," demanding a "suspension or defeat of those fixed laws of Nature which are our only safeguard against the assaults of chaos and the dæmons of unplumbed space."[1] The drastic environmental changes that have occurred in recent decades have given rise to the notion of "global weirding," an ecocultural understanding addressing doubts regarding the abilities either of science to explain these massive shifts or of humans to manage them.[2] These recent crises have also encouraged scholars to become more attuned to the ecopolitical perspectives offered by weird works from more than a century ago.

A diversity of factors contributed to the 1890s flourish of the weird, as James Machin observes,[3] including the growing economic investment in environmental policy, the rise of popular occulture, and the strong general interest in the biological, geological, meteorological, and astronomical sciences that were inspiring new notions of, among other subjects, species coreliance, vegetal ontology, and the possibility of nonhuman consciousness. While not part of an environmentalist initiative, the weird nevertheless brings forward perspectives on animal, vegetal, and atmospheric ontology in which natural elements are subjects worthy of recognition and respect. The fin-de-siècle weird was driven not by the question of what protections or rights should be extended to nonhuman elements of the ecologies in which we participate, but rather, more disconcertingly for many, by considerations regarding what agency these other forces – many mysterious or yet unrecognized – enact and perhaps even assume for themselves. Artists and authors of the 1890s such as Machen, Simes, William T. Horton, Robert Murray Gilchrist, M. P. Shiel, and Vernon Lee continued the Victorian literary interest in questioning and often undermining middle-class self-confidence and productivist assumptions. However, they take the exploration in a new direction by addressing assumptions regarding humans' entitlement and capabilities regarding environmental management. In doing so, works of weird art and fiction themselves at times take on the role of ecocriticism – analyses of and commentaries on the relationship between the environment and the arts.[4] Not only the subjects and perspectives but also the forms, tones, and styles of these works sustain in their audiences the moral uncertainty in which weird ecology finds its fit.

Mainstream Environmentalism at the Fin de Siècle

Victorians thought and acted in ways we could now recognize as environmentalist, but they did so through their own methods and cultural matrices of understanding. As Lawrence Buell proposed in 2005, "the environmental turn in literary studies is best understood less as a monolith than as a concourse of discrepant practices," affirming that environmentalist works have always existed and, importantly, have refused to cohere into any sort of "totalizing rubric."[5] Thus, Richard Kerridge argues, the ecocritic "wants to track environmental ideas and representations wherever they appear, to see more clearly a debate which seems to be taking place, often part-concealed, in a great many cultural spaces."[6] The late-Victorian shift in ecological vision – spurred on by industrial and urban innovations, extraction technologies, and global imperialist anxieties – exposed one of these partially hidden cultural developments as the weird.

In the second half of the nineteenth century, environmental consciousness gained momentum through the efforts of politically invested groups driven to establish protective legislation regarding specific locations deemed worthy of preservation, such as lakes, mountains, and urban green spaces. Some Victorians, Pierre Desrochers observes, were also considering ways of making industrialization more compatible with environmental sustainability. "Perhaps no institution ever," he writes, "did more to promote the discussion of by-product development than the British Society for the Encouragement of Arts, Manufactures and Commerce . . . in the second half of the nineteenth century."[7] The chemist Lyon Playfair and journalist Peter Lund Simmonds, for example, "not only anticipated concepts and debates that now occupy a prominent place in contemporary literatures on corporate social responsibility, environmental management, and sustainable development, but they also ended up by challenging some of the fundamental premises of modern-day theorists" (Desrochers, "Victorian Pioneers," 704). The narrative of Victorian modernization, Desrochers suggests, had incorporated its own subplot of responsible extraction and processing – albeit one driven as much by a wish to maximize the use value of resources than by a sense of responsibility to the welfare of the ecology of which one was a part.

This vision of resource efficiency accords to some degree with the dominant model of early environmentalism characterized by stewardship and conservation, the view that people had a duty not to waste or abuse nature but to manage it – a process that included preservation, but also control, containment, and often modification with the aims of maximizing the welfare of various acknowledged sentient beings. A growing segment of the middle class viewed stewardship as not only a duty, but also a right often seen as bestowed to people by some more-than-human force, spiritual or otherwise, that thereby implied a form of essential ownership. As Thomas Hardy makes amply apparent in works such as *Tess of the d'Urbervilles* (1891) and *Jude the Obscure* (1895), most of the rural poor – struggling to maintain their lifestyle and simply to survive – would not have found their intimate relations with the organic ecology as being characterized by the rights and privileges of stewardship.

If Victorians were not environmentalists by current definitions of the term, they were still well aware of the growing amount of damage humans were causing to the ecology in which they participated and were developing practical and rhetorical strategies for dealing with it. As Wendy Parkins observes, "it was the Victorians who first contemplated the widespread environmental despoliation brought by industrialization."[8] Citing John Stuart Mill, John Ruskin, and William Morris, Parkins contends that "nineteenth-century writers grappled with this emerging awareness of the deleterious impact of human activity on the environment." Throughout the nineteenth century, we find a steady increase in legislation regarding issues such as land stewardship and conservation. We also find concerns regarding issues such as labor rights and healthy living conditions for humans, as well as, equally important, a growing awareness of the interconnectivity across species. Sanitation science during the second half of the century was spurred by efforts to address urban living conditions and threats of cholera and other diseases, developing into considerations of how human bodily waste can be viewed and used as an agricultural resource.[9] As early as 1849, Ruskin proposed, in *The Seven Lamps of Architecture*, that humans' inherent ethical "duties" included "practicing present economy for the sake of debtors yet unborn, of planting forests that our descendants may live under their shade. . . . It belongs as much to those who are to come after us."[10] An awareness of such ecological contingencies across processes, space, and (distant and speculative) time fostered a collective shift in Western economic thought to an appreciation of human's coreliance with the rest of the natural world, and then to an environmental conscience or ethics, a sense of a responsibility not to sacrifice the health and contentment of other humans or sentient beings for personal profit. Caring for what was seen as nature became recognized, by the late nineteenth century, as fundamental to caring for other people.

Environmental movements were motivated not only to conserve pristine regions of land, but also to develop practices in both urban and nonurban regions that enhanced the health and wellbeing of humans (and, often, other species). As James Winter envisions the situation: "The city cover[ed] over the remaining patches of nature and ... the ever more congested streets. ... It seemed in the eyes of many to have become a great pump that, in the morning, drew in people, goods, nutrients, and, in the evening and after dark, expelled wastes of every kind."[11] An example of this perspective in action can be found in the debates that arose in 1890 around plans to build a dam on Lake Thirlmere in the Lake District in order to supply drinking water to the expanding industrial town of Manchester. Harriet Ritvo observes that "the opposing parties could be (and usually were) understood as representing powerful and incompatible icons: the Lake District, a symbol of natural beauty and unspoiled countryside, and Manchester, a symbol of modern industrial progress."[12] The seeming conflict between maintaining pristine green space versus supplying more usable water was, however, also recognized as something of an oversimplification of the controversy. The Thirlmere Defense Society was formed not only to protect the lake from more human intrusion but also to promote a more general environmentalist agenda and to gain support for its mission from prominent citizens. Moreover, defendants of the lake's state were not unanimous in their rationale, with pragmatic and idealistic interests not always being closely aligned. Well-known conservation activist Octavia Hill forewarned that "aesthetic arguments ... would have no effect on the politicians unless it could be shown that the health and future prosperity of Manchester did not depend on the destruction of wild beauty" (Winter, *Secure from Rash Assault,* 182). Ultimately, the value of Romanticist aesthetics was not recognized as a sufficiently important factor, and eventually the dam was built in light of what would have been deemed an ethically responsible aid to the welfare of the local citizens.

Various key associations impacted 1890s attitudes to the environment. The Commons Preservation Society, founded in 1864, was created "with the intention of defending open spaces in urban areas" and "was one of the first national organizations to actively promote landscape preservation ... [that] achieved numerous successes in protecting open spaces."[13] The Selborne Society, established in 1885, with Alfred Tennyson becoming president in 1888, emphasized education, legal pressure for environmental change, and gathering information from nature observation as opposed to collection. In 1891, the Selborne Society cited a speech by its founder G. A. Musgrave in declaring in its *Nature Notes* that:

> "The influential position of the Society has been vastly increased in the year 1890, through the co-operation of members of high position in the literary and scientific worlds; while its numerical strength has steadily grown." ...

> The truth is that a great deal of the most difficult part of the Society's work has been done. The idea that we are a band of sentimentalists or faddists, if it ever was entertained, is as dead as Julius Cæsar. ... The public press is altogether with us.[14]

These efforts were further buttressed by the garden city movement that began to flourish at the century's end; Aya Sakai notes that the main goals of the Metropolitan Gardens and Playgrounds Association in the late 1890s was "securing available vacant plots of ground within the Metropolitan area and obtaining the right to lay out gardens and to provide seating in all discussed burial grounds, churchyards, and enclosed squares."[15] An 1893 article in the *Saturday Review* argues,

> The stream of civilization ever deepening and broadening, flows on – whither? Weary sometimes of the fatness and ease of our environment, we lift our eyes wistfully to those far-off peaks whence it flows, and imagine the lives of shepherds and hunters of old full of that freshness and simplicity of which modern life has long been bereft. ... Now, since our land has become one large farm, there are not wanting symptoms of an altered taste; people have begun to spend money as freely in restoring asperities as their grandfathers did in removing them, in creating ponds and marshes where they had been laboriously drained away.[16]

Regarding the damages of industrialization, an article published in the *Spectator* in 1897 declares that "sixty years have shown that the evil results even of these destructive agencies are not permanent. The coal is worked out, the scrap-iron foundries, collieries, and bottle-works are deserted, and the ground once more in process of being replanted with trees, and restocked with flowers, birds, and even game."[17] While these associations see their mission as addressing modern abuses of the natural ecology, the discourse itself more often than not maintains an assumption of human authority and competence. Nature beyond the human, meanwhile, is configured as perhaps not always passive, but nevertheless domesticated through combined discourses of management and aesthetics. These seemingly logical formulations stand in distinct contrast to the creative offerings arising from such overlapping developments as Symbolism, decadence, apocalyptic and science fiction literatures, and of course the weird. Weird works of the 1890s prove neither escapist nor particularly hopeful, instead often offering a sense of inevitable doom tinged by an exasperation with the limits of most humans' imaginations. And yet, as the following examples suggest, there is more to this than resignation, as the works propose a range of alternatives to models built on a foundation of human authority and economic growth, alternatives that demand living in uncertainty.

The Tentacles of Weird Ecology in Art and Literature

Weird authors and artists of the 1890s evoke a distinct sense of irritation regarding common perspectives on the British environment. Their creative renderings of the ecofantastic, disastrous, and apocalyptic stand in contradiction with the rational, economically sensitive efforts to formulate pragmatic projects aimed at accommodating both a respect for (aspects of) nature and perpetual industrial growth. While practitioners of the weird often appear to demonize the natural environment, they are principally driven to sustain a reader's sense of a loss of self-coherence, a succumbing to the experience of a powerful force beyond their ken. Roger Luckhurst has described this immersiveness, as presented in twenty-first-century works, as "tentacular alterities [that] were introjected or embraced rather than phobically expelled."[18] Ecological introjection – the adoption of the perspective and experience of something recognized as otherwise distinct from the self – demands the frightening possibility of an absorption having already occurred before one's judgment, let alone permission. This consideration can be found in the works of authors recognized as some of the earliest contributors to the weird, such as Edgar Allan Poe, Edward Bulwer-Lytton, and authors of the Decadent Movement. The decadents are of particular interest here since they were themselves especially influential in the 1890s.

For decades now, academic scholarship of the British fin de siècle has emphasized topics such as decadence, aestheticism, New-Woman feminism, queer sexuality, new technology and media, and consumerism – all of which have been predominantly associated with the cultural dynamics of city life. Stewardship, as I have suggested, similarly engaged with and was shaped by urban and industrialist concerns. But if one focuses instead on the weird ecologies of the 1890s, an alternative perspective becomes apparent not only within the period's art and literature, but also in its environmental conception and politics. Elsewhere I have analyzed the ecological perspectives of decadence (reflective of its centuries-old association with paganism and organic processes of decay, regeneration, flourishing, and excess).[19] Decadent hedonism, I argue, produces a finer sensitivity to the natural world, its power, and its own aspirations and intentions. In this context, the human subject often appears vulnerable to being overwhelmed by the eco-other, forced to acknowledge its reliance for its sense of self on ecological relationality. Dustin Friedman and Neil Hultgren note the emergence, at the end of the century, of a particularly decadent form of the weird, a "Paterian weird" that "signals the surprising intersections of the natural landscape and supernatural forces."[20] As they argue: "The scale and impact of the weird can, then, vary drastically in the way that it explores the erosion of received accounts of the relationship between humanity and the natural world. It can ask readers to rethink the space and time of the entire universe" (Friedman and Hultgren, "Decadence and the Weird," 41). The weird more than decadence has been invested in decentering the subject by, as Simes's art for Machen's cover suggests, evoking a sense of an alternative source for ecological understanding. In the process, it shifts the conceptual fulcrum of agency from the human (whether that of the capitalist, imperialist, steward, or somebody else) to other beings, or to the elemental, the meteorological, and especially – when it comes to the weird – that which exists beyond human comprehension.

In the context of the visual arts, Simes, Aubrey Beardsley, William T. Horton, and others were recognized even in their own time as contributing to the stylization and reification of this disconcerting eco-aesthetic. Consider the second piece from Horton's *Three Visions*, a set of drawings that appeared in 1896 in Arthur Symons's journal the *Savoy* and that effectively captures this weird state of discord (Figure 9.2).[21] The minimalist, black-and-white image portrays a person's head and shoulders with a creature suggestive of a nautilus wrapping its tentacles around their scalp and dangling them downward. The human figure has an expression of aggravated acceptance. The image, however, is accompanied by the quotation "Giving head to seducing spirits – 1 Timothy, iv. I," suggesting that the creature has taken over the subject's mind or imagination, and that acceptance was never on the table. The fixed stare of the nautilus, the most frightening aspect of the image, offers no hint of emotional intentionality; its blank gaze directed at the viewer is neither seductive, nor aggressive, but instead suggests a lack of any communication between the creature and the human as individuals. And yet, the tight attachment of the creature to the human's scalp and the echo of its wrapped tentacles in the figure's furrowed brow imply a sort of mind-meld or ego-absorption.

The issue of the *Savoy* containing the image was published a month after Horton had become a member of the Hermetic Order of the Golden Dawn, the most influential occult society of the decade. While he left the Order soon after, his investment in occult thought remained throughout his life, with him often exploring occult opportunities with W. B. Yeats.[22] In addition to designing a tarot deck, his works appear in various occult-associated periodicals such as the *Green Sheaf*, the *Annals of Psychical Research*, and the *Occult Review*. In this context, the work demarcates a

"Giving heed to seducing spirits."—I TIMOTHY, iv. I.

Figure 9.2   William T. Horton, second image from *Three Visions*, *Savoy* 2 (April 1896): 75. Courtesy of Special Collections, McFarlin Library, University of Tulsa.

link, for Horton, between the ecological tentacular, on one hand, and the mysteries of the otherworldly, on the other. In 1898, Horton published *A Book of Images*, which offers a number of illustrations, such as *The Wave* and *The Gap*, that focus less on the ecological seduction of the human and instead emphasize the disturbing sense of expansiveness and mystery that the ecological evokes for so many. While these other works capture the anxious awe, akin to the sublime, that humans feel when attempting to comprehend the vastness of nature, the image of the human and the nautilus that I have discussed induces more forcefully the emotional and intellectual abyss of the nonsignifying eco-other central to the weird.

The sense of global or astronomical horror is not unique to the weird. Benjamin Morgan notes that "Victorianists have long been historicizing and theorizing the Anthropocene under other names. . . . These new scalar frameworks suggest the necessity not only for closer attention to the history of industrialization but also to the history of the planetary imaginaries that developed in relation to it."[23] As his key example of such imaginaries, Morgan turns to M. P. Shiel's *The Purple Cloud* (1901), "a forerunner of horror and weird fiction" (Morgan, "Fin du Globe," 623), in which the central character ultimately considers the planet as a never-wholly-comprehensible force and himself as a not-so-self-determining "small earth, precisely her copy, extravagantly weird and fierce" (626). Shiel's weird fiction explores the immeasurability of ecological force with greater emotional detail than that of most 1890s authors, with some prime examples to be found among his stories in *Prince Zaleski* (1895) and *Shapes in the Fire* (1896). "Vaila," from the latter collection, captures with particular effectiveness the sinister quality of the ecological weird as a transspatial, transtemporal disorientation. The narrator, a scientist, recalls an acquaintance, Haco Harfager, who curiously requested he be present for the impending death of the man's mother. During the narrator's northward journey to the family home on the island of Vaila in the Shetlands, he senses "a spectral something in the unreal aspect of silent sea and sunless dismalness of sky which produced upon my nerves the impression of a voyage *out* of nature, a cruise *beyond* the world."[24] Arriving at the desolate house, situated "at the very throat of some yelling planet" (Shiel, "Vaila," 87), our hero is met by Haco, his mother, and his aunt – the last three of the family line. With echoes of Poe's "Fall of the House of Usher," the remaining narrative steadily torques the reader's sense of foreboding as the story moves unstoppably toward an existential collision of the mechanical, ecological, meteorological, and psychological.

The House of Harfager, it turns out, has been constructed by one or more medieval architects as a sort of clockwork barometer, hung from massive chains and able to spin in reaction to the wind and lashing rains, all centered around an immense hourglass slowly dripping leaden balls into a pool deep in the bowels of the structure. The existential dread that Shiel hopes to evoke is made apparent by the fact that the model echoes a case, described to our narrator by a famous scientist, involving a toymaker who loses his mind in an obsession with "this earth – I had almost said this universe" as but a "Machine of Death," a "running shriek of Being" in which each person's existence is but a "little whisk of life" (71). Indeed, an inscription on the stone of Haco's home reads "'harfager-hous: 1389-188.'" (the last digit illegible due to a spot of tarnish), establishing the date of the building's construction but also its destruction, as well as that of the family line (98). Using Archimedes's principle of buoyancy and equilibrium, Haco has deduced the end date as 1889 – the hourglass having been designed to measure a 500-year period. "By what algebra of despair," our narrator asks Haco, "do you know that the last date must be such, was intended to be such, as to correspond with the stoppage of the horologe? And, even if so, what is the significance of the whole. It has – it can have – *no significance!*" (100). The narrator's angst arises from the "intended" demise of the family – a sort of preordained murder on the part of the medieval architects – but it is emotionally extrapolated by the implication of the sheer insignificance of death itself.

As the destined moment arrives during an intense tempest, with the reeling, gyrating building smashing against its own supports, the human sense of scale is itself demolished: "It was the levity of hugeness! It was the mænadism of mass! Swift – ever swifter, swifter – in ague of urgency, it reeled and raced, every portico a sail to the storm, vexing and wracking its tremendous frame to fragments" (120). Shiel's fatalism is driven by the indeterminate agency of an astronomical system with no investment in human life. It is not a question of whether there is an essential morality to humans, but what possible intentions, and likely none, might drive the ecological actions of nature, the planet, and the universe in general. That said, "Vaila" also carries a curious but undeniable caveat – that at least some humans, such as the medieval architects, have had the knowledge and ability to engage and work with the weird as it maneuvers on its transhistorical, atmospheric, and astrological scales. In another sense, Shiel suggests that the people engaging on this other level are alchemists of some sort such as occultists, spiritual philosophers, or – in perhaps the most profound component of 1890s weirdness – artists and authors with the imaginative capabilities to conceive of and represent the indeterminate.

The Weird's Own Ecocriticality

The weird is characterized by an anxiety arising from the sense of a force operating beyond our comprehension, but the whisper of an intellectual understanding in "Vaila" also signals the possibility of a place for the human within these machinations. In this sense, some weird works are themselves ecocritical analyses of the relationship of art and literature to their organic ecology. Geography scholar Nigel Clark has proposed that we recognize "an active exchange between earth and cosmos, . . . a new sense of the unpredictability and open-endedness of this interaction. . . . Exorbitant events point to an excess that can never be contained or accounted for, thus injecting an element of abyssal undecidability into all our deliberations."[25] He asks:

> Where does this leave worldly contingencies and ambivalences which may *not* be of our own making? Are there not also forces and processes with the potential to escape the closure of a fully subsumed nature, we might ask? Can we be so sure that there is no unassimilated materiality capable of veering in or rearing up and catching us unaware? (Clark, "Ex-orbitant Globality," 172)

The concern that Clark renders here as some monstrosity looming large from the lagoon of our own scalar instability was appreciated, even revered by various weird authors and artists of the 1890s, as W. T. Horton's illustrations *The Wave* and *The Gap* suggest. Clark's argument helps clarify why weird works have often portrayed such conceptual indeterminacy as enticingly elusive, and yet, collectively, have also developed rather rigid formal characteristics. This simultaneous investment in both the leaky supernatural and generically formulaic is linked to the weird's ecocritical exploration and whether the human or culture is an inevitable part of its processes or just a reassuring means of imagining its containment. The plot structure of weird works aims to sustain a sense of terror laced with foreboding and defeatism. Central characters are often isolated, obsessed with affirming the facticity of science (including the occult), medicine, or history (including genealogical fatalism). These characters are generally either, on one hand, desperate to uncover the materialist logic and order of reality or, on the other, open to their own inevitable annihilation or, more precisely, their embodied ego's reconfiguration as but a temporary nodule, at most a resource, for some sort of operations so vast as to be inconceivable. Under the constrictions of these formal characteristics, we find the weird offering commentary on the interfusion between the natural environment and its cultural renderings.

One author of the 1890s who turned to the weird to explore the place of the artistic in the ecological was Robert Murray Gilchrist. Acquainted with Henry Harland, Richard Le Gallienne, William Sharp, and other members of the 1890s literary scene, Gilchrist built his early reputation on a series of strange tales marked by a decadent aesthetic. As one contemporary summarized, in Gilchrist's first story collection *The Stone Dragon and Other Tragic Romances* (1894) "you may distinctly trace the influence of Poe, and perhaps also Villiers de l'Isle Adam and Charles Baudelaire. Indeed, if there is a man who could catch and cage the spirit of *Fleurs du Mal* in our Saxon tongue, it is the author of *The Stone Dragon*."[26] Hugh Lamb more recently summarized the same collection as "one of the most singular volumes of weird tales in English literature."[27] Gilchrist's "The Crimson Weaver," which first appeared in 1895 in the *Yellow Book*, offers a particularly imaginative rendering of ecological absorption within a nightmarish Pre-Raphaelite aesthetic. A page describes how he and his master, an aged knight, "roam aimlessly" until they eventually "wander from our track and lose ourselves" in a frighteningly disorienting landscape.[28] Despite ominous signs, our two brave adventurers proceed. When one character warns them of the dangers, the knight declares, "The evil she hints cannot exist. There is no fiend" (Gilchrist, "Crimson Weaver," 269) and later, after additional disturbing signs of trouble, the page affirms, "You are strong, Master – no evil can touch us" (271). Warnings and unpleasantness pile up but, by the time the two men finally question their decision, it is too late and they find they have been absorbed by the alien environment. "The atmosphere became almost tangible: I could scarce breathe" (276), the page declares.

The foreign ecology is a parkland of grotesque excess with "satyrs vomiting senilely, nymphs emptying wine upon the lambent flames of dying phoenixes, creatures that were neither satyrs nor nymphs, nor gryphins, but grotesque adminglings of all, slain by one another, with water gushing from wounds in belly and thigh" (270). A statue of Diana sits with head and shoulders "white with the excrement of a crowd of culvers that moved as if entangled in a snare" (271). The Crimson Weaver herself exudes some "unspeakable horror" (272), donning a robe she weaves with thread made of the blood of men's hearts. One recognizes in Gilchrist's story an echo of Alfred Tennyson's "Lady of Shalott," with a female artist confined to a tower weaving eternally for her life. In Gilchrist's version, however, the artist is more powerful, the multiple lovers being absorbed by her, becoming her very lifeblood. Moreover, she operates not in isolation, but is mentally in tune with the perverse landscape that she maintains. Even within the context of the Decadent Movement, the sheer foulness of Gilchrist's imagery is original, the repulsiveness marking the overwhelming incomprehensibility of the ecological. The abject becomes the aesthetic, insides pour outside, species barriers break down, while our wanderers absorb and are absorbed by the very atmosphere that is also the mind of the seducer. The crimson thread weaves together the artistry of the loom, the self-invested ecological spirit, and the human heart, with the greatest emotional force coming from the inescapable sway of the weird itself, its combination of attraction and dread. This macramé of the macabre, in Gilchrist's rendering, does not demarcate a broader level of conception that somehow contains the eco-weird. Rather, the author intertwines the threads of the artistic and ecological as a critical commentary on the naïve confidence with which these adventurers into foreign lands succumb to the influences of the unfamiliar and are ultimately subsumed by its indeterminate drives.

Vernon Lee's contribution to the weird is especially insightful regarding the relation of ecology and the arts because, in addition to her fiction, she wrote volumes of essays addressing humans' psychological and affective engagements with both nature and art, while offering serious arguments for a recognition of the weird and haunting as real yet inexplicable elements of one's lived experience. In her essay "The Lie of the Land" (1897), she describes the way in which sensitivity to an ecological context can shift one's sense of place beyond the explainable. "The order of time and space is sometimes utterly subverted," she writes, "the power of outdoor things, their mysterious affinities, can change the values even of what has been and what has not been, can make one live for a moment in places which have never existed save in the fancy. Have I not found myself suddenly taken back to certain woods which I loved in my childhood simply because I had halted before a great isolated fir?"[29] In addition to acknowledging the self-determining drive of the imagination, creating conduits the individual does not necessarily recognize, Lee also suggests the force of the environment itself, the "power of outdoor things" arising in particular in the coreliances and mutual integrations in which she herself participates. Lee begins her essay collection *The Enchanted Woods* (1905) with a similarly supernatural observation about forests: "When one is in them they seem to march nowhere with reality; and after issuing one is tempted to deny their existence. For they are full of spells and of adventure without end, drawing one, up that dark, gliding river, into their hidden heart."[30] Lee's exploration of the self's relation to the spirit of a place renders the environment as disorienting, mysterious. But this organic expansion, for Lee, extends even into the very artistry of her own concep-tion. As she continues, "The soil into which the thousand-year-old oaks strike their gnarled roots, is the soil of romance itself. Rinaldo or Sir Guyon was steered along those translucent, brown waters[;] ... the foun-tain of Merlin is hidden among the twisted whitehorns; perhaps Merlin himself." Lee not only articulates the means of the weird's seductiveness, but also suggests its discord with more common narrative structure: "One follows now one path, now another, through marshland or underwood, up and down, endlessly, aimlessly, much as one reads, listlessly turning pages, the suddenly broken off, suddenly resumed narrative" (Lee, "Introduction," 4). The language and ideas bring to mind the meanderings of the two adventurers in Gilchrist's "Crimson Weaver." Just as the weird is often defined by its evocation of inevitable ecological uncertainties, it also undermines the reader's familiarity with generic conventions, the lie of the narrative landscape.

Lee repeatedly characterizes what she calls "hauntings" as an interweaving of the ecological and cultural, of "weird places" and "strange stories." "The genuine ghost?" Lee asks in the preface to her short story collection *Hauntings* (1890), "And is not this he, or she, this one born of ourselves, of the weird places we have seen, the strange stories we have heard?"[31] In "Oke of Okehurst" (1890), a family portrait leads the "weird, exquisite" heroine Alice Oke, "a weird creature, visibly not of this earth," to allow her immersion into the past, utterly absorbed by the identity of an ancestor.[32] Meanwhile in "Prince Alberic and the Snake Lady" (1896), a royal youth entrapped by his jealous grandfather becomes fully invested in the landscape depicted in a tapestry hanging on the wall, and particularly in a snake in the image.[33] When later exiled, Alberic finds himself living in the actual landscape rendered in the wall-hanging and so proceeds to consummate his relationship with the snake, who proves to be a woman ensnared by a curse. In this story, the artwork becomes the environment, and the transspecies status that Gilchrist demonized here functions as an extension of the intermediations between the weird and the world, and the ecological and the cultural. While the links might appear to serve as an affirmation of the place of the artist within the experience of the unknowable, Lee presents the ego as in fact a structural contribution to the very systems against which it self-defines. The most anxious element of the weird, in Lee's oeuvre, resides in the individual being usurped by the environment into which it, like Prince Alberic, has been led by its own imagination.

Among the eco-weird authors of the 1890s, Arthur Machen perhaps most forcefully plunges the artist into this conceptual abyss. Like Horton, Machen was rather underwhelmed by his experience as a member of the Golden Dawn but maintained his intensive studies of the occult and alchemical throughout his life. He believed in the existence of an other-worldly reality, but vehemently opposed those such as spiritualists who claimed direct communication with it. He himself turned to symbolism to suggest these inarticulate forces without actually representing them. He is still best known for his horrifying novella *The Great God Pan* (1894), in which the weird is portrayed as the classical pagan deity of nature, the wild, and the pastoral, with Pan seducing and then either shaming various upright, middle-class male professionals or leading them to their deaths.[34] But it is in *The Hill of Dreams* (written 1897; published 1907) that Machen most richly explores weird artistry. In the novel, an aspiring young writer named Lucian Taylor falls asleep among the gorse and moldering moss atop the eponymous hill and has a dreamlike sexual encounter with a faun. Later, on his return to the site, it is clear his experiences are being regulated by the ecology itself: "The bramble bushes shot out long prickly vines, amongst which he was entangled, and lower, he was held back by wet bubbling earth. He had descended into a dark and shady valley, beset and tapestried with gloomy thickets; the weird wood noises were the only sounds, strange, unutterable mutterings, dismal, inarticulate."[35] Machen refers to the geography as the "weird wood" three times in total, while we are also informed of "a weird suggestion that had once beset him, that his very soul was being moulded into the hills" (Machen, *Hill of Dreams*, 182–83). Not only does *The Hill of Dreams* utterly enmesh weirdness and the natural environment into each other, but it acknowledges more than once the way in which ecological agency overrides that of the writer.

Escaping to the London suburbs, Lucian turns his energies to his writing, only to realize that his absorption into the ecological has already occurred, and that his sentences only satisfy him when they educe "a weird elusive chanting" (196). Upon the impoverished, hallucinating artist's death, we are told the writings he has produced are "illegible hopeless scribblings" (308), as "inarticulate" to his readers as he himself earlier had found "the weird wood's noises" (68). The hill of Lucian's eco-erotic dreamscape, has, in short, infiltrated his own identity as an artist, who now produces writing that, from a human standpoint, lacks articulation, let alone direction, because it communicates, we are drawn to conclude, on the vaster ecological scale of the hill of dreams. Lucian's art does not offer a controlling, explanatory commentary on the ecological; its commentary resides, if at all, in its absorption into the "weird elusive" form of nature itself. For Machen as occultist, the effort of a writer, nature lover, or whomever to contain or assume an understanding of the ecological can only result in succumbing to the "wet bubbling earth" and what other humans, with their limited comprehension, will see as "hopeless scribbling."

Just as the weird as a mode of understanding has permeated today's ecocriticism, we have recently seen a developing awareness of the ecological investments within weird works of the 1890s. Roger Luckhurst observes that the "growing concern at the fragile ecology of human existence on the planet has increasingly favored Gothic, horror, and weird modes. Ecocriticism might have started with high Worsdworthian Romanticism, but it has come to recognize that horror can powerfully figure the kinds of global changes that the domestic scales of realist fiction cannot see" (Luckhurst, "Gothic, Horror, and the Weird," 90).[36] Notably Vernon Lee, writing in 1890, had similarly proposed that

> the supernatural, in order to call forth those sensations, terrible to our ancestors and terrible but delicious to ourselves, skeptical posterity, must necessarily, and with but a few exceptions, remain enwrapped in mystery. Indeed, 'tis the mystery that touches us, ... while the figure itself wanders forth, scarcely outlined, scarcely separated from the surrounding trees; or walks, and sucked back, ever and anon, into the flickering shadows. (Lee, "Preface," viii)

As Lee suggests, the chief characteristic of the weird is not its alien quality but its disturbing familiarity. One is drawn to sense within the evocative uncertainties of the narrative something uncanny in its configuration, something almost but not quite operating along an expectant pattern, the central figure of the scenario seeming familiar to the reader yet also, evocatively, an integrated aspect of their ecology. From an environmentalist standpoint, we are drawn to shift from discussing human responsibilities to considering not simply the rights of other-than-human beings, but what these others might deem to be the rights of humans, if anything. We are going through a time, globally, when the ecological is making it painfully apparent that we are not the sole authors of our experiences. Whether it is the climate crisis, the mutating coronavirus, or some other force no doubt out there but yet to be realized, our story is never utterly ours to narrate. As weird works of the 1890s demonstrate, this realization fostered a similar set of sustained uncertainties at the fin de siècle. What is most disorienting in these century-old materials is not the atmospheric ambiguities of the mysterious presences, but the amorality. Authors and artists such as Horton, Shiel, Gilchrist, Lee, and Machen intensify our discomfort by refusing to reify the threat, thereby sustaining the sense of the otherworldly functioning outside human systems of classification and organization. The reader's anxiety arises not from knowing what the threat is, but from being excluded from the possibility of knowing.

Notes

1 H. P. Lovecraft, *Supernatural Horror in Literature*, 1927, revised and expanded 1933–34 (New York: Dover, 1973), 15.

2 A recent discussion of global climate change and the fantastic can be found in Gerry Canavan and Andrew Hageman, "Introduction: 'Global Weirding,'" *Paradoxa* 28 (2016): 7–13.

3 James Machin, *Weird Fiction in Britain 1880–1939* (London: Palgrave Macmillan, 2018).

4 Analyses of Victorian ecocriticism – Victorian writing addressing the relationship of literature and art to the physical environment – has blossomed in the past two decades. Relevant essay collections include Laurence W. Mazzeno and Ronald D. Morrison, eds., *Victorian Writers and the Environment: Ecocritical Perspectives* (London: Routledge, 2017); Wendy Parkins, ed., *Victorian Sustainability in Literature and Culture* (New York: Routledge, 2018); and Dewey W. Hall, ed., *Victorian Ecocriticism: The Politics of Place and Early Environmental Justice* (Lanham, MD: Lexington Books, 2017). See also Lynn Voskuil, "Why Victorian Ecocriticism Matters," in *The Routledge Companion to Victorian Literature*, eds. Dennis Denisoff and Talia Schaffer (New York: Routledge, 2020), 506–16.

5 Lawrence Buell, *The Future of Environmental Criticism: Environmental Crisis and Literary Imagination* (Malden, MA: Blackwell, 2005), 11.

6 Richard Kerridge, "Introduction" in *Writing the Environment: Ecocriticism and Literature*, eds. Richard Kerridge and Neil Sammells (London: Zed Productions, 1998), 1–10 (5).

7 Pierre Desrochers, "Victorian Pioneers of Corporate Sustainability: Lyon Playfair, Peter Lund Simmonds and the Society of Arts' Waste Products Initiatives," *Business History Review* 83, no. 4 (2009): 703–29 (704).

8 Wendy Parkins, "Introduction: Sustainability and the Anthropocene," in *Victorian Sustainability in Literature and Culture*, ed. Wendy Parkins (New York: Routledge, 2018), 1–13 (1).

9 See Henry Austin, *Report on the Means of Deodorizing and Utilizing the Sewage of Towns* (London: George E. Eyre and William Spottiswoode, 1857); and Christopher Hamlin, "Providence and Putrefaction: Victorian Sanitarians and the Natural Theology of Health and Disease," *Victorian Studies* 28, no. 3 (Spring 1985): 381–411.

10 John Ruskin, *The Seven Lamps of Architecture* (New York: John Wiley, 1849), 154.

11 James Winter, *Secure from Rash Assault: Sustaining the Victorian Environment* (Berkeley, CA: University of California Press, 2002), 190.

12 Harriet Ritvo, "Manchester v. Thirlmere and the Construction of the Victorian Environment," *Victorian Studies* 49, no. 3 (2007): 457–81 (457).

13 Ben Cowell, "The Commons Preservation Society and the Campaign for Berkhamsted Common, 1866–70," *Rural History* 13, no. 2 (2002): 145–61 (146).

14 "The Selborne Society and Its Publication," *Nature Notes: The Selborne Society Magazine* 13, no. 2 (January, 1891): 1–7 (1).

15 Aya Sakai, "'Re-Assessing' London's Squares: The Development of Preservation Policy 1880-1931," *The Town Planning Review* 82, no. 6 (2011): 615–37 (621).

16 "Home-Made Alps," *Saturday Review of Politics, Literature, Science and Art*): 76, no. 1971 (1893): 150–51 (150).

17 "'Sixty Years' Change in Landscape," *Spectator* 3599 (June 19, 1897): 865–66 (865).

18 Roger Luckhurst, "Gothic, Horror, and the Weird," in *The Routledge Companion to Victorian Literature*, eds. Dennis Denisoff and Talia Schaffer (New York: Routledge, 2020), 83–94 (87).

19 See my *Decadent Ecology: Decay, Desire, and the Pagan Revival* (London: Cambridge University Press, 2022). I thank Kristin Mahoney for her insights regarding the ecological forces behind decadent works, including those that do not explicitly engage with the place of the human in organic ecological systems.

20 Dustin Friedman and Neil Hultgren, "Decadence and the Weird: Introduction," *Studies in Walter Pater and Aestheticism* 4 (Summer 2019): 35–43 (38).

21 William T. Horton, "*Three Visions*," *Savoy* 2 (April 1896), 75.

22 Jon Crabb, "The Strange Case of Mr William T. Horton," *The Public Domain Review* (2016), https://publicdomainreview.org/essay/the-strange-case-of-mr-william-t-horton.

23 Benjamin Morgan, "Fin du Globe: On Decadent Planets," *Victorian Studies* 58, no. 4 (Summer 2016): 609–35 (610–11).

24 M. P. Shiel, "Vaila," *Shapes in the Fire* (London: John Lane, 1896): 67–121 (81). Further citations appear in the main body of the chapter.

25 Nigel Clark, "Ex-orbitant Globality," *Theory, Culture, & Society* 22, no. 5 (2005): 165–85 (179, 167).

26 "Mr. R. Murray Gilchrist," *Academy: A Weekly Review of Literature and Life* 57 (December 9, 1899): 689–90 (690).

27 Hugh Lamb, ed., *Victorian Nightmares* (New York: Taplinger, 1977), 43.

28 Robert Murray Gilchrist, "The Crimson Weaver," *Yellow Book* 6 (July 1895): 269–77 (269).

29 Vernon Lee, "The Lie of the Land," in *Limbo and Other Essays* (London: John Lane, 1908), 43–62 (61).

30 Vernon Lee, "Introduction," in *The Enchanted Woods, and Other Essays on the Genius of Places* (London: John Lane, 1905), 2–11 (3).

31 Vernon Lee, "Preface," in *Hauntings: Fantastic Tales*, 1890 (London: John Lane, The Bodley Head, 1896), x.

32 Vernon Lee, "Oke of Okehurst," in *Hauntings: Fantastic Tales*, 1890 (London: John Lane, The Bodley Head, 1896), 109–91 (128, 173).

33 Vernon Lee, "Prince Alberic and the Snake Lady," *Yellow Book* 10 (July 1896): 289–34.

34 Arthur Machen, *The Great God Pan* (London: John Lane, 1894).

35 Arthur Machen, *The Hill of Dreams* (London: E. Grant Richards, 1907), 68.

36 See also Roger Luckhurst, "The Weird: A Dis/orientation," *Textual Practice* 31, no. 6 (2017): 1041–61.

CHAPTER 10

Queer Theories of the 1890s

Simon Joyce

As Richard Ellmann famously wrote at the end of his 1987 biography of Oscar Wilde, its subject belonged "to our world more than Victoria's," and if there's a connecting thread running through much of the explosion of interest in Wilde in the past few decades it is surely this: that whether we consider him (as he sometimes thought of himself) as a martyr for a cause yet to be publicly fought or simply a figure out of time, Wilde's sexual and gender politics (among other aspects of his life and writing) speak clearly now in a way they struggled to in the late nineteenth century.[1] They have apparently spoken even when Wilde himself could not be spoken of, if we take Alan Sinfield's suggestion in *The Wilde Century* of a silence that was "Wilde-shaped" and yet managed to provide a template for gay male style and sensibility in the twentieth century to which Ellmann thought that Wilde better belonged. The difficulty of reading silence apparently doesn't stand in the way of our hearing it clearly, with Sinfield ready to supply its contours: "The inhibiting of debate took a certain shape," he posits, "one determined by the notions that had accrued around Wilde," with the consequence that "between 1900 and 1960, a dandified manner afforded by far the most plausible queer identity."[2]

This is an inverse account of male homosexuality to the one David Halperin has provided in which we are supposed to have moved in the opposite direction, away from the gender transitivity of dandyism and toward an image that is "straight-acting and -appearing," in a shift that he subsequently clarified as one that "privileges sexuality over gender."[3] Reversing Ellmann, then, we might conclude with Halperin that the dandy Wilde belongs squarely to his own century and has little to tell us about how to navigate the present currents of gender and sexual politics. I will be arguing something along those lines, but for very different reasons than might be implied by Halperin. If we set aside their inverse trajectories, he and Sinfield agree on a transformation that's evident in gay male self-presentation during the century after Wilde, but we surely need to pose the question more broadly than that, given present investments – which are not universally shared – in an alliance linking Ls, Gs, and Bs (lesbians, gay men, bisexuals) on one axis of sexual orientation with Ts, Is (transgender and intersex people), the nonbinary and genderqueer along another of gender identity. Both Halperin and Sinfield have registered this coalitional framework, the former by admitting that "it is looking more and more as if the model of (homo)sexuality with which I grew up, and whose genealogy I have tried to map in the essays that follow, never had more than a narrowly circumscribed reach." A definition centered on object-choice, he acknowledged, never succeeded in wholly excluding "considerations of gender identity, gender presentation, gender performance" or disentangling "sexuality from matters of gender conformity and gender deviance" (Halperin, *How To*, 22). Sinfield made a similar course correction with his 2004 *On Sexuality and Power*, which tried (not entirely successfully) to think about gender identity and expression alongside the cathexes of sexual desire in terms of Freud's distinction between the desire-to-be and the desire-for. Like Halperin, Sinfield recognized a renewed attention to gender that upended late twentieth-century gay male culture, pointing to a confused imaginary that simultaneously made space for the hypermasculine "clone look" and for cross-gender dissonance, as expressed through camp and drag: the incoherence, he concluded, "seemed to suffice, until the 1990s when transgender people, by declaring themselves, made the illogicality blatant."[4]

I propose to look back from our present moment of a fragile (and perhaps unraveling) coalition to see what models of sexual and gender identity from the 1890s might be useful to us now, and for this project returning to and canonizing Wilde does not appear especially helpful.[5] Indeed, in some ways, he might personify the *least* useful mode of thinking, one that was already regressive in the 1890s on account of its deep investment in asymmetrical relationships and status hierarchies: the pederastic model. Rethinking the decade requires us to look elsewhere, in other words, than to Wilde. The difficulty is mostly that pederasty requires dominant and subordinate partners, with all the power differentials such terms imply: one figure who is older, wealthier, better educated, more cultured, and perhaps all the above; another who is younger, poorer, with less education and experience of the world. Gender presentation is harder to fit into this schema because the terms are in many ways reversible – a cisnormative older man with a boy whose youth types him as feminized, or an older queen paired with the hypermasculinity of rough trade – but in either case the relationship is still one based in structured asymmetry, as are many of the equivalent lesbian pairings, most obviously butch/femme. Wilde was not the only figure in the late nineteenth century to subscribe to the pederastic mode of thinking about same-sex relations; indeed, if we follow the lead of Linda Dowling in *Hellenism and Homosexuality in Victorian Oxford* (1994) we might see it as fairly hegemonic within the educational institutions that catered to – and, not coincidentally, reinforced the sense of entitlement of – young men of privilege. But it's also fair to say that others, including Wilde's near-contemporary John Addington Symonds, tried more to resolve its inherent problems.

Wilde tended to resist programmatic statements, but one of the few he made after his release from prison displays little evidence of introspection or regret. Writing to his loyal friend Robert Ross when others close to him expected him to renounce Lord Alfred Douglas, Wilde commented that "a patriot put in prison for loving his country loves his country, and a poet in prison for loving boys loves boys. To have altered my life would have been to have admitted that Uranian love is ignoble. I hold it to be noble – more noble than other forms."[6] The assertion is oddly hybridized, mixing in equal parts the elevated language of Wilde's famous speech in court (holding Uranian love to be as or more noble than its heterosexual counterpart) with the prosaic and tautologous self-evidence of boy-loving. It is also worth pointing out that Douglas himself would have been twenty-seven when this letter was written. In these respects, the letter signals the emergence of an idea of sexual preference (someone who loves boys) that is narrower than most invocations of same-sex desire and in this sense a quite precise reaffirmation of a pederastic identity that required a differential such as age in order to map the relationship between its constitutive partners.

As a first step toward revising our understanding of the 1890s, I turn to Symonds, who would develop a sexual self-understanding that was more closely tied to sexological models that were less hostile to gender dissonance. In the process, I argue that he and others were at the same time engaged in adapting – and sometimes consciously mistranslating – German materials in response to a more general hostility to male effeminacy that Dowling and others have shown to be endemic among the British upper classes. A truer and more useful reworking of sexology can be found in the waning part of the decade, particularly in the years after the Wilde trials, when Edward Carpenter placed German sources such as Karl Heinrich Ulrichs and Magnus Hirschfeld in dialogue with insights he derived from close contacts with feminist and New Woman thinkers of the period. Arguing against a tendency to highlight and magnify the shifts of emphasis performed by someone like Symonds, I suggest a different historical trajectory that signals a productive alignment of German sexology and the British homophile movement, in which gender transitivity could be thought in relation – and not in opposition to – sexual identity.

Asymmetrical Partnerships and the Problem with Pederasty

Symonds was in many respects the product of a similar background and educational system to Wilde's, with private schooling at Harrow the inevitable pathway to Oxford. His views about gender, sexuality, and particularly same-sex desire were shaped by the same forces, including a transformative exposure to Plato that he recalled as having saved him from indulging the "animalism of boyish lust" he witnessed around him at school. In his secret and posthumously published *Memoirs*, he recorded that a providential encounter with the *Symposium* and *Phaedrus* felt "as though the voice of my own soul spoke to me through Plato," producing the insight "that masculine love had its virtue as well as its vice, and stood in this respect upon the same ground as normal sexual appetite."[7] Three aspects of this description define Symonds' processing and reworking of the pederastic tradition, especially as he would put it into dialogue with new work in sexology that had begun to appear in Germany: first, that male homosexuality needed to be thought of as properly "masculine" as opposed to both "boyish lust" and also the impulse to identify same-sex desire with cross-gender identification; second, the attempt at the same time to define it as the equivalent of heterosexuality even as it specified an equivalence between partners as opposed to a structuring difference; and third, a contrary attempt to place the "virtue" of same-sex desire figuratively above the "ground" of heterosexual appetite. If part of Wilde's formula echoed the last point in asserting the "more noble" form of Uranian love, his insistence on identifying as a poet who "loves boys" did little either to shift the gendered dynamic of classical pederasty or to place partners in a relation of equivalence.

A key to Symonds's reworking of the pederastic model can be found in his gloss on Pausanius's famous speech from *The Symposium*, which is likely one of the key passages that he had encountered at Harrow. Two decades later, in his *A Problem in Greek Ethics* (1873), he expounded on Plato's development of two modes of love that were derived in turn from different versions of the goddess Aphrodite. The first was the daughter of Zeus and the Titan Dione, whereas the second – the child of Uranus alone – was the inspiration for the descriptor "Uranian" that Wilde used, most likely drawing upon Edward Carpenter's popularizing of a term from Ulrichs's *Riddle of Man-Manly Love*.[8] In the translation of Plato by his Oxford mentor Benjamin Jowett, Symonds would read that Uranian lovers:

> love not boys, but intelligent beings whose reason is beginning to be developed, much about the time at which their beards begin to grow. And starting from such a choice, they are ready, I apprehend, to be faithful to their companions, and pass their whole life with them, not to take them in their inexperience, and deceive them, and make fools of them, and then run away to others of them.[9]

The lovers that descended from what Jowett translated as "the common Aphrodite," however, were those whom Pausanius saw as "apt to love women as well as youths, and the body rather than the soul," in a formulation that links nonreciprocated relationships structured by age or gender difference. Symonds's immediate interpretive inference was that in classical Greece "the love of boys is held to be ethically superior to that of women," although in a more developed commentary he noted that the nobler form was marked by "the belief in the possibility of permanent affection between paiderastic friends," on the assumption that they were closer in age than man to boy and capable of sustaining a relationship beyond the developmental turning point suggested by Pausanius's phrase "about the time at which their beards begin to grow."[10]

The obvious point of weakness is that Pausanius focuses solely on one figure in the couple and says little about a potential partner, who is a "companion" in Plato's text but not necessarily what Symonds terms a "paiderastic friend" in a phrasing suggesting a relation of equals. In his reworking, Symonds was responding to a problem that also runs through Ulrichs's early works in the mid-1860s, that of the Uranian's attraction to others who might be alike in the broadest sense (the "same sex," allowing for "man-manly" love) but are otherwise unlike and as such incapable of reciprocation or sustained affection. In his earliest schema, Ulrichs figured the homosexual man as an *Urning* who – on account of the feminine soul (*anima muliebris*) – desired cisnormative partnters, *Dionings*. The difficulty in this formulation flowed from the assumption of a natural right to express and act upon such a desire that could be legally defended as sharing the same justification as heterosexuality, on the basis that the gendering of the soul dictated its appropriate sexual orientation; if this worked as a tool of rhetorical and legal advocacy for the *Urning*, however, its weak spot is the *Dioning* object of desire, who by the same logic has to act against his own nature to consent to the relationship. As Ulrichs highlighted in his first published pamphlet *Vindex* (1864), "subjectively, it is unnatural for the Dioning, since the Dioning does not enjoy sex with his own kind," and his initial solution is unconvincing: the act would instead have an "objective naturalness . . . grounded in the fact that nature has bestowed upon the Dionian youth the ability to enjoy sexual pleasure with women as well as Urnings and hermaphrodites," although it is unclear why they alone have such an intrinsically promiscuous nature (Ulrichs, *Vindex*, 47).

A second explanation quickly followed which tried to parse the various channels of *Dioning* desire: here, Ulrichs distinguishes between "the necessity of the species to mate" and "the fulfillment of nonreproductive, natural, sexual activity, i.e. the sexual needs of the individual," which could be satisfied by and with *Urnings*. This allowed him to conclude that "nature did not create Dionings for women alone, *but also for Urnings*, namely, to fulfill the [second] need" (91; emphasis in original). Tellingly, this revision shifts the emphasis from the active role of the *Dioning* ("the ability to enjoy sexual pleasure") to the passive (created to fill the needs of others), in effect conceding that it is only the rights of *Urnings* that are at issue. In his focus on reproduction, Ulrichs was also making a Darwinian distinction between natural and sexual selection that proved attractive to British homophile writers of the period, including Charles Kains-Jackson, Carpenter, and Wilde. If, as Dowling suggests, the Malthusian thesis on overpopulation relieved the urgency for species reproduction, a counteracting argument could be made for the value of what in the Platonic framework she terms "spiritual procreancy," the creation of art and ideas; this in turn grounded a homosexual apologetics in which "Greek love" could be repurposed "as the animating spirit of a new chivalry, a warfare to be fought out . . . on a higher plane of ideas. In this realm," Dowling concludes, "a strategically revived idiom of Greek ideality stands to reinvigorate English civilization far more effectually than any martial force of arms."[11] In "The New Chivalry" (1894), Kains Jackson used this framework to argue for the superiority of boys as objects of desire by pointing out that pederasty does not ask "that very plain question of the Marriage Service, 'Will it lead to the procreation of children?' . . . Where boy and girl are of equal outward grace," he continued, "the spiritual ideal will prevail over the animal and the desire of influencing the higher mind, the boy's, will prevail over the old idea to add to the population."[12] Without taking it to this implicit conclusion in terms of the preferred object of desire, Wilde developed a similar line of thought at the end of "The Critic as Artist" in an extended analogy that linked aesthetics to ethics as sexual to natural selection: like the latter, he suggested, ethics "make existence possible," whereas aesthetics, "like sexual selection, make life lovely and wonderful, fill it with new forms, and give it progress, and variety and change."[13] The former (and, implicitly, heterosexual reproduction) fall in the realm of duty; the latter into the far superior one of pleasure.

Translating Sexology: Anglo-German Exchange Networks

Hearing these Darwinian echoes in German and British writing under-scores the way that evolutionary thinking acted as a transnational body of thought, much as the classical Greek and Latin traditions would have done for those with the privilege of a nineteenth-century higher education. Histories of homophile politics often assume a definitive national differ-ence that made Britain inhospitable to German sexological thinking, especially when it emphasized cross-gender identification as an intrinsic component of same-sex desire. Gert Hekma, for instance, has suggested that "in England, John Addington Symonds and the other poets of Uranian love were inspired by classical examples and came nearer to ideals of friendship and Greek eros than to those of the third sex" that were posited not only by Ulrichs but also in different ways by Richard von Krafft-Ebing and Magnus Hirschfeld.[14] This resistance was arguably stronger in Wilde than Symonds, who would develop a self-understanding that was essentially a modified version of Ulrichs, as I shall show. Hekma sees the mainline of British thinking as closer to the minor position in Germany that was grouped around Adolph Brand's journal *Der Eigene* and promoted a hypermasculine and militaristic model of male homosexuality derived from the classical Greeks and developed in reaction to "third sex" thinking; if such a model might have clearer echoes with Wilde's classical pederasty, *Der Eigene* ironically turned against him in the period following Richard Strauss's operatic version of *Salomé*, mostly, as Yvonne Ivory has suggested, because Wilde was at the same time being tied by Hirschfeld to "prevailing medicals models of homosexuality" for which cross-gender presentation was central.[15]

As opposed to standard accounts of the fin de siècle that counterpose what Julia Serano has termed "femmephobia" in Great Britain to a German "effemimania," in which there is a "cultural obsession" with "people who express femininity," I read these impulses as existing in a productive tension in both countries and nurtured by complex transna-tional exchange networks.[16] There were, to be sure, local conditions that helped determine which might be dominant: Dowling has written persua-sively, for instance, about a centuries-old British hostility to the figure of the male "effeminatus" that has little to do with gender or sexuality, while Heike Bauer has usefully suggested some of the political and cultural conditions subtending the forms in which early sexological arguments were advanced in the principalities (such as Ulrichs's Hanover) that were amalgamated into modern-day Germany.[17] But the question of influence is typically considered a unidirectional one, in which a predominantly German sexological discourse is shown to have been resisted in Britain. This misses, among other things, the ways that Ulrichs in particular revised and refined his polemical arguments and categories through an expanding set of encounters with self-defined *Urnings* across Europe, including Britain, many of whom failed to recognize themselves exactly in his speculative work. This is especially true of his writing between 1866 and 1868, when some of his rigid binaries began to break down under pressure from self-reporting that clarified that *Urnings* might desire each other, those of a similar physical appearance as themselves, and men and women simultaneously, all of which produced a more complicated charting of categories. At the same time, he tentatively recognized a category that marked the extreme of the feminine-presenting *Weibling* that more clearly anticipated the modern transwoman, and here his evidentiary archive is derived from a medley of classical sources (the Roman emperor Heliogabalus), a Berlin contemporary Frederike Blank (who petitioned to dress as a woman, be recognized under a female name, and legally marry a male fiancé), and reports of London-based "Mary Annes" (307).

One item from Ulrichs's archive summarized newspaper accounts of a fairly routine British case from 1867 against what he terms "two womanly types" for whom the arresting officer acknowledged he had trouble determining "whether they were males or females," with one being charged as Henry Maltravers but preferring to be called Kate Smith (307).[18] A letter from an "intermediate urning" from London the following year claimed to have met them and to have read them parts of Ulrichs's own work in a striking example of a closed feedback loop in which the people that served as the empirical evidence for his sexological categories came to recognize and identify themselves in the terms that he was producing.[19] This letter also highlights part of Ulrichs's problem in delineating this particular category, which his correspondent termed "true *Weiblings* who are women through and through," people he imagined as having not only "utterly feminine facial expressions [and] girlish complexion" but also "feminine structure of limbs" (192, 194). In the absence of a concept comparable to the twentieth-century idea of gender identity, it was common for early sexologists to imagine this kind of willed physical transformation occurring on the strength of a cross-gendered identification: Ulrichs, for instance, puzzled over his witnessing of a *Weibling* from Munich whom he observed as having a trachea that "as far as it can be seen externally, is thoroughly structured as a female's," an anomaly that led him to qualify the separation of *anima* and *corpore* in order to suggest that in extreme cases there might be an overlap or spillage between the two and to designate such people as a "bridge" between *Urnings* and intersex people (384).

This line of thinking calls into question Hekma's assertion that, compared to other third sex theories, in Ulrichs's thinking gender inversion "was limited: only the soul, not the body belonged to the other sex," as a marker only of sexual preference and thus "not visible in signs of the body or the mind" (Hekma, "Female Soul," 220). In some ways, this was the dream of somebody like Symonds, who strenuously argued against the common assumption that male homosexuals would "carry their lusts written in their faces" by counterposing that most "differ in no detail of their outward appearance . . . from normal men."[20] He could make such a claim only by jettisoning the *Weibling* from his model, which in turn required him to exaggerate the extent to which cross-gender identity (unlike same-sex desire) might be written on the surface of the body; paraphrasing Krafft-Ebing's description of the most intensified form of gender-nonconformity (*Androgyne/Gynandrier*), for instance, Symonds describes it as a stage in which the *anima* of spirit "modifies the bony structure of the body, the form of the face, the fleshly and muscular integuments," whereas the original is clear that such changes are only projections of physical transformation occurring in the brain (160–61).[21] This misreading is a useful example of the process that Bauer has described in which the universalizing aims of sexology were repurposed and mistranslated to suit local interests and prejudices.

It is worth asking at this point how exactly someone like Symonds could access German texts that (in the case of Krafft-Ebing's *Psychopathia Sexualis*) were not translated into English until the year before his death and (in the case of Ulrichs) until long after. Bauer offers two intersecting explanations. First, that "as a result of the Romantic legacy, middle- and upper-middle-class education, particularly in nineteenth-century Britain, often included knowledge of German," which for Symonds would have been furnished by a German governess Sophie Girard who was hired when he was ten.[22] Bauer's second thesis, especially in relation to Ulrichs, is more interesting: that his ideas "were easily understandable within different contexts without needing translation," instead having an aspect of "a-translatability [which] derives from the fact that they are based on an older

Platonic concept" (399). Knowing some German, but more importantly the Latin and Greek sources on which sexology depended for so much of its terminology would thus have enabled people like Symonds or Edward Carpenter (whose father was a scholar of German idealist philosophy) to translate – and, when necessary, mistranslate – sexology for themselves.

Symonds, Carpenter, and Male Effeminacy

A close reading of Symonds's *Memoirs* indicates some areas of mistranslation and can help to locate the terms of his resistance. Symonds is unreliable about when he first encountered Ulrichs's work and how far it influenced the composition of his sexual autobiography. Archly titling his second chapter "Containing Material which None but Students of Psychology and Ethics Need Peruse," as if to parody the scientific stance adopted by Krafft-Ebing, he insisted at its conclusion that, while writing it, "I had not read the extraordinary writings of Ulrichs, who maintains that the persons he calls Urnings form a sex apart" and that from self-examination "I do not recognize anything which justifies the theory of a female soul" (Symonds, *Memoirs,* 102–3). Another statement of ignorance was appended to the twelfth chapter on "Emotional Development," where Symonds stipulates that "This was written by me at Venice in May 1889," when "I had not then studied the cases of sexual inversion recorded by Casper-Liman, Ulrichs, and Krafft-Ebing." It was, he felt, important to leave the chapter as is ("What I wrote, I now leave as it stands") on the basis that it would be a misrepresentation "to mix it up with the discussion of theories unknown to me at the time of writing" (372). This seems a sensible precaution against the feedback loop I mentioned in the section "Translating Sexology" (and which Symonds worried about when he was writing *Sexual Inversion* with Havelock Ellis) until we check the dates, which raise questions about what he had read and when.[23] The idea of writing an autobiography was first floated in a letter to his friend Graham Dakyns just two months before he wrote the "Emotional Development" chapter in Venice and a note appended that August already described his friend Claude Cobham as "certainly what Ulrichs calls a *Weibling,*" so he quickly came to understand and utilize the German's specialist vocabulary (377); a year later he would criticize Richard Burton for having "never heard (when I last saw him) of either Ulrichs or Krafft-Ebing."[24]

Having rejected the idea of retroactively recoding his sexual autobiography in terms derived from sexological theory, Symonds nonetheless avers that in Ulrichs's "peculiar phraseology, I should certainly be tabulated as a

Mittel Urning, holding a mean between the *Mannling* and the *Weibling,"* an acknowledgment that simultaneously registers a distance from the idea of being "tabulated" at all and how he saw a use in such classificatory efforts. In seeking this middle ground, however, Symonds disavowed any suggestion of gender complementarity in favor of the love of same for same: he was, he declares, somebody "who is not marked by an effeminate passion for robust adults or by a predilection for young boys" and was thus driven by what (following Walt Whitman) he termed "comradely instincts" (103). Although he uses a German term, the closest to this "Mittel" figure in Ulrichs is actually the *Zwischenurning* that he writes about in *Memnon* as similarly marking "the midpoint in the chain whose furthest points are called Mannling and Weibling," and yet the figure is offered not as a vehicle for dismantling gender binaries but instead for restabilizing them. For Ulrichs, the heuristic purpose of the in-between was not to call into question the *Mannling/Weibling* distinction in which he had invested so much, but to clarify that each of the pair does not necessarily desire the other. In terms of object choice, the passage reconceptualizes desire as a vector of age as well as gender, so that *Weiblings* are attracted to older youths (designated by the Latin term *draucus*) and *Mannlings* to younger ones (*puer*) who are implicitly feminized; the "Zwischen" accordingly splits the difference, desiring the *Bursch* who is a combination of conventionally masculine and feminine qualities, "muscular, strong, and handsome" while also having "beautiful eyes, lips, and cheeks" with just "a little beard" that recalls Pausanius's use of facial hair to denote the onset of adult development (103). It may be that this is what Symonds was driving at in insisting his attraction was neither to "robust adults" nor to "young boys," but in designating desire for each as "effeminate" he was also claiming for himself an implied hypermasculinity: "I am," he proudly declared, "more masculine than many men I know who adore women" (103).

When it comes to narrating himself, however, Symonds' self-portrait covers attributes that were remarkably similar to the ones that Ulrichs offers of himself as a young *Weibling,* a resemblance that again raises the question of whether recognizable diagnostic questions had begun to harden into orthodoxies. Ulrichs writes of the generic type that the "feminine nature" is "by no means confined to his sexual love for men. ... He also possesses a so-called feminine personality, from childhood on, which can be observed through an inclination to girlish preoccupations, a dislike of boyish games, fights and snowball throwing, in manners, in gestures, in a certain softness of the boy's character, etc." In the case history he supplied for *Sexual Inversion*, Symonds covered similar ground, echoing some of the details and reversing signs of others as if in a deliberate strategy to occupy the middle ground: thus, he acknowledged having "avoided games and the noisy occupations of boys, but [being] only non-masculine in his indifference to sport, was never feminine in dress or habit." The *Memoirs* similarly detail a "slight" muscular build and inability to "throw a ball or a stone like other boys" and yet the section concludes with the statement "and yet I was by no means effeminate," a telling conjunctive phrasing indicating that he might have expected readers to draw the opposite conclusion (Symonds, *Memoirs,* 146).

The pattern here is less an evasion of sexology than a conscious (mis)translation of its insights that aims to keep the key terms and categories in place but sever any connection with gender transitivity. To conclude, I want to consider an alternative pathway that was taken by a contemporary of Symonds, Edward Carpenter, partly in response to the Wilde trials. As the products of similarly privileged backgrounds, there are reasons to see these men as part of a distinctive cohort, and yet each responded differently to new sexological research in Europe. In the early years of the 1890s, after corresponding with Symonds and Ellis, Carpenter delivered a series of lectures on women, marriage, sex-love, and homogenic love in a free society, seemingly planning to collect them in a book, but it was derailed by the publicity from the trials and concerns over the inclusion of the chapter on "Homogenic Love," which Carpenter had published independently. His biographer Sheila Rowbotham notes that as a consequence of the trials the chapter "had to wait until 1908 before joining the others in a revised form in *Love's Coming-of-Age.* So while the latter gathered a wide readership, *Homogenic Love* – the first British statement by a homosexual man, linking emancipation to social transformation – was destined only for friends and acquaintances," but the consequences were more dramatic than this. When a complete volume was first issued (in 1906, not two years later) it was not the chapter on homogenic love that was included but a reworked version of another Carpenter essay, now retitled "The Intermediate Sex."[25] Tracking the changes to both essays in the context of the larger argument of *Love's Coming-of-Age,* we see him turning away from older – and, as 1895 showed, unsuccessful – defenses of pederasty in favor of a sustained engagement with sexology and the feminist politics of the New Woman.

As Figure 10.1 shows, Carpenter made his revisions by literally writing over his earlier pamphlets, in this instance repurposing "Homogenic Love" for a new volume on *The Intermediate Sex* (1908) in which he referred to

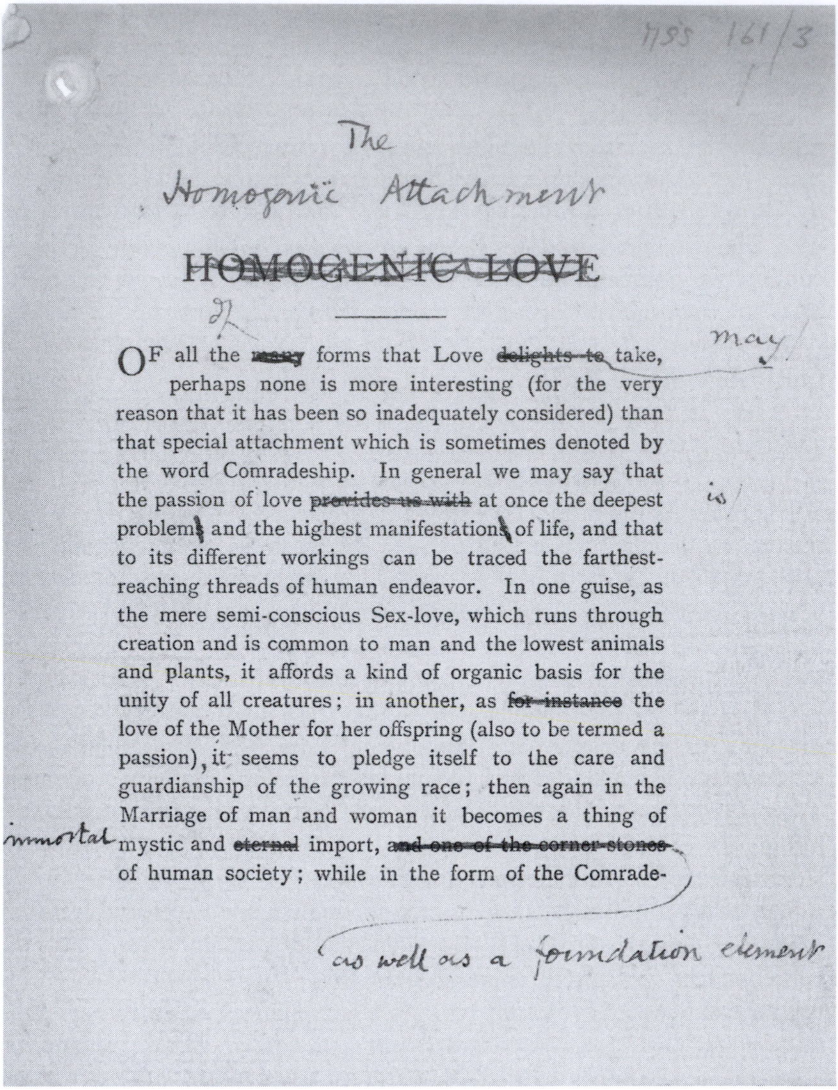

The
Homogenic Attachment

HOMOGENIC LOVE

OF all the many forms that Love delights to take, may
perhaps none is more interesting (for the very
reason that it has been so inadequately considered) than
that special attachment which is sometimes denoted by
the word Comradeship. In general we may say that
the passion of love provides us with at once the deepest is
problems and the highest manifestations of life, and that
to its different workings can be traced the farthest-
reaching threads of human endeavor. In one guise, as
the mere semi-conscious Sex-love, which runs through
creation and is common to man and the lowest animals
and plants, it affords a kind of organic basis for the
unity of all creatures; in another, as for instance the
love of the Mother for her offspring (also to be termed a
passion), it seems to pledge itself to the care and
guardianship of the growing race; then again in the
immortal Marriage of man and woman it becomes a thing of
mystic and eternal import, and one of the corner-stones
of human society; while in the form of the Comrade-

as well as a foundation element

Figure 10.1   Title page for chapter of *The Intermediate Sex*, reflecting new title and
opening. Edward Carpenter Collection. Image courtesy of Sheffield City Archives.

Ulrichs as author of the "only theory . . . which has at all held its ground in
this matter . . . that in congenital cases of sex-inversion there is a mixture of
male and female elements in the same person."[26] This realignment can
similarly be seen in added references to Magnus Hirschfeld across

successive versions of the essay. Unavailable when he published the original pamphlet, that body of work would only recently have become accessible to somebody like Carpenter and only in German. His response was initially unfavorable, as is clear from a handwritten note running vertically up the manuscript page insisting "I do not mention here some later and partly scientific writers in favour of the Urning movement like Dr. Hirschfeldt [sic], because their work is perhaps too partisan in character"[27] (see Figure 10.2). In 1908, however, he substituted a new footnote reversing his assessment, declaring that Hirschfeld's approach "though avowedly favourable to the Uranian movement, is in a high degree scientific and reliable in character" (54). This shift from thinking of Hirschfeld as "partisan" to "scientific and reliable" indicates Carpenter's search for new forms of advocacy in the wake of the Wilde trials and readiness to break with British instincts to distrust German sexology especially over issues of gender expression. This engagement challenges the standard view that (as Jeffrey Weeks puts it) "effeminacy, the usual characteristic for male homosexuality, was not necessarily linked with homosexuality" in Carpenter's thinking.[28] Such an assessment is tied to passages in *Love's Coming-of-Age* that survived from the earlier pamphlet contrasting "normal" and "extreme" models of male and female homosexuality, with the latter in each case recycling homophobic and transphobic repudiations of cross-gender expression: an "extreme" gay man, for instance, would be "mincing in gait and manners," "the voice inclining to be high-pitched," and "skillful at the needle and in woman's work."[29] Such passages are impossible to defend, but only suggest one part of the intervention that Carpenter was making in his revision for the newly integrated and complete text of *Love's Coming-of-Age*. Its new opening insisted that the appearance of "New Woman" thinking in the 1890s, the peak of which roughly coincided with the Wilde trials, raised the possibility of a rapprochement between gender roles that had been moving apart, with modern women now "a little more masculine" and "modern man (it is to be hoped), while by no means effeminate . . . a little more sensitive in temperament and artistic in feeling than the original John Bull" (Carpenter, *Love's Coming-of-Age*, 114). By the chapter's end, this optimism has drained away, speaking of "an alienation of the sexes from each other, of which complaint is so often made to-day" (133). Squaring this circle requires distinguishing between Carpenter's descriptive and prescriptive agendas: either the general complaint misses evidence of a progressive movement to combat alienation or that movement is something his book wants to will into being. Either way, its motor forces are the

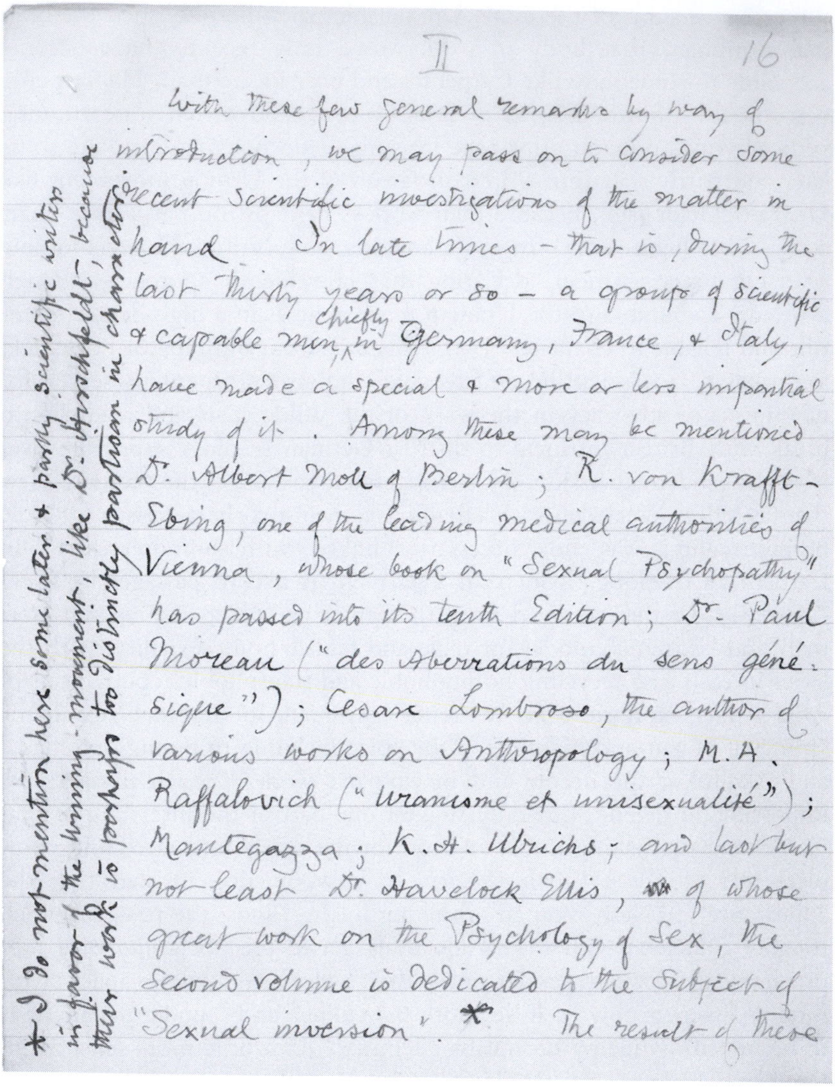
II 16

With these few general remarks by way of introduction, we may pass on to consider some recent scientific investigations of the matter in hand. In late times – that is, during the last thirty years or so – a group of scientific & capable men, chiefly in Germany, France, & Italy, have made a special & more or less impartial study of it. Among these may be mentioned Dr. Albert Moll of Berlin; R. von Krafft-Ebing, one of the leading medical authorities of Vienna, whose book on "Sexual Psychopathy" has passed into its tenth Edition; Dr. Paul Moreau ("des Aberrations du sens génésique"); Cesare Lombroso, the author of various works on Anthropology; M.A. Raffalovich ("Uranisme et unisexualité"); Mantegazza; K.H. Ulrichs; and last but not least Dr. Havelock Ellis, of whose great work on the Psychology of Sex, the second volume is dedicated to the subject of "Sexual inversion". * The result of these

* I do not mention here some later & partly scientific writers in favor of the uraning movement, like Dr. Hirschfeldt, because their work is perhaps too distinctly partisan in character.

Figure 10.2 Material added in revision for *The Intermediate Sex*, including note on Hirschfeld, running up left-hand side. Edward Carpenter Collection. Image courtesy of Sheffield City Archives.

New Woman and the invert, both of whom "can do much to fill the gap" between men and women. In his most Utopian strain, Carpenter elevates such inverts, "through their double nature, command of life in all its phases, and a certain freemasonry of the secrets of the two sexes," to a position as "reconcilers and interpreters" who can explain genders to each other (134).

If the "extreme" versions were being jettisoned, perhaps into a new category defined by something like gender identity, this was not, as is often imagined, a simple retrenchment of cisnormativity. For Carpenter, inversion was in and of itself bi-gendered, and as such could anticipate a future marked less by gender antipathy and more by mutual understanding. In this future, he suggested in the chapter immediately preceding "The Intermediate Sex" (on "Marriage: A Forecast"), even heterosexual marriage and monogamy might have a chance, but they needed the example of inversion to indicate new forms of mutual respect and love. In similar ways, another of the earlier chapters ("On Woman in Freedom") upheld a surprisingly queer and gender-transitive version of the New Woman – "rather mannish in temperament," perhaps "homogenic," to some of whom "children are more or less a bore; to others, man's sex-passion is a mere impertinence" – as the forerunner of new domestic arrangements: Carpenter felt that, freed from the burden of species reproduction, their efforts could "result in a tremendous improvement in the general position of their more commonplace sisters." A decision not to "devote itself to the work of maternity" thereby held out hope for a revised "notion of motherhood far more dignified than before," just as inverts might save heterosexuality by situating themselves outside of it (67).

There is a lot in Carpenter that is hard to defend or make use of today, but I would nonetheless argue that his work has more promise than that of either Symonds or Wilde. Uniquely among the possibilities on offer, his thinking allows for the interaction between same-sex advocacy and gender-based progressive activism, to the extent of seeing the two struggles as fully integrated with each other. He got there in part by taking on board the insights of sexology, demonstrating comparatively little of the resistance that marks much of the British homophile movement in the nineteenth century. On this issue, his denigration of the "extreme" versions of male and female homosexuality is the most significant blot, and perhaps only recuperable in the context of the similar differentiations that were being elaborated by people such as Ulrichs and Hirschfeld, both of whom struggled to imagine a category like the transsexual, who would be simultaneously distinct from, yet allied to, the *Urning* or invert. Looking back at the 1890s from a moment when our own imagining of such a coalitional model is under pressure, it would be here, and not to a more recognizable figure such as Wilde, that I would look for guidance.

Notes

1 Richard Ellmann, *Oscar Wilde* (London: Hamish Hamilton, 1987), 553.

2 Alan Sinfield, *The Wilde Century: Effeminacy, Oscar Wilde, and the Queer Moment* (London: Cassell, 1994), 124–25.

3 David Halperin, *One Hundred Years of Homosexuality* (New York: Routledge, 1989), 8–9; and *How to Do the History of Homosexuality* (Chicago, IL: University of Chicago Press, 2002), 109.

4 Alan Sinfield, *On Sexuality and Power* (New York: Columbia University Press, 2004), 93.

5 An ominous sign of this unraveling would be the increasing visibility of so-called LGB Alliances. For a useful discussion of such developments in the UK, see Finn McKay, *Female Masculinities and the Gender Wars: The Politics of Sex* (London: I. B. Taurus, 2020), ch. 4.

6 Oscar Wilde to Robert Ross (? February 18, 1898) in *Complete Letters of Oscar Wilde*, eds. Merlin Holland and Rupert Hart-Davis (New York: Henry Holt, 2000), 1019.

7 Amber K. Regis, ed., *Memoirs of John Addington Symonds* (New York: Palgrave Macmillan, 2016), 152.

8 Ulrichs acknowledged *The Symposium* as his source by citing the passage in question as the epigraph of the tenth in his series of pamphlets, "Prometheus" (1870). See Karl Heinrich Ulrichs, *The Riddle of Man-Manly Love*, trans. Michael A. Lombardi-Nash (Amherst: Prometheus Books, 1994), 542.

9 Plato, *The Symposium, in The Dialogues of Plato*, trans. Benjamin Jowett (Oxford: Clarendon Press, 1953), 1:513.

10 John Addington Symonds, *A Problem in Greek Ethics*, reprinted in *John Addington Symonds (1840–1893) and Homosexuality*, ed. Sean Brady (London: Palgrave MacMillan, 2012), 39–121 (76).

11 Linda C. Dowling, *Hellenism and Homosexuality in Victorian Oxford* (Ithaca, NY: Cornell University Press, 1994), 30–31. *The Symposium* is again the key text, especially Socrates's recounting of a conversation with Diotima in which she noted that "there are men who are more creative in their souls than in their bodies." Jowett's translation suggests the homosocial context for the former, as opposed to the explicitly heterosexual basis of physical reproduction: "When he finds a fair and noble and well-nurtured soul, he embraces the two in one person, and to such a one he is full of speech about virtue and the nature and pursuits of a good man, and he tries to educate him" (*Dialogues*, 1: 541).

12 Charles Kains-Jackson, "The New Chivalry" (1894), reprinted in *Nineteenth-Century Writings on Homosexuality*, ed. Chris White (New York: Routledge, 1999), 154–58 (157).

13 Oscar Wilde, "The Critic as Artist," in *The Collected Works of Oscar Wilde* (Ware: Wordsworth Press, 1997), 963–1016 (1015).

14 Gert Hekma, "A Female Soul in a Male Body: Sexual Inversion as Gender Inversion in Nineteenth-Century Sexology," in *Third Sex, Third Gender:*

Beyond Sexual Dimorphism in Culture and History, ed. Gilbert Herdt (New York: Zone Books, 1994), 213–39 (220).

15 Yvonne Ivory, "The Trouble with Oskar: Wilde's Legacy for the Homosexual Rights Movement in Germany," in *Oscar Wilde and Modern Culture: The Making of a Legend*, ed. Joseph Bristow (Athens, OH: Ohio University Press, 2008), 133–53 (146). "In their treatment of Wilde," Ivory argues, "the two movements made public their ideological differences; Wilde's being championed by [Hirschfeld] ultimately led to his being rejected by [Brand] – by the very organization, ironically, whose ideas best reflected his own philosophy" (135).

16 Serano defines these terms in her "A Transgender Glossary," accessible at http://www.juliaserano.com/terminology.html.

17 See Dowling, 8–12, on the *effeminatus*. Heike Bauer has argued through careful comparison of German and English versions of Krafft-Ebing's *Psychopathia Sexualis* that translations into English, beginning in the 1890s, emphasized a social-Darwinist focus on same-sex desire as a potential index of national and imperial degeneration that was absent in the original German. See Heike Bauer, "'Not a Translation but a Mutilation': Translation and the Discipline of Sexology," *Yale Journal of Criticism* 16, no. 2 (2003), 381–405.

18 The appearance of Maltravers/Smith and Claire Montague before the Marlborough Street magistrate in London was reported in *The Sun* (October 18, 1867), 3 under the heading "RIDDING TOWN OF A BRACE OF DANGEROUS FELLOWS." Charged with causing a disturbance of the peace for frequenting "urinals" and arguing with prostitutes in Piccadilly, they were bound to be of good behavior for six months on sureties of £100 each.

19 The danger of requiring an identification in terms that precede and override the individual's experience is a familiar complaint in trans writing. See, for instance, Sandy Stone, "The 'Empire' Strikes Back: A Posttranssexual Manifesto," in *Transgender Studies Reader*, eds. Susan Stryker and Stephen Whittle (New York: Routledge, 2006), 221–35.

20 John Addington Symonds, Problem in Modern Ethics, in *John Addington Symonds (1840–1893) and Homosexuality*, 123–208 (134–35).

21 For comparison, see Richard von Krafft-Ebing, *Psychopathia Sexualis*, trans. Franklin S. Klaf (New York: Arcade Publishing, 2011), 216.

22 See Phyllis Grosskurth, *The Woeful Victorian: A Biography of John Addington Symonds* (New York: Holt, Rinehart and Winston, 1965), 9. Intriguingly, Matthew Sturgis's recent biography records that Wilde and his brother also had "a succession of governesses, usually foreign, [who] introduced them at least to both French and German." See Matthew Sturgis, *Oscar Wilde* (New York: Knopf, 2021), 24.

23 "I framed a set of questions upon the points which seemed to me of most importance after a study of Ulrichs and Krafft-Ebing," Symonds wrote in 1892, but he also recorded his concern that the "diffusion" of sexological texts "may tend to the formation of a kind of 'fixed style' in these confessions."

Correspondence reprinted in Havelock Ellis and John Addington Symonds, *Sexual Inversion, A Critical Edition*, ed. Ivan Crozier (New York: Palgrave Macmillan, 2008), 250.

24 Symonds to Dakyns (September 24, 1890), in *Letters of John Addington Symonds*, eds. Herbert M. Schueller and Robert L. Peters (Detroit, MI: Wayne State University Press, 1969), 3:500.

25 Sheila Rowbotham, *Edward Carpenter: A Life of Liberty and Love* (London: Verso, 2008), 190.

26 Edward Carpenter, *The Intermediate Sex: A Study of Some Transitional Types of Men and Women* (London: George Allen and Unwin, 1908), 66.

27 Carpenter, handwritten MS of *The Intermediate Sex*, Carpenter Collection MSS 161 (p. 16). To the extent that he would have read Hirschfeld's work by this point, it was most likely a text like *Der Uranische Mensch* (1903–04) or contributions to the *Jahrbuch für Zwischenstufen*, which he had been publishing since 1897.

28 Jeffrey Weeks, *Coming Out: Homosexual Politics in Britain, From the 19th Century to the Present* (London: Quartet, 1977), 49.

29 Edward Carpenter, *Love's Coming-Of-Age: A Series of Papers on Relations of the Sexes* (London: Swan Sonnenschein, 1906), 127.

Eugenics and Degeneration in Socialist-Feminist Novels of the Mid-1890s

Diana Maltz

It is a troubling but accurate claim that before the specter of the Nazi Final Solution, many British intellectuals at the fin de siècle perceived eugenics as forward-thinking and liberating.[1] Ample evidence is found in the records of the radical Men and Women's Club, led by statistician Karl Pearson, a protégé of the founder of eugenic theory Francis Galton.[2] As the Fabians reorganized state government into the 1910s, this eugenic goal would permeate their implementation of the "endowment of motherhood," a scheme to support new mothers and reduce infant mortality and malnutrition.[3] The link between eugenics and aspirations for a rural utopia further undergirded some of the earliest proposals for town planning.[4] Eugenicist ideologies pervaded various literary projects: H. G. Wells's and George Bernard Shaw's works reflected a strain of eugenic thinking,[5] as did the writings of their socialist-feminist contemporaries. In such works, we observe the sometime coalescence between late-Victorian concerns about degeneration and emerging eugenic solutions.

This chapter looks to progressive women writers who framed the male decadent as an enervated, parasitical specimen and an obstacle to social, evolutionary advancement. In 1979, literary critic Linda Dowling posited the figures of the decadent and New Woman as allies against the status quo in the 1890s, and this claim has carried weight with critics ever since.[6] Yet, depending on how they defined decadence, some New Women writers of the fin de siècle would have recoiled at the pairing.[7] In their fictions, Gertrude Dix (1867–1950) and Emma Frances Brooke (1844–1926) respectively endorsed ideas of degeneration and eugenics in the service of promoting an ideal healthy body within a rural utopian schema. What sets their novels apart from those of better-known New Women novelists Sarah Grand, George Egerton, and Mona Caird is that these authors subscribed to socialism as well as feminism, particularly revering Edward Carpenter's ethos of simple living.[8]

The subject of relatively meager scholarly attention, socialist-feminist novels constitute a subspecies of realist fiction in the 1890s.[9] Unlike the middle-class New Woman novel, they frequently chronicle women's participation in radical movements. They feature industrial strikes, rural communes, anarchist violence, and free-love relationships. Although some authors espoused Fabian "gas-and-water" state socialism, others were less driven by theories of taxation and more by the prospect of the moral perfection of the individual. These ethical socialists met in groups like the Fellowship of the New Life (FNL, 1883–97), where they imagined ways of performing their conscience, whether through servantless housekeeping, refusal to eat animal products, coeducating their children, or communal living. They embraced a late Victorian millenarian optimism that historian Stephen Yeo has called "the religion of socialism."[10]

During their lifetimes, many socialist-feminist authors were better known as activists. Edith Lees Ellis belonged to the FNL; Emma Frances Brooke had leadership roles in the Fabian Society; Gertrude Dix was active in the Bristol Socialists; and Katharine St. John Conway was a Bristol Socialist, a Fabian, and a founding member of the Independent Labour Party.[11] Although their locales and formal affiliations divided them,[12] a unifying influence appears to have been Edward Carpenter, who sustained an association with all their organizations.[13]

Socialist-feminist novelists embraced Carpenter's belief in a simpler, healthier life as a chosen daily ethics and paired this with an apprehension about the inadequate, defective male body. In Gertrude Dix's *The Girl from the Farm* (1895), the narrator admires the athletic, ethically evolved protagonist Katharine Marchant at the expense of her feeble, irresolute brother. His moral failings are manifested in his deficient body, and it is suggested that this deficient body generated those moral failings. In Emma Frances Brooke's *A Superfluous Woman* (1894), the protagonist Jessamine Halliday marries a degenerate aristocrat and gives birth to children with severe disabilities (one of whom later murders the other). As lurid as this scenario appears, in earlier scenes, Brooke has envisioned an alternative to her heroine's degradation, suggesting a return to a more authentic, egalitarian, unselfconscious rural life. In sum, both Dix and Brooke use the unsavory figure of the decadent to reject middle- and upper-class convention in favor of health and liberation, and in this way, they anticipate twenty-first-century social critiques of decadence.[14] Their visions are not altogether unified, however: whereas Dix simply dismisses her flimsy, immature dandy, Brooke advocates a more radical "negative eugenics" with an eye to her decadent's diseased offspring.[15] While Dix's heroine ultimately sets her sights on the cultured metropolis, Brooke never ceases idealizing a rural retreat.

As socialists, these novelists were ironically appropriating eugenicist thinking and turning it against its originators. Francis Galton had proposed that arranged marriages among the upper classes ensured a genetically superior race, but Dix and Brooke argued that wealthy men were less likely to be "eminent" (Galton's word) and more likely to be degenerate.[16] Their fictional middle- and upper-class men are louche and languishing, morally and genetically unfit. As a foil to Jessamine's dissipated aristocratic husband, Brooke presents a young poor Scottish farmer defined by his honesty and robust constitution. A concern for eugenic marriage was simultaneously emerging in other New Woman fictions as well. Sarah Grand's *The Heavenly Twins* (1893), with its treatment of a syphilitic rake, anticipates the preoccupation with hereditary disease that we will find in Brooke's novel a year later.[17] In Ménie Muriel Dowie's *Gallia* (1895), the progressive Girton-educated protagonist shrewdly selects a future husband on eugenic grounds. But neither she nor any of *Gallia*'s other urbane characters expresses a romantic desire for the simple life or opprobrium for profligate gentry. Simplification and praise of the healthy body in nature were specific to these socialist writers, who took their cues from Edward Carpenter.

Edward Carpenter and the Simple Life

Edward Carpenter catalyzed the counterculture as it existed at the turn of the century. In writings and lectures, he advocated the social benefits of such innovations as wool-wearing, back-to-the-land settlement, cooperativism, vegetarianism, the eradication of hired servants, free love, and women's rights. Drawing on an eclectic assortment of social movements and philosophies, he synthesized them into a complex bohemian subculture. He read up on new inquiries into the afterlife and spirit world and Theosophy's foray into merging esoteric, non-Western religious beliefs. He studied Lamarckian evolution, which claimed that the biological organism adapts to social circumstance. He familiarized himself with advances in the field of sexology. He absorbed John Ruskin's reverence for the medieval crafts guild, and he studied the economic materialism of Marx and Engels. There were his direct ventures into Indian philosophy and Hindu mysticism. In 1890, he visited Ceylon and India, where he sat at the feet of a swami. Carpenter was a central player in the fin-de-siècle English quest for spiritual awakening.

Perhaps most striking was Carpenter's idea that small daily practices were themselves revolutionary ways of living ethically. Carpenter and his friends believed that one got closer to aesthetic and spiritual enlightenment through the minute and ordinary, and this influenced their daily choices of cups, plates, beds, and foods, and even the fabrics they wore. In *England's Ideal* (1887) and *Civilisation: Its Cause and Cure* (1889), he anticipated society shedding its middle-class values. Newly self-conscious, everyone was longing for and edging closer to a "higher morality" and a "better conception of human dignity."[18] Ultimately, the return to the primitive would be the key to our spiritual renewal: "The meaning of the old religions will come back to [man]. On the high tops once more gathering he will celebrate with naked dances the glory of the human form and the great processions of the stars, or greet the bright horn of the young moon."[19]

At the heart of his mission of "simplification" was a faith in the vital body. In his essays, Carpenter itemized the meager costs of his homegrown vegetarian diet and proclaimed the comfort of sandaled feet and clothes that breathed. He lauded uncluttered spaces and bare floors, the satisfactions of physical labor, and implicitly, the class redemption inherent in rural self-sufficiency. Although Carpenter encouraged people to find their own methods of living, devotees eagerly interpreted these statements as directives. His praise of a simpler lifestyle coalesced into several interlocking ethical imperatives: the reification of a pure English countryside, the return to older rhythms of life, and the liberation of the body from the constraints of modernity. A closer look at the social circles he occupied, however, underscores the complexity of late-Victorian progressive ethics. For some, the predominant belief in healthful vitality would be closely allied with eugenics.

Carpenter himself did not espouse eugenic theory. In an addendum to his rereleased *Civilisation* in 1920, it was his friend, the sexologist and fellow "New Lifer" Havelock Ellis, who suggested why modern societies lacked robustness:

> In the ancient civilisations, was the practice of infanticide applied to inferior babies and the habit of allowing sick persons to die. That was evidently the secret of the natural superiority of the savage and of the men of the old civilisation, for the Greeks and Romans were very stringent in this matter. The flabbiness of the civilised and the prevalence of doctors and hygienists ... is due to the modern tenderness for human life which is afraid to kill off even the most worthless specimens and so lowers the whole level of "civilised" humanity. Introduce a New Hardness in this matter and

we should return to the high level of savagery, while the doctors would disappear as if by magic. I don't myself believe we *can* introduce this hardness; and that is why I attach so much importance to *intelligent* eugenics, working through birth-control, as the only *now possible* way of getting towards that high natural level you aim at. (78)

Notably, while grateful for the clarification, Carpenter gingerly called our "modern tenderness" only "*one* cause . . . of the failure of modern civilisations" (78; italics in the original). As the eugenic movement solidified with the establishment of the Eugenics Educational Society in 1907, Ellis published works such as "The Sterilisation of the Unfit" (1909), *The Problem of Race-Regeneration* (1911), and *The Task of Social Hygiene* (1912).[20] Yet he had already anticipated his eugenic advocacy through sexological writings at the fin de siècle.[21] His volume *The Criminal* (1890) also paraphrased ideas about congenital depravity from Cesare Lombroso's *Criminal Man* (1887). By the mid-1890s, socialist-feminist novelists united Ellis's concerns about hereditary weakness with Carpenter's desire for the simple life. This healthy life required intentionality.

The Girl from the Farm

Scholars of the 1890s know *The Girl from the Farm* (1895) as a New Woman novel and a text in the radical Keynote Series from John Lane's press The Bodley Head. It has received hardly any critical attention, perhaps because of its static setting in a cathedral town, its simple plot, and its mostly bourgeois characters. Dix's follow-up novel *The Image Breakers* (1900) featured men and women in free unions, hints of same-sex eroticism, the collapse of a rural commune, and an anarchist bomb-maker's descent into manic insanity.[22] In 1900, Dix daringly left Britain to homestead in the California Sierras with her new husband Robert Nichol, who disseminated Carpenter's pamphlets on "homogenic love" across the American West. If *The Girl from the Farm* appears a tame beginning, it is nevertheless a bridge to her later work. The novel interrogates genetic inheritance, sexual fallenness, class inequality, and decadence. In contrast to her later life experiment in America, *The Girl from the Farm* gestures to the ideal of rural utopia only briefly before steering its protagonist to the metropolis as the locus of real social change.

In this story, Hilary Marchant, a dean's dissolute son, seduces and impregnates a young country woman. When his sister, Katharine, discovers the girl homeless and penniless, she saves her from drowning and shelters her in her bedroom. But her parents recoil from harboring a fallen woman in their home, wary that her presence will attract gossip. Although his mother guesses Hilary might be responsible for the pregnancy, the farm girl never exposes his sin to his parents. Katharine's father, whose sight has been failing throughout the novel, collapses and dramatically goes blind just as Hilary arrives on the scene. Katharine, perceiving the truth, quickly shepherds the girl off to a new life in London. The novel's complexity lies in the slow burn leading up to this flight.

Dix associates Hilary's moral weakness with his physical feebleness. Mrs. Marchant, who dotes on him, regrets that he "had not inherited her excellent constitution. Indeed, he was far less robust than his sister, and among other characteristics, like his father, had long and nervous hands, never for a moment still."[23] His nervous hands are metonymic of a sensibility that is high-strung to a fault. Like his father's weak, white "bloodless" hands (Dix, *Girl,* 51), they hint that the family has gone through progressive stages of degeneration. Indeed, notwithstanding the fact that Dean Marchant is gradually descending into blindness, he has always been "a man of an originally delicate constitution, rendered still more feeble by a life of sedentary labour" (38). Mrs. Marchant consequently frames Hilary as a potential invalid; she is gratified that he looks "handsome *and well*" (30, my emphasis); she urges him to continue his long walks as "too close study is not good for you" (30).

Dr. Marchant identifies a simultaneous character defect through Hilary's failure to build a career for himself: "His achievements at College had amounted to nothing except in the matter of debts, by which his resources had been crippled for some time to come. Irresolute, unstable as water, he loved to dabble first with one thing and then with another, till the novelty of his occupation had worn off, and he would throw it up for something else" (50). Apart from the cunningly displaced word "crippled" here, the understanding is that the unproductive, indebted Hilary is a dilettante.

This story is in fact grounded in Hilary's decadent subjectivity. The opening scene, during which he is on one of his country rambles, shows his inclination to view the world as spectacle rather than truly engage with it. He responds to the vista before him as if it were artificial: "as he might have walked through some gallery of *mediocre* paintings" (2; italics in the original). He is jolted out of his ennui when he surveys a derelict farmhouse, whose ugliness transfixes him:

> He tried to find some explanation for the curious attraction which rooted
> him to the spot. The air of tragedy which hung about it was due, he

thought, to some other cause than the mere disposition of its stones and the signs of neglect and decay about them. Once or twice in his life, other places, with no peculiarities in their physical details, had seemed to single themselves from the rest to appeal to him in this remarkable way with suggestions of horror and crime. He was alive to impressions conveyed thus mysteriously as the sensitised plate is receptive of more than can be perceived by the eyes. He tried to recall the *quasi*-scientific theory which he had himself formed to account for the phenomenon. Wearied however, in his attempt to pick up the threads, he relapsed into vague speculations as to the sordid drama of lust or cruelty of which he felt sure this farm of fallen fortunes had been the theatre. (3–4)

As with the rural setting that had led him to it, Hilary also positions the farmhouse as a "theatre," again conveying his desire to aestheticize and rewrite the world around him as artifice. Further, in the passage, terms like "curious," "impressions," "sensation," and "suggestions" seem allusive of Walter Pater's prescriptive Conclusion to *Studies in the History of the Renaissance* (1873). Tellingly, Hilary gravitates to sights that mirror his own degeneration and around which he can concoct thrilling, crude narratives. In this regard, he embodies Max Nordau's earlier insight into the decadent sensibility: whereas "the ordinary man always seeks to think, to feel, and to do the same as the multitude [,] the decadent seeks exactly the contrary."[24] Less than a decade before the novel, Oscar Wilde had theorized the appeal of the ugly, claiming that a good artist could effectively aestheticize ugliness.[25] Indeed, the decadent pursuit of the sensations, by definition, would include the quest not only for beauty, but also for repulsion. Wilde's Dorian Gray visits opium dens and lowlife slums to truly know ugliness. Like Dorian, Hilary Marchant undertakes a "*quasi*-scientific" diagnosis of his own responses, an act that confirms him as decadent in thought and feeling. He dispassionately compares his enjoyment of the ugly to the technical receptivity of a photographic "sensitised plate."

In this dismal scene, Hilary encounters the girl: "He observed to himself that she was a lily on a dung-hill; that she belonged to the picture; that in certain ways the influence of the strange house was upon her, though in others she had escaped it" (8). Hilary suspects that she might have been "the victim of frequent hard words, even of blows" (8), correlating her with the tales of crime and cruelty he had fantasized about the house. Because of her class abjection, she embodies a taste of the repellent and aesthetic at the same time.

Hilary is not diabolical or even wholly amoral; in his earliest exchange with the girl, he is anxious to assuage her tears and he later has pangs of conscience over deflowering her. He had not actively sought her ruination but had been careless: his seducing her was "the mere drifting on an unhindered current of inclination" (114); however, this drifting itself seems symptomatic of a decadent solipsism. Later, after a stormy night during which the girl confronts him outside his home and he nearly confesses the affair to Katharine, he awakens refreshed, though nothing has really changed: "He remembered it now as an evil dream, which continues to affect the nerves only as long as one broods about it in the dark" (115). This easy dismissal of his own sin resembles Dorian Gray's parallel reasoning, "If one doesn't talk about a thing, it has never happened."[26] Like Dorian's secrecy over the portrait, Hilary destroys the evidence of his illicit affair by burning his sketches of the girl's face (Dix, *Girl*, 114).

Hilary's temperament recalls symptoms in Nordau's *Degeneration* (1892). He is persistently twitchy: he first encounters the girl while driven by "restless discontent" on his walk; he remains "restless and disinclined to sit still" after arriving home (2, 35). At the piano, he "play[s] one thing after another by fits and snatches"; he generally experiences only a "fitful energy which came in restless spurts" (31, 67). This jumpiness is also borne of his compulsion to return to the farm and see the girl again. When he does so, covertly, the exposure to damp brings on fever and he is bedridden for a month. Hilary's illness is at least partly fueled by his torment at what he has wrought, since he has caught a glimpse of the girl's "altered" condition (157). Physically weakened, he is also tearful at his mother's questioning, driven by a "morbidly quick intuition of intense nervous irritability" (153).

Meanwhile, it is ironic that characters mistakenly attribute restlessness to Katharine. Her father, anxious that she will desert him and their philological work together, worries that she has caught "the restless, modern spirit" (130). But Katharine maintains a cool head, despite her active, athletic body. Her moral compass is clearer than Hilary's and her destiny less elusive to her. She has graduated from the university and sees her sojourn at home in Allerton helping her father complete his manuscript as merely temporary. From the start, she looks forward to a London life that will suit her New Woman predilections; she anticipates teaching, journalism, and solving social problems among the urban poor. Katharine's understanding of social duty is continuously juxtaposed against her mother's more conventional forms of charity. The societies that Mrs. Marchant subscribes to, such as the Penitent's Home Association, sustain the status quo, and she uses them to shore up her middle-class respectability. Although Katharine shares a similar desire to perform good works, her urban aspirations elicit her mother's suspicion because they would ostensibly threaten Katharine's marriageability and social standing in Allerton.

Katharine has "ideas about humanity," her mother says vaguely (116). We can gain a sense of what they are through allusions to Katharine's friends and influences. Mrs. Marchant complains:

> Ah . . . people talk a great deal of nonsense about Nature and simplification of life. Of course you don't mean it, Hilary; but it is the sort of thing one should be on one's guard against. There is that Mr. Gardener Katharine knows, who writes books about it, and goes to *absurd* extremes. He was an Oxford man, yet he actually lives with quite poor people in their *hugger-mugger* way (I do not like that term, but I don't know else how to express what I mean), and earns a living by market-gardening – or was it making sandals? – calls himself a socialist, and positively declines to live on some property which was left him. I do not think it could have been much, or he would not be so foolish. A friend of mine who met him said she was surprised to find him quite a gentleman, and that of course makes it all the more regrettable.

> "I wish", said Hilary, "one need not have the bother of peeling one's apples. It seems a thing that ought to be done *for* one." (30–31; italics in the original)

Mr. Gardener is, of course, Dix's fictionalization of Carpenter, whose eager rejection of his class status is distasteful and unfathomable to Mrs. Marchant. Hilary's response confirms the class complacency his mother has taught him and demonstrates his aspirations to dandiacal idleness.

Katharine's sensibility has been shaped by Carpenterian ideals. Walking with "long, swinging strides," she rejoices in the beautiful countryside surrounding her parish home (101). She discards "unnecessary draperies" in her dress and opts for "plainly-coloured walls and polished floor[s]," assuring her mother, "I think them lovely . . . they remind me of my college rooms" (101, 93). This austerity is redolent of Carpenter's writings on the home, and Mrs. Marchant seems aware of this when she admits, "I suppose it is aesthetic . . . but to me it looks bare" (93).[27] Katharine's attempt at New Life simplicity in her parents' home is a workable compromise until she confronts their small-mindedness; ultimately, these two worlds cannot be reconciled.

Mr. Gardener may have modeled the simple life for Katharine, but he never gets another mention in the book or makes a real appearance there. She never theorizes retreating to an agricultural commune as others did in her generation (and as characters do in Dix's second novel). For young, privileged Katharine, London signifies the future for a progressive New Woman. The city also affords ample means for intellectual stimulation and pleasure: a circle of friends instead of loneliness; the latest plays as opposed to penny literature sold off the cart of an itinerant peddler (123, 7). In this regard, Katharine departs from the general trend of Carpenterian pastoralism.

Nevertheless, she retains some allegiance to Carpenter's ethics and sensibility. When Katharine defies her family's values by sheltering the pregnant girl, they call her quixotic (213) – a claim that had been leveled at Carpenter's own projects. Katharine is in fact more modern than her mother, who would banish the pregnant girl to a refuge for fallen women and expect her to atone for her sins. Katharine argues that the girl has no need of repentance and that she is pure, even if she is longer a virgin. Meanwhile, the girl sleeps upstairs in her bedroom, watched over by a Madonna and a "Buddh[a] from an Indian shrine" (220). The latter gestures not only to Katharine's university education, but also to her exposure to Carpenterian counterculture. The Buddha gazes "in unruffled contemplation" at the girl in the bed (220). Katharine, too, would ideally move her parents from agitation at the girl's presence to thoughtful tranquility. Seeing their parochialism, she opts for London instead. Her charged leave-taking with the girl is akin to the dramatic door slam at the end of Henrik Ibsen's *A Doll's House* (1879). Escaping to the city, Katharine censures her parents' disingenuousness, as they condone Hilary's decadence under the pretense of respectability. Katharine's clear-sighted renunciation of her family contrasts with the troubled complicity of Brooke's heroine, as we will see.

A Superfluous Woman

Emma Frances Brooke came to the Fabian Society in 1885 by way of the Hampstead Historic Club, where she had read Marx with the anarchist Charlotte Wilson. She was well integrated in British radical circles. Beyond her association with the Men and Women's Club (through which she would have known Olive Schreiner), Wilson's *Freedom* magazine would have granted her an acquaintanceship with Carpenter and the Tolstoyan anarchists in the Croydon Brotherhood (who sought to forge a utopia through rural settlement and who were themselves an offshoot of the Fellowship of the New Life).[28] Nevertheless, Brooke had a vexed history with members of the FNL.[29] Her novel's advocacy of the simple life demonstrates how one might selectively embrace one ideological tenet of a group while renouncing others.

A Superfluous Woman relies on a pastoralism that critics until now have simply bypassed as incidental to the plot rather than critical to her socialist vision. The sage Dr. Cornerstone advocates for progressive late-Victorian ideologies, including women's education and restoration of the body through meaningful work. Although he never prescribes a flight to the country specifically, living simply while in London has not proven effective for the heroine. She needs the rural retreat to distance herself from the lure of the London season. Ultimately, the novel's claims for a new modern purity rest on both eugenic and environmental ideals.

The book begins with the words, "Dying? H'm!" uttered by the world-weary and wise doctor who has been summoned to the bedside of Jessamine Halliday, a socialite wasting away from an unnamed illness.[30] Dr. Cornerstone surveys the luxuries of her home and determines that she has suffered "a splenetic seizure brought on by *ennui* and excessive high breeding. ... Her imagination had been touched by the picturesque interest of mortal decay upon aesthetic furniture" (11; italics in the original). Cynical as the doctor's words are, they pinpoint the two central problems in Jessamine's life. She is at the mercy of the fashionable world, and her disposition lends itself to it. Jessamine is a distillation of the worst of high society: she is flighty, insincere, willful, narcissistic, an expert poseur.

Spurred by Cornerstone, she awakens to a life of action. But even then, her new commitment to service is erratic and self-conscious, a new sequence of poses as she restlessly jumps from one trend to the next. At one point, Jessamine reads Thoreau and dresses in "unbleached calico and prints at twopence a yard," efforts redolent of Carpenter's stripped-down aesthetic (13). Although she is fundamentally healthy in body, aristocratic living has muddied her instincts, producing a hysterical, pathological subject. She is deficient in what Cornerstone calls "mind-energy": the ability to use her intellect and resist the call of her own vanity (15). Yet Jessamine does, in fact, intermittently perceive her life with discernment. The crux of the novel is her vacillation between earnestly wanting to free herself from Society and yearning for the socialite role she has perfected so well. Following one of her moments of clarity and conscience, Jessamine secretly flees her impending engagement to a debauched aristocrat and spends some months as a lodger at a modest croft in the Scottish Highlands (34, 45). If her early effort at simplicity had been mere performance, this is her second chance to pursue an authentically modest life, now without an audience of posh admirers.

The months in Scotland are a time of wholesome physical work and reflection. Upon meeting the love interest of the book, Colin Macgillvray, Jessamine registers how he sees her – "a picture, an art product, an object which it was well for him to have seen, and no more" – and this recognition of her irrelevance and customary vanity smites her (50). As Jessamine's acquaintanceship with Colin grows, Brooke repeatedly highlights his physical stature: "It was the lights and touches in his face and manner which revealed his nature, as the sun falling upon a rock will discover its secret beauty. He stood out from the triviality of the conversation with all his qualities large, deep, massive" (57). Colin's uncomplicatedness, sturdiness, and reticence put Jessamine's coquetry to shame, and she is confounded by him. Their relationship takes a turn when she joins him in trying to recapture a runaway sheep, and she mistakenly foresees his death from an oncoming train. She finds herself comforted and overwhelmed by "the mere sense of mass in the nature of this man" (75). In a later chapter, he distinguishes himself by his athletic prowess at the Highland Games while Jessamine looks on. Colin's genetic inheritance is later spelled out through Brooke's allusions to his father Rorie's rugged Viking heritage ("Culture had given but the hastiest daub to his once splendid animal physique" [182]).

Colin feels an intense emotional connection to the land. He is described as "slaw" [slow] by his neighbors, which signifies not ignorance, but attachment to tradition (326). He is in harmony with the cycles of planting and harvest. Although fellow villagers perceive him simply as hardworking and practical-minded, at several points in the story, he gazes at the mountains and fields with something akin to worship and certainly with love. He looks to be Jessamine's conduit to a more authentic future, one that would include a heightened appreciation of nature, rewarding labor, unselfconscious love, and easy companionship. In this novel, Colin embodies the life promised by Carpenter.

That said, the Highlands never truly fulfill the Carpenterian ideal of radical self-determination heralded by fin-de-siècle intellectual circles. The croft offers no self-conscious community for philosophizing about one's daily work and choices.[31] Mrs. McKenzie treats Jessamine's cross-class passion for Colin with reserve, perhaps a sign of her class deference (88–89, 104–05). Beyond this, the McKenzies are strict Sabbath-keepers. They have adorned Jessamine's room with a Calvinistic map of the saved and the damned, reflective of their own puritanism (79). Even as their daily lives are occupied by the farm tasks that Carpenter would have found wholesome and honest, there is little fun and spontaneity among them. On the Sunday after the incident with Colin, Jessamine awakens in her bed "as bare to feeling as any pagan girl," "conscious only of warmth and well-being," but this culture hardly encourages her to lead by feeling (78). Like her hosts, Colin subscribes to local tradition and earnestly looks to the Sabbath service to steady him and prevent him being distracted by his new affections for her.

The arrival of Colin's peasant father at the McKenzies' farm spurs Jessamine's first movement away from a possible union with Colin. To marry Colin would mean sharing a house with his parents. Rorie Macgillvray, with his worn, greasy work garb and coarse accent, terrifies Jessamine and drives her back to her familiar class snobberies. Shortly after seeing Rorie, she makes the fateful move of requesting that Mr. McKenzie purchase a society paper when he is in town. This magazine reacquaints her with the world she has missed and stimulates her old longings for admiration by her former suitor Lord Heriot. Jessamine's revived hunger for the aristocratic life is figured both as a lapse into an old addiction and as a kind of newly awakened atavism: "Nature mocks us with this trick of reversion" (123). On reading the magazine, she knows that she must return to London. She sees that Colin outshines all the gentry; but undone by her ambition, she gives up her efforts to "live a human life humanly" (121). Instead, "the thing [her innate corruption], all claws and fangs and horror, leapt like a wolf on Jessamine's newborn passion [for Colin and an honest life]" (126).

Just as seeing Colin's father acts as a catalyst to Jessamine's rejection of a marriage to Colin, another episode, seemingly small, shapes how she will reenvision her relations with Colin. While in the village, Jessamine meets a little girl who, it turns out, is the product of two unmarried parents, neither of whom seems ostracized by the villagers for having had sex out of wedlock. This union appears to be the inspiration for Jessamine's later desire to forego a conventional marriage and simply be sexually intimate with Colin (an idea he finds unthinkable and forbids). Jessamine has showered affection on the little girl, and this anticipates a passage some chapters later when she imagines returning to London society bearing her own baby through Colin:

> I carry in my arms my little baby, and I say, "This is the child of the man I love, and for whom forever, though I see him no more, I shall live as a true wife. He was the best and truest man I ever met, and the finest to look upon; and he took my heart by storm. ... Such a power of goodness went

out from him that he had but to look at me and I grew better. I could not marry him, because I was not fit for the duties of his wife; but, yes, I loved him so that I united myself to him with trembling joy. And this is my baby." Supposing I said this. (164)

Here she may even foresee marrying the wealthy Lord Heriot while carrying and raising Colin's baby, whose purity would be an antidote to the vice around her. However, unlike Dowie's Gallia, Jessamine does not knowingly, transparently cultivate Colin's courtship as a means to pregnancy. Jessamine's thinking is extemporaneous, erratic, and only semi-conscious.

To identify the perversity of her subsequent marriage to Lord Heriot, one must return to the descriptions of other upper-class weddings in *Society's Whispers*, the gossip magazine she had read while on the farm. These marriages function as they had hundreds of years ago, to bridge great properties and produce an heir. At this point, however, the couples' genetic lines are weak, dissolute, and diseased:

> [The list of marriages] was headed by an account of a very grand ceremony and important alliance. This was between a middle-aged man of enormous wealth, who was familiarly recognised in private circles as – next to Lord Heriot – the biggest rake in Great Britain, and a beautiful girl in her teens, whose family were permeated with hereditary insanity, and who was herself said – in strict confidence – to have had her moments. The object of the alliance was to connect two splendid land properties, and to unite the blue blood, which it was said the bride brought, with the immense amassed capital of the bridegroom, with the further object of producing a single unit of the race to inherit in his own person all these pleasing consolidated privileges. The alliance had received the highest and most signal support; royalty had appeared at the ceremony, and all the best nobility had been present. As to the clergy, they had assembled in such august and over-whelming numbers that there had hardly been a sentence apiece for them to read over the happy pair. The law also had been assiduous in confirming the alliance, and in tying the two together in a complication of bonds and red tape. (119–20)

This passage underscores not only Brooke's eugenic beliefs but also her socialist abhorrence of inherited wealth and institutions that sanction it. Jessamine, too, sees how repulsive these marriages are, but driven by instinct, almost bestially, she sets her sights on regaining Lord Heriot from a coquettish American rival.

When the novel jumps ahead ten years, we see what Jessamine's ambitious marriage has wrought. Jessamine had sought to redeem her union to Heriot through virtuous motherhood, but Heriot's sins and those of his antecedents eclipsed her efforts (269). She has given birth to an "idiot" girl with a "drooping" head and a "malicious" disposition, and a "poor malformed" boy "who lived in pain" (271). Both are imprinted by the "crimes and debauchery of generations" (271). They are sequestered away, cared for by attendants who are sworn to secrecy about their existence. Jessamine's patience and gentleness with her children, even as they arouse her own "terror and horror," have been her daily penance for the marriage itself (272).

Jessamine's third and final pregnancy inspires her with even greater aversion and self-loathing, and she ultimately gains her freedom, dying some months after a miscarriage. (This miscarriage, following the murder of the boy by his sister and the sister's death in the chaos, has dispelled any chance of Heriot gaining an heir.) On her deathbed, Jessamine hallucinates the presence of the sturdy, smiling little boy she would have had with Colin. It is an additional tragedy of the story that Colin, loyal to the end after Jessamine's unexplained return to England, has never married or had children and has thus deprived the world of his issue. What is left then? Simply: his intimacy with nature and solace in it. Colin's last act in the book, after learning of Jessamine's death, is to gaze at the mountains with the observation, "The hills look butifully" and to "[raise] his hand quietly in the peasant's salute" (336). Jessamine, Heriot, and their corrupted progeny have waned and wasted by the novel's end. Colin, conversely, has the last word, and so do Carpenterian values of simplicity, rurality, and well-being.

Conclusion: The Decadent and Socialist-Feminist Fiction

In the hands of another novelist, Lord Heriot would be witty and glib – another Lord Henry Wotton from *The Picture of Dorian Gray*. But he is a minor character and characterized by his lack of agency. His decadent persona intersects with his invalidism (273). Near the end of the book, his voice is "saturated with mental disease and feebleness" and his lips are likewise "wandering and feeble" (243). An emblem of bodily degeneration – balding, aged, querulous – he is nevertheless well turned-out:

> [Lord Heriot] had fallen asleep upon his chair, the table napkin spreading over one knee, his hands dangling, and his legs crossed, the dainty shoe being pointed stiffly and with singular aimlessness upward. His immaculate shirt front, with the diamond sparkles at regular intervals, hooped outward, and his head – the hair most carefully tended – nodded sideways.

> "The best valeted man I ever beheld!" said the doctor.

> All that the tailor and a priceless personal attendant could do had been done to turn Lord Heriot into a reputable figure of a man. If starch, fine cloth, and shaving could have erased the traces of a past, that past would have vanished under the applications as completely as breath on a well-rubbed mirror. (276)

Heriot is a dandy with no especial alliances with art movements or opinions about them. We never learn of his friends or interests. We know only his appetites; he succumbs to alcoholism with an early death ahead (286). He fulfills his family's notorious trajectory, joining "his drunken younger brother, . . . his sister, a microcephalous idiot, . . . his father [dead] of paralysis and ungovernable temper" (120). Indulging in behaviors closely allied with late-Victorian notions of cultural decadence and degeneration, Heriot even meets literary markers of atavism. Dr. Cornerstone concludes that, stripped of the trappings of family wealth, he is merely a "semi-criminal loafer" (277) – words that social cartographer Charles Booth used to describe the animalistic "Class A" residuum residing on the poorest streets of London. Cornerstone imagines transplanting Heriot from the House of Lords into the casual ward (277).

One might situate Brooke's Lord Heriot and Dix's Hilary Marchant on a spectrum of degeneracy, and conclude that at his worst, the neophyte Hilary aspires to Heriot's decadence and is only just spared its fatal costs. It is aristocratic lineage that differentiates Heriot from Hilary. While Hilary has inherited his poor constitution from his privileged father, Heriot's people have defiled themselves for centuries. Heriot's sartorial efforts to hide his physiological weakness are also inherited: "Lord Heriot's past was a long one; it did not begin with himself. There had been a sameness in the history of the Heriots for generations; it was varied only by the differences in manifestation caused by the different tastes and fashions of the time" (276–77).

Although Brooke goes so far as to advocate eugenic correctives, in *The Girl from the Farm* Dix simply observes Hilary's degeneration without fearing the condition of his child-to-be, even if its mother is "no broad-shouldered, strapping country wench" (221). Here, far-off eugenic concerns cede to pressing current moral ones. Taking the girl under her wing as they depart for London, Katharine dictates, "Now you will come with me, and be perfectly good for the sake of the little child that is coming to you" (227–28). The fetus, rather than a vessel of Hilary's vice, is as innocent as its mother, and there is hope for it.

The 1890s accordingly mark a point at which believers in degeneration could advance into eugenic activism. While eugenic enthusiasts spanned the political spectrum, socialists were among its most vocal exponents, propelling it into state policy and mainstream culture.[32] Reviewers of *A Superfluous Woman* thus praised its "primal passion" and reproduced its atavism: "One ... devours the whole at a sitting."[33] Another commended its "*virile* grasp on the problems of life," implying two things.[34] First, "problem" novels now necessarily addressed the crises of social class *and* sex; second, as an expression of counterdecadence, eugenics had entered the popular discourse and readers were primed for it.

Notes

1 Michel Freeden, "Eugenics and Progressive Thought: A Study in Ideological Affinity," *Historical Journal* 22, no. 3 (September 1979): 645–71.

2 Angelique Richardson, *Love and Eugenics in the Late Nineteenth Century: Rational Reproduction and the New Woman* (Oxford: Oxford University Press, 2003).

3 L.J. Ray, "Eugenics, Mental Deficiency and Fabian Socialism between the Wars," *Oxford Review of Education* 9, no. 3 (1983): 213–22.

4 Wolfgang Voigt, "The Garden City as Eugenic Utopia," *Planning Perspectives* 4, no. 3 (1989): 295–312. Patrick Geddes, the father of the British town planning movement, had been a member of the socialist Fellowship of the New Life.

5 J. Jopson, "The Language of Degeneration: Eugenic Ideas in *The Time Machine* by H.G. Wells and *Man and Superman* by George Bernard Shaw," *Galton Institute Newsletter* 51 (June 2004): 1–16.

6 Linda Dowling, "The Decadent and the New Woman in the 1890s," *Nineteenth- Century Fiction* 33, no. 4 (March 1979): 434–53.

7 By publishing *The Girl from the Farm* in John Lane's Keynotes series, Dix signaled her professional alliances with literary-decadent circles. Its cover and title page were designed by Aubrey Beardsley.

8 Angelique Richardson's *Love and Eugenics in the Late Nineteenth Century* focused primarily on Grand, Egerton, and Caird.

9 See Judy Greenway, "No Place for Women? Anti-utopianism and the Utopian Politics of the 1890s," *Geografiska Annaler: Series B, Human Geography* 84, no. 3–4 (2002): 201–09; Angela Ingram and Daphne Patai, eds., *Rediscovering Forgotten Radicals: British Women Writers, 1889–1939* (Chapel Hill, NC: University of North Carolina, 1993); Jo-Ann Wallace "The Case of Edith Ellis," in *Modernist Sexualities*, eds. Hugh Stevens and Caroline Howlett (Manchester: Manchester University Press, 2000), 13–40; Jana Smith Elford, "'Waking Dreams': Networked Feminists and Idealist Feminism in Late-Nineteenth Century London," PhD dissertation, University of Alberta, 2018. Barbara Tilley's edition of Emma Frances Brooke's *A Superfluous Woman* features a critical introduction and contextual appendices (Brighton: Victorian Secrets, 2015). Socialist feminists have been

afforded more comprehensive attention by historians; see Anna Clark, *Alternative Histories of the Self: A Cultural History of Sexuality and Secrets, 1762–1917* (London: Bloomsbury, 2017); and Sheila Rowbotham, *Rebel Crossings: New Women, Free Lovers, and Radicals in Britain and the United States* (London: Verso, 2016).

10 Stephen Yeo, "A New Life: The Religion of Socialism in Britain, 1883–1896," *History Workshop Journal* 4, no. 1 (Autumn 1977): 5–56.

11 One might add Olive Schreiner to this list, as she belonged to the FNL between 1885 and 1886. One might also include the Scottish novelist Jane Hume Clapperton, if only for her novel *Margaret Dunmore: or a Socialist Home* (1888). However, Clapperton seems not to have belonged to any organized socialist association, though she was a member of suffrage societies from the 1870s on. Her treatise *Scientific Meliorism* (1885) developed from Galton's eugenic theory.

12 On the pluralism of reform communities, see Jana Smith Elford, "The Late-Victorian Feminist Community," *Victorian Review* 41, no. 1 (2015): 32–35; Ruth Livesey, "Morris, Carpenter, Wilde and the Political Aesthetics of Labor," *Victorian Literature and Culture* 32, no. 2 (2004): 601–16; Wendy Parkins, "Edward Carpenter's Queer Ecology of the Everyday," *19: Interdisciplinary Studies in the Long Nineteenth Century* 26 (2018): 1–18 (2).

13 The Fabian Society began in 1884 as a breakaway group from the FNL. Many sustained memberships in both societies. While not a formal Fabian, Carpenter associated with Fabians. See Sheila Rowbotham, *Edward Carpenter: A Life of Liberty and Love* (London: Verso, 2008), 90.

14 Regenia Gagnier, *The Insatiability of Human Wants: Economics and Aesthetics in Market Society* (Chicago, IL: University of Chicago Press, 2000), especially ch. 5. Matthew Potolsky contextualizes the social critique of decadence in his introduction to *The Decadent Republic of Letters: Taste, Politics, and Cosmopolitan Community from Baudelaire to Beardsley* (Philadelphia, PA: University of Pennsylvania Press, 2013).

15 Positive eugenics encouraged breeding among the most desirable populations; negative eugenics discouraged unwanted populations through efforts like sterilization. See Neil MacMaster, "The White Race: Degeneration and Eugenics," in *Racism in Europe 1870-2000* (Basingstoke: Palgrave, 2001), 42–43.

16 Francis Galton, *Hereditary Genius* (London: Macmillan, 1892).

17 Syphilis was thought to be a hereditary disease at this time, though it is now believed to be infectious.

18 Edward Carpenter, *England's Ideal and Other Papers on Social Subjects* (London: Swan Sonnenshein, Lowrey, and Co., 1887), 59.

19 Edward Carpenter, *Civilisation: Its Cause and Cure* (London: Allen and Unwin, 1921), 73.

20 On this history, see Lucy Bland and Lesley Hall, "Eugenics in Britain: The View from the Metropole," in *The Oxford Handbook of the History of Eugenics,*

eds. Alison Bashford and Philippa Levine (Oxford: Oxford University Press, 2010), 213–27 (214).

21 Ivan Crozier, "Havelock Ellis, Eugenicist," *Studies in History of Philosophy of Science Part C: Studies in History and Philosophy of Biological and Biomedical Sciences* 39, no. 2 (June 2008): 187–94.

22 See Diana Maltz, "Ardent Service: Female Eroticism and New Life Ethics in Gertrude Dix's *The Image Breakers* (1900)," *Journal of Victorian Culture* 17, no. 2 (June 2012): 147–63.

23 Gertrude Dix, *The Girl from the Farm* (London and Boston: John Lane, Roberts Bros [American, 2nd ed.], 1896), 30.

24 Max Nordau, *Degeneration* (New York: Appleton, 1895), 306.

25 Oscar Wilde, "A Note on Some Modern Poets," *Woman's World* 2 (1889): 108–12 (108).

26 Oscar Wilde, *The Picture of Dorian Gray*, ed. Joseph Bristow (Oxford: Oxford Worlds Classics, 2008), 92.

27 On simple life aesthetics, see Diana Maltz, "Living by Design: C. R. Ashbee's Guild of Handicraft and Two English Tolstoyan Colonies, 1897–1907," *Victorian Literature and Culture* 39, no. 2 (September 2011): 409–26; and Diana Maltz, "The Newer New Life: A. S. Byatt, E. Nesbit, and Socialist Subculture," *Journal of Victorian Culture* 17, no. 1 (March 2012): 79–84. See also Parkins.

28 Sheila Rowbotham claims that Brooke did not know Carpenter before sending him a fan letter praising *Sex-Love* in 1894 (Rowbotham, *Edward Carpenter*, 212). However, this seems unlikely given her wider alliances; see Mark Bevir, *The Making of British Socialism* (Princeton, NJ: Princeton University Press, 2011), 260; Elford, "Waking Dreams," 19.

29 The FNL formed in 1883 out of a study group enthusiastic about the writings of the late philosopher James Hinton. In an 1885 letter to Karl Pearson, Brooke recounted Hinton's predatory behavior toward her years before. See Kay Daniels, "Emma Brooke: Fabian, Feminist and Writer," *Women's History Review* 12, no. 2 (2003): 163; see also Ruth First and Ann Scott, *Olive Schreiner, a Biography* (New York: Schocken, 1980), 152.

30 [Emma Frances Brooke], *A Superfluous Woman* (Cassell, 1894), 1.

31 Cf. Salome Hocking's *Belinda the Backward* (1905); Gertrude Dix's *The Image Breakers* (1900); Edith Lees Ellis's *Attainment* (1909), where characters collectively debate their radical choices.

32 G. R. Searle, *Eugenics and Politics in Britain, 1900–1914* (Leyden: Noordhoff, 1976).

33 "The New Books of the Month," *Review of Reviews* 9 (January–June 1894): 192; the citation about devouring from the *Queen* appears in an unpaginated ad for the novel, which its publisher Heinemann placed at the end of several novels, e.g., Henry James's *The Other House* (1897).

34 *Gentlewoman*, my emphasis, from the same ad cited in endnote 33.

CHAPTER 12

The Conservative and Patriotic 1890s

Alex Murray

Logan Pearsall Smith would in 1924 profess himself a little bemused at the posthumous reputation of the 1890s:

> It is a curious experience to find that one has lived through an important literary epoch and never known it. When I now read about the decadent nineties, the impropriety of that epoch, its enthusiasm for style and form, and the baleful countenance it gave to Art for the sake of Art, I wonder a little, for I remember those years which led on to the war in South Africa as a period of imperialism and of Kipling's glory; a decade throughout which a strong east wind of Philistinism blew over England, without any noticeable remission or shifting to the south. I can recall no evidence of popular enthusiasm for Art, no encouragement given to the cultivation, however guiltless, of literary form.[1]

As far as Smith was concerned, the Aesthetic or Yellow Nineties were a myth, perhaps manufactured by those early literary historians of the decade, perhaps a curious accident of collective memory. At any rate, to many who lived through them, the decade might have been better dubbed the Khaki Nineties, or as I am labeling it here, the Conservative and Patriotic Nineties. But, of course, the decade was aesthetic *as well* as conservative and patriotic. These two seemingly opposed ideological tendencies, or perhaps more accurately structures of experience, were coexistent. It has been commonplace in literary criticism to see them as opposed, involved in some sort of culture war that came to the surface in the Oscar Wilde trials of spring 1895. Yet, as I will argue in this chapter, these two versions of the 1890s were thoroughly imbricated.

But, of course, there were more than two politico-literary tendencies to the decade. Searching for an appropriate metaphor to capture the "creative revolutionary energy" of the 1890s, Richard Le Gallienne happened on a "ten-ringed circus, with vividly original performers claiming one's distracted attention in every ring." Yet, he conceded, that metaphor gave the illusion of a unity of purpose that did not exist. Better to "compare it to a series of booths at a fair, each with its vociferous 'barker' inviting us in to the only show on earth." Outside one stood W. E. Henley "beating the big drum of Imperialism," while outside another "mystic-looking booth" stood W. B. Yeats, "musically talking of Rosicrucianism, fairies, Celtic folklore, and an Irish theatre." A little along the way was George Bernard Shaw, "advertising Fabian socialism as a nostrum for all our national ills and discoursing on Wagner and the 'Quintessence of Ibsenism' by the way." Other booths were given over to Socialist clergymen, and to James Abbott McNeil Whistler "declaiming paradox."[2] The literary 1890s were incorrigibly plural; there was no dominant literary movement, no towering personality, no quintessential work of art. Even an individual writer might move from one booth to another as they sought new audiences or experimented with new forms. Yet literary criticism tends to prefer clear – if illusory – demarcations. We want our decadents to be aloof from the imperialists, our realists and mystics facing each other with daggers drawn. The danger is that we partition literary production in such a way that deracinates it from the social, cultural, and political context that gives it meaning. The writers and artists we associate with the decadent and aesthetic 1890s were as prone to political despair, populist enthusiasms, and ideological volte-face as anyone else. Literary critics, however, have tended to search for ideological commitment, if not purity, in the authors they study. Yet, as this chapter demonstrates, ideology at the fin de siècle was rarely pure and never simple. In tracing the gamut of conservatisms, from Nietzschean-inspired celebrations of the violence of empire, to jeremiads against bourgeois modernity, and quietist retreats into the pastoral, I aim to show how multifarious conservatism itself could be. In our own age of rancorous political division and hardening ideological positions, it is simultaneously bracing, surprising, and instructive to think alongside and against the conservatism and patriotism of the 1890s. The more we make space for a capacious conservatism in our study of the fin de siècle, the greater our sense of productive confusion as to the intersection of politics and aesthetics that runs like a fault line through the decade.

Politics and History

My methodology in this chapter is hardly breaking new ground; given the predominance of historicism – broadly conceived – over the past forty years, it would be disingenuous to pretend that my approach is radically novel. Yet there has been a development over the last ten or so years of a wider, and more historically aware, approach to the interaction between literature and cultural politics in the 1890s. This was a method pioneered by an earlier generation of scholars whose work recovered the forgotten writers of the period and placed them firmly in their historical context. Works such as Karl Beckson's *London in the 1890s* (1993) and Murray G. H. Pittock's *Spectrum of Decadence: The Literature of the 1890s* (1993) demonstrated the efficacy of reading the authors of the 1890s as deeply engaged with broader cultural politics. Since then, we have had Nick Freeman's deep history of that most pivotal year of the decade. Freeman reads the significant political and cultural events of 1895 – the summer election, Wilde's trials in April and May – alongside football results and extreme weather events to create a far more variegated picture of that year, and to read those events in their immediate context. As he notes, with hindsight we might see Wilde's trials as a pivotal event in the development of modern sexuality, but for most residents of the British Isles in 1895 his works, and his downfall, were of little concern.[3]

Wilde might have been of little importance to the majority of the electorate in 1895, but Wilde himself was a shrewd observer of British politics. Recent criticism has shown us just how politically engaged a writer Wilde was. Deaglán Ó Donghaile has made a compelling case for Wilde as an anticolonial writer whose work demonstrates a deep-seated commitment to the downtrodden and a sustained hostility to the political establishment.[4] This documenting of Wilde's political commitments is an important corrective to the tendency to deny Wilde held any strong beliefs. Wilde's awareness of the political issues of his day was shared with just about every other writer of the 1890s. Even the most ardent aesthete was engaged with contemporary politics, even if that engagement manifested itself as an antidemocratic jeremiad against modernity, as in the case of a writer like Frederick Rolfe, the self-styled Baron Corvo. As Matthew Potolsky has noted, we need to be careful not to parcel writers of the fin de siècle into neat left–right political positions, for in "fin-de-siècle pubs and coffee houses across the United Kingdom and Europe utopian socialists rubbed shoulders with republicans, anarchists, throne-and-altar conservatives, liberals, and populists, and party-line positions on any given issue could be difficult to predict."[5] But there are some clearly dominant political positions that contemporary criticism is bringing to light. Stefano Evangelista has made a striking case for the centrality of cosmopolitanism to the literature of this period, exploring how literary cosmopolitanism "took on a political dimension, translating into a desire to challenge and undo the alliance between literature and nationalism." As he notes, this work is essential in challenging "the charge of apolitical formalism" that has dogged aestheticism and decadence since Adorno's withering critique.[6] The work that I am modeling here is, then, a contribution to recent criticism's attempt to expand what the political might be when we look at the 1890s. That is not an attempt to replace models which explored the politics of sexual dissidence, but to think about how sexual politics might intersect with other political concerns. While my focus is on the patriotic and the conservative, I hope it will be understood as working alongside, not against, those critics who are undertaking important work on anticolonial thought, on utopian socialism, antivivisectionists, rational reproduction, or anarchist activism.[7] All of these political ideas were eddying around the 1890s and writers were responding to a great many of them, often simultaneously.

Counter-Decadence

Perhaps the most likely place to look for literary conservatism in the 1890s is in the writings of those who attacked literary decadence and Wilde in particular. While it might seem to us that Wilde and the decadents were everywhere in the 1890s, the reality was that being outraged about their antics was far more popular (and lucrative) than being a decadent writer. Marie Corelli's most famous novels of the 1890s were vituperative attacks on the sensual egoism of decadence. *Wormwood: A Drama of Paris* (1890) anatomized the amoral novelists of Paris, while *The Sorrows of Satan* (1895) offered a relentless assault on the pretensions of literary London. In the former, the absinthe-addicted narrator Gaston Beauvais lambasts his reader at every turn, reminding them that while they may view him as a "skulking pariah of the slums and back streets of Paris," they share with him that indulgent egoism – "the worship of the self" – that is corroding modern life.[8] In the latter novel the Satan of the title, Prince Lucio Rimânez, is able to eviscerate the materialism and hedonism of London in the 1890s while encouraging Geoffrey Tempest – the aesthetic novelist who he has recently made a millionaire – to cynically capitalize on its vapid fads and fashions: "You belong to the age, Tempest, – it is a decadent ephemeral age, and most things connected with it are decadent and ephemeral. Any era that is dominated by the love of money only, has a rotten core within it and must perish."[9] Corelli's attacks on progressive art and her hysterical Francophobia sold exceptionally well. At the end of the century her books were averaging 175,000 sales. Yet, as Annette R. Federico notes, Corelli was borrowing – stylistically and thematically – from those literary movements she was attacking: "her manipulation of almost every feature of literary decadence challenges antithetical genres, styles, audiences, and sexualities."[10] Even counter-decadence relied on channeling the amoral deviance of that which it critiqued.

The year *The Sorrows of Satan* was published, and Wilde was tried and imprisoned, also saw the first translation of Max Nordau's *Entartung* (*Degeneration*) appear in English. While it had been a subject of some literary debate since its publication in German, its translation saw it become one of the publishing sensations of the British 1890s: there were to be seven more editions of *Degeneration* by the end of the decade. While Nordau's screed was attacked by many writers – most famously George Bernard Shaw's "open letter," *The Sanity of Art* (1895) – it provided conservative commentators with a powerful new lexicon with which to lambast progressive art. Perhaps most memorable among them was Hugh E. M. Stutfield, whose "Tommyrotics" in *Blackwood's* offered a relentless attack on the eroticism, neuroticism and posturing of the New Woman and the decadent. Nordau was his inspiration: "Just as the world seems most in need of him a new prophet has arisen to point out some of the dangers which lie on the path of modern civilisation." *Degeneration* might have been deserving of some of the hostile criticism it had received, Stutfield conceded, but he defended the proliferation of "unsavoury topics" in the volume because Nordau had handled them with "the spirit of fierce hatred and horror which characterise a Juvenal."[11] Nordau's bitter, at times deranged, attacks on Nietzsche, Symbolism, decadence, and other purveyors of artistic egoism flirted – stylistically at least – with the very art he claimed to despise.

The Wilde trials saw the floodgates open, and a stream of anti-decadent diatribe showered the Victorian reading public. One of the most notorious was the short attack in W. E. Henley's *National Observer* on the April 6, 1895: "Of the Decadents, of their hideous conceptions of the meaning of Art, of their worse than Eleusinian mysteries, there must be an absolute end."[12] The irony was that even in this volume of the *National Observer* the egoistic mysticism of decadence was being featured. Four pages on from this attack the reader would come across two of Arthur Symons's "Venetian Nights": "Veneta Marina" and "Alla Dogana."[13] The proximity of decadent and anti-decadent writers and sentiments underscores just how heterogeneous the media ecology of the 1890s was. Examples of progressive artists contributing to conservative and patriotic publications abound. Arthur Symons might have referred to the popular press as "the plague, or black death of the modern world," but he was dependent on it for his income, reviewing music-hall entertainments and theater for the evening paper the *Star*;[14] Max Beerbohm, Symons, George Egerton, Francis Thompson, William Archer, and Joseph Conrad all contributed to the *Outlook*; Beerbohm penned a weekly "Commentary" for the *Daily Mail*; Reggie Turner wrote for the *Daily Telegraph*; Ada Leverson contributed witty satires of her fellow decadents to *Punch*.[15] While, as Matthew Kibble has noted, modernists such as Ezra Pound and H. D. had, by the time of the First World War, settled into attacking what they saw as the impoverishment of the language at the hands of Harmsworth's *Daily Mail*, the 1890s presents a much messier picture.[16] The inverse was also true: writers of a less than radical hue featured in the *Yellow Book*, including Arthur Waugh, Arnold Bennett, George Gissing, and John Buchan. As I have noted elsewhere, decadent writers such as Symons, Vincent O'Sullivan, W. B. Yeats, and Paul Verlaine all contributed to the archly conservative periodical the *Senate* (1894–97).[17] One of the more amusing decadent attacks on decadence, Lionel Johnson's "The Cultured Faun," in which he mocked the "flowery Paganism, such as no 'Pagan' ever had," was published in the rabidly conservative the *Anti-Jacobin*.[18] As these examples all demonstrate, even counter- or anti-decadent literature of the 1890s was not as clearly demarcated from that it would purport to lambast.

Conservatism in the 1890s

While it is a fool's errand to categorize decades in absolute political terms, the 1890s can lay claim to being one of the more conservative decades of the nineteenth century. In 1893, the Conservative-dominated House of Lords threw out William Gladstone's Second Home Rule Bill proposing a system of home rule for Ireland, precipitating a political crisis for Victorian liberalism. In the summer election of 1895 that followed, the Conservative and Liberal Unionist coalition gained 114 seats, almost all taken from the Liberals, giving them a massive majority in the House of Commons. The Conservatives and Liberal Unionists were to maintain this advantage in the "Khaki Election" of 1900, held at a point when the Boer War between Britain and the Boers in Southern Africa looked certain to be won (the conflict would in fact carry on until May 1902 when the Treaty of Vereeniging was signed). The 1895 election saw disastrous results for the Independent Labour Party (ILP) with its leader Keir Hardy losing his parliamentary seat. In the years that followed there was a dramatic decline in membership of the ILP. As David Cannadine puts it: "In the era of the Diamond Jubilee and the Boer War it was popular Toryism that seemed more appealing to many members of the working class."[19] Key to the success of the Conservatives had been the evolution of popular or "One Nation" Conservatism that was to be a defining feature of Benjamin Disraeli's second term as Prime Minister (1874–80). By the 1890s, it had fundamentally transformed the nature of parliamentary politics in England. The Conservative Party was no longer the party of the gentry; as Disraeli had grasped, electoral reform necessitated a Toryism that used empire and patriotism as its key ideological principles.

Yet conservatism – as a broad-ranging set of social values – was (and still is) multifaceted, and often at odds with the political party with which it shares a name. The populist tenor of Disraelian Toryism was anathema to many who saw the duty of conservatives as the preservation of England's aristocratic social order and/or its traditions. For such conservatives, tradition should function as a bulwark against modernization and democratization. The principles of conservatism might be summarized as: a skepticism toward progress and claims of novelty; a reverence for the past; a strong, if at times idiosyncratic, nationalism; the belief in the sanctity of individual liberty and freedom from excessive state control. In an expansive understanding of conservatism – conceived as a critique of modernity and the myth of progress – we can find some of the more unexpected alliances between conservatism and progressive art. Conservatism as it manifested itself in the 1890s was not exclusively the preserve of the political right. To argue for the conservation and preservation of the past – both in its physical traces and its values – was a fundamental element of Fabian socialist challenges to the corrosive, alienating effects of exploitative capitalism. William Morris, for example, would routinely turn to the past to find alternatives to the horrors of industrialized modernity. As he put it in "How I Became a Socialist" (1894), "the leading passion of my life has been and is hatred of modern civilization." Yet, as Morris conceded, to retreat into "the study of history and the love and practice of art" would lead to nostalgia, to "turn history into inconsequent nonsense, and make art a collection of the curiosities of the past, which would have no serious relation to the life of the present."[20] In a similar fashion, John Ruskin would famously open *Praeterita* (1885): "I am, and my father was before me, a violent Tory of the old school."[21] This was not a Toryism that incorporated the late-Victorian Conservative Party. Like Morris, Ruskin saw his conservatism as a living, sensuous relationship between past and present that functioned as a critique of modernity.

However, not all forms of 1890s conservatism that dovetail with aestheticism share the egalitarian principles of Fabian socialism. One of the most common features of conservatism is a reverence for pre-Reformation social organisation and spiritual belief. These writers were following Edmund Burke who had famously lamented in *Reflections on the Revolution in France* (1790) that "the age of chivalry is gone. ... Never, never more, shall we behold that generous loyalty to rank and sex, that proud submission, that dignified obedience, that subordination of the heart, which kept alive, even in servitude itself, the spirit of an exalted freedom!"[22] Some writers of the 1890s saw modernity as opening the possibility for a return of sorts to medieval chivalry, but perhaps not a version that Burke would have recognized. Uranian writers of the fin de siècle saw their own age as offering possibilities for queer living that had not been seen since the dissolution of the monasteries. Charles Kains Jackson argued in 1894 that since the need to increase the population of England had finally come to an end for the first time in at least 437 years, society was able to embrace human love without the burden of procreation: "Wherefore just as the flower of the early and imperfect civilization was in what we may call the Old Chivalry, or the exaltation of the youthful feminine ideal, so the flower of the adult and perfect civilization will be found in the New Chivalry or the exaltation of the youthful masculine ideal." The 1890s would not return to, but rather would perfect the medieval by embracing a queer idealism in which the "tenderness" of the older man for the younger was of the "highest value."[23] The queer valences of medievalism and its foundation in Christian idealism were, however, often tied to asymmetrical power relations, with Uranianism often involving exploitation of working-class youth, particularly in southern Europe and north Africa.

Other writers associated with the Decadent Movement saw their literary practice as an assault on the Liberal mantra of change for change's sake. Arthur Machen used decadent-occult literary forms to explore the ways in which modernity was forever haunted by the past. This was undertaken as part of a broader critique of science, rationality, and materialism. Machen's journey toward conservatism was dramatic. He recalled that "the great victory of Gladstone in 1880 warmed my heart. I was an earnest young Liberal." As such he was strongly in favor of the Municipal Corporations Act of 1882, championed by Lord Rosebery, which granted greater power to local governments to acquire land and make bylaws. The new corporation replaced the Portreeve of Usk, a position and a structure of local government dating back to the fourteenth century. "I knew then, suddenly," Machen writes, "that I was no longer an earnest young Liberal. I knew that I hated the notion of destroying old things, just because they were old; and that, I believe, is not a Liberal frame of mind. But to abolish the Portreeve of Usk! Why, the Chief Magistrate of the City of London was the Portreeve of London before Mayors, much less Lord Mayors, were born or thought of. And I don't believe that Usk is any the happier for having a Local Government Board instead of a Portreeve and two Bailiffs."[24] Elsewhere he would rail against "that vile 'Liberal' objection to splendour as splendour."[25] From this point on Machen attacked the myth of progress through a series of narratives that dramatize the dangers of attempting to overcome or erase the past.

Machen's scandalous novella *The Great God Pan* was, along with *The Inmost Light*, published as the fifth volume in John Lane's Keynote Series in 1894. The early parts of the novella were first published as a short story in the short-lived decadent-conservative newspaper the *Whirlwind* in December 1890. In the novella, Dr. Raymond, drawing on the latest advances in "the physiology of the brain," performs a surgical operation on a seventeen-year-old girl Mary with disastrous consequences. In trying to bridge "the world of sense" and some sort of spirit realm, he leaves the young girl "a hopeless idiot" who has, during the experiment, copulated with the Great God Pan, conceiving Helen Vaughan who will become the evil tormenter of the great and good of London society, leading to a spate of tragic suicides. The temporal frame of the novella is important: the experiment takes place in 1864–65 and Helen takes her own life (under compulsion) in 1888. In Machen's narrative, the scientific curiosity of the high Victorians returns at the fin de siècle to wreck its revenge. The desire of these men of science to penetrate the mysteries of the spirit in the name of progress leads to an attack on the social structure through the most destructive of femmes fatales. Toward the end of the narrative, Villiers explains that Helen Vaughan and her possession by Pan are "an old story, an old mystery played out in our day, and in dim London streets instead of amidst the vineyards and olive gardens." In attempting to access "the most secret forces that lie at the heart of all things," they have trespassed on the realms of religion and poetry, for these forces "cannot be names, cannot be spoken, cannot be imagined except under a veil and a symbol, to the most of us appearing as a quaint, poetic fancy, to some a foolish tale."[26] Machen's conservative gothic serves as a warning to those who would try to meddle with the natural and spiritual order of things.

Lionel Johnson's "By the Statue of King Charles at Charing Cross" stands as one of the most important expressions of the conservative decadent aesthetic. The poem was published in *The Book of the Rhymers' Club* in February 1892 in which it is in august decadent company. It first, however, appeared a month earlier in the January 30 edition of the

Royalist, a magazine dedicated to the Stuart cause. The King stands at that busy London intersection as a rebuke to its modern citizens, and as a model for an alternative way of living:

> Our wearier spirit faints,
> Vexed in the world's employ:
> His soul was of the saints;
> And art to him was joy.

As exhausted as the speaker might feel as he tries to come to terms with fin-de-siècle London, the statue of King Charles offers succor: "And through the night I go, / Loving thy mournful face."[27] Francis O'Gorman has argued that the poem is a site-specific response to the experience of modern upheaval. Written in 1887 in the wake of riots in Trafalgar Square, and set in a location plagued with traffic, the poem should be read as a pointed avoidance of modernity. O' Gorman persuasively inter-prets Johnson's turn to the Stuart monarch and away from the Square where socialists had only a few years earlier called for reform as a transla-tion of "seventeenth-century Stuart absolutism into unobtrusive support for the forces that swept away political dissenters, as well as the violent 'vulgar cads' that attended them."[28] As O'Gorman notes, Johnson's poem is not simply nostalgic for a lost past but a monument to those preserving the social order of the 1890s against democratic change.

Patriotism in the 1890s

The 1890s were a deeply patriotic decade, and patriotism, imperialism, even jingoism, were an integral part of the literary landscape. Disraeli had latched onto imperialism as a key component of his one-nation conserva-tism after 1867. It didn't take long for the Liberals to see the electoral value of patriotic rhetoric; Gladstone had proclaimed in 1878 that "the senti-ment of empire may be called innate in every Briton. If there are excep-tions, they are like those of men born blind or lame among us. It is part of our patrimony: born with our birth."[29] Queen Victoria's Golden Jubilee of 1887 further fostered such patriotic feeling, and by the 1890s it infiltrated every arena of public, and private life. There were, of course, many writers who were appalled by the rising jingoistic sentiments, such as Max Beerbohm who mocked Rudyard Kipling.[30] However, we should be careful about reading Kipling as himself outrightly opposed to literary decadence; as Neil Hultgren and Jesse Oak Taylor have noted, Kipling drew on aestheticist tropes and form across his oeuvre.[31] Wilde, as ever, was as inconsistent and paradoxical about patriotism as he was any other political ideal. While he may have famously declared his allegiance to cosmopolitanism in "The Critic as Artist," his much less quoted reflections on the role of national identity in art, in the context of a discussion of Shakespeare's plays, are worth recalling: "Patriotism, I need hardly say, is not a necessary quality of art; but it means, for the artist, the substitution of a universal for an individual feeling, and for the public the presentation of a work of art in a most attractive and popular form."[32] Wilde understood very well the power of patriotism to bind together artist and readers into imaginary communities. So many writers of the 1890s did use patriotism as a means – they thought – of fostering forms of empathy and common understanding (or of attracting new readerships).

Katharine Bradley and Edith Cooper, who wrote as Michael Field, saw their aesthetic project as wholly intertwined with the vitality of the nation. At the close of the 1890s they were able to see the state of the nation at war as analogous to their own battle to write a new verse drama. As Cooper wrote on the last day of 1899: "Like our country we shall face the difficulties of empire building when circumstances are stubborn. I believe both England and Michael Field will win."[33] Their belief in the supremacy of the English resulted in a patronizing address "To America" in which they reminded their transatlantic cousins to "Remember whence ye came."[34] Other nations fared no better. In the 1890s, the perennial debate over whether or not the Elgin Marbles (appropriated in the first decade of the century from the Acropolis in Athens by Lord Elgin) should remain in the British Museum or be returned to Greece rumbled on. Boldly did Michael Field step into the fray. Byron may have lamented the violence done to the Parthenon – "Dull is the eye that will not weep to see / Thy walls defaced, thy mouldering shrines removed / By British hands"[35] – but for the Fields who else but the English could truly respect the culture which had produced the marbles? Apostrophizing the "Great Master of the Parthenon," they ask:

> Do not the heroes of thy land belong
> To us, whose loftiest lyric poet's song
> Honours divine Erechtheus? Or, to speak
> Of our twain hoary prophets, who as these
> Have sung Tiresias and Pheidippides?
> Who tells the tale of Jason's wondrous crew?
> Who, if not Landor, guards Aspasia's grace
> Perfect from soil? Is it too much for you
> To trust your darkening torsos to our race?[36]

Surely, they intimate, the English civilization of the 1890s is so strikingly like that apogee of human creative expression in the fifth century BCE that it would be unthinkable for the marbles to reside anywhere else. They provide as evidence for this claim Algernon Charles Swinburne's *Erechtheus* (1876) and poems by Robert Browning and Alfred Tennyson. English exceptionalism here is grounded in its poetic achievements, and Michael Field would see themselves as part of the exceptional literary tradition of an exceptional nation. As Greece still waits in the twenty-first century for the return of the its marbles (not to mention the many other countries seeking to regain ownership of cultural treasures stolen by the British across its empire and beyond), we should remember that for many in the 1890s – even those who celebrated cosmopolitan culture and challenged the restrictive view of gender and sexuality dominant at the time, as Bradley and Cooper did – British exceptionalism was unquestioned and seemingly unassailable.

Michael Field's nationalism grew over the course of the 1890s, reaching an apex with the almost hysterical jingoism that greeted the outbreak of the Second Anglo-Boer War in October 1899. They were not alone among fin-de-siècle poets otherwise known for their progressive sexual and social politics who greeted the outbreak of war with unabashed patriotism. Foremost here is Algernon Charles Swinburne. The *enfant terrible* of British literature in the 1860s and 1870s, by the 1890s he was deeply nationalistic. It is a struggle to reconcile the radical republicanism of *Songs before Sunrise* (1871) with the unrepentant xenophobia of a number of verses in *A Channel Passage and Other Poems* (1904). Francis O'Gorman has argued that it is "not difficult, at the beginning of the twenty-first century, to construct Swinburne as a kind of liberal hero, writing bravely against 'Victorian values' on behalf of freedom and self-expression, liberty, and self-determination," yet to do so means politely neglecting his Unionist, anti-Irish prose and poetry written from the 1880s through to his death.[37] Swinburne's six poems on the war in South Africa appeared in prominent national outlets, two in *The Times* and four in the *Saturday Review*, which gives some sense of his conservatism and alignment with national(ist) sentiment. Published in *The Times* the day after the outbreak of the conflict, "The Transvaal" set the tone for the rest of Swinburne's Boer War verse, marked by venomous invective and righteous anger. "Patience, long sick to death, is dead," the poem opens. The nation should return to the great example of Oliver Cromwell and his naval commander Robert Blake, who oversaw "a commonweal that brooked no wrong / From foes less vile than men like wolves set free." Swinburne conjures up

what he sees as a tradition of righteous republican British anger in the face
of tyranny. The characterizations of the Boers as uncivilized animals is
confirmed in the infamous final lines in which the country must "scourge
these dogs, agape with jaws afoam, / Down out of life. Strike, England, and
strike home."[38]

While the Boer War might have seen some strident critiques of empire
emerge, particularly following the brutal treatment of Boer women and
children in British concentration camps, for others it was a chance to reflect
on the dynamism and vitalism of the imperial project. John Davidson had
challenged Victorian sexual hypocrisy throughout the 1890s, and in his own
way he was to challenge hypocrisy around empire. There was no point, he
thought, pretending it was a benign, "civilising" force. In the dog days of the
Boer War, he penned *The Testament of an Empire Builder* (1902), a
monologue of the eponymous man of Empire, modeled, a number of
scholars conjecture, on Cecil Rhodes. As John Holmes argues, the Empire
Builder is "a Nietzschean superman, a frankly martial imperialist driven to
conquest by a will for power."[39] In the poem, Heaven and Hell exist in no
celestial or demonic realm, but on earth, and the Empire Builder's ruthless
ascension is the survival of the fittest: "I clambered into Heaven at once /
And stayed there" (l. 696–97).[40] The ruthless desire to make money
("reaped millions before my time") opens up the possibilities of Empire:

> Then, being English, one of the elect
> Above all folks, within me fate grew strong.
> The authentic mandate of imperial doom
> Silenced the drowsy lullaby of love[.]
>   (Davidson, "Testament," l. 702–06)

The Empire "undid my simple, immature design" and made me "What!
tenfold a criminal? / No other name for Hastings, Clive and me!" (l.
713–14). But the criminality of Robert Clive, Warren Hastings, and
Cecil Rhodes (who is named as the third in this triumvirate in "On
Poetry"[41]) is not to be condemned; it could only be considered criminal
by those who fail to embrace the will to power. In a final dialectical reversal
that reads as a Nietzschean revision of William Blake's theory of contraries,
the Empire Builder exhorts his readers to:

> Secure your birthright; set the world at naught;
> Confront your fate; regard the naked deed;
> Enlarge your Hell; preserve it in repair;
> Only a splendid Hell keeps Heaven fair.
>   (l. 722–26).

Davidson's poem was interpreted by his contemporaries as an example of the influence (pernicious or otherwise), of Nietzsche on English letters. Cecil Rhodes as Superman might seem repugnant to many today, but it is an amoralism that was wholly in keeping with the decadent attempt to overthrow sentiment and conformism, to transvaluate all values. It is a form of decadence that we need to acknowledge and incorporate into our literary histories of the 1890s, rather than embarrassedly wishing it away.

Many writers were more circumspect; they lamented the rising tide of nationalist sentiment but could see very clearly that it was the keynote of the age. George Gissing's novel *The Whirlpool* (1897) sees the central character Harvey Rolfe reading aloud, "with no stinted expression of delight, occasionally shouting his appreciation," Kipling's *Barrack-Room Ballads* (1892) to his son Hughie, and his old friend Morton. An excited Rolfe prophesizes:

> The average Englander has never grasped the fact that there was such a thing as a British Empire. He's beginning to learn it, and itches to kick somebody, to prove his Imperialism. The bully of the music-hall shouting "Jingo" had his special audience. Now comes a man of genius, and decent folk don't feel ashamed to listen this time. We begin to feel our position. We can't make money quite so easily as we used to; scoundrels in Germany and elsewhere have dared to learn the trick of commerce. We feel sore, and it's a great relief to have our advantages pointed out to us. By God! we are the British Empire, and we'll just show 'em what *that* means![42]

The novel, beginning in 1886, traces the cynical, dandiacal Rolfe's marriage to the musician and proto-New Woman Alma Frothingham and his increasing disillusionment with modern life – the "whirlpool" – in late-Victorian London. Rolfe's transition from an idle, cynical bachelor with progressive attitudes toward gender relations to, by the end of the novel, a jingoistic widower is offered up by Gissing as something of a parable. Here as well as in *The Year of Jubilee* (1894) and *The Crown of Life* (1899), Gissing offers a bitter, sardonic take on the simultaneous rise of jingoism and middle-class suburban comfort. As John Sloan notes, "the very absence of an alternative ideal or way of life that might resist these vortical influences serves to deprive the reader of any final privileged perspective for resolving the conflicts explored."[43] Gissing was, in his own way, conservative and patriotic. The final work published in his lifetime, *The Private Papers of Henry Ryecroft* (1903), offers perhaps the consummate articulation of a conservative-quietist worldview. The solution for the autobiographical titular character of that novel to the vulgarity of urban modernity with its materialism and jingoism, its dirt and noise, was to retreat into the Devon countryside. Gissing might have despised the rancorous jingoism of Swinburne and Kipling, but he was to solemnize the deep beauty of the English landscape where the true spirit of the country was to be found. The narrator of *The Crown of Life* would celebrate the Sussex countryside as "the perfect loveliness of that rural landscape which is the old England, the true England, the England dear to the best of her children."[44] Gissing's gentle, rural, antimodern reactionary position was antithetical to the brash celebrations of empire in a writer like John Davidson, which only serves to underscore that there was a spectrum of conservatism and patriotism in the 1890s.

Conclusion

The movement of some artists from decadence to jingoism did not go unremarked. A biography in the *Speaker* of the fictional decadent poet Malvolio Malséant captured something of the amused confusion. Malséant had run the gamut over the course of the fin de siècle from aesthete to decadent, to Catholic Symbolist, to Neo-Celt, before the arrival of "the crisis" when he "began to display symptoms of a craving for energy and vitality." The biographer's friendship with Malséant had always proceeded on the understanding that the former was a Philistine, the latter a decadent. But Malséant's "evolution" had rendered their relationship impossible: "If the Archdecadent himself can turn Philistine and quote Kipling, then the rest of us have no place in the scheme of things." While there was hope that another revolution in Malséant's tastes might rectify the situation, he "remains a nightmare living contradiction in terms, a Decadent turned Philistine, yet no less a Decadent than before."[45] By the turn of the twentieth century many of the ideological fault lines of the 1890s had blurred. But then, as I have suggested over the course of this chapter, those fault lines were never stable. As in our own day, the culture wars of the 1890s were manufactured and propagated for strategic reasons by both progressive writers and their establishment critics. When we start to dig down a little, we can see decadent conservatives, patriotic aesthetes, and any manner of hybrid aesthetic-political dispositions. These hydra-headed creatures can disrupt our comfortable categories for reading the past – and the present – and that is precisely why we need to be open to their existence.

Notes

1 Logan Pearsall Smith, *Reperusals and Re-collections* (London: Constable & Co., 1936), 85.
2 Richard Le Gallienne, *The Romantic '90s* (New York: Doubleday, 1925), 138–39.

3 Nick Freeman, *1895: Drama, Disaster and Disgrace in Late Victorian Britain* (Edinburgh: Edinburgh University Press, 2011).

4 Deaglán Ó Donghaile, *Oscar Wilde and the Radical Politics of the Fin de Siècle* (Edinburgh: Edinburgh University Press, 2020).

5 Matthew Potolsky, "Decadence and Politics," in *Decadence: A Literary History*, ed. Alex Murray (Cambridge: Cambridge University Press, 2020), 152–66 (153).

6 Stefano Evangelista, *Literary Cosmopolitanism in the English Fin de Siècle: Citizens of Nowhere* (Oxford: Oxford University Press, 2021), 30, 24.

7 For example: Elizabeth Carolyn Miller, *Slow Print: Literary Radicalism and Late Victorian Print Culture* (Stanford, CA: Stanford University Press, 2013); Anna Feuerstein, *The Political Lives of Victorian Animals: Liberal Creatures in Literature and Culture* (Cambridge: Cambridge University Press, 2019); Angelique Richardson, *Love and Eugenics in the late Nineteenth Century: Rational Reproduction and the New Woman* (Oxford: Oxford University Press, 2003); Leela Gandhi. *Affective Communities: Anti-colonial Thought, Fin-de-Siècle Radicalism, and the Politics of Friendship* (Durham, NC: Duke University Press, 2006).

8 Marie Corelli, *Wormwood: A Drama of Paris*, ed. Kirsten Macleod (Peterborough: Broadview, 2004), 224.

9 Marie Corelli, *The Sorrows of Satan*, ed. Julia Kuehn (Kansas City, MO: Valancourt, 2008), 55–56.

10 Annette R. Federico, *Idol of Suburbia: Marie Corelli and Late-Victorian Literary Culture* (Charlottesville, VA: University of Virginia Press, 2000), 2.

11 Hugh E. M. Stutfield, "Tommyrotics," *Blackwood's Edinburgh Magazine* 157 (June 1895): 833–45 (833).

12 "Notes," *National Observer*, April 6, 1895: 547.

13 Arthur Symons, "Venetian Nights," *National Observer*, April 6, 1895: 551.

14 Arthur Symons, "Introduction: Fact in Literature," in *Studies in Prose and Verse* (London: J. M. Dent, 1904), 1-4 (3).

15 For a study of the relationship between decadence and the press see Nick Freeman, "Fighting like Cats and Dogs: Decadence and Print Media," in *Decadence: A Literary History*, ed. Alex Murray (Cambridge University Press, 2020), 87–101.

16 Matthew Kibble, "'The Betrayers of Language': Modernism and the *Daily Mail*," *Literature & History* 11, no. 1 (2002): 62–80.

17 Alex Murray, "Decadent Conservatism: Politics and Aesthetics in *The Senate*," *Journal of Victorian Culture* 20, no. 2 (2015): 186–211.

18 Lionel Johnson, "The Cultured Faun," *The Anti-Jacobin* (March 14, 1891): 156-7 (157).

19 David Cannadine, *Victorious Century: The United Kingdom 1800–1906* (London: Penguin, 2018), 462

20 William Morris, "How I Became a Socialist," in *Selected Writings and Designs* (Harmondsworth: Penguin, 1961), 33–40 (36).

21 John Ruskin, *Praeterita*, ed. Francis O'Gorman (Oxford: Oxford University Press, 2013), 7. As O'Gorman notes, these sentiments were first aired years earlier in *Fors Clavigera* of October 1871 (O'Gorman, "Introduction," xvi).

22 Edmund Burke, *Reflections on the Revolution in France*, ed. Conor Cruise O'Brien (London: Penguin, 2004), 170

23 Charles Kains Jackson, "The New Chivalry," *The Artist and Journal of Home Culture* 15, no. 172 (April 2, 1894): 102–04 (104).

24 Arthur Machen, "The Custom of the Manor," in *Dog and Duck* (London: Jonathan Cape, 1926), 173–80 (174, 176).

25 Arthur Machen, *Far Off Things* (London: Martin Secker, 1922), 80.

26 Arthur Machen, "*The Great God Pan*," in *Decadent and Occult Works*, ed. Dennis Denisoff (Cambridge: MHRA, 2018), 43–88 (81).

27 Lionel Johnson, "By the Statue of King Charles at Charing Cross," in *Poetical Works* (London, Elkin Matthews, 1915), 14–15.

28 Francis O'Gorman, "Lionel Johnson and Charing Cross," *Journal of Pre-Raphaelite Studies* 24 (2015): 78–96 (88).

29 William Ewart Gladstone, "England's Mission," *Nineteenth Century* (September 1878): 560–84 (569).

30 On Beerbohm's "queer indifference" as a riposte to Kipling's jingoism see Kristin Mahoney, *Literature and the Politics of Post-Victorian Decadence* (Cambridge: Cambridge University Press, 2015), 29–32.

31 Neil Hultgren, *Melodramatic Imperial Writing From the Sepoy Rebellion to Cecil Rhodes* (Athens, OH: Ohio University Press, 2014), 109–14; Jesse Oak Taylor, "Kipling's Imperial Aestheticism: Epistemologies of Art and Empire in *Kim*," *English Literature in Transition, 1880-1920* 52, no. 1 (2009): 49–69.

32 Oscar Wilde, "The Truth of Masks," in *The Soul of Man Under Socialism and Selected Critical Prose*, ed. Linda Dowling (London: Penguin, 2001), 280–304 (295).

33 Michael Field, "Works and Days" (1899) British Library, Add MS 46788, 145v.

34 Michael Field, "To America," *Academy* (January 4, 1896): 12.

35 Lord Byron, "Childe Harold's Pilgrimage," Canto XV, *The Major Works* (Oxford: Oxford University Press, 2008), 81.

36 Michael Field, "On a Proposal to Restore the Elgin Marbles to Athens," *Academy* (January 3, 1891): 13.

37 Francis O'Gorman, "Swinburne and Ireland," *Review of English Studies* 64, no. 265 (2013): 454–74 (473).

38 Algernon Charles Swinburne, "The Transvaal," *The Times* (October 11, 1899): 7.

39 John Holmes, *Darwin's Bards: British and American Poetry in the Age of Evolution* (Edinburgh: Edinburgh University Press, 2009), 44–45.

40 John Davidson, "The Testament of an Empire Builder," in *The Poems of John Davidson*, vol. 2, ed. Andrew Turnbull (Edinburgh: Scottish Academic Press, 1973), 334–49. This and all subsequent citations are given parenthetically with line numbers.

41 John Davidson, "On Poetry," in *Holiday and Other Poems* (London: Grant Richards, 1906), 131–56 (155).
42 George Gissing, *The Whirlpool* (London: Hogarth, 1984), 449, 450.
43 John Sloan, *George Gissing: The Cultural Challenge* (London: Palgrave Macmillan, 1989), 128.
44 George Gissing, *The Crown of Life* (London: Methuen, 1899), 166.
45 H.F.C. "Malvolio Malséant; Or, The Degenerate Regenerated," *Speaker* (June 1, 1901): 244–45.

CHAPTER 13

Decadence and the Antitheatrical Prejudice

Adam Alston

Theater has long been thought to be inadequate or injurious because of its tendency to go wrong, or to run along lines that are deemed to be, in some way, aesthetically or morally wrong. The theater historian Jonas Barish's magisterial study *The Antitheatrical Prejudice* (1981) is the most comprehensive chronicle of theater's manifold wrongness, a subject that the theater scholar Nicholas Ridout later pulled front and center in his wonderfully engaging book, *Stage Fright, Animals, and Other Theatrical Problems* (2006). For Ridout, the precarious liveness of theater – its tendency to break down with the forgotten line or the child performer taking matters into their own hands – forms the very basis of its queasy ontology.[1] But in the late nineteenth century, theater's wrongness had less to do with the mesmeric pull of liveness's vulnerabilities, and more to do with its relationship to the ascendency of bourgeois morality, the perception of declining artistic standards, and a society transformed by industry. Of particular note were those champions of fin-de-siècle decadence and symbolism, like Anatole Baju and Maurice Maeterlinck, who believed that the materiality of theater obstructed the poet's aesthetic and spiritual aspirations. Arthur Rimbaud put their desired solution best when he proposed to embrace the domestic setting as a "a stage-set of sorts," fit for flights of pseudotheatrical fancy.[2]

Each of these considerations – moral, aesthetic, and metaphysical – identify theater's wrongness as a form of impurity, and considering them together can potentially shed some instructive light on core issues of relevance to this volume. Firstly, such an approach enables us to better understand how theater pertained to decadence over the course of the fin de siècle, which, in turn, can help with illuminating the cultural politics of the 1890s. Secondly, a cross-disciplinary methodology that cuts across Literary Studies and Theater and Performance Studies has plenty to teach us about a few misleading assumptions regarding the 1890s – including the extent to which theater was (and in some quarters still is) regarded as a minor or inappropriate topic in the study of decadence and related areas, like symbolism, where literature tends to steal the limelight – as well as the unfortunate neglect of decadence in Theater and Performance Studies, which has remained stubbornly resistant to even recognizing "decadent theater" as a relevant subject of study. What makes this latter point especially galling leads me to the final issue that this chapter is looking to address: how perceptions of theater as a decadent institution (in the sense of it being in artistic decline or causing some kind of moral corruption) tie in with what Barish identifies as an "antitheatrical prejudice," on the one hand, and an *apparent* rejection of a decadent theater among theatrical modernizers in the 1890s, especially self-professed decadents and symbolists, on the other. As it turns out, this very prejudice was generative in the evolution of theater itself as a site for aesthetic experimentation, which is part and parcel of what makes the 1890s such a fascinating period of study in addressing the early development of modernism.

Of particular concern in addressing each of these areas is discourse *about* theater and decadence, which forms this chapter's primary focus. This discourse threatened the survival of particular theaters after influential voices prompted the enforcement of legislation that led to their closure, just as it threatened the survival of those involved in making theater. It also exposes cultural and political attitudes, be it with regard to the cultivation of bourgeois morality, taste, or a desire for or resistance to industrial "progress." At the same time, plenty of artists and writers associated with fin-de-siècle decadence expressed the view that theater was not decadent enough, which again offers clues as to their values and beliefs. What interests me most in all this is how theater produces not just artistic representations, but the bases upon which those representations and those who do the representing are judged, along with the institution of theater itself. In other words, I am interested in what the discursive conjunction of "decadence" and "theater" can tell us about taste, discrimination, and the attribution of value in the 1890s, and beyond.

Part of the problem in considering how decadents and critics of decadence were thinking about theater's wrongness has to do with the semantic promiscuity of decadence as a concept. The theater and literary critic Richard Gilman is particularly probing in expressing his frustration with the protean qualities of the term "decadence," describing it as "an unstable word and concept whose significations and weights continually change in response to shifts in morals, social and cultural attitudes, and even technology," existing "precariously and almost cabalistically" in and beyond a promiscuous set of words like "world-weary," "self-indulgent," "ultrarefined," "overcivilized," "debauchery," "effeteness," "depravity," "hedonism," "luxuriousness," "decay," "degeneration," and "retrogression."[3] As this list suggests, "decadence" is essentially a placeholder term that depends on a specific context for meaning. It also has a theatrical quality insofar as it tends to represent, and often mask, something else: a prejudicial attitude, perhaps, in which the word is used as a generic pejorative that might be linked to any of the other terms that Gilman outlines; or an aesthetic style or genre; or perhaps a taste that can be cultivated – such as a taste for decay or delight in disgust, which the literature scholar David Weir identifies as a key facet of fin-de-siècle decadence in Europe, and which might help with moving "the conceptual difficulty that attaches to decadence" from an "intellectual liability" to "an aesthetic asset ... more a matter of sensibility than rationality."[4] Equally, though, we might ask what this intellectual liability has to say about the beliefs and values of a given interlocutor. This might help in ascertaining the cultural politics of decadence, staging the ways in which it is imbued with different meanings – for instance, with regard to those who condemn decadence when they see it, and those who embrace its potentialities, not least when such a concept is embodied, and put into practice as a cultural force. Of particular interest in the context of this chapter is the extent to which the semantic promiscuity of decadence informs not just the relationship of theater to decadence, but the cultural politics of the 1890s more broadly, be it with regard to ethics, the emergence of modernism, or the extent to which this emergence was driven by how the relationship of ideas and concepts to their material realization were understood. The ways in which theater's wrongness plays into all three areas invite us to reconsider how we envisage the creativity and cultural tumultuousness of the 1890s, the significance of decadence as a generative aesthetic concern in its own right (and not simply as a poor cousin of symbolism), as well as our understanding of decadence itself, which is still cast in the long shadow of antitheatrical prejudice.

One reason for the relative neglect of or resistance toward the study of theater and decadence has to do with the fact that there is no coherent style, genre, or aesthetic category to which decadence refers.[5] As Sos Eltis, who is an important scholar in the context of this chapter, observes:

> "Decadent theatre" is not an established genre or commonly used category within British theatre studies. ... Though the word "decadent" was frequently used to bemoan the "foul boulevard cynicism" and "debauched palates" of fashionable playwrights and audiences, it did not delineate an artistic school or movement, but simply a sense that moral and artistic

standards were dropping; even the pantomime was diagnosed as "decadent" in 1896.[6]

The sense that theater is somehow complicit in the decline of moral and artistic standards is as old as theater itself. It can be found from Plato's condemnation of theater's duplicity and moral dubiousness, right through to debates of our own age about the distribution of public subsidy in periods of austerity and crisis.[7] At the same time, as Barish suggests, "the most active and sustained hostility" toward the stage tends to be provoked in the very moments "when it becomes a vital force in the life of a community."[8] The prominence of decadence as a point of reference in late nineteenth-century theater practice and criticism is no exception. Many writers associated with decadence wrote works for the stage – which is to say, works intended to be embodied and enacted, rather than merely read as verse dramas – and many theater makers and performers either affiliated themselves with decadence's inner circles, or were recognized as embodying the reasons why decadence and associated concepts have been both lauded and condemned. Those associated with decadence in the 1890s may not have formed a coherent artistic movement *as theater makers*, although many came to be associated with both decadence and symbolism by leading critics of the day, captured most clearly in the retitling and development of Arthur Symons's "The Decadent Movement in Literature" (1893) into *The Symbolist Movement in Literature* (1899);[9] but the extent to which *any* movement of the fin de siècle can be definitively taxonomized is up for debate, as the coterminous bed-hopping of naturalists, symbolists, and decadents goes some way toward illustrating. For instance, the playwright Henrik Ibsen might have "had no aspiration towards or association with the Decadent movement," but, as Eltis observes, he remains a key reference point in the study of theater and decadence despite being more generally regarded as a progenitor of realism (Eltis, "Theatre and Decadence," 205). In the eyes of his critics, at least, Ibsen's work was the very epitome of decadence – laced with venereal disease, incestuousness, and with the look and feel of "an open drain; of a loathsome sore unbandaged; of a dirty act done publicly"[10] – but, as Eltis goes on to note, "the distinctions between expelling, exploring and exploiting decadence were often so fine as to exist only in the viewer's mind" (Eltis, "Theatre and Decadence," 207).

So "decadence" is both an unruly concept, and promiscuous in its attachment to genres, styles, and categories. Hence, rather than establishing decadent theater as a coherent concept or practice, it would be better,

I argue, for us to discover how decadence is refracted in the hands of different playwrights, performers, and theater makers; how it travels across countries and decades; how it is shaped by the material circumstances of its production and reception; how it is condemned, appropriated, and queered relative to the dominant tastes and conventions of its day; and how it exceeds the textual as embodied or enacted phenomena. Decadence's penchant for boundary crossing is one of the things that makes decadence decadent, and the "active and sustained hostility" toward the very idea of a decadent theater gives us an excellent starting point for discovering it as a vital force in the artistic exploration of perversity, transgression, and gloriously subversive ruination. Moreover, such an approach to decadence might have something important to tell us about the charge of theater being in some way wrong, with the codification of this wrongness over the course of the fin de siècle being as good a place as any to start.

Moral Scourge

Theater's wrongness is embedded in commonplace metaphors and frames of reference. To "put on an act" or to describe something as "stagey," "melodramatic," or "theatrical" is usually intended to cast doubt on the authenticity or integrity of a person, behavior, or situation. Unruly children or subjects at the end of their tether might also find themselves reprimanded for "making a scene" or "making a spectacle" of themselves. These are all expressions of what Barish calls "the antitheatrical prejudice," and they are confined neither to the English language, nor to recent history. As Barish writes, "European languages abound in such expressions, most of them pejorative. They embody, in current terms, the vestiges of a prejudice against the theater that goes back as far in European history as the theater itself can be traced" (Barish, *Antitheatrical*, 1). Outside of Europe, actors in India, Southeast Asia, and China have been associated with baseness or vileness in ways that excluded them from full social integration (Barish, *Antitheatrical*, 1), and the sheer extent of the antitheatrical prejudice – its historical as much as its geographical reach – suggests that it constitutes more than an aberration. Rather, as Barish puts it, it forms the very basis of an "ontological malaise, a condition inseparable from our beings" that one can trace from Tertullian's theologically motivated condemnation of spectacles as "instruments of malign spirits" to the "saving salt of antitheatricalism" in the work of twentieth-century playwrights like Peter Handke (Barish, *Antitheatrical*, 2, 45, 464). To this we might add the hyperbolic diatribes of seventeenth-century puritans like William Prynne, who believed theater audiences to be "contagious in quality" and more "apt to poison, to infect all those who dare approach them, than one who is full of running Plague-sores";[11] Friedrich Nietzsche's critique of "theatrocracy" in *The Case of Wagner* (1888), concerned as it is with Richard Wagner as "*the artist of decadence*";[12] and Michael Fried's "Art and Objecthood," his famously disparaging assessment of the theatrical condition in (1967)[13] – these being just a few of the best-known examples.

Antitheatricality still haunts the practice and study of theater and performance, not least at a time when actor-statesmen and reality TV presidents demand that we recognize how theatricality has both problematized and become "central to our imagining of the historical *real*."[14] As performance historian and live artist Dominic Johnson acknowledges, "solo performance, body art and performance art have often prompted scholars to imagine that such work is motivated by a seemingly atavistic attempt at embodying truth, presence or authenticity," reclaiming each from a reality blemished by theatricality, be it with regard to the performance maker Ron Athey's self-obliterative martyrdoms, which "attempt to get beyond representation *through representation* itself," or Marina Abramović's insistence on the artist's presence, or in the work of canonical avant-garde playwrights like Handke and Samuel Beckett.[15] I highlight this merely to stress that the "ontological malaise" Barish identifies reaches deep within the study and practice of theater and performance as well as literature, and might even be said to define the emergence of Performance Studies as a discrete discipline in the late twentieth century, not least in the disparagement of theater as "the string quartet of the 21st century: a beloved but extremely limited genre, a subdivision of performance," to borrow from performance scholar Richard Schechner.[16] In Schechner's hands, theater reads as an outmoded institution – a decadent institution at odds with the supposed radicalism of performance in art, protest, and everyday life.

Antitheatricalism, then, is not so easily consigned to the history books; nonetheless, it has a habit of spreading at specific historical junctures. The late nineteenth century is just such an example, when puritanical diatribes against theater's "decadence" had serious consequences for its makers and stakeholders. For instance, the power exercised by the Lord Chamberlain's Office, which had the prerogative of censoring plays in Britain from 1737 until the 1968 Theatres Act abolished theater censorship, disincentivized or posed an obvious hurdle to the production of controversial theater performances in fin-de-siècle Britain. Those who took the plunge in legally permissible private performances often did so at no small risk to themselves – for instance, when J. T. Grein's Independent Theatre Society staged the 1891 London premiere of Ibsen's *Ghosts* (1881), or when Grein's career was effectively ruined during the notorious Pemberton-Billing trial in 1918 following a production of Wilde's *Salomé* (1891) starring the dancer Maud Allan. The trial was initiated when Grein and Allan tried to sue the Conservative Member of Parliament Noel Pemberton-Billing for libel after he permitted his newspaper to publish outrageous attacks on their character, although the trial soon became a platform for Pemberton-Billing to subject them to absurd and explicitly homophobic slander that condemned both as antipatriotic degenerates in a time of war. Likewise, the 1895 trials of Oscar Wilde for "gross indecency" had already set a precedent – with Wilde ultimately imprisoned in Reading Gaol, and regarded as a pariah thereafter – making abundantly clear what was at stake for those associated with a decadent theater.[17]

As literature scholar Matthew Brinton Tildesley points out, the 1888 Local Government Act also gave local councils in Great Britain control over the issuing of music hall licenses, while adherents to a resurgent moral purity movement lobbied local councils "in a partially successful attempt to close down the music halls (distinctly reminiscent of the original puritans' closing of the theaters of the seventeenth century)":

> The mouthpiece for this campaign was Laura Ormiston Chant, who opposed the license for *The Empire* on the grounds that "the place at night is the habitual resort of prostitutes in pursuit of their traffic, and that portions of the entertainment are most objectionable, obnoxious, and against the best interests and moral well-being of the community at large."[18]

For activists like Chant, the performer embodied licentiousness and performed material was prone to spreading moral corruption, prompting temporary closures of music halls while investigations were undertaken concerning the performed material and comportment of the performers. In the case of *The Empire*, this involved making "structural alterations to the building in an attempt to screen off prostitutes from the theater's clientele. This was, however, pulled down by the crowds when the theater reopened" (Tildesley, "Decadent Sensations," 164). (One can imagine the many defenders of sensuous or erotic artistic practice at the time, like Symons and Selwyn Image, being among the first in line to do so).[19]

The early twentieth century, too, was rife with the antitheatrical prejudice in contexts ranging from the political arena, to cultural production. For instance, in a speech delivered to the House of Commons in 1900,

Liberal politician and social purity advocate Samuel Smith condemned "the growing tendency to put upon the stage plays of a demoralising character" – he mentions Arthur Wing Pinero's *The Gay Lord Quex* (1899), along with a couple of touring performances from the United States – calling for stricter supervision of theater performances, and deploring what theater critics had long since recognized as "the decadent character" of "degrading" and "foul and corrupting plays." He goes on:

> The moral standard of a country is largely affected by the drama. Multitudes of young men and young women form their ideas of what is right and wrong in no small degree from what they witness on the stage; and when they see the purest and holiest things of life turned into derision, and disgusting licentiousness treated as the normal rule of life, is it likely that their own moral standard will remain high? Is it not certain that the same effects will follow in London as in Paris in that a decadent drama, and, what always accompanies it, a decadent literature, will produce a decadent nation?[20]

Smith's opprobrium was no doubt exacerbated by a significant rise in the number of theaters in London, where his scorn is largely poured, nearly doubling between 1860 and the mid-1880s (Quilter, "The Decline of Drama," 547). As a consequence, theater itself was seen to take on a virulent quality.

Although Smith set the tone for his remarks in an 1888 speech on literary decadence – in which he publicly deplored the rapid spread of "demoralising" and "pernicious" French literature – the emphasis that he places on plays *in performance* tends to elude the attention of scholarly commentators.[21] "The written words of a play do not really show its moral tendency," he writes: "That depends on dress, gestures, and suggestive acting" (Smith, "Mr Samuel Smith, M.P.," 7). In other words, it is not the metaphysical theater conjured into consciousness when reading verse dramas that is ultimately at stake for Smith in this particular rant, but a theater of bodies in a shared space, and all that means for the potential transmission of affect from a corrupt stage to an impressionable audience. Hostility, then, but at the same time a recognition of theater's place and power as a moral technology not just within an elite metropolis, but, in Smith's hyperbolic assessment, with regard to the very fiber and moral backbone of a nation – a theme that Arthur Balfour, the former Tory Prime Minister, would later pull front and center in his 1908 Henry Sidgwick Memorial Lecture on political and national decadence.[22]

As with most examples of the antitheatrical prejudice, Smith identifies a threat to established structures of power and privilege in ways that acknowledge theater's potentially transformative power, priming the rhetorical toolbox for subsequent critiques of theater and theatricality in the twentieth century, including the theatrical or performative presentation of self. For instance, in 1935, the North American art critic Thomas Craven took aim not just at paintings, but at the dandyish demeanor and mannerisms of painters. His vitriol targeted the "shapely, slender hands" of male artists, their sensitivity, and involvement in what he dubbed "the modern cult of effeminacy."[23] As the performance historian Amelia Jones has persuasively argued, examples like this evidence a clear connection between decadence and homophobic antitheatricality, in which Wildean dandyism came to be seen as the glue connecting "effeminate and implicitly homosexual weakness in artistic execution to the supposed decadence of European art" and literature, *especially* with regard to the "threat" of theatricality.[24] As Jones puts it, in such contexts theatricality is understood to be "debased because it is connected implicitly to femininity or to gay men who are effeminate; in turn, femininity and gay masculinity are assumed to be theatrical, lesser versions of human embodiment and subjectivity" (Jones, *In Between Subjects*, 131). Here, theatricality stands as the "perverted" cousin of self-formation, aligning more with "the artificial, the unnatural, the abnormal, the decadent, the effete, the diseased," always and forever "infected with queerness."[25]

Theater in Decline

Moral purity advocates had a particular axe to grind in condemning theater's supposedly inherent wrongness, but a very different set of diagnoses come into play when we turn to theatrical declinism, especially with regard to the creative sclerosis of an industry dominated by commercial incentives and the popularity of melodrama. There is no shortage of examples of theater critics and impresarios condemning the "decadence" of theater as an outmoded institution buckling under the weight of declining artistic standards. Examples range from Louis Charpentier mourning the "decadence" of taste in eighteenth-century France, to Peter Brook's influential condemnation of "deadly theater" in *The Empty Space* (1968).[26] Eltis has usefully drawn attention to a number of other examples that are specific to the late nineteenth century, including the English critics Harry Quilter and Oswald Crawfurd.[27] Quilter diagnosed late nineteenth-century theater in London as being subject to an insidious process of decay: the contemptible consequence of neglecting tragic drama and "genuine" comedies in favor of "the decadence of the lighter forms of dramatic representation," and an unhealthy favoring of Gallic dramas

(Quilter, "Decline," 552). His xenophobia and snobbery are thinly veiled, as is his chauvinism in perceiving "that decadence in national spirit and taste, which has made of us late years think that all artistic products emanating from France must of necessity be superior to those of our own country" (Quilter, "Decline," 552). Crawfurd, too, thought that appeals to the taste of rural and working-class audiences at the cost of "educated" metropolitan counterparts, the prioritization of melodramas suited to long runs, and the actor-manager system were all causes of theater's decadence" (Crawfurd, "The London Stage," 501–06). Bigotry clearly guides their diagnoses of theater's decadence, as it did with the moral puritans, but Quilter and Crawfurd were really taking aim at what they saw as declining standards in the quality of playwriting and theater making.

It is the insistence on theater's unique characteristics as an art form – a temporal and material art of bodies acting in space – that tends to be highlighted by these critics as a particularly worrisome concern. Quilter was not just taking aim at the moral dubiousness or derivative qualities of plays; rather, he traced the decadence of London theater to "the conditions of the stage itself" (Quilter, "Decline," 554–55). Putting aside the xenophobic perception of foreign influence on the composition of plays, it was the "upholsterer" of theater (who we might now call a scenographer, although he really means anyone other than the playwright) who was ultimately to blame for the degradation of English drama (Quilter, "Decline," 556). Similarly, Crawfurd reserves his most stringent criticism for the actor-manager. In other words, recognizing the fact that these critics advocate for putting art before profit,[28] the very assets that distinguish theater from dramatic literature stand as primary culprits in the diagnosis of theater's decadence (Crawfurd, "The London Stage," 510–11).

The Italian performer Eleonora Duse is an important figure in this discussion, as she exemplifies how an individual decrying artistic stultification can be acknowledged in turn as the very embodiment of decadence.[29] Her commentaries and influence on the theater of the 1890s is also a fascinating example to consider in appreciating the counterintuitively generative role played by the antitheatrical prejudice in the emergence and development of modernism. In words that would go on to inspire Symons and the theater designer Edward Gordon Craig, she famously declared that "to save the Theatre, the Theatre must be destroyed, the actors and actresses must all die of the plague. They poison the air, they make art impossible."[30] This is typical of the rhetoric favored by avant-gardists and modernists of the period, who found the making and reception of theater to be unbearably sclerotic. Better, they thought, to start over in the pursuit of a craft worthy of the name, which for Duse led to the pioneering of a modern, naturalistic performance style. However, where stock references to a need for theater to be "cleansed" reek of macho and fascistic grandstanding (Filippo Tommaso Marinetti being a prime example), Duse's mid- to late career – after her split with the decadent author and playwright Gabriele d'Annunzio – lends a feminist edge to her demands for innovation. Her attitude toward feminist activism in Europe may well have been conflicted, but, as Susan Bassnett acknowledges, she was determined to celebrate women on stage "who impose their will upon the world around them," surviving *in spite* of their suffering.[31]

Duse's association with New Womanhood was fostered through her predilection for playing roles like Pinero's Paula Ray, or Ibsen's Nora Helmer and Hedda Gabler. Although her fame was linked to her naturalistic depiction of these roles, which was considered innovative and was celebrated as such, her gendered association with modernity and modernism also fueled disparaging allusions to decadence and disease in the eyes of contemporaries. She was seen as "the woman of modern times," as fellow actress Adelaide Ristori put it, "with all her complaints of hysteria, anaemia and nerve trouble and with all the consequences of those complaints; she is, in short, the fin de siècle woman."[32] It is as though the role that helped establish her career – a portrayal of the consumptive Camille in Alexandre Dumas *fils*'s play *La dame aux camélias* (1852) – had "infected" her playing of a very different kind of woman in search of agency and autonomy, at least in the eyes of commentators for whom the New Woman was both subject to sickness as well as a kind of disease. With Duse and her critics, the cultural politics of decadence and disease played out as a battleground over which the relationship of a modern theater to its past was fought.

Discontent with theater – the kind that prompted Duse to say that "the Theatre must be destroyed" – had a formative role to play in the evolution of modernism, not least modernist theater and drama. As literature and theater scholar Martin Puchner writes: "Even the most adamant forms of modernist antitheatricalism feed off the theater and keep it close to hand. The resistance registered in the prefix *anti* thus does not describe a place outside the horizon of the theater, but a variety of attitudes through which the theater is being kept at arm's length and, in the process of resistance, utterly transformed."[33] Puchner's remarks offer vital insight into the relevance of the antitheatrical prejudice for modernist theater and drama – and indeed the period of modernism – but equally they offer insight into those strands of theatrical and literary experimentation in the late nineteenth century that have been misleadingly described as intermediaries between the agony of romanticism and the early years of modernism, respectively: namely, decadence and symbolism.[34] What is more, as the section "Metaphysical Impurity" explores, the antitheatrical prejudice played an important role in how poets, playwrights, and theater makers associated with decadence and symbolism were thinking about their practice, including the innovativeness of that practice (a counterintuitive notion that has been amply substantiated in Vincent Sherry's work on the "essentially progressive energy" of a decadent modernism turned against modernity).[35] In fact, it had a formative role to play in how these poets, playwrights, and theater makers were thinking about a wide range of transformations, be it with regard to the self, cultural expression, or the forward march of industrial progress.

Metaphysical Impurity

Several important playwrights and commentators associated with decadence had an uneasy and at times confrontational relationship with theater. In part this is due to the close intersections between decadence and symbolism – or, as I put it in this chapter's opening section, the tendency for fin-de-siècle playwrights to bed-hop, experimenting with multiple affiliations between and within different artistic and intellectual communities. For example, Wilde and Rachilde championed the leading symbolist theater of the day – the Théâtre d'Art – and wrote plays that became closely associated with symbolism, but at the same time they were recognized as decadents, and these very same works are routinely folded into the orbit of decadence. The bifurcation of symbolism and decadence – especially the former's association with modernist beginnings, and the latter with crepuscular endings – is really the product of "literary polemic," as Sherry puts it, rather than adversarial struggle (Sherry, *Modernism*, 7). And an important cornerstone of this polemic was the antitheatrical prejudice.

As theater historian John Stokes explains in an elucidating commentary on the "Paterian paradox," the symbolist yearning for a disembodied voice became "an intolerable ideal, a contradiction even, once the Decadent was given the opportunity of assuming a public presence, an identifiable and vocal personality" (Stokes, "The Legend of Duse," 151). Many symbolists regarded the search for metaphysical purity as being in some way tainted once expressed, or made public, not least when sullied by a public art of bodies in space, like the theater. Theater renders the Paterian paradox particularly acute, which explains why many symbolists and decadents were resistant to the prospect of staging. Thus we find Anatole Baju, who founded the literary review *Le Décadent* (1886–89), suggesting that "life itself was theatre, or at the very best circus"; reason enough, he thought, to abandon theater's material trappings.[36] It is worth stressing that Baju's writing on decadence lacked any real consistency, and he came to see *décadisme* and *symbolisme* as rival literary schools;[37] nonetheless, as a self-professed decadent, his call for the abandonment of theater is odd given the theater's various associations with sensuousness and perversity of the kind surveyed in this chapter. It is even more odd given how many of his peers in France and neighboring countries were committed playwrights, including Wilde, Rachilde, Jean Lorrain, Remy de Gourmont, Maurice Maeterlinck, Hugo von Hofmannsthal, and Gabriele d'Annunzio.

Many of the primary culprits for propagating the pursuit of metaphysical purity in symbolist art and literature held a more complex relation to theater than outright dismissal, like Stéphane Mallarmé. Mallarmé's "systematic retreat from the stage" only started after the Théâtre-Français rejected two fragmentary plays that he had been writing between 1864 and 1867 – *Hérodiade* (1871) and *L'Après-midi d'un faune* (1876) – prompting him "to formulate the famous doctrine of symbolism: "To paint not the object, but the effect it produces."[38] Interestingly, as Puchner acknowledges, the evolution of *Hérodiade* from a rejected play to a closet drama, which was eventually published in 1871, is characterized by the removal of stage directions, "as if to prove how little he was thinking of theatrical representation" (Puchner, *Stage Fright*, 59). Puchner sees this transition as encapsulating a view of theater withdrawn from reality that was to reach its apogee in the decadent protagonist of Joris-Karl Huysmans's *À Rebours*, Des Esseintes, "whose favorite activity resides in reading Mallarmé's poetic dramas in the solitude of his own closet" (Puchner, *Stage Fright*, 59). But the reverence with which Mallarmé viewed and valued "the effect" produced by an object of symbolist interest was still deeply invested in *the idea* of the performing body, and was inspired by encounters with its movements. For instance, Mallarmé regarded Loïe Fuller's dances as an exceptional form of poetry, and although he was more interested in the dancer as a metaphorical figure than he was in their physicality, it was their physical being which prompted his metaphysical interests. In other words, Baju's antitheatrical-ism (in 1887, at least) reduced a more complex antinomy – the Paterian paradox – to a caricature of Mallarmé's more nuanced sense of this antinomy *as* an antinomy, which depends on the performing body in the crafting of a mimetically impossible enterprise.[39]

The best-known example of a playwright concerned with the aesthetic "wrongness" of theater is the Belgian playwright Maurice Maeterlinck, whom Eltis describes "as the pre-eminent Decadent dramatist" of fin-de-siècle Paris (Eltis, "Theatre and Decadence," 201). Maeterlinck suggested in his writings that theater should be no more than a "temple of dreams," and that the "mystic density of a work of art" risked being jeopardized by the corporeality of living actors.[40] This is in fact typical of modernist antitheatrical prejudice, which tended to center on the actor – albeit not always for the same reason as Maeterlinck, who viewed the actor as an impediment to ethereality. This is why, as Frazer Lively notes, Maeterlinck "refused to let his first play be produced in the theater, and for a time he resisted having any of his works staged. He envisioned his dramas as plays for marionettes" (Lively, "Introduction," 10), or shadows – but this did not stop him from becoming one of the foremost playwrights of his age, perhaps *because* he held fast to a belief that "the more uncompromisingly one dismisses theater, the more triumphantly one can claim it back" (after all, he was as much a master of atmosphere and the scenographic technologies needed to produce it as he was of poetry).[41] In light of Puchner's observations about modernist antitheatricality, perhaps we might think of Maeterlinck's apparent antitheatrical prejudice less in terms of being a call to abandon theater, and more as a basis for its redemption. Read along these lines, decadent theater emerges not simply as the regressive underside of those genres typically regarded as "modernist," like naturalism, but as an important cornerstone in a theater aspiring toward a state as yet unrealizable, and for that reason all the more appealing to those interested in transgressing the recognized limits of theatrical possibility.

Redeeming Decadent Theater

Once we read Maeterlinck's relationship with theater as being predicated on a desire to transform its potential, we can begin to appreciate why he permitted the impresario Paul Fort to stage his works with his Théâtre d'Art. The Théâtre d'Art produced eight varied programs between 1890 and 1892, presenting plays by several writers associated with decadence and symbolism, including Maeterlinck, Rachilde, Pierre Quillard, Remy de Gourmont and Catulle Mendès. And it did so in ways that were, as cultural historian Patrick McGuinness recognizes, "interestingly staged, innovatively designed and thoughtfully performed," (McGuinness, "Mallarmé," 151), while at the same time actively supporting a community of peers – for instance, by holding benefit performances for decadent playwrights and poets, like Paul Verlaine.[42] Decadent glitterati were also closely involved in promoting and supporting the Théâtre d'Art, including Rachilde and Wilde. Rachilde's reputation, which was firmly established by 1890, brought their programs to the attention of literary and intellectual elites who were drawn to the staging of her own plays. She also joined the theater's programming committee and wrote favorable reviews of productions. Wilde, too, served as an artistic advisor. If, as literature scholar Matthew Potolsky argues, decadence is less a coherent mode of production than it is "a characteristic mode of reception," or "stance,"[43] then the communities that built around theaters like the Théâtre d'Art provided a forum for cultivating and even enabling this stance. Hence, while an international and cosmopolitan "republic of letters" fostered cross-pollination in the development of this mode of reception, excuses for gathering and supporting one another as a community with shared interests – be it at the theater, the café, or the salon – were at least of equal significance. This invites us to put to rest more reductive characterizations of decadence, due in no small part to the influence of Paul Bourget, that celebrate it merely as an atomistic literary tendency advanced by solipsistic antiheros.[44]

However much symbolist poets and their affiliates lauded metaphysical purity, and however much they denigrated theater's necessarily public means of expression, it is notable that reviews of work performed at a "temple" of symbolist theater, the Théâtre d'Art, tended to appraise it on the basis of the physical attractiveness of a performer. It was ultimately the "skinniness" of Georgette Camée as the leading role in Percy Bysshe Shelley's supposedly unperformable play *The Cenci* (1819), and the "disproportionate size" of Lucie Dénac as The Wife in the 1890 premiere of Rachilde's *La Voix du sang (Voice of Blood)*, that drew the staunchest criticism (Lively, "Introduction," 13–16). As Lively puts it, "no matter how 'cerebral' or 'ideal' the symbolists intended a production to be, the libidinal effect of the actors on the audience could still make or break a show" (Lively, "Introduction," 16). And it was not just the performers on stage who drew attention. The audience, too, appeared eccentrically dressed, described by one critic, Georges Roussel, at the opening night of Rachilde's *Madame La Mort* (1891), as "decadentish-instrumentish-Maeterlinckish-symbolist poets, painters, neo-traditionalist, pointillist-impressionist or not pointillist! So many revolutionary mops of hair! All those floppy felt hats, in colors which strangely complement one another!" (Lively, "Introduction," 20). To attend the premiere of a work that might claim its seat at the table of decadent theater was also to participate in the formation of a decadent *socius*, performing allegiance with a "decadentish" crowd in ways that ought to prompt pause for thought about decadent atomization. Theater's publicness made decadent cosmopolitanism explicit – it performed it – just as it had a hand in its very possibility.

It is important to add that some of the leading lights of fin-de-siècle aestheticism and decadence were also critics and theorists of theater and performance. For instance, Symons, in an essay on Wagner, describes how

> the drama written as literature, at a distance from the theatre, and with only a vague consciousness of the actor, can be no other than a lifeless thing. . . . Wagner's best service to drama, in his theories as in his practice, is the insistence with which he has demonstrated the necessary basis of the play in theatre. . . . No one has seen more clearly the necessity of "tempering the artistic ends to be realised" to the actual "means of execution" which are at the artist's disposal.[45]

In other words, the emphasis so often placed on the preservation of metaphysical purity in studies of decadence and symbolism, such as those famous studies advanced by Symons himself, ought at least to be colored by recognition of the fact that he was an advocate not just of drama, but the creation of "beauty for an instant" in live performance (Symons, *Plays, Acting, and Music*, 3). Even when writing about Maeterlinck's plays, "which do all they can to become disembodied," Symons insists on the importance of their being staged, aspiring toward "atmosphere without locality . . . [which] Mr. Craig can give us so easily" (Symons, *Studies*, 358). And this recognition of the *potential* for theater to provide a home for even the most extravagant or "unperformable" scenes is ultimately what prompts him to find a potentially exciting compromise with the sceno-graphic, inviting us to resist thinking about decadent or symbolist drama as a drama of the mind only. This accounts for Symons's desire to draw pantomime (a wordless art) into dialogue with poetic drama (a metaphys-ical literature), just as it accounts for why he dedicates his essays on theater in *Studies in Seven Arts* (1906) to considerations of Wagner, Duse, Craig, and Alfred Jarry, all of whom, with the possible exception of Craig, have been associated with decadence in some form or another. These artists were interested in more than contemplation; for them, sensational experi-ence came first and foremost, as did the practice of theater *as a practice*.

*

Theater should not be dismissed as an erroneous or marginal topic in the study of late nineteenth-century decadence. The cultural politics of decadent rhetoric clearly affected what plays were staged, and how they were staged – if they were staged at all – but there is no shortage of examples of plays and indeed a whole host of performance forms that might usefully be reclaimed as important examples of decadent theater and performance, especially when we consider decadence as a concept and a practice that travels across styles, genres, movements, and aesthetic categories.[46] Such an endeavor demands that we pull into focus the grounding of theater in particular historical moments, particularly those that subject decadence to conflicting cultural associations and instrumentalist political uses, as was clearly the case in Britain and France in and around the 1890s, when decadence served as a cultural-political crucible that evolved in tandem with the antitheatrical prejudice. It also demands that we recognize the important discursive roles played by decadence and the antitheatrical prejudice in the fostering of a modern theater, at once opposed to modernity's valorization of commerce, and invested in the transformational impulses of modernism.

For moral puritans of the 1890s, the relationship of theater to decadence was black-and-white: theater is a moral technology, and hence capable of advancing the decadence of a community, society, or nation. But for playwrights or would-be playwrights and poets like Maeterlinck and Mallarmé, the antitheatrical prejudice takes on a paradoxical character of a kind that does not merely signal the atrophy or decline of artistic innovativeness; rather, as Puchner recognizes, antinomy toward theater and the theatrical plays into the evolution of theater itself. To this end, theater's decadent wrongness – moral, aesthetic, or metaphysical – and indeed theater's standing as an embodied and enacted practice, may be the best starting point we have for appreciating its role in a nascent modernism. Equally, theater's decadent diagnoses in the late nineteenth century invite reconsideration of movements and categories, like naturalism and symbolism, that are so often taken for granted in Theater and Performance Studies as coherent and stable points of reference. In short, dwelling on theater's decadent wrongness might stand as a corrective for theater's omission from studies of decadence, as well as the disregard for decadence that has for so long affected the study of theater and performance.

Acknowledgment

Research for this chapter was generously supported by an Arts and Humanities Research Council Fellowship (AH/T006994/1).

Notes

1 Nicholas Ridout, *Stage Fright, Animals, and Other Theatrical Problems* (Cambridge: Cambridge University Press, 2006), 3. Ridout borrows the notion of an "ontological queasiness" from Barish.

2 Arthur Rimbaud, "VIGILS (*Illuminations XX: Veillées*)," in *Arthur Rimbaud: Selected Works in Translation*, ed. and trans. A. S. Kline (London: Poetry in Translation, 2008), 168.

3 Richard Gilman, *Decadence: The Strange Life of an Epithet* (New York: Farrar, Straus and Giroux, 1975), 19, 33.

4 David Weir, "Afterword: Decadent Taste," in *Decadence and the Senses*, eds. Jane Desmarais and Alice Condé (Cambridge: Legenda, 2017), 219–28 (220).

5 For exceptions, see "Staging Decadence," https://www.stagingdecadence .com/blog (accessed July 21, 2021); Adam Alston and Alexandra Trott, eds. "Decadence and Performance," special issue of *Volupté: Interdisciplinary Journal of Decadence Studies* 4, no. 2 (Winter 2021).

6 Sos Eltis, "Theatre and Decadence," in *Decadence: A Literary History*, ed. Alex Murray (Cambridge: Cambridge University Press, 2020), 201–17. See also Harry Quilter, "The Decline of Drama," *Contemporary Review* 51 (April 1887): 547–60 (551–52); Oswald Crawfurd, "The London Stage," *Fortnightly Review* 47, no. 280 (April 1890): 499–516 (506); Charles Dickens, "On the Decadence of Pantomime," *Theatre* 27 (January 1896): 21–25.

7 See, for instance, Assed Baig, "During Times of Austerity Art is Just Middle-Class Decadence," *Huffington Post* (February 20, 2013), https://www .huffingtonpost.co.uk/assed-baig/during-times-of-austerity_b_2349132.html (accessed February 8, 2019).

8 Jonas Barish, *The Antitheatrical Prejudice* (Berkeley, CA: University of California Press, 1981), 66.

9 Arthur Symons, "The Decadent Movement in Literature," *Harper's New Monthly Magazine* (November 1893), 858-67; Arthur Symons, *The Symbolist Movement in Literature* (London: Archibald Constable & Co., Ltd., 1908).

10 Editorial Comment," *Daily Telegraph* (March 14, 1891)," in *The Fin de Siècle: A Reader in Cultural History C. 1880–1900*, eds. Sally Ledger and Roger Luckhurst (Oxford: Oxford University Press, 2000), 127.

11 William Prynne, *Histriomastix: The Player's Scourge, or Actor's Tragedy* (New York: Johnson Reprint Corporation, 1972 [1632]), 152.

12 Friedrich Nietzsche, "The Case of Wagner (1888)," in *The Nietzsche Reader*, ed. Keith Ansell Pearson and Duncan Large (Oxford: Blackwell Publishing, 2006), 451–55 (453), emphasis in original. For a complete version of this text with the postscripts referencing "theatrocracy," see https://archive.org/stream/ thecaseofwagnern25012gut/25012-pdf_djvu.txt, (accessed June 3, 2021).

13 Michael Fried, "Art and Objecthood,"in *Minimal Art: A Critical Anthology*, ed. Gregory Battock (Berkeley, CA: University of California Press, 1968), 116–47.

14 Alan Ackerman and Martin Puchner, "Introduction: Modernism and Anti-Theatricality," in *Against Theatre: Creative Destructions on the Modernist Stage*, eds. Alan Ackerman and Martin Puchner (Basingstoke and New York: Palgrave Macmillan, 2006), 1–17 (4), emphasis in original.

15 Dominic Johnson, "Introduction: Towards a Moral and Just Psychopathology," in *Pleading in the Blood: The Art and Performances of Ron Athey*, ed. Dominic Johnson (London: Live Art Development Agency; Bristol: Intellect, 2013), 10–41 (12–13), emphasis in original; see also Ridout, *Stage Fright*, 5–6.

16 Richard Schechner, "A New Paradigm for Theatre in the Academy," *TDR* 36, no. 4 (Winter 1992): 7–10 (8).

17 See Philip Hoare, *Wilde's Last Stand: Scandal and Conspiracy During the Great War* (London and New York: Duckworth Overlook, 2011).

18 Laura Ormiston Chant, quoted in Matthew Brinton Tildesley, "Decadent Sensations: Art, the Body and Sensuality in the "Little Magazines,'" in Desmarais and Condé, *Decadence and the Senses*, 162–81 (164).

19 See Joseph Bristow's writing on Symons's "addiction" to The Empire: Joseph Bristow, '"Sterile Ecstasies": The Perversity of the Decadent Movement', in *The Endings of Epochs*, ed. Laurel Brake (Cambridge: D. S. Brewer, 1995), 65–88 (74–75). See also John Stokes, *In the Nineties* (Hemel Hempstead: Harvester-Wheatsheaf, 1989), 60–61; Arthur Symons, 'The Paris Music Hall', in *Plays, Acting, and Music* (London: Duckworth and Co., 1903), 123–26 (123).

20 Samuel Smith, 'Mr Samuel Smith, M.P., on immoral plays', *Rhyl Record and Advertiser*, May 19, 1900, 7, https://newspapers.library.wales/view/3638338/3638345/50 (accessed January 9, 2021); see also Eltis, 'Theatre and Decadence', 207. 9

21 Quoted in Simon Heffer, *The Age of Decadence: Britain 1880 –1914* (London: Random House, 2017), 502. Julie Stone Peters's brilliant chapter on "the theatrical obscene" does not address Smith's speeches, but it nonetheless speaks to this point; see Julie Stone Peters, "Performing Obscene Modernism: Theatrical Censorship and the Making of Modern Drama," in *Against Theatre*, eds. Ackerman and Puchner, 206–30.

22 Arthur James Balfour, *Decadence* (Cambridge: Cambridge University Press, 1908). I am borrowing the term "moral technology" from Terry Eagleton, via Ridout's discussion of theater as a moral technology. See Nicholas Ridout, *Scenes from Bourgeois Life* (Ann Arbor, MI: University of Michigan Press, 2020), 68–73 passim.

23 Thomas Craven, "Effeminacy?," *The Art Digest* (October 1, 1935): 10.

24 Amelia Jones, *In Between Subjects: A Critical Genealogy of Queer Performance* (London and New York: Routledge, 2021), 152.

25 Eve Kosofsky Sedgwick and Andrew Parker, "Introduction," in *Performativity and Performance*, eds. Eve Kosofsky Sedgwick and Andrew Parker (New York and London: Routledge, 1995), 1–18 (5, 6); see also Jones, *In Between Subjects*, 133.

26 Louis Charpentier, *Causes de la décadence du goût sur le theatre (Causes of the decadence of taste in theatre* (Paris: Dufour, 1768); Peter Brook, *The Empty Space* (London: Penguin, 2008).

27 See Eltis, "Theatre and Decadence."

28 Both Quilter and Crawfurd condemn the commercialization of the English stage; however, Crawfurd goes further in calling for a robust system of public arts subsidy as the only sensible means of remedial action that might be taken.

29 See John Stokes on Duse's being "firmly identified with Decadence as an international phenomenon." John Stokes, "The Legend of Duse," in *Decadence and the 1890s*, ed. Ian Fletcher (New York: Holmes and Meier, 1979), 151–71 (154).

30 Eleonora Duse quoted in Arthur Symons, "Eleonora Duse," *Contemporary Review, 1866–1900* 78 (August 1900): 196–202 (198).

31 Susan Bassnett, "Eleonora Duse," in *Bernhardt, Terry, Duse: The Actress in Her Time*, eds. John Stokes, Michael R. Booth, and Susan Bassnett (Cambridge: Cambridge University Press, 1988), 119–70 (167).

32 Quoted in Meredith Conti, *Playing Sick: Performances of Illness in the Age of Victorian Medicine* (London and New York: Routledge, 2019), 74.

33 Martin Puchner, *Stage Fright: Modernism, Anti-Theatricality, and Drama* (Baltimore, MD: Johns Hopkins University Press, 2002), 2.

34 See, for instance, Mario Praz, *The Romantic Agony*, 2nd ed., trans. Angus Davidson (London and New York: Oxford University Press, 1970). To paraphrase Edmund Wilson, we might say instead that decadence and symbolism thrived in one another's teeth. Edmund Wilson, *Axel's Castle: A Study of the Imaginative Literature of 1870–1930* (New York: Farrar, Straus and Giroux, 2004), 10.

35 Vincent Sherry, *Modernism and the Reinvention of Decadence* (Cambridge: Cambridge University Press, 2015), 24–25.

36 Quoted in Frantisek Deak, *Symbolist Theater: The Formation of an Avant-Garde* (Baltimore and London: Johns Hopkins University Press, 1993), 22–23. See also Anatole Baju, *L'Ecole décadente* (Paris: Vanier, 1887), 31.

37 See David Weir, "Decadent Anarchism, Anarchistic Decadence: Contradictory Cultures, Complementary Politics," in *Anarchism and the Avant-Garde: Radical Arts and Politics in Perspective*, ed. Carolin Kosuch (Leiden and Boston: Brill, 2019), 129–52 (141).

38 Mallarmé quoted in Puchner, *Stage Fright*, 59.

39 "[*Hérodiade* is] absolutely scenic, not possible in the theater, but requiring the theater." Mallarmé quoted in Puchner, *Stage Fright*, 60.

40 Quoted in Frazer Lively, "Introduction," in Rachilde, *Madame La Mort and Other Plays*, ed. and trans. Kiki Gounaridou and Frazer Lively (Baltimore and London: Johns Hopkins University Press, 1998), 10.

41 Patrick McGuinness, "Mallarmé, Maeterlinck and the Symbolist *Via Negativa* of Theatre," in *Against Theatre*, eds. Ackerman and Puchner, 149–67 (150). Maeterlinck's pact with theatre also speaks to Petra Dierkes-Thrun's writing on the "postmetaphysical." Petra Dierkes-Thrun, *Salome's Modernity: Oscar*

Wilde and the Aesthetics of Transgression (Ann Arbor, MI: University of Michigan Press, 2011), 3, 28.

42 The Théâtre d'Art held a benefit performance for Paul Verlaine and Paul Gauguin in 1891, presenting Maurice Maeterlinck's *L'Intruse* (1891), Verlaine's *Les Uns et les Autres* (1884), and Charles Morice's *Chérubin* (1891). See Théâtre d'art, printed serial, March 20, 1891, https://gallica.bnf .fr/ark:/12148/bpt6k1051560v/f4.item (accessed May 28, 2021).

43 Matthew Potolsky, *The Decadent Republic of Letters: Taste, Politics, and Cosmopolitan Community from Baudelaire to Beardsley* (Philadelphia, PA: University of Pennsylvania Press, 2013), 4.

44 Paul Bourget, "The Example of Baudelaire," trans. Nancy O'Connor, *New England Review* 30, no. 2 (2009), http://cat.middlebury.edu/~nereview/30-2/ Bourget.htm (accessed April 20, 2021). For a study of the same tendency in Symbolism, see Wilson, *Axel's Castle*, 211.

45 Arthur Symons, *Studies in Seven Arts* (London: Archibald Constable and Company Ltd., 1906), 283–84.

46 For a much broader and more international range of examples not covered in this chapter, see the website for the Staging Decadence project, https://www .stagingdecadence.com.

CHAPTER 14

Religion and Science in the 1890s

Anne Stiles

In the late twentieth century, literary scholars generally maintained that Victorian scientific progress threatened the dominance of religion as a social force and personal belief system. These writers took their cue from J. Hillis Miller's *The Disappearance of God: Five Nineteenth-Century Writers* (1963), which argues that the nineteenth and twentieth centuries witnessed "the gradual withdrawal of God from the world," due in part to "the rise of science and technology."[1] The post-Darwinian 1890s, with its apocalyptic sensibility and upheavals in art, gender norms, and social mores, seemed especially vulnerable to this sense of divine absence.

Miller's influential work exemplifies a larger scholarly trend known as the secularization thesis, which assumes that "religious institutions, beliefs and practices decline with modernity," as Lori Branch explains.[2] According to this narrative, "industrialization, urbanization, and material science" were the key forces behind religion's "inevitable decline."[3] While some critics have seen this alleged waning of religious faith as a progressive development, Miller dwelt on a collective sense of loss. In premodern times, Miller argues, God was viewed as a "transcendent and immanent" presence permeating nature and society (Miller, *Disappearance*, 7). This sense of God's nearness and ability to intervene in human life was what Victorians – even the most devout believers – sought in vain in the bustle and anonymity of urban life.

The secularization thesis emerged in mid-twentieth-century sociology and soon spread to neighboring social science and humanities disciplines (Branch, "Postsecular Studies," 94). But it echoed concerns voiced by religiously conservative Victorians themselves. Take, for instance, Marie Corelli, the bestselling novelist of the 1890s, who dedicated her book *The Mighty Atom* (1896)

> To *those self-styled "progressivists,"* who by precept and example assist the infamous cause of *education without religion,* and who, by promoting the

idea, borrowed from French atheism, of denying to the children in board schools and elsewhere, *the knowledge and love of God* as the true foundation of noble living, *are guilty* of a worse crime than murder.[4]

The novel's protagonist, 10-year-old prodigy Lionel Valliscourt, receives a Gradgrindian science-based education. He is taught that "there was no God, and that the first cause of the universe was merely an Atom, productive of other atoms ... shaping worlds indifferently" (Corelli, *The Mighty Atom,* 66).[5] The idea of an apparently purposeless universe with no hope of an afterlife eventually leads Lionel to commit suicide.

Coming on the heels of Corelli's blockbuster success, *The Sorrows of Satan* (1895), *The Mighty Atom* quickly became a fan favorite in its own right.[6] Yet its portrayal of the clash between science and religion obscures the ways in which these seemingly opposing forces came together, or at least peacefully coexisted, during the 1890s – a misunderstanding reinforced by twentieth-century historians. By contrast, the twenty-first-century "religious turn" in the humanities encourages us to reevaluate the secularization thesis. Recent scholarship by Mark Knight, Frances Knight, Christine Ferguson, Jill Galvan, Charles LaPorte, Sebastian Lecourt, and others paints a more nuanced picture of the interactions between science and religion in the late nineteenth century that leaves room for collaborations and compromise. Frances Knight observes, for instance, that the Free Churches (Presbyterians, Methodists, and Baptists, for instance) reached "the peak of their social, cultural, and political influence" at the fin de siècle rather than receding into the background of English life.[7] Roman Catholicism likewise gained influence, especially among aesthetes, as the examples of Michael Field, Baron Corvo, John Gray, and Oscar Wilde suggest. Anglicanism lost some of the political power it had wielded at the beginning of the Victorian period, but proved malleable enough to absorb new artistic and scientific ideas. Across the board, Christians of different denominations became more willing to work together on common causes, such as social purity activism or the plight of Armenian Christians massacred in Turkey (Knight, *Victorian Christianity*, 229). "Rather than being a period of 'crisis of faith,'" Frances Knight suggests, "the English fin de siècle was a time when Christian faith became a means for intellectual and cultural integration" (228).[8]

Nontraditional faiths also proliferated at the fin de siècle. The 1890s witnessed revived interest in new religious movements such as Spiritualism, Theosophy, Christian Science, New Thought, and the Hermetic Order of the Golden Dawn. As Lecourt explains in Chapter 5 of this volume and elsewhere,[9] the 1890s witnessed revived interest in new religious movements. Britons approached heterdox faiths such as Spiritualism, Theosophy, Christian Science, New Thought, and the Hermetic Order of the Golden Dawn with varying degrees of seriousness. While dabblers attended séances or Theosophical society meetings out of curiosity, believers embraced Theosophy, Spiritualism, or Christian Science as substitutes for or complements to traditional creeds. Such new religious movements enabled believers to preserve aspects of traditional Christianity – including belief in an afterlife or an immortal soul – in a rapidly changing world. Victorian authors such as Wilde, Sir Arthur Conan Doyle, H. Rider Haggard, Bram Stoker, and Corelli herself were influenced by these movements and wove them into their fiction. More strikingly, perhaps, the Society for Psychical Research (SPR), founded in 1882, brought scientific methods to bear on the study of occult phenomena such as haunted houses, Ouija boards, clairvoyance, and telepathy. Members of this group included illustrious physicists Oliver Lodge and William Barrett, chemist Sir William Crookes, and psychologist William James. While ostensibly objective in their research, some members of the SPR hoped to prove the immortality of the soul upon scientific grounds.[10] As these examples suggest, the pseudoscientific and occult practices popular during the 1890s were not necessarily opposed to faith. More often, they were expressions of belief that testify to the period's ongoing investment in religion.

These examples suggest why we might wish to reevaluate fiction by fin-de-siècle authors not typically viewed as religious, especially those who dabbled in pseudoscience or the occult. They also demonstrate the need to reexamine longstanding assumptions about the conflict between religion and science in late-Victorian life. But delving into each of these new religious movements and pseudoscientific trends would require multiple volumes (in fact, much excellent work has already been written on these subjects).[11] This chapter's more modest aim is to trace conflicts and confluences between science and religion in two landmark novels of the 1890s: Wilde's *The Picture of Dorian Gray* (1890, 1891) and Corelli's *The Sorrows of Satan,* often described as the first modern bestseller.[12] Both works explore the compatibility of Christianity (or aspects thereof) and heterodox practices with mainstream scientific ideas, from Darwinian natural selection to hereditary degeneration to Santiago Ramón y Cajal's neuron doctrine. With their occult and pseudoscientific content, both novels strain the boundaries of "science" and "religion" in ways that encourage us to rethink these terms. They also call into question the secularization thesis, in which progress accompanies religious decline.

At first glance, Wilde and Corelli seem to have little in common. By pairing a bestselling novelist often viewed as an arch-conservative with a decadent provocateur, I suggest how scholarly approaches blending religion and science can apply to authors across the late-Victorian ideological spectrum.[13] Such approaches can also uncover unsuspected similarities between diametrically opposed literary figures.

In fact, Wilde's *The Picture of Dorian Gray* and Corelli's *The Sorrows of Satan* have much in common, especially when viewed from a religious standpoint. Both draw on late-Victorian Gothic tropes and on the much older Faustian tradition, dating back to the Renaissance, in which a young man sells his soul for worldly gain. This essentially Christian framework encompasses the ideas of God, sin, damnation, and the soul as separate from the body. Both novels contain a Mephistopheles figure (Lord Henry in *Dorian Gray,* the devil himself in *Sorrows of Satan*) who tempts the protagonist but is not fully responsible for his downfall, as well as a tragic female love interest named Sybil who commits suicide (Karschay, *Degeneration,* 168–69). Each contains striking examples of the corrupting power of fiction. Each book arguably has a moralistic conclusion, Wilde's protest against "ethical sympathies" in art notwithstanding.[14] Finally, both works combine elements of traditional Anglican or Roman Catholic theology with ideas derived from new religious movements like Spiritualism, Theosophy, and the Hermetic Order of the Golden Dawn. Such blending is typical of fin-de-siècle spirituality as a whole and key to reconciling religion and science (however that term is understood) within each novel. Reading through this interdisciplinary lens gives us a richer sense of the 1890s by showing how major literary figures had more complicated relationships to questions of faith and morality than we generally allow.

The Picture of Dorian Gray

For modern readers, Wilde is perhaps the defining figure of the 1890s, whose name telegraphs countercultural artistic movements like decadence and aestheticism as well as sexual dissidence, thanks to his 1895 trials and incarceration for "gross indecency" with other men. The leading playwright of the decade, Wilde was also a proponent of *l'art pour l'art* ("art for art's sake") who famously wrote in the 1891 preface to *The Picture of Dorian Gray* that "There is no such thing as a moral or immoral book" and that "an ethical sympathy in an artist is an unpardonable mannerism of style" (Wilde, *Dorian,* 3). Thanks to his irreverent witticisms and love of Hellenic culture, "it is extremely difficult to tie down Wilde's religious attitudes with any certainty," as Hilary Fraser observes.[15]

Some scholars, like biographer Richard Ellman, have questioned the sincerity of Wilde's deathbed conversion to Catholicism and viewed him as an atheist or agnostic.[16] But it is probably more accurate to say that Wilde embraced an iconoclastic, highly personal version of Catholicism mingled with heterodox faith traditions. Born into an Anglo-Irish Protestant family, Wilde maintained a "prolonged flirtation with the Roman Catholic Church" beginning at Oxford and ending with his conversion to Catholicism in November 1900 (Fraser, *Beauty and Belief,* 206). Like many British decadents, Wilde was drawn to Catholicism for its Continental exoticism, outsider appeal, and embrace of paradox that echoed a decadent aesthetic. For such individuals, Ellis Hanson explains, the Catholic Church was "at once modern yet medieval, ascetic yet sumptuous, spiritual yet sensual, chaste yet erotic, homophobic and yet homoerotic, suspicious of aestheticism and yet an elaborate work of art."[17] Catholicism also offered gay and lesbian aesthetes a "queer religious space" encompassing the monastery and the convent as well as same-sex desire expressed through the love of God.[18] Yet decadent converts to Catholicism like Wilde, Gray, and Michael Field have largely been ignored by literary historians engaged in mapping "the trajectory from Victorian doubt to modernist disbelief," as Martin Lockerd observes.[19] Such scholarship overlooks the real draw of faith for major countercultural figures of the decade, thereby reinforcing the secularization thesis and the cliché of the "Naughty Nineties."

As these examples show, Wilde was representative of many British decadents and aesthetes in his attraction to the Catholic Church. His works testify to his ongoing investment in Catholicism and in heterodox trends like Spiritualism, Theosophy, and the Hermetic Order of the Golden Dawn, with which he and his wife Constance were involved. In *Dorian Gray* and elsewhere, Wilde weaves together Christianity and aestheticism, seeing Christ as an artist or as a work of art who indelibly alters the beholder (Knight, *Victorian Christianity,* 56–57). This view is most clearly expressed in *De Profundis,* written in 1897 and published in 1905, where "Wilde finds in Christ the very ideal of the romantic artist, a sexually ambiguous individualist and aesthete much like himself" (Hanson, *Decadence and Catholicism,* 5). Science fits into Wilde's unconventional faith when scientific ideas and objects are inherently beautiful, as in Dorian's contemplation of a "pearly cell in the brain" (Wilde, *Dorian*, 113). Wilde also warns, however, against using scientific theories and methods to rationalize one's misdeeds, as Dorian and Lord Henry often do.

Wilde was better informed about science than most of his peers. His father, Sir William Wilde, was a prominent eye and ear specialist who founded a Dublin hospital and was knighted in 1864.[20] As Elisha Cohn observes, Wilde's upbringing and education brought him into contact with theorists of science such as W. K. Clifford, Ernst Haeckel, T. H. Huxley, and John Tyndall and kept his writing "*au courant* with scientific debates."[21] Wilde kept a notebook during his Oxford years that tracked his developing interests in aestheticism *and* emergent scientific debates about evolution, microscopy, and the materiality of mind. Like Corelli, Wilde was particularly fascinated by tiny particles (atoms, molecules, and brain cells) both for their aesthetic beauty and their implications for human subjectivity (Cohn, "Wilde and the Brain Cell," 23–29). These scientific interests eventually found their way into fictions like *Dorian Gray*.

The Picture of Dorian Gray has generated controversy ever since it first appeared as a thirteen-chapter serial in *Lippincott's Magazine* in 1890 and later as an expanded, twenty-chapter book in 1891. The novel revolves around three upper-class young men: artist Basil Hallward, his former Oxford classmate Lord Henry, and his muse Dorian Gray, who meet in the London studio where Basil is finishing his painting of Dorian. After Lord Henry awakens the handsome youth to a sense of his beauty and its impermanence, Dorian wishes that the portrait would grow old and ugly in place of himself: "If it were I who was to be always young, and the picture that was to grow old ... I would give my soul for that" (Wilde, *Dorian*, 25). Dorian's Faustian bargain comes true as years pass and he commits a series of escalating crimes, egged on by Lord Henry and his philosophy of "new Hedonism" (22). While Dorian remains young and handsome, the portrait gradually changes into a "foul parody" of the original, as if "the leprosies of sin were slowly eating the thing away" (133). When Basil sees the changed painting and urges Dorian to repent, Dorian murders the painter and blackmails chemist Alan Campbell to dispose of the body with nitric acid. (Intriguingly, Wilde learned from a "friendly surgeon" how one might dissolve a corpse by chemical means, suggesting how social connections to scientists and physicians kept him up-to-date in scientific matters [Ellman, *Oscar Wilde*, 314].) Finally, overcome by guilt, Dorian stabs the painting that serves as his externalized conscience. The servants discover "hanging upon the wall a splendid portrait of their master as they had last seen him, in all the wonder of his exquisite youth and beauty. Lying on the floor was a dead man . . . withered, wrinkled, and loathsome of visage. It was not till they had examined the rings that they recognized who it was" (Wilde, *Dorian*, 188). By stabbing the portrait, Dorian has inadvertently committed suicide, thus proving his supernatural connection with the painting.

As "the pre-eminent example of an English decadent fin-de-siècle novel," *Dorian Gray* introduced many readers to French poet Théophile Gautier's ideas about the independence of art and morality, a theme also championed by Pater, Wilde's mentor at Oxford (Knight, *Victorian Christianity*, 45). Victorian readers used to viewing art as moral or improving were troubled by this message. They were also disturbed by the pleasure-seeking, subtly homoerotic behavior of the novel's main characters. Initial reviewers criticized the novel's "effeminate frivolity" and "studied insincerity," complaining that it held every "good and holy impulse . . . up to ridicule."[22] Most damningly, the reviewer for the *Scots Observer* accused Wilde of "grubbing in muck-heaps" and alluded to the Cleveland Street Affair of 1889, in which police discovered that wealthy, aristocratic men had been paying telegraph boys at the local post office for sexual favors (quoted in Bristow, "Introduction," xxi). Such comments prompted Wilde to tone down the homoerotic elements of the book-length version in 1891, such as Basil's obvious crush on Dorian in the opening chapters (Bristow, "Introduction," xxv–xxvi).

But while some critics considered the book offensive or indecent, others viewed it as a morality tale whose hedonistic protagonist meets a deservedly terrible end. Seen in this light, the book condemns the amoral pleasure-seeking extolled by Lord Henry and enacted by Dorian at great cost. It also serves as a call for moderation in all things. Responding to criticism of the first, serial edition of his novel, Wilde acknowledged, "Yes, there is a terrible moral in *Dorian Gray* – a moral which the prurient will not be able to find in it, but which will be revealed to all whose minds are healthy. Is this an artistic error? I fear it is" (quoted in Bristow, "Introduction," xxiii).

While not as didactic as *The Sorrows of Satan*, *Dorian Gray* can certainly be read within a Christian framework of sin, redemption, and punishment. Mid-twentieth-century critics, for instance, emphasized Wilde's investment in the Faust myth, the figure of the doppelgänger, and Dorian himself as tragic antihero, thereby eliding the work's controversial gay overtones.[23] A quick internet search reveals that this approach is still popular in high schools. Reading *Dorian Gray* against the grain of the secularization thesis recuperates aspects of these older, moralistic interpretations, with a crucial difference. By consulting more recent Wilde scholarship, I illuminate, rather than obscure, connections between the author's scientific knowledge, religious views, and sexual inclinations.

Dorian Gray's treatment of science at times reinforces a moralistic reading. For instance, Lord Henry likens his unwholesome influence over Dorian to an experiment:

> [Lord Henry] had been always enthralled by the methods of natural science, but the ordinary subject-matter of that science had seemed to him trivial and of no import. And so he had begun by vivisecting himself as he had ended by vivisecting others. Human life – that appeared to him the thing worth investigating. (Wilde 50)

This passage suggests that Lord Henry sees Dorian as an "interesting study" as opposed to a friend or even a feeling human being (Wilde, *Dorian,* 50). Vivisection (the dissection of live animals for scientific purposes) was a controversial topic for Wilde and his contemporaries thanks to recent, well-publicized trials involving prominent scientists. In 1881, neurologist Sir David Ferrier was hauled into court for allegedly violating the 1876 Anti-vivisection Act. Since 1873, Ferrier had engaged in cerebral localization experiments involving electrical stimulation and surgical mutilation of the brains of monkeys, dogs, and other animals, sometimes without anesthetic.[24] Though Ferrier was ultimately acquitted, the grisly details of his trial lingered in the public imagination. By describing himself as a vivisector, Lord Henry indicates his disregard for Dorian's wellbeing and fulfills the worst fears of antivivisection activists, who argued that scientists who experimented on animals might similarly exploit vulnerable human beings (Otis, "Howled," 32).

Like his aristocratic mentor, Dorian occasionally invokes science to justify his misconduct. For instance, he muses on Darwinism and the anatomy of the nervous system following his cruel rejection of actress Sybil Vane and her subsequent suicide:

> For a season he inclined to the materialist doctrines of the *Darwinismus* movement in Germany, and found a curious pleasure in tracing the thoughts and passions of men to some pearly cell in the brain, or some white nerve in the body, delighting in the conception of the absolute dependence of the spirit on certain physical conditions, morbid or healthy, normal or diseased. (Wilde, *Dorian,* 113)[25]

The suggestion here, Cohn notes, is that "materialism renders sin unavoidable and thus excusable" (32). At the same time, the passage aestheticizes the bodily structures it renders visible: "a pearly cell in the brain," "some white nerve in the body."

This passage is found in chapter eleven, in which Dorian amasses collections of perfumes, jewels, musical instruments, tapestries, and ecclesiastical vestments in emulation of the "poisonous book" given to him by Lord Henry (Wilde, *Dorian*, 107). This book is commonly assumed to be Joris-Karl Huysmans's *À Rebours* (1884), which Wilde's contemporary Arthur Symons called "the breviary of the Decadence" (quoted in Knight, *Victorian Christianity*, 42). This groundbreaking French novel concerns a "bored, bisexual aesthete," Duc Jean Des Esseintes, who engages in a series of bizarre activities designed to absorb his senses, such as decorating a live tortoise with gemstones (42). Like Des Esseintes, Dorian seeks exotic sensory experiences to distract him from growing fear and *ennui*: "these treasures . . . were to be to him means of forgetfulness, modes by which he could escape, for a season, from the fear that seemed to him at times to be almost too great to be borne" (Wilde, *Dorian*, 119). Intriguingly, this is also the chapter in which Dorian voyeuristically attends Catholic mass due to his interest in "Roman ritual," though his flirtation with Catholicism is less serious than Wilde's own (Wilde, *Dorian*, 112; Lockerd, *Decadent Catholicism*, 26).

In the context of chapter eleven, the "pearly cell in the brain" sounds like one of Dorian's aestheticized collectibles. The description of the cell as singular and isolated rather than plural or connected also sheds light on how Dorian views cells and selves. Around 1890, there was considerable debate among scientists as to whether nerve cells were individuated or whether they touched to form a web or reticulum. In 1889, Spanish scientist Santiago Ramón y Cajal proposed that nerve cells are individuated, each one "an absolutely autonomous canton."[26] He also posited that impulses pass from one neuron to another unidirectionally along axons and dendrites, although the exact means of this communication was unclear. He based these claims on newly discovered silver staining techniques that made nerve fibers more clearly visible (Stiles, *Popular Fiction*, 159; Finger, *Origins*, 45–46). Whether or not Wilde was aware of these discoveries, his depiction reflects this "new understanding of the brain cell as a self-contained structure, its interior inaccessible, and its connection to other cells unexplained," as Cohn observes (Cohn, "Wilde and the Brain Cell," 31). If one takes the cell as a metonym for the self, as both Corelli and Wilde tended to do, this view of the cell in isolation as opposed to part of a broader community or network suggests a larger problem with Dorian's thinking.[27] Viewing himself in isolation allows Dorian to ignore the effects of his actions on others.[28]

But the aestheticization of the brain cell also had positive overtones at a time when neuron doctrine and the emergent field of neuroscience more broadly were sources of fear and fascination for religious Victorians. As I have written elsewhere, late-Victorian Gothic novels including *Dracula* (1897) and *Strange Case of Doctor Jekyll and Mr. Hyde* (1886) traded on the frightening idea that automatic brain functions (e.g., reflex actions, unconscious thought processes) undermined the Christian idea of the soul or free will.[29] If our brains are no more than collections of neurons, where does individual autonomy come into play? At what point does God intervene in the workings of human physiology? Wilde effectively neutralizes these questions – or at least puts them on pause – by regarding the brain cell as beautiful object.

This is not the first or only time Wilde aestheticizes the brain cell. Cohn notes that the image of the ivory cell first appeared in Wilde's 1884 poem "Roses and Rue," and resurfaces in "The Critic as Artist" (1891), where Wilde refers to "one single ivory cell of the brain" in which "there are stored away things more marvellous and more terrible than even they have dreamed of, who ... have sought to track the soul into its most secret places" (quoted in Cohn, "Wilde and the Brain Cell," 31). This passage suggests that for Wilde, an up-to-date understanding of cerebral anatomy need not undermine spirituality. The brain cell as Wilde envisions it retains the sense of mystery that the soul or will once had for religious Victorians. It is also manifestly beautiful, speaking to Wilde's purposeful blending of aestheticism and Christianity in *Dorian Gray* and elsewhere. Because *Dorian Gray* also explores the dangers of aestheticism, however, a beautiful object cannot always be taken at face value, as the contrast between Dorian's changeless beauty and corrupt soul make clear.[30] This ambiguity suggests Wilde's ambivalence about scientific theories and methods, whose value depends on the intentions of the person invoking them as well as their inherent beauty.

Christianity is not the only religious framework that helps make sense of *Dorian Gray*. Eleanor Dobson argues that the novel contains overtones of Spiritualism, Theosophy, and the Hermetic Order of the Golden Dawn, all of which interested Wilde and his wife, Constance.[31] At various times, Wilde attended séances, participated in thought-reading experiments, and purchased a copy of Helena Blavatsky's *The Key to Theosophy* (1889). None of these activities were necessarily incompatible with Christian beliefs, Dobson observes (Dobson, "Cultures of Spiritualism," 144). Constance, meanwhile, attended meetings of the Theosophical Society (sometimes accompanied by Oscar) and in 1888 was initiated into the Hermetic Order of the Golden Dawn, a magical order that was a major influence on modern practices such as Wicca. After Constance was kicked out of the

Golden Dawn in 1889, she joined the SPR, which, as mentioned, was dedicated to the scientific study of occult phenomena (Dobson, "Cultures of Spiritualism," 144–45). Through his wife, Wilde was socially connected to influential members of these and other esoteric societies.

Predictably, elements of these heterodox traditions surface in *Dorian Gray*. The magic portrait at the heart of the novel "conform[s] to the Golden Dawn's belief in the supernatural power of images" and the Theosophical maxim that "the material world cannot be separated from its spiritual counterpart," Dobson suggests (Dobson, "Cultures of Spiritualism," 145). Though it is a painting, not a photograph, Dorian's portrait also evokes the tradition of Spiritualist photography, in which ghostly shapes and shadows appeared in the background of sitters' portraits. Such photographs were often taken in the presence of mediums and produced by incomplete exposures or by applying paint or chemicals to the photographic plate (143). Like these pictures, which purported to capture images of actual spirits, Dorian's portrait "reveal[s] to him his own soul" over the course of the novel (Wilde, *Dorian*, 91).

Wilde's mixture of Catholicism, neuroscience, and occultism in *Dorian Gray* suggests the need to rethink his legacy. His fluent handling of theological and scientific debates complicates his reputation as consummate dandy and provocateur, and suggests that irreverent wit can flourish alongside religious introspection. Wilde's blend of science and religion also links him with Corelli, whose readers relished her mixture of science, Anglicanism, and heterodox spirituality. But each author had separate aims befitting their target audiences. Whereas Wilde the aesthete could see beauty and thus divinity in science, Corelli imagined an otherworldly religious cosmology in which science played an important supporting role. For her middle-class fan base, Corelli's works provided both escapism and religious consolation bolstered by (sometimes spurious) scientific logic.

The Sorrows of Satan

Though now less well known, Corelli was arguably more famous than Wilde in her heyday, admired by Queen Victoria, the Prince of Wales, William Gladstone, George Meredith, and even Wilde himself, who wrote that Corelli told "marvellous things in a marvellous way" (quoted in Kuehn, "Introduction," x).[32] According to biographer Brian Masters, "While Queen Victoria was alive, Miss Corelli was the second most famous Englishwoman in the world; afterwards, there was no one to approach her" (Masters, *Now Barrabas*, 6). Annette Federico, meanwhile, emphasizes that "Corelli broke all publishing records" with book sales averaging 175,000 copies a year around the turn of the century.[33]

For her predominantly middle-class readership, Corelli's unprecedented appeal lay partly in her old-fashioned religious attitudes. The author presented herself as an orthodox member of the Church of England and a champion of morals that were eroding in a godless, scientific age. Witness, for instance, her production of *Praise and Prayer: A Simple Home Service* (1923), a short liturgical book containing a series of Christian prayers, hymns, and blessings. Many of Corelli's other works, including *The Mighty Atom* and *The Sorrows of Satan,* quote scripture, often at length.[34] Yet critics have more often noticed Corelli's interest in heterodox faiths like Spiritualism, Theosophy, Rosicrucianism, and even Christian Science, elements of which surface in her novels.[35] These heterodox faiths and her own personal belief system, the so-called Electric Creed of Christianity, helped Corelli reconcile religion and science in ways that comforted her world-weary readers. As she confided in an 1888 letter to her first publisher, George Bentley, "people appear to revel in and gloat over anything that has to do with an admixture of science and religion."[36] She recognized that heterodox believers formed a large part of her fan base, though she generally denied affiliation with their creeds. Shortly before the appearance of her novel *Ardath* (1889), she wrote to Bentley that "spiritualists . . . are all waiting for my new book, as cats for a poor little mouse."[37]

Despite her moralistic self-presentation, Corelli lived as eccentric a life as Wilde himself. She and her best friend, Bertha Vyver, inhabited a luxurious residence in Stratford-upon-Avon, where they worked to preserve Shakespeare's legacy. Some have speculated that Corelli and Vyver were romantically involved and even appeared as a "recognized couple" at public gatherings.[38] Corelli, however, was not forthcoming about her personal life. As Federico notes, Corelli scrupulously controlled her public image, dodging photographers and interviewers and portraying herself as younger and more cosmopolitan than she actually was.[39]

As this description suggests, Wilde and Corelli had surprising similarities, from their nonnormative sexual identities to their creative self-fashioning, fraught relationships with the press, and ongoing interest in new religious movements. But they were separated by insuperable barriers of class, gender, and education. Corelli was the illegitimate daughter of journalist Charles MacKay. Her formal education consisted of a series of governesses followed by a stint in a French convent school (possibly an English establishment staffed by French nuns [Masters, *Now Barrabas,*

33]). Like most middle-class women, she was taught music, modern languages, and polite literature rather than the latest scientific theories. Therefore, when she heard about new scientific developments, she often misunderstood or creatively reinterpreted them to suit her needs, as in *The Sorrows of Satan.*

I am hardly the first to notice parallels between *The Picture of Dorian Gray* and *The Sorrows of Satan.* Federico, for instance, describes Corelli's bestseller as "*The Picture of Dorian Gray* meets *New Grub Street*" (Federico, *Idol of Suburbia,* 83). Reviewer W. T. Stead, meanwhile, compared the novel to Milton's *Paradise Lost* (1667) because it makes a hero of Satan, who is more sympathetic than most of the human characters (Masters, *Now Barrabas,* 141). The narrator is struggling novelist Geoffrey Tempest, an Oxford-educated classicist (like Wilde himself) who has fallen on hard times. Tempest suddenly inherits five million pounds on the same day that he meets mysterious Prince Lucio Rimânez, whose cynical *bon mots* recall Lord Henry but whose personal beauty rivals Dorian Gray. With Lucio's guidance, Tempest publishes his novel to glowing reviews and meets London's "swagger" society. He embraces a hedonistic lifestyle, purchasing a landed estate, meeting the Prince of Wales, and marrying beautiful Lady Sybil Elton. He also meets his literary rival, Mavis Claire, a thinly veiled stand-in for Corelli whose wholesome books win popular acclaim despite harsh reviews. After the tragic suicide of Lady Sybil – whose erotic advances are scornfully rejected by Lucio – the Prince entertains Tempest on his yacht, where Rimânez reveals his true identity as Satan and forces Tempest to choose between himself and God. When Geoffrey chooses God, he is abandoned in the mid-Atlantic and rescued by a passing steamer. Tempest returns to England to find his fortune stolen by his bankers and himself poor once again. But his literary career is revived when a "slashing" review brings new attention to his novel. Lucio, meanwhile, moves on to new targets; the novel's conclusion finds him cozying up to a Cabinet minister.

The Sorrows of Satan is an entertaining, fast-paced melodrama that allows readers to vicariously enjoy undreamt-of luxuries. It is also an angry book lacking "restraint of any kind," as Stead observed (quoted in Masters, *Now Barrabas,* 142). Corelli's many targets include dandies, aesthetes, and decadent writers who eschew bourgeois morality and the "unsexed" New Women who read their works. For instance, she condemns the poetry of Algernon Charles Swinburne and dismisses Pater's *Marius the Epicurean* (1885) for its "cliquey" following and "public failure," as measured by limited sales.[40] To achieve success, Lucio explains, a novel must be a "judicious mixture of Zola, Huysmans, and Baudelaire," or have a heroine who is "a 'modest' maid who considered honourable marriage a 'degradation,'" like the protagonist of Grant Allen's 1895 *succès de scandale, The Woman Who Did* (Corelli, *Sorrows,* 44).

The novel's characters demonstrate the destructive effects of such unwholesome reading. Lady Sybil describes herself as "a contaminated creature trained to perfection in the lax morals and prurient literature of my day" (Corelli, *Sorrows,* 147). As if to prove it, she shamelessly throws herself at Lucio. Tempest, meanwhile, feels an undeniable homoerotic attraction to Rimânez akin to Dorian's initial fascination with Lord Henry (Federico, *Idol of Suburbia,* 79). When they first meet, Tempest declares himself "amazed and fascinated" by the Prince's appearance: "I thought I had never seen so much beauty and intellectuality combined in the outward personality of any human being" (Corelli, *Sorrows,* 14). Though never acted upon, Tempest's attraction to Lucio increases Satan's power over him. Therefore, one might view Corelli's novel as a response to the homosexual panic generated by Wilde's 1895 trials, which took place six months prior to the publication of her book. Corelli worried that the trials would distract the public from *The Sorrows of Satan* and reduce her sales, fears that proved not entirely unfounded (Karschay, *Degeneration,* 168).

Despite its apparent rejection of aestheticism and decadence, the novel exploits public fascination with these trends, much as George Du Maurier's *Trilby* (1894) had done a year earlier (Federico, *Idol of Suburbia,* 60). It also caters to the popular appetite for religious subject matter, however unconventional. *The Sorrows of Satan* takes a sympathetic view of the devil, who is condemned to tempt human beings against his will. Only if they refuse his temptations – which they seldom do – can he ascend to heaven. Ironically, Lucio/Satan emerges as one of the novel's staunchest defenders of the existence of God, though he scorns organized religion: "Though I am not a Christian I never said I doubted the existence of Christ. That knowledge was forced upon me," he tells Tempest (Corelli, *Sorrows,* 184).

The novel also takes an unusual view of the afterlife, eschewing conventional depictions of Heaven and Hell. "I should decline to go to any heaven which was only a city with golden streets," Lucio scornfully declares. He does insist, however, upon the existence of "a different kind of heaven," and of other worlds inhabited by beings who worship God (Corelli, *Sorrows,* 110). Hell, meanwhile, is depicted as "a black and hollow cavern, glittering alternately with the flashings of fire and ice," mixing Dante's frozen ninth circle of Hell with the more traditional idea of infernal flames (201). The novel also includes a sort of limbo, the world's end, where damned souls have an occasional moment of respite.

Here and elsewhere in Corelli's oeuvre, reincarnation and karma play an important role, suggesting the influence of Theosophy (Ferguson, "New Religions and Esotericism," 421). Lucio explains that men and women "live on through a myriad worlds, a myriad phases, till they learn to shape their destinies for Heaven!" (Corelli, *Sorrows*, 338). His exotic pet – a winged beetle that once dwelt in the body of a 4,000-year-old mummy – allegedly contains the transmigrated soul of an Egyptian princess.[41] An even more dramatic example comes from Corelli's bestseller *Ziska* (1897), in which ancient Egyptian dancing girl Ziska-Charmazel kills painter Armand Gervase, who is the reincarnation of the faithless lover who murdered her thousands of years before. Her murder of Gervase is ultimately a selfless act, freeing him "from an incessant cycle of punitive incarnations" (Ferguson, "New Religions and Esotericism," 422).

In Corelli's heterodox cosmology, science plays an ambivalent role. Lucio and other characters frequently decry scientific materialism as eroding public morals. At Tempest's lavish wedding fête, Rimânez arranges a tableau vivant called "Faith and Materialism" wherein materialism is pictured as "a human skeleton, bleached white and grinning ghastly mirth upon us as! While we yet looked, the skeleton itself dropped to pieces, – and one long twining worm lifted its slimy length from the wreck of bones, another working its way through the eye-holes of the skull" (Corelli, *Sorrows*, 203). The disgusting spectacle evokes "murmurs of genuine horror" throughout the audience, and causes "a distinguished professor of science" to walk out in a huff (203). Explaining his choice of imagery, Lucio calls out the hypocrisy of those who "accept Materialism as their only creed" yet become offended by the natural decay of the body after death (203). Ironically, the devil himself decries scientific materialism in favor of faith, which appears in the tableau as a beautiful soaring spirit backed by a chorus of joyful voices.

Here and elsewhere in the novel, Corelli goes to great lengths to illustrate the horrors of "education without religion," much as she would later do in *The Mighty Atom*. But science does play a part in her eccentric cosmology. Take, for instance, Lucio's magnificent yacht, "The Flame," which Tempest describes as "a vessel whose complete magnificence filled me, as well as all other beholders, with bewildered wonderment and admiration. She was a miracle of speed, her motive power being electricity" (Corelli, *Sorrows*, 315).

Corelli was fascinated by electricity, going so far as to build an entire religion based upon it. Corelli's "Electric Creed," which she described in the introductions to her novels *A Romance of Two Worlds* (1886) and *The Life Everlasting* (1911), posits that "all the wonders of Nature are the result of *light and heat alone*," and that light, heat, and electricity are equated with God's love.[42] The Creed also depicts neural networks as channels of telepathic communication with Christ. This religion took on a life of its own outside of Corelli's fiction, becoming the basis of a small church in Colorado and informing Corelli's own beliefs. In a 1923 letter to journalist John Cuming Walters, written a week before her death, Corelli wrote: "I am sending you *The Life Everlasting*. If you read the 'prologue,' only, you will grasp my faith," which she said she had been developing and following "all my life."[43]

Corelli's creation of the Electric Creed invites comparison with other female religious innovators of the nineteenth century, such as Mary Baker Eddy and Ellen White (the founders of Christian Science and Seventh-day Adventism, respectively). It also suggests the high degree of inventiveness with which novelists of her generation blended religion, science, and liberal doses of fantasy. In keeping with Corelli's creed, electricity has wondrous applications in *The Sorrows of Satan*. In the novel's climactic scene, Lucio's electric-powered yacht instantly transports Tempest to the world's end, "the last spot on earth left untainted by Man's presence!" (Corelli, *Sorrows,* 343). In this "landscape ... like a glittering dream of fairy-land," Tempest sees the spirits of his departed friends, damned souls who have been allowed a momentary release from their punishment (342).

Electricity was not the only scientific phenomenon to interest Corelli. Like Wilde, Corelli was fascinated by neurons, atoms, and tiny particles more generally, though her understanding of these entities was limited. For instance, Lucio explains that bodily death is not the end of human existence due to "the regeneration of atoms. The brain-cells are atoms, and within these, are other atoms called memories, curiously vital and marvellously prolific!" (Corelli, *Sorrows,* 276). This passage blatantly misrepresents Ramón y Cajal's neuron doctrine, which posited that nerve cells were separate entities, not that they possessed occult powers. But this example shows how Corelli creatively revised scientific ideas to bolster her Electric Creed. In *The Sorrows of Satan*, brain cells ensure the immortality of the soul by acting as storehouses of electricity, divine love, and memories that somehow survive bodily death.

These are just a few examples of how Corelli's novels attempt to reconcile science and religion for her world-weary readership. But her works sometimes lack clarity about what "science" really is. For example, Lucio declares that "in all matters scientific I [am] an 'absolute master'" (Corelli, *Sorrows*, 153). But his much-vaunted scientific feats blur into black magic. For instance, the spectacular fireworks and tableaux vivants he arranges for Tempest's wedding party are actually performed by denizens of hell disguised as human beings; similarly, his electric yacht is piloted by a demon.

By contrast, Corelli's earlier novel, *A Romance of Two Worlds,* takes a more positive but equally vague view of science. In her author's prologue, Corelli declares that "the light of Science must be brought to bear on the New Testament, in which its glorious pages will grow bright with hitherto unguessed mystical meanings" (Corelli, *Romance,* 10). The novel's unnamed neurasthenic protagonist recovers health and strength through revitalizing herbal tonics and electrotherapy. Following the Electric Creed of her mentor Heliobas, she frees her soul from her body and travels through the galaxy, viewing life on other planets. Once again, the science depicted here seems more akin to pseudoscience or magic than to actual science practiced by Corelli's contemporaries, though there are overlaps (such as the use of electrotherapy to treat neurasthenia). Clearly, Corelli took creative liberties to bridge the gap between science and religion and console readers beset by doubt, like the Anglican clergyman who wrote to her that *A Romance of Two Worlds* rescued him from suicide.[44]

Conclusion

The examples of Wilde and Corelli suggest the fascinating ways in which fin-de-siècle Britons navigated faith and doubt across the political and ideological spectrum. For all their differences, both Wilde's and Corelli's works challenge the secularization thesis: Wilde by blending Christianity, neuroscience, and aestheticism; Corelli by creatively revising scientific theories to align with her heterodox faith. With their occult and pseudo-scientific leanings, *The Picture of Dorian Gray* and *The Sorrows of Satan* ask us to reconsider what counts as religion or science during the 1890s, and to redraw the boundaries of faith to encompass individuals and trends that fall outside the pale of orthodoxy.

Notes

1 J. Hillis Miller, *The Disappearance of God: Five Nineteenth-Century Writers* (Cambridge, MA: Harvard University Press, 1963), 1, 4.
2 Lori Branch, "Postsecular Studies," in *The Routledge Companion to Literature and Religion*, ed. Mark Knight (New York: Routledge, 2016), 91–101 (93, 94).

3 Charles LaPorte, "Victorian Literature, Religion, and Secularism," *Literature Compass* 10, no. 3 (2013): 277–87 (277).

4 Marie Corelli, *The Mighty Atom* (Philadelphia, PA: J.B. Lippincott, 1896), 3, emphasis in original.

5 As the structure of atomic particles was not fully understood in 1896, Corelli presumably invokes the older definition of the atom as "a hypothetical particle, minute and indivisible," which dates back to ancient Greece and India (Oxford English Dictionary).

6 Brian Masters, *Now Barrabas was a Rotter: The Extraordinary Life of Marie Corelli* (London: Hamish Hamilton, 1978), 148–51.

7 Frances Knight, *Victorian Christianity at the Fin de Siècle: The Culture of Religion in a Decadent Age* (London: I.B. Tauris, 2016), 229.

8 Thanks to a wave of Jewish immigration to London in the 1880s, Judaism was also an increasingly significant cultural force at the fin de siècle, despite widespread antisemitism. See Mark Knight, "Studies of Christianity and Judaism," in *The Routledge Companion to Victorian Literature*, eds. Dennis Denisoff and Talia Schaffer (New York: Routledge, 2020), 426–35.

9 See also Charles LaPorte and Sebastian Lecourt's "Introduction: Nineteenth-Century Literature, New Religious Movements, and Secularization," *Nineteenth-Century Literature* 73, no. 2 (2018): 147–60.

10 Jill Galvan, *The Sympathetic Medium: Feminine Channeling, the Occult, and Communication Technologies, 1859-1919* (Ithaca, NY: Cornell University Press, 2010), 4.

11 For an overview of the substantial literature on Spiritualism, see Christine Ferguson, "Recent Studies in Nineteenth-Century Spiritualism," *Literature Compass* 9, 6 (2012): 431–40. On occult and new religious movements more generally, see LaPorte and Lecourt's "Introduction" as well as Christine Ferguson, "New Religions and Esotericism," in *The Routledge Companion to Victorian Literature*, eds. Dennis Denisoff and Talia Schaffer (New York: Routledge, 2020), 414–25.

12 Julia Kuehn, "Introduction," in Marie Corelli, *The Sorrows of Satan* (Kansas City, MO: Valancourt Books, 2008), vii–xvii (viii).

13 On Corelli's and Wilde's relative ideological positions, see Stephan Karschay, Degeneration, Normativity and the Gothic at the *Fin de Siècle* (New York: Palgrave, 2015), 168–69.

14 Oscar Wilde, *The Picture of Dorian Gray,* ed. Joseph Bristow (Oxford: Oxford University Press, 2008), 3. Of course, not all critics see a clear-cut moral in *Dorian Gray.* Joseph Bristow's essay "Wilde, *Dorian Gray,* and Gross Indecency," for instance, ascribes Dorian's unhappy fate to improper mentoring by Basil and Lord Henry, combined with internalized homophobia. See *Sexual Sameness: Textual Differences in Lesbian and Gay Writing*, ed. Joseph Bristow (New York: Routledge, 1992), 44–63.

15 Hilary Fraser, *Beauty and Belief: Aesthetics and Religion in Victorian Literature* (Cambridge: Cambridge University Press, 1986), 209.

16 See, for instance, Ellman's *Oscar Wilde* (New York: Vintage, 1988), 583–84.

17 Ellis Hanson, *Decadence and Catholicism* (Cambridge, MA: Harvard University Press, 1997), 7.

18 Frederick S. Roden, *Same-Sex Desire in Victorian Religious Culture* (New York: Palgrave, 2002), 125. Roden points out that some queer Catholic aesthetes – Christina Rossetti and Gerard Manley Hopkins, for instance – may not have physically acted upon their same-sex desires. For others, including Wilde, "passionate desire for mortal men was a means for discovering . . . Catholic religious life" (126).

19 Martin Lockerd, *Decadent Catholicism and the Making of Modernism* (London: Bloomsbury Academic, 2020), 10.

20 Anne Stiles, *Popular Fiction and Brain Science in the Late Nineteenth Century* (Cambridge: Cambridge University Press, 2012), 58.

21 Elisha Cohn, "Oscar Wilde and the Brain Cell," in *Literature, Neurology, and Neuroscience: Historical and Literary Connections*, eds. Anne Stiles, Stanley Finger, and François Boller (Amsterdam: Elsevier, 2013), 19–39 (21).

22 Quoted in Joseph Bristow, "Introduction," in Oscar Wilde, *The Picture of Dorian Gray*, ed. Joseph Bristow (Oxford: Oxford University Press, 2008), ix–xxxii (xx).

23 For a representative article in this vein, see Dominick Rossi, "Parallels in Wilde's *The Picture of Dorian Gray* and Goethe's *Faust*," *CLA Journal* 13, no. 2 (December 1969): 188–91.

24 Laura Otis, "Howled Out of the Country: Wilkie Collins and H.G. Wells Retry David Ferrier," in *Neurology and Literature, 1860-1920*, ed. Anne Stiles (New York: Palgrave, 2007), 27–51 (27).

25 The German term *Darwinismus* (Darwinism) suggests Haeckel as one source of Dorian's musings, as Bristow notes in his 2008 edition of *Dorian Gray* (Wilde, *Dorian*, 214).

26 Quoted in Stanley Finger, *Origins of Neuroscience: A History of Explorations into Brain Function* (Oxford: Oxford University Press, 1994), 47.

27 On Corelli's unorthodox views of the neuron, see chapter five of Stiles, *Popular Fiction and Brain Science*.

28 There are two subsequent references to brain cells in *Dorian Gray*. The first follows Dorian's murder of Hallward, as he makes his way to an opium den: "From cell to cell of his brain crept the one thought . . . the wild desire to live" (Wilde, *Dorian Gray*, 156). At the opium den, "every cell of the brain, seems to be instinct with fearful impulses" (Wilde, *Dorian Gray*, 160). Notably, the first of these references implies the connectedness of brain cells, suggesting that Dorian is finally beginning to grasp the consequences of his actions on others.

29 See the introduction and first two chapters of Stiles, *Popular Fiction and Brain Science*.

30 On *Dorian Gray* as a critique of aestheticism, see chapter twelve of Ellman, *Oscar Wilde*.

31 Eleanor Dobson, "Oscar Wilde, Photography, and the Cultures of Spiritualism: 'The most magical of mirrors,'" *English Literature in Transition, 1880-1920* 63, no. 2 (2020): 139–161.

32 Wilde evidently changed his initial view of Corelli, as suggested by an anecdote from his time in Reading Gaol. Asked if Corelli was a great writer, Wilde replied, "Now don't think I've anything against her moral character ... but from the way she writes she ought to be here" (quoted in Masters, *Now Barrabas was a Rotter* 12).

33 Annette Federico, *Idol of Suburbia: Marie Corelli and Late-Victorian Literary Culture* (Charlottesville: University Press of Virginia, 2000), 2.

34 Mark Knight, "The Limits of Orthodoxy in a Secular Age: The Strange Case of Marie Corelli," *Nineteenth-Century Literature* 73, no. 3 (December 2018): 379–98 (387).

35 Regarding whether Corelli should be considered primarily as an orthodox Anglican or as a proponent of new religious movements, see M. Knight, "The Limits of Orthodoxy in a Secular Age."

36 Marie Corelli to George Bentley, March 5, 1888, Corelli Collection (Cat. No. GEN MSS 332), Yale University, Beinecke Rare Book and Manuscript Library.

37 Marie Corelli to George Bentley, December 29, 1888, Corelli Collection (Cat. No. GEN MSS 332), Yale University, Beinecke Rare Book and Manuscript Library.

38 Lillian Faderman, *Surpassing the Love of Men* (New York: Triangle Classics, 1994), 214.

39 See chapter two of Federico, *Idol of Suburbia.*

40 Marie Corelli, *The Sorrows of Satan* (Kansas City, MO: Valancourt Books, 2008), 179.

41 One wonders if this detail inspired Richard Marsh's 1897 Gothic novel, *The Beetle,* in which an ancient Egyptian female shapeshifter takes the form of the titular insect.

42 Marie Corelli, *A Romance of Two Worlds* (New York: A. L. Burt, 1887), 162.

43 Marie Corelli to J. Cuming Walters, December 6, 1923. Marie Corelli Papers (Collection 748), Department of Special Collections, Charles E. Young Research Library, UCLA. For more on Corelli's Electric Creed, see chapter five of Stiles, *Popular Fiction and Brain Science.*

44 "Appendix" to Corelli, *A Romance of Two Worlds,* 311–24 (314).

CHAPTER 15

Little Magazines and/in Media History

Lorraine Janzen Kooistra

Giving 1862 as the entry's date, the Oxford English Dictionary (OED) identifies Henry Holland's declaration "We are living in *an age of transition*" as the first to define the experience of constant change as a temporal condition.[1] A British physician and travel writer, Holland (1788–1873) took a transnational perspective on the "period when changes, deeply and permanently affecting the whole condition of [humanity], are occurring more rapidly, as well as extensively, than at any prior time in human history," impacting "the relations of races and communities of [people] over the whole face of the globe."[2] With its compelling connection to the extraordinary technological, meteorological, environmental, and species change that characterizes contemporary life, Holland's "age of transition" emerges from the historical record to describe the ongoing experience of modernity. My point about the age of transition, however, is theoretical and methodological as much as it is historical. Although the OED locates this initial usage in Holland's *Essays on Scientific and Other Subjects*, a book published in 1862, its first appearance in print was actually 1858, in the *Edinburgh Quarterly Review*. By situating the historical record within the book collection rather than the periodical essay, the OED manifests a print culture bias toward so-called permanent (codex, authored) over ephemeral (serial, edited) forms, a privileging reinforced by literary history. The slippage in the dictionary entry usefully illuminates Laurel Brake's insight that "Print is, of course, *always* in transition."[3] Holland's work transitioned from periodical *Review* to a collection of *Essays* in the space of four years. Since then, it has been excerpted and reprinted in the global press, microfilmed, and digitized. Thus, the work that announced the age of transition in the nineteenth century continues to circulate in various media in the twenty-first, including its instantiation within this chapter, which you may be reading in print or on screen. Situating little magazines as media in transition – emerging in the 1890s in the midst of massive technological and cultural change and continuing to circulate today in both material archives and digital editions – this chapter examines the form within the framework of media history. While literary history tends to canonize only those periodical items that effected the transition from serial to book and to ignore or downplay those that did not, a media-based approach takes the periodical itself as the object of study.

The little magazine is usually characterized as a serial of art and literature produced by countercultural artists, writers, editors, and publishers for a relatively small immediate readership. Counterpointing its limited circulation, and in consequence of its ongoing relationship with global mechanisms of remediation, the little magazine also manifests international connections and impact. As a marginal media form contesting, but always engaging, mainstream print culture, the little magazine emerged in the second half of the nineteenth century, developed internationally as a countercultural publishing genre in the twentieth, and continues to thrive, in both print and digital media, in the twenty-first. Little magazines produced as print objects in the previous two centuries are now being remediated digitally, making these ephemeral publications with limited print runs newly – and differently – available to contemporary audiences on the worldwide web. The *Modernist Journals Project* (MJP), for example, provides open-access visual scans and metadata of selected transatlantic periodicals published between 1890 and 1922.[4] The *Blue Mountain Project* (BMP) offers an international, multilingual range of avant-garde periodicals from 1848 – the year of revolutions in Europe – to 1923.[5] On a much smaller scale than these electronic resources, *Yellow Nineties 2.0* (Y90s) publishes marked-up digital editions of eight little magazines produced in Great Britain between 1889 and 1905 – the *Dial* (1889–97), the *Evergreen: A Northern Seasonal* (1895–96), the *Green Sheaf* (1903–04), the *Pagan Review* (1892), the *Pageant* (1896–97), the *Savoy* (1896), the *Venture* (1903–1905), and the *Yellow Book* (1894–97) – within a robust editorial apparatus of born-digital scholarship.[6] Using an interdisciplinary methodology informed by book history, the digital humanities, and periodical and media studies, I draw on these titles as case studies in the little magazine as a fin-de-siècle media form. In an effort to undiscipline the "literatures in transition" narrative in which little magazines progress from Victorian aestheticism and decadence to modernist achievement, I examine them "as a form of technology in transition,"[7] moving across boundaries of space, time, and media to engage a complex network of makers and readers.

While boutique scholarly sites such as the BMP, the MJP, and the Y90s show networks of practice and influence across little magazine titles, periods, and geographies, mass digitization illuminates crucial connections between marginal and mainstream media across Britain, Europe, and North America. The dissident content of little magazines circulated in the reviews, letters, and essays of international periodicals, just as the countercultural media form itself responded to, critiqued, and engaged mass print in diverse ways. Digitization allows us to see 1890s little magazines within this larger media history, one in which the form not only marks "an important shift in periodical creation," as Evanghélia Stead argues, "but also, just as significantly if not more so, in media communication"[8] – that is, a shift in both material format and modes of production, and in intermedial networks of local/global exchange. Increasingly, scholars recognize the 1890s little magazine as an international new media phenomenon. Stead has led the way in analyzing the media form in comparative French and British perspectives, situating the "petite revue" and "little magazine" in historical context and showing their crucial relationship to "big" periodicals across nations and languages. Kirsten Macleod's pioneering work on fin-de-siècle American little magazines shows their significance as a cultural phenomenon in their own time and place as well as in relation to similar movements in Europe.[9] Focusing on the British publishing context, Koenraad Claes argues that the fin-de-siècle little magazine marked its alterity precisely through its material form as a "Total Work of Art."[10] Supported by specialist sites such as the BMP and the MJP as well as the massive digital archives of historic print culture, modernist critics have likewise begun to situate little magazines within larger media contexts.[11]

As a media form designed to express transition in its seriality, ephemerality, topicality, and miscellaneity, "the periodical emerged as *the* characteristic form of print" in the modern age.[12] Caroline Levine's definition of form as *"an arrangement of elements – an ordering, patterning, or shaping"* – provides a useful theoretical framework for understanding the shifting formations of the little magazine through the ordering determinants of "whole, rhythm, hierarchy, network."[13] A magazine's whole is made up of the totality of its print run, which itself comprises a series of related wholes, known as volumes or issues; its rhythm is constituted in the regular temporal release of these individual issues, as well as by the arrangement of elements within and across them; hierarchy orders both a magazine's aesthetic patterns and its sociopolitical relations; and its network encompasses the complex interconnections across the wholes, rhythms, and hierarchies that situate the magazine in the world and make it available to readers in particular times, places, and media. A study of the little magazine as a media form begins with the recognition that its heterogeneous visual and verbal materials were produced collaboratively through social and technological processes; mediated by editors, publishers, printers, and engravers; and offered to the public as a commodity on a serial cycle of publication aimed at creating and retaining an audience of reliably returning readers.

If we recognize little magazines as highly mediated objects of fin-de-siècle print culture, we also need to acknowledge the complex processes and distinct affordances created by their remediated digital status. Since scholars today largely rely on digital editions in their study of material artifacts, understanding remediation as a critical dialectic between old and new media is vital.[14] "Situating the little magazine in its remediated past," as Eric Bulson observes, "involves thinking about it as an object for intellectual inquiry (both in its material and virtual formats) ... [and] in relation to its archives" and the processes involved "in bringing so many titles back to life again and again and again."[15]

The nonliterary systems of communication that constitute a periodical become immediately obvious in the digital editing process. In contrast to a book, the periodical "text" does not derive from an authorial entity, but from a series of nested formal elements: the title's print run; the volumes that comprise it; and the individual items arranged within each issue. In the process of building a digital edition of the Y90s' first and largest magazine, the *Yellow Book,* I learned how much remains to be discovered about the periodical that gave its color to the decade – the *yellow nineties* – and contributed to the international development of the little magazine as a countercultural media form. Conventional *Yellow Book* scholarship has focused almost exclusively on London-based authors and artists, principally decadent men and New Women, who developed the modern short story, experimented with poetic form, popularized art nouveau design, and participated in the fine printing revival. This highly selective narrative cannot account adequately for the *Yellow Book*'s numerous provincial and international contributors or the incredible variety of its literary and artistic contents. With a few notable exceptions, literary history has largely filtered out the magazine's creative nonfiction, religious legends, folk tales, and untranslated works, as well as its pastoral landscapes, children's book illustrations, and reproduced genre paintings. These outliers, the irreconcilables of literary traditions and canonical interests, invite us to examine little magazines as always-in-transition formations of cultural value, whose meanings are made contextually, contingently, and even contradictorily, within the miscellaneity of the media form.

With the expansion of the Y9os magazine rack to include digital editions of seven other little magazines, the *Yellow Book* becomes situated within a range of artistic, social, institutional, and political networks and regional, national, and international connections. Although each title is unique, Y9os magazines collectively manifest what Eric B. White describes as the form's contrapuntal interest in localism and transnationalism.[16] Three of these magazines – the *Dial,* the *Green Sheaf,* and the *Pagan Review* – illuminate a countercultural practice of self-publishing in direct challenge to the industrial mainstream press. Together with a small group of friends, life partners Charles Ricketts and Charles Shannon produced the *Dial* out of their home at The Vale, Chelsea, inscribing the magazine's queer making in its mode of production, material design, and avant-garde French connections. Pamela Colman Smith created the hand-colored issues of the *Green Sheaf* at her studio in Milborne Grove, which housed her Green Sheaf Press and Green Sheaf School of Hand Colouring as well as her oral performances of West Indian tales for London's bohemian community. Born in London to American parents, Smith grew up in England and Jamaica, then studied art in New York before beginning her career in Great Britain. Although she had neither Celtic heritage nor nationalist politics, her *Green Sheaf* magazine circulated as an organ of the contemporary Irish revival movement. Bringing together the regional and the transnational, the particular and the universal, Smith's magazine challenged the boundaries that contain ethnic, national, and personal identities. Some of these fluidities and challenges are also present in William Sharp's *Pagan Review,* the magazine he produced at a cottage in Buck's Green, West Sussex, supplying all editorial content himself under an array of pseudonyms. While Ricketts and Smith each troubled the notion of fixed identity in their magazines by publishing some of their own work anonymously or pseudonymously, Sharp went further, creating a female alter-ego to express the Highland Gaelic concerns that he, as a Lowland English speaker, could not articulate in his own person.[17] When Sharp joined the *Evergreen*'s editorial team in Edinburgh, his dual contributions – in his own name and that of his avatar, the renowned Celtic revivalist Fiona Macleod – constituted a queer challenge to national and sexual identities. The alternative modes of production, local/transnational intersections, and deliberate disruptions of identity displayed in these little magazines characterize the media form as a technology in transition.

Although they were not as intensely do-it-yourself as the *Dial* and the *Green Sheaf,* both the *Evergreen* and the *Venture* were committed to asserting the value of the human over the machine and the interests of the creative community over commercial commodity culture. Patrick Geddes, publisher of the *Evergreen,* established a School of Art in Old Town Edinburgh to support his Scottish Renascence project. Here a small group of mostly women artists created the Celtic-inspired textual ornaments that weave throughout the *Evergreen's* pages. In keeping with the magazine's local/global vision, Geddes relied on a community-based, collaborative, editorial practice for the selection and arrangement of the *Evergreen's* contents, and drew on participants in his International Summer School for its multilingual, multimedia, and interdisciplinary contributions. Approaching the *Venture* as a total work of art within the fine-printing revival, New Zealand artist and London-based gallery owner John Baillie sidestepped established publishing houses to bring out his own annual of art and literature. In contrast, the *Pageant* and the *Savoy* align their mode of production with that of the *Yellow Book,* cultivating their markets through the technological and commercial publishing systems of modern print culture. Acutely aware of their position in relation to mainstream media, and eager to reach European and North American as well as British buyers, each magazine aggressively promoted itself as a unique title, while also acting as a serial advertisement for its publisher: Henry & Co., Leonard Smithers, and The Bodley Head, respectively. Individually and collectively, the eight titles on the Y90s magazine rack express their countercultural ideas through local communities and material practices of making, while simultaneously inserting themselves into global networks of communication and their associated aesthetic and political structures. In the following examples, I map some of the ways in which the little magazine's formal elements – whole, hierarchy, rhythm, and network – situate the form within media history as a technology in transition.

Whole

About the same time that Henry Holland introduced the "age of transition" in the *Edinburgh Quarterly Review,* Charles Baudelaire was analyzing modernity in *Le Figaro,* a mainstream French paper. In "The Painter of Modern Life," Baudelaire celebrated the anonymous periodical illustrator Constantin Guys (1802–92) for his sketches capturing "the fugitive, the ephemeral, the contingent"[18] – the very characteristics of modernity that mark the little magazine as a form of technology in transition. The posthumous appearance of Guys's "A Sketch" in the *Yellow Book*[19] three years after the artist's death provides insight into how a magazine makes its meanings as a *whole* – that is, both as an entire print run directed by an ordering editorial agenda, and as an individual volume within the totality represented by the title. In this section, I show how Guys's "A Sketch" negotiates its meaning in relation to the *Yellow Book*'s overall branding, Beardsley's editorial selection and placement of the work in Volume 5, and the intermedial impact of Oscar Wilde's arrest in the month of its publication, April 1895.

Positioned about three-quarters of the way through Volume 5, Guys's "A Sketch" is the twelfth of fourteen works of art in the issue, which stretches to over 300 pages. The halftone print shows an apparently chance meeting, on an indistinct urban street, between two men walking arm in arm and another man coming toward them (Figure 15.1). Guys captures the fleetingness of their encounter (suggested by the horizontal parallel lines across their feet), their masculine fashion, and their cosmopolitan pose. A momentary fragment, this sketch of everyday life encodes a particular gender, ethnicity, and class within the modern "urban aesthetic" that Mark Turner aptly ascribes to the magazine.[20] In this sense, Guys's drawing is "on brand" for the *Yellow Book*, regardless of its original production for another periodical a generation before the British magazine set out to dazzle consumers with contemporary contents encased within bold yellow-and-black covers.

Moreover, the posthumous appearance of Constantin Guys in the *Yellow Book* is not entirely anomalous to the little magazine as a media form. Emerging in a decade self-consciously aware of its transition into a new century, little magazines demonstrated a marked interest in their relation to the historical past as well as to their present moment and imagined future. Incorporating handmade paper, wide margins, and old-face typography, their material formats aligned more with preindustrial books than contemporary periodicals. They declared their aesthetic lineage and positioned themselves within an ongoing historical tradition by reprinting, citing, or reviving historic creators, works, and methods. Despite the *Green Sheaf*'s affiliation with the contemporary Irish revival, for instance, editor Smith included posthumous excerpts from William Blake (1757–1827) and Anna Barbauld (1743–1825); these selections asserted her magazine's affinity with the former's self-published symbolic works and the latter's legacy as a woman of letters in the public sphere. Aligning their title with symbolism, broadly construed, *Savoy* editors Arthur Symons and Aubrey Beardsley reprinted artwork generated earlier in the century by both Blake and the Pre-Raphaelites. As part of the *Pageant*'s effort to represent "the survival of the pre-Raphaelite idea in

Figure 15.1   Constantin Guys, "A Sketch," *Yellow Book* 5 (April 1895): 261. Courtesy of
Toronto Metropolitan University Libraries Archives and Special Collections. *Yellow
Nineties 2.0*.

art and literature,"[21] coeditors Charles Shannon and Gleeson White remediated works by Dante Gabriel Rossetti and John Everett Millais and educated readers in a history of wood-engraved illustration extending from Renaissance Florence to Victorian London.[22] Rather than including work by earlier artists, the *Dial* and the *Venture* situated themselves in a tradition of artistic practice by reviving wood engraving as an original artform. In contrast, all the images in the *Evergreen: A Northern Seasonal* were photomechanically reproduced drawings by contemporary Scottish artists. Seizing on design rather than mode of production, this Scottish revival magazine inscribed its aesthetic lineage in the Celtic-inspired textual ornaments it commissioned and circulated. As modern versions of an ancient form, these designs made a visible connection to the nation's past while looking forward to a transnational future. Like the *Evergreen,* the *Yellow Book* featured art by living artists, with one exception: Constantin Guys's "A Sketch" in Volume 5.

Margaret Beetham reminds us that each item, each volume, and each title of a periodical "was and is part of a complex process in which writers, editors, publishers and readers engaged in trying to understand themselves and their society" – in other words, "the periodical press was and is part of a wider process of negotiation and struggle over meaning" (Beetham, "Theory of the Periodical," 20). As a mediated work, Guys's "A Sketch" makes its meaning contingently, within the context of the *Yellow Book* as a whole, the volume in which it appeared, and the ongoing moments of its reception, from April 1895 print object to today's digital screen. By selecting Guys's work for publication in Volume 5, art editor Beardsley aligned the *Yellow Book* with Baudelaire's historic perspective on the value of visual art in modernity's ephemeral print culture. At the same time, Beardsley orchestrated contiguous relationships in his arrangement of the volume's contents. Immediately preceding Maurice Baring's essay about French man of letters Anatole France, and the following story by France himself, "L'Evêché de Tourcoing" (The Bishopric of Tourcoing),[23] Guys's "A Sketch" visually introduces the magazine's French connections to readers. These adjacent items – halftone print, review essay, and untranslated French story – can be read in relation to each other, but they might also be read within the larger whole of the volume's twenty-seven literary pieces and fourteen artworks. Not surprisingly, literary scholars have analyzed English in preference to French works and short stories and poetry in preference to essays, so Baring's and France's contributions to the *Yellow Book* have not been closely scrutinized. Similarly, critics have tended to favor line-block reproductions of pen-and-ink drawings over the process engravings of tonal works, and this may account for the lack of attention given to Guys's "A Sketch." Even Turner, in his compelling analysis of Baudelaire's influence on the *Yellow Book*'s aesthetic under Beardsley's editorship, does not discuss the magazine's publication of art by the celebrated "Modern Painter" himself. And yet this work appeared within one of the most consequential issues of the *Yellow Book*'s thirteen-volume print run, the transitional Volume 5 marking the before and after of Beardsley's art editorship.

The historical record tells us that Beardsley was art editor when Guys's "A Sketch" was selected for and arranged within Volume 5, but not when the issue reached its first public in April 1895. As is well known, Beardsley was fired, and his artistic contributions to the volume dramatically excised before publication, in consequence of the media storm occasioned by Wilde's arrest with, as reported in the press, "*Yellow Book* under his arm."[24] In this early instance of fake news having wide-ranging personal and political effects, *yellow* and *book* act as nonhuman agents of change within interlinked networks of human lives, sociopolitical formations, and intermedial expressions.

Despite his eviction from the magazine's staff, however, Beardsley remains an unacknowledged presence in the *Yellow Book*'s transitional fifth volume, with his editorial selections and arrangements left intact. A critical reading of Volume 5, taking into account its transnational media moment, heterogeneous editorial content, and paratextual materials, has yet to be attempted; such an analysis could provide a model for interpreting little magazines in media history. While author-based literary methods tend to mine serials for extractable content, approaching the media form in terms of Levine's "whole" enables scholars to analyze the contingencies and contradictions of a magazine's fugitive pieces as they relate to each other within an individual volume and the title's editorial agenda. Whether publishing in historic print or contemporary digital media, editors work on the level of design, and their decisions have evident designs on their targeted readers. An interdisciplinary, media-based methodology recognizes the complex systems of mediation and design that participate in the meaning-making processes of the little magazine as a whole.

Hierarchy

As a categorical term, "little magazine" implies a big/small hierarchy determined by sociocultural values. From the perspective of the commercially driven mainstream press, a large audience base and market share place "big" at the top of the media hierarchy. For the countercultural avant-garde, on the other hand, "little" rises to the top of an aesthetic hierarchy based on selective contents "meant for the rare few, capable of empathetic appreciation, who understand" (Stead, "Reconsidering," 1). Charles Ricketts confirmed the latter view in his "Apology" in the first issue of the *Dial*: "The sole aim of this magazine is to gain sympathy with its views."[25] As editor-publisher, Ricketts understood this goal could only be achieved through design: that is, through the material, nonlinguistic systems of communication that mediate a magazine's contents. In a media interview, Ricketts elaborated that the purpose of the *Dial* was "to emphasise and re-emphasise the importance of design in art."[26] Taking the *Dial* as my example, I now consider how hierarchical form, described by Levine as the patterns and arrangements that organize aesthetic and cultural value (Levine, *Forms,* 13), operates in the design structures of little magazines and their digital surrogates.

Like the creation of the original print object itself, its digital remediation is all about design. As Alan Galey and Stan Ruecker remind us in "How a Prototype Argues," design "positions us in a potent space between past and future," but its manifestations also demand critical analysis. "Failing to recognize design as a hermeneutic process means failing to understand how our inherited cultural record actually works."[27] Little magazines, in both original print and digital editions, offer scholars an opportunity to think critically about the larger systems of design that impact a work's meaning. The highly mediated sites that make little magazines available today are created out of a complex series of editorial and technological decisions in the backend that combine to create a graphic interface through which users can access data and affordances. Although their technologies, objectives, and audiences differed, little magazines also manipulated design to convey their argument to readers – in effect, to manifest the manifestos of their makers. A media-informed methodology approaches little magazines as material objects designed to be, as Koenraad Claes has shown so persuasively, "Total Works of Art" aiming to integrate "medium and message, form and content, ethics and aesthetics" (Claes, *Late Victorian Little Magazine,* 1).

Makers of 1890s little magazines leveraged design as a strategy of engagement, aware that it had the capacity to activate the affordances latent in the materialities of the medium. They designed their titles to interact with readers through the form's paratextual elements: covers, title pages, lists of contents, textual ornaments, layouts, advertisements, and so on. As a countercultural media form, the little magazine was designed to be modernity's other. Fundamental to a title's design strategy was its built-in challenge to the values governing modern systems of communication, modes of production, and social formations. The architecture of the *Dial* deliberately deployed strategies of inversion to challenge both aesthetic and cultural hierarchies.

Physically, the *Dial* presented itself to readers as an artist's portfolio, wrapped in brown paper covers and loosely bound so that its prints could easily be removed for study and display. Although the *Yellow Book* and its followers contested the longstanding hierarchy of verbal over visual media by segregating contents into "Letterpress" and "Pictures," the *Dial*'s design made an even more radical argument about relative value. Insisting on the primacy of visual art, the magazine demoted literature to the bottom of the traditional hierarchy. The Contents for the *Dial*'s first volume listed only its artwork; the Contents for the ensuing four volumes included a separate list of literary items, but located it in a secondary position, *after* the list of illustrations. In Volumes 2 and 5, both lists were displaced to the back pages of the magazine, where they were printed in such a small font that the tiny textual block on the wide expanse of laid paper appeared more decorative than functional. Disrupting received notions of centrality and marginality, the design of the *Dial* invited, even required, readers to look before they read, and to absorb before they sought out the metadata of titles and creators. Through their artisanal approach to circulating art in multiples as prints (as opposed to reproduced copies), the last four volumes of the *Dial* also staged a resistance to the large-scale practices of the commercial press and its drive to speed, efficiency, and standardization. Modeling the integrity of manual methods and material media, these volumes of the *Dial* revived wood engraving as an original artform that could reach readers, as the Prospectus claimed, "directly from the hands of the artists."[28]

The fin de siècle witnessed a dramatic shift in image reproduction technology: in less than a decade, mass print abandoned facsimile wood engraving in favor of photomechanical processes. In its revival of wood engraving as an original artform, the *Dial* asserted human values over mechanical ones and sought to close the widening gaps between art and labor, design and execution, creator and consumer. For Ricketts, "the final carrying out of a design by the designer is a desirable thing in itself," as "the "warmth" of the line may be preserved thereby."[29] Crucially, Ricketts rejected the commercial practice of casting metal stereotypes from the woodblocks and printing from the resulting metal plate; in the *Dial*, he insisted, "all woodcuts have been printed from the wood to ensure the greater sweetness in printing" (Prospectus for the *Dial,* n.p.). For Ricketts, only art that expressed the integrity of its medium could mitigate against the material and cultural stereotypes generated in and by mass print. Using his medium of wood engraving – a form of relief printing that requires designs to be cut in reverse on the block – Ricketts encoded the alterity of the sexual invert into selected images of the *Dial.* Beginning with the 1892 volume, which was the first to rely on wood-engraved textual ornaments, Ricketts carved his monogrammed initials in natural order on selected designs, knowing that they would appear backwards when printed. An expert engraver, Ricketts could only have created these inverted signatures deliberately. Moreover, his editorial arrangement of contents accentuates this message to discerning readers. The first of his designs to bear this coded mark appears on the volume's first textual page, which features Ricketts's Asian fairy tale of forbidden love and toppled hierarchy, "The Marred Face" (Figure 15.2).[30] In the bottom left corner of this marginal illustration for a fantastic work from his own hand, the artist's reversed initials play with ideas of marring and mirroring to assert the value of queer design and human individuality.

My case study of the *Dial* suggests some of the ways in which material affordances and editorial shaping inform the design structures of little magazines and correlate to the "powerful *hierarchies*" that organize society, "including gender, race, class, and bureaucracy" (Levine, *Forms,* 21). I now move from spatial patterning to temporal rhythms to show how the little magazine, as a technology in transition, manipulated seriality itself to contest modernity's standardization of time.

Rhythm

In April 1894, when Henry Harland and Aubrey Beardsley issued the first Prospectus for the *Yellow Book,* they articulated the ideal temporality of periodicals: duration over time, expressed through patterns of repetition and difference. The volumes of the magazine would be published on the fifteenth of July, October, January, and April each year, they promised, "and so from quarter to quarter, it is hoped, *ad infinitum.*"[31] Ephemerality and permanence, interval and pause, set the rhythm of serial publication. Periodicals connect with readers at regular and predictable intervals – annually, quarterly, monthly, weekly, daily – in order to establish and maintain a reliable circulation across a targeted audience. Periodical rhythms work to "reinforce the importance of a time-regulated society" while simultaneously promising "that this is not the end, there will be

So So THE MARRED FACE So So

So So So

MY MOUNTAINS ARE MY OWN
AND I WILL KEEP THEM
TO MYSELF
W . BLAKE

I

BOTH city and suburbs re-
joiced. From roof to roof-
top swayed the bell-like
weight of large lanterns that
mimicked the languorous
airs of lilies on the nod, yet
more duskily, like fruit again become blossom,
against a faint pink sky still pale with the
lingering trail of sunset; for Chang Tei had
laid low that haughty head of his upon Mount
Torment, below the prison gates; and with the
dawn of even, when a wan moon-crescent
beckoned to clustering stars, and mimic lights
from the bridges swam with them in the river,
a glow from his still burning house put a dull
redness in the air, through which, now and
again, shot rapidly a light more acute, when a
charred wall crumbled in.

This was watched, long after curfew and into
the night, for some beggars sat at a town gate.
The sound of the patrol's retreating footfalls was echoed by overhanging
eaves, with this the tremulous expostulations of some belated tippler hurried
away; the night-wind swept past, and the stillness from circling hills sank
upon the city.

"Curse me!" quoth beggar Foo, "but Ling must have found a sweetheart." At this the pent hatred of the others clamoured against those limbs,
that whole nose of his: "He a sweetheart forsooth!" They glanced hate-
fully at each other's maimed limbs; as the wind tosses dead tree-branches,
so their arms became shaken, for with Ling was their common fund for food.
AH! curse him; to hide thus from the patrol since sun-down was not
pleasant, for the night became cold when the pre-morning wind, that shudders
in the chimneys, adds its shriller coolness to the air.

Their hoarse clamour soon spluttered, and gradually ceased; dull gleams
only answered the fixed gleam of hungry eyes; one idea only troubled their
shrivelled lips: then with tacit consent the beggars bent towards the place

I

Figure 15.2   Charles Ricketts, "The Marred Face," *Dial* 2 (1892): 1. Courtesy of Mark
Samuels Lasner Collection, University of Delaware Library, Museums, and Press. *Yellow
Nineties 2.0.*

another number" (Beetham, "Theory of the Periodical," 30). "These distinct temporalities in print media," Mark Turner observes, "suggest and construct different socio-cultural understandings about time, in a period in which temporal shifts and disruptions were a sign of its modernity."[32] As a countercultural media form emerging in the age of transition, the fin-de-siècle little magazine imagined time differently. In a variety of compelling ways, its makers used the serial form to contest the underlying assumptions of industrial time.

Undermining the notion of seriality itself, the *Pagan Review* issued only a single number. The *Dial,* subtitled an "Occasional Publication," declared it would not publish at regular intervals at all. Rather, as its title suggested, it would appear only when the generative sun was able to put creative shadows into play – in other words, in its own time. Periodical intervals were also unsettled by the *Savoy,* which – in imitation of the *Yellow Book* – began as a quarterly but switched to monthly publication after the first two numbers. Notably, the quarterly format was outdated by the 1890s. As Brake points out, the *Yellow Book* "was a quarterly at a moment when timeliness, topicality, and the news were paramount; and it looked like a book when the ephemeral periodical was at its apogee" (Brake, *Print in Transition,* 155). In both material format and temporal rhythm, the *Yellow Book* announced itself as a technology in transition: an ephemeral serial aspiring to the permanence of codex, an old-fashioned quarterly circulating new art and literature. The *Pageant* and the *Venture* similarly reimagined a long-established publishing format: the illustrated annual targeted at gift buyers willing to pay a premium for a high-quality, au courant publication on offer to middle-class art lovers in the holiday season. But it was the two titles associated with the fin-de-siècle Celtic revival, the *Evergreen* and the *Green Sheaf,* that deliberately set out to disrupt modernity's periodical rhythms with older understandings of time. These two magazines contested the basic premise of serial publication – a fixed starting point with an infinite number of repetitions appearing at regular intervals – by announcing the limits of their print runs at the outset and employing idiosyncratic temporal measurements derived from natural, rather than industrial, cycles.

Patrick Geddes and his collaborators designed the *Evergreen: A Northern Seasonal* as a set of four volumes, "to be complete in a little over a year and a half."[33] Sometimes inaccurately described as a quarterly, the *Evergreen* came out semi-annually, with each volume organized around one of the four seasons. The magazine's serialization did not present its seasons chronologically in calendar sequence, however; following the solar-oriented temporality of the Celts, its issues appeared in relation to seasonal equinoxes and solstices. Published in 1895, the first two volumes, Spring and Autumn, appeared more-or-less in line with their respective equinoxes. Summer and Winter, the two solstice volumes, came out the following year and brought the print run to an end. Just as the magazine's whole was divided into four issues, each volume's Table of Contents was organized in thematic quadrants, exploring the Season's manifestations "In Nature," "In Life," "In the World," and "In the North" (Figure 15.3). In a diverse array of scientific and historical essays, folklore and fiction, poetry and pictures, each issue explored its season from a variety of perspectives, crossing temporal, national, and geographic borders as well as disciplinary ones in order to achieve an inclusive comprehensiveness. As *Evergreen* contributor and botanist Victor Branford explained, the *Evergreen*'s "four-fold division" contested modernity's fragmentation and isolation, aiming to express "the naturalistic" and "the humanistic view" in "a harmonious whole."[34]

The periodical rhythm of Pamela Colman Smith's the *Green Sheaf* was also shaped by a temporality older than, and uncontained by, standardized units of industrial time: the cycles of the moon. The year between the appearance of the magazine's first issue in May 1903 and its final number in 1904 saw thirteen full moons. By bringing out thirteen issues in the year rather than the standard twelve, the title conveyed an alternative seriality associated with the creative power of women and a mystical understanding of natural processes. Smith highlighted the significance of the number thirteen by setting the magazine's annual subscription rate at thirteen shillings and selling individual issues for thirteen pence apiece. It is likely that occult meanings for the number thirteen were also behind the *Green Sheaf*'s periodical intervals and price points. As a member of the Hermetic Order of the Golden Dawn, Smith was immersed in a world of symbolic correspondences expressed by the tarot cards; in 1909, she was to design the famous Rider-Waite deck, which continues to be used in divinations by the occult community today. Notably for a magazine associated with the Irish revival, Number 13 in the tarot deck is the Death Card; far from signaling the end of life, it represents "rebirth, creation, destination, renewal."[35] As Smith's manifesto declared, the *Green Sheaf* aimed to bring together the ancient and the eternal in symbolically illustrated pages featuring "ballads of the *old world*" that are "green for ever"[36] (Figure 15.4). The periodical rhythm of the *Green Sheaf* circulated the Irish revival as part of a wider effort to reset the alienating patterns of modern life through the intersection of localized story and universal symbol.

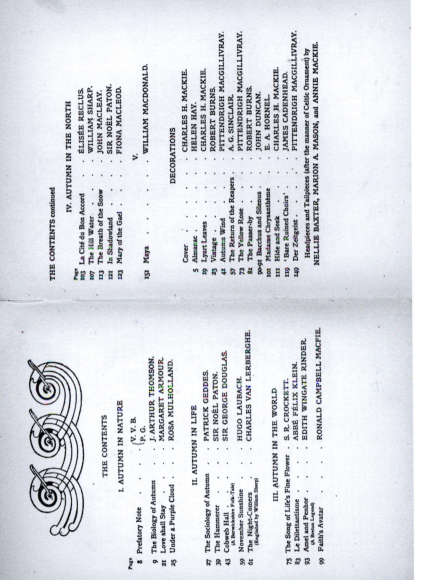

THE CONTENTS

I. AUTUMN IN NATURE

Page
8   Prefatory Note   .   { V. V. B.
                             { P. G.
9   The Biology of Autumn   .   J. ARTHUR THOMSON.
21   Love shall Stay   .   MARGARET ARMOUR.
25   Under a Purple Cloud   .   ROSA MULHOLLAND.

II. AUTUMN IN LIFE

27   The Sociology of Autumn   .   PATRICK GEDDES.
39   The Hammerer   .   SIR NOËL PATON.
43   Cobweb Hall   .   SIR GEORGE DOUGLAS.
      (A Berwickshire Folk-Tale)
59   November Sunshine   .   HUGO LAUBACH.
61   The Night-Comers   .   CHARLES VAN LERBERGHE.
      (Englished by William Sharp)

III. AUTUMN IN THE WORLD

75   The Song of Life's Fine Flower   .   S. R. CROCKETT.
83   Le Dilettantisme   .   ABBÉ FÉLIX KLEIN.
93   Amel and Penhor   .   EDITH WINGATE RINDER.
      (A Breton Legend)
99   Faith's Avatar   .   RONALD CAMPBELL MACFIE.

THE CONTENTS continued

IV. AUTUMN IN THE NORTH

Page
103   La Cité du Bon Accord   .   ÉLISÉE RECLUS.
107   The Hill Water   .   WILLIAM SHARP.
113   The Breath of the Snow   .   JOHN MACLEAY.
121   In Shadowland   .   SIR NOËL PATON.
123   Mary of the Gael   .   FIONA MACLEOD.

V.

151   Maya   .   WILLIAM MACDONALD.

DECORATIONS

Cover   .   CHARLES H. MACKIE.
5   Almanac   .   HELEN HAY.
19   Lyart Leaves   .   CHARLES H. MACKIE.
23   Vintage   .   ROBERT BURNS.
41   Autumn Wind   .   PITTENDRIGH MACGILLIVRAY.
57   The Return of the Reapers   .   A. G. SINCLAIR.
73   The Yellow Rose   .   PITTENDRIGH MACGILLIVRAY.
81   The Passer-by   .   ROBERT BURNS.
90-91   Bacchus and Silenus   .   JOHN DUNCAN.
101   Madame Chrysanthème   .   E. A. HORNEL.
111   Hide and Seek   .   CHARLES H. MACKIE.
119   'Bare Ruined Choirs'   .   JAMES CADENHEAD.
149   Der Zeitgeist   .   PITTENDRIGH MACGILLIVRAY.

Headpieces and Tailpieces (after the manner of Celtic Ornament) by
NELLIE BAXTER, MARION A. MASON, and ANNIE MACKIE.

Figure 15.3   Table of Contents, *Evergreen: A Northern Seasonal* 2 (Autumn 1895): 3–4. Courtesy of Toronto Metropolitan University Libraries Archives and Special Collections. *Yellow Nineties 2.0.*

No. 4.

The Green Sheaf

1903

My *Sheaf* is small . . . but it is green.
I will gather into my *Sheaf* all the young fresh things I can—*pictures*,
verses, *ballads*, of *love* and *war* ; tales of *pirates* and the *sea*.
You will find ballads of the *old world* in my *Sheaf*.   Are they not
green for ever . . .
Ripe ears are *good* for *bread*, but green ears are good for *pleasure*.

LONDON
EDITED, PUBLISHED, AND SOLD BY
PAMELA COLMAN SMITH
& SOLD BY ELKIN MATHEWS, VIGO STREET, W.

Figure 15.4.   Pamela Colman Smith, cover design for the *Green Sheaf* 4 (1903).
Courtesy of Mark Samuels Lasner Collection, University of Delaware Library, Museums, and Press.
Yellow Nineties 2.0.

Network

"As a form that first and foremost affords connectedness," Levine observes,
"the network provides a way to understand how many other formal
elements – including wholes, rhythms, and hierarchies – link up in larger

formations" (Levine, *Forms*, 113). The affordances of digitization have exponentially enhanced our ability to investigate the little magazine within transnational, multilingual, and intermedial networks. Keyword searches of unstructured data (texts) and metadata (bibliographic information) enable scholars to discover connections across media forms, opening up new avenues of investigation and analysis. But the sheer size of the ever-expanding digital archive also invites a methodological shift to reading patterns at scale. Working at the level of distant rather than close reading, computer processes can visualize the high-level social formations and relationships that enmeshed little magazines in intersecting local, national, and international networks. As periodicals scholars have long recognized, both human and machine reading are crucial to the study of magazines as a media form. Brake describes periodicals as networks in Friedrich Kittler's terms: "the technic whereby cultural exchange takes place," or the mediality that makes literary and artistic forms possible in specific historical and material situations.[37] Expanding on Brake's work, Rebecca N. Mitchell argues that "the technic not only supplements the meaning of the artefact, but also impinges on the very possibility of the existence of the artefact or its mode of production."[38] Her work compellingly demonstrates the impact of the *Century Guild Hobby Horse* (1884–94) "as a hub from which a variety of new, more specialized forms emerged" – including the little magazines and fine-printing presses of the fin de siècle and beyond (Mitchell, "Crafting Generic Networks," 76). J. Stephen Murphy, meanwhile, urges scholars to study magazine networks through computational analysis. With its capacity to visualize the links that connect entities or nodes and to reveal hubs, network analysis can discover patterns of order within larger, and apparently chaotic, systems. These visualizations, he argues, "provide a new way to reveal the social constructedness of literary history and literary value."[39]

The affordances of *Yellow Nineties 2.0* offer multiple ways to read, navigate, discover, and analyze the site's eight little magazines and their makers. Volumes are available for close reading and analysis in both the virtual facsimile flip-book that mimics page turns and preserves layout, and in the continuous scroll familiar to online readers. Hyperlinks create a complex network of connections across individual items, contributors, paratextual elements, and born-digital scholarship. Relational databases, meanwhile, support data visualizations. Modeling the ways in which 1890s little magazines worked to produce graphic knowledge systems in an age of technological transition, the *Database of Ornament* allows users to study textual decorations within and across titles.[40] The *Y90s Personography*, a biographical database, enables users to query the relationships, connections, and social networks of magazine contributors of all kinds – authors, artists, engravers, editors, publishers, and so on – and to visualize their personal and professional affiliations for further analysis.[41] Because this dataset is structured in linked open data, it leverages the power of the semantic web to discover and infer high-level patterns of association between local and cosmopolitan communities, not only in Great Britain, but across the world. As datasets proliferate online and computational tools become increasingly accessible to scholars more familiar with close reading strategies than network analysis, computer visualizations will play a significant role in understanding the fin-de-siècle little magazine as a media form, and its ongoing role in media history.

In an editorial for the first number of the *Savoy*, Arthur Symons asserted the magazine's resistance to the limits of stylistic and historical categories. "We are not Realists, or Romanticists, or Decadents," he insisted. "For us, all art is good which is good art."[42] This chapter has argued that the 1890s little magazine is not Victorian, or decadent, or modernist. It is not even literary. While such disciplinary tags may be applied to selected contents, they cannot contain or comprehend the totality of the media form that emerged at the fin de siècle and continues to thrive today. Understanding the little magazine as a countercultural form within media history requires the scholarly analysis of the "whole" of a title's editorial agenda and mode of production in relation to individual volumes, while paying due attention to the sociopolitical hierarchies expressed in its aesthetic design, the ways in which its serial rhythms position bodies in relation to time, and the complex, ongoing, and changing networks of its makers and readers. Enabled by the electronic resources of our digital age, we have the opportunity to study these remediated print objects as new media in their own day, responding to, and expressing, modernity's age of transition.

Notes

1 "transition, n." *OED Online*, Oxford University Press, September 2021, www.oed.com/view/Entry/204815 (accessed November 16, 2021); (emphasis in Holland).

2 Henry Holland, *Essays on Scientific and Other Subjects, Contributed to the Edinburgh and Quarterly Reviews* (London: Longman, Green, Longman, and Roberts, 1862), 1–2.

3 Laurel Brake, *Print in Transition, 1850–1910: Studies in Media and Book History* (New York: Palgrave, 2001), xiv.

4 *The Modernist Journals Project,* directed by Susan Smulyan (Brown) and Jeff Drouin (Tulsa), https://modjourn.org.

5 *Blue Mountain Project,* directed by Clifford E. Wulfman, Princeton University Library, https://bluemountain.princeton.edu/bluemtn/cgi-bin/bluemtn.

6 *Yellow Nineties 2.0,* directed by Lorraine Janzen Kooistra, Toronto Metropolitan University Centre for Digital Humanities, https://1890s.ca. I gratefully acknowledge the generous funding provided by the Social Sciences and Humanities Research Council of Canada in support of this project and the ongoing support of the University Library.

7 Faye Hammill, Paul Hjartarson, Hannah McGregor, "Introducing Magazines and/as Media: The Aesthetics and Politics of Serial Form," *ESC: English Studies in Canada* 41, no. 1 (2015): 1–18 (6).

8 Evanghélia Stead, "Reconsidering 'Little' versus 'Big' Periodicals," *Journal of European Periodical Studies* 1, no. 2 (2016): 1–17 (12).

9 Kirsten Macleod, *American Little Magazines of the Fin de Siècle: Art, Protest, and Cultural Transformation* (Toronto: University of Toronto Press, 2018).

10 Koenraad Claes, *The Late-Victorian Little Magazine* (Edinburgh: Edinburgh University Press, 2018), 1.

11 Peter Brooker and Andrew Thacker, eds. *The Oxford Critical and Cultural History of Modernist Magazines: Vol. 1, Britain and Ireland 1880–1955* (Oxford and New York: Oxford University Press, 2008); Robert Scholes and Clifford Wulfman, *Modernism in the Magazines* (New Haven, CT: Yale University Press, 2010).

12 Margaret Beetham, "Towards a Theory of the Periodical as a Publishing Genre," in *Investigating Victorian Journalism,* eds. Laurel Brake, Aled Jones, and Lionel Madden (Basingstoke and London: Macmillan, 1990), 19–32 (19).

13 Caroline Levine, *Forms: Whole, Rhythm, Hierarchy, Network* (Princeton and Oxford: Princeton University Press, 2015), 3, 21. (emphasis in original)

14 Jay David Bolter and Richard Grusin, *Remediation: Understanding New Media* (Cambridge, MA: MIT Press, 1992), 14–15.

15 Eric Bulson, "The Little Magazine, Remediated," *Journal of Modern Periodical Studies* 8, no. 2 (2017): 200–25 (201–02).

16 Eric B. White, *Transatlantic Avant-Gardes: Little Magazines and Localist Modernism* (Edinburgh: Edinburgh University Press, 2013), 1.

17 Michael Shaw, "William Sharp's Neo-Paganism: Queer Identity and the National Family," in *Queer Victorian Families: Curious Relations in Literature,* eds. Duc Dau and Shale Preston (New York: Routledge, 2015), 77–95 (78).

18 Charles Baudelaire, *The Painter of Modern Life and Other Essays,* trans. and ed. Jonathan Mayne (London: Phaidon Press, 1964), 13.

19 Constantin Guys, "A Sketch," *Yellow Book* 5 (1895): 261, in *Yellow Book Digital Edition,* ed. Dennis Denisoff and Lorraine Janzen Kooistra, https://1890s.ca/YB5-guys-sketch.

20 Mark Turner, "Urban Encounters and Visual Play in *The Yellow Book*" in *Encounters in the Victorian Press,* eds. Laurel Brake and Julie Codell (London: Palgrave Macmillan, 2005), 138–160 (139).

21 "A 'Pageant' and How it is Made," *Pall Mall Gazette* (November 6, 1895): 3, *British Library Newspapers,* https://go.gale.com/ps/i.do?p=GDCS&u=udalhou sie&v=2.1&it=r&id=GALE%7CY3200463564&asid= 1637211600000-9cb7bc8e (accessed July 30, 2018).

22 See Alfred W. Pollard, "Florentine Rappresentazioni and their Pictures," *Pageant* 1 (1896): 163–83, *Pageant Digital Edition,* ed. Frederick King and Lorraine Janzen Kooistra, https://1890s.ca/pag1-pollard-florentine; Gleeson White, "The Work of Charles Ricketts," *Pageant* 1 (1896): 79-93, https://1890s.ca/pag1-white-ricketts; and Charles Ricketts, "A Note on Original Wood-Engraving," *Pageant* 2 (1897): 253–66.

23 Maurice Baring, "M. Anatole France," *Yellow Book* 5 (April 1895): 263–79, *Yellow Book Digital Edition,* https://1890s.ca/YBV5_baring_anatole; Anatole France, "L'Evêché de Tourcoing," *Yellow Book* 5 (April 1895): 283–89, *Yellow Book Digital Edition,* https://1890s.ca/YBV5_france_eveche.

24 J. Lewis May, *John Lane and the Nineties* (London: John Lane The Bodley Head, 1936), 80; Simon Wilson, "A Case of Jaundice: What was Wilde really reading while awaiting his arrest? Pierre Louÿs's Aphrodite? Another French novel? A book with a yellow cover? Or...*The Yellow Book*?" *The Wildean: A Journal of Oscar Wilde Studies,* 58 (Jan 2021): 1–18 (5–6).

25 Charles Ricketts, "Apology," *Dial* 1 (1889): 36, *Dial Digital Edition,* ed. Lorraine Janzen Kooistra, https://1890s.ca/dialv1-apology.

26 Temple Scott, "Mr. Charles Ricketts and the Vale Press (An Interview)," *Bookselling* (December 1896), in *Charles Ricketts, Everything for Art: Selected Writings,* ed. Nicholas Frankel (London: Rivendale Press, 2014), 333–41 (339).

27 Alan Galey and Stan Ruecker, "How a Prototype Argues," *Literary and Linguistic Computing* 25 (2010): 405–24 (421).

28 Charles Ricketts, Prospectus for *Dial* 2 (1892), n. p., included among ephemera in the British Library bound copy of H.C. Marillier, *The Vale Press and the Modern Revival of Printing,* 1900.

29 Charles Ricketts, "A Defense of the Revival of Printing," in *Charles Ricketts, Everything for Art,* ed. Nicholas Frankel, 110.

30 Charles Ricketts, "The Marred Face," *Dial* 2 (1892): 1–7, *Dial Digital Edition,* https://1890s.ca/dialv2-ricketts-marred.

31 Prospectus to the *Yellow Book* 1 (April 1895), n. p., *Yellow Nineties 2.0,* https://1890s.ca/wp-content/uploads/YB1-prospectus.pdf.

32 Mark Turner, "Time, Periodicals, and Literary Studies," *Victorian Periodicals Review* 39, no. 4 (2006): 309–16 (312).

33 Prospectus to the *Evergreen: A Northern Seasonal* 1 (Spring 1895): n. p., *Yellow Nineties 2.0,* https://1890s.ca/egv1-prospectus.

34 Victor Branford, "Old Edinburgh and *The Evergreen*," *Bookman* 9, no. 51 (December 1895): 88–90, *Yellow Nineties 2.0,* https://1890s.ca/eg2_review_bookman_1895.

35 Arthur Edward Waite, *The Pictorial Key to the Tarot* (Stamford, CT: U.S. Games, 2008), 97.

36 Pamela Colman Smith, ["Manifesto"], *Green Sheaf* 4 (1903), front cover, *Green Sheaf Digital Edition,* ed. Lorraine Janzen Kooistra, https://1890s.ca/green-sheaf-volumes.

37 Laurel Brake, "'Time's Turbulence': Mapping Journalism Networks," *Victorian Periodicals Review* 44, no. 2 (2011): 115–27 (116).

38 Rebecca N. Mitchell, "The *Century Guild Hobby Horse*: Crafting Generic Networks in Fin-de-Siècle England," *Bibliographic Society of America* 112, no. 1 (2008): 75–94 (78).

39 J. Stephen Murphy, "Introduction: Visualizing Periodical Networks," *Journal of Modern Periodical Studies* 5, no. 1 (2014): iii–xv (v).

40 *The Database of Ornament,* ed. Lorraine Janzen Kooistra, *Yellow Nineties 2.0,* https://ornament.library.ryerson.ca.

41 *Y90s Personography,* ed. Alison Hedley, *Yellow Nineties 2.0,* https://personography.1890s.ca.

42 Arthur Symons, "Editorial Note," *Savoy* 1 (January 1896): 5, *Savoy Digital Edition,* ed. Christopher Keep and Lorraine Janzen Kooistra, https://1890s.ca/savoyv1-symons-editorial.

CHAPTER 16

Fin-de-Siècle Visuality (and Textuality) and the Digital Sphere

Rebecca N. Mitchell

Credo in unam Artem, multipartitam, individibilem.[1]

In "The Unity of the Arts," a review of an 1887 lecture on Modern Art given by designer Selwyn Image, Oscar Wilde summarized the speaker's aesthetic philosophy with this phrase, offered in Latin, that he termed "the central motive of [Image's] creed": "I believe in one art, indivisible." As John Stokes and Mark Turner note in their edition of Wilde's journalism, the line is "a parody of the Nicene Creed: 'I believe in one God, the Father Almighty, Maker of heaven and earth and of all things visible and invisible,'"[2] poking mild fun at the seriousness with which Image and his ilk were committed to this belief. Yet in the years leading to the 1890s, the idea of the "unity of the arts" held enormous sway in leading literary and artistic circles in Britain. Almost certainly drawing on Walter Pater's discussion of the shared formal aspiration of the arts,[3] versions of this tenet were voiced in countless articles, lectures, and ideological manifestos of the period, applied to people and practices across a range of artistic media and styles. In an 1888 address to the National Art Congress, Royal Academy President Sir Frederic Leighton "had much to say about the unity of the arts in the Middle Ages—a unity which the admirable 'Arts and Crafts' movement hopes to restore,"[4] reported the *Pall Mall Gazette*, and upon his death in 1896, an obituary noted that "the unity of the Arts was realized in his career as in that of some of the masters of the Renaissance."[5] Bernard Partridge, perhaps best known as a cartoonist for *Punch* but also as a trained architect and stained-glass designer, was praised in 1888 for his acting ability with the invocation of the phrase: "To be a passable actor, and so excellent a draughtsman, is a nearer approach to the 'unity of the arts' than is often attained in this specializing age."[6] A decade later, coverage of the 1898 first exhibition of the Northern Art Workers' Guild noted that the group's "gospel" is "the essential unity of all of the arts and their true foundation in vital handicraft."[7]

Wilde himself, in the review of Image's lecture, glosses the speaker's point, writing that "the true unity of the arts is to be found, not in any resemblance of one art to another, but in the fact that to the really artistic nature, all the arts have the same message, and speak the same language, though with different tongues" (Wilde, "Unity of the Arts," 34). In Wilde's formulation, as in fin-de-siècle practice, there is tension between the idea of unity, on the one hand, and the manifestation of difference in the resulting arts, on the other hand. It is a sort of unity that embraces, and should result in, diversity of expression, though the complexity that results from that tension can be difficult to trace among the evidence of 1890s visual culture, thanks to a myopic critical and popular focus on decadent iconography.

One might be forgiven if the first 1890s visual referents that spring to mind are the striking, curvilinear designs of Aubrey Beardsley (1872–98), who has come to have an outsized influence in shaping today's understanding of the visual landscape of the period. Beardsley's style used stark contrasts (in an mostly monochromatic oeuvre), frequent employment of negative space, and an only-sometimes playful invocation of sexual dissidence. Among his best-known compositions are his illustrations of Oscar Wilde's *Salomé* (see Figure 16.1), which affiliated Beardsley's work with that of the playwright, despite the fact that Beardsley ultimately had little regard for Wilde. The connection nevertheless helped to fix Beardsley in the mind of the public with a Wildean decadence. This aspect of Beardsley's career was recently summed up in the reviews of the Tate Gallery's major 2020 retrospective exhibition of his work, with periodicals across the ideological spectrum agreeing on Beardsley's place within the artistic canon. The conservative *Evening Standard* declared him "the epitome of what critics defined as fin-de-siècle Decadence"[8] and the liberal *Guardian* critic noted that his career "has become synonymous with fin-de-siècle decadence."[9] The Tate itself stated that his "charismatic persona played a part in the phenomenon that he and his art generated, so much so that the 1890s were dubbed the 'Beardsley Period.'"[10] Foremost among the evidence for these conclusions were his involvement with and contributions to the literary and artistic quarterly (1894–97) the *Yellow Book*, which has become a symbol for the broader movement and indeed the decade itself. References to the term "Beardsley Period" may be scarcely used today outside of the Tate's own website, but the "Yellow Nineties" remains in frequent usage in criticism characterizing the period.[11] Beardsley's vision has perhaps come to exemplify fin-de-siècle visuality, but it was in many ways not at all typical of the broader artistic movements

Figure 16.1   Aubrey Beardsley, "John and Salome" (1894) from *A Portfolio of Aubrey Beardsley's Drawings Illustrating "Salome" by Oscar Wilde* (John Lane, 1907). Public domain image courtesy of the British Library.

of the decade. For one thing, he did not embrace the "unity of the arts": though he contributed some written pieces to little magazines of the period, his artistic efforts did not range nearly as widely as those of other artists and craftspeople. Since 2005, PDFs of the *Yellow Book* have been available via open-access websites such as *Yellow Nineties 2.0* and archive. org (which incorporates digitized volumes from *Yellow Nineties 2.0*). So significant is the reach of these works that the characterization of the so-called Beardsley Period risks overwhelming the multivalent, multimodal aspects of fin-de-siècle visual culture.

Beardsley's example points to some of the ways that the complexity and nuance of 1890s visual culture is both reinvigorated and narrowed by advances in digital scholarship. As in Beardsley's case, the amplification of certain artists and styles through recent digitization has helped to reframe their work to be received anew, with the resulting emphasis falling differently than in decades past. That the British artistic and textual worlds of the 1890s were committed to a kind of proto-interdisciplinarity is well known, and digital advances are poised to capitalize on that promise. Exploring these links to clarify the diversity as well as the interconnectedness of fin-de-siècle literary and artistic cultures is a rich area for current and future research, but some practical factors make such work more difficult. Part of the difficulty is due to the discipline-based training of scholars, which tends to focus on the art historical *or* the literary, with little truly interdisciplinary research plumbing the connections or engaging methodologically with both. Other obstacles – such as access to rare works – can be more readily addressed through digital means. The digitization of periodicals, both from the exploding Victorian mass media (as in the British Newspaper Archive, which has digitized over fifty million pages) or niche artisan productions (as in *Yellow Nineties 2.0*; see Chapter 15 of this volume), has given access to an enormously larger audience than was possible previously, including those outside of the reach of archives. In other ways beyond mere access, the digital landscape proposes routes to maximize the potential of the unity of the arts vaunted by fin-de-siècle creators. Fine art objects, furniture, art manufacture, and even late-Victorian ephemera are frequently held in museum collections; even in instances where high-quality digital artifacts (e.g., digital images, 3D digital scans) have been produced, they are often subject to the proprietary restrictions of collections management systems, where even scant metadata (searchable text appended to the digital images) is frequently inaccessible to the researcher. Emerging digital protocols, though, promise to unlock digital images and thus these collections, in part by creating a platform for extensive metadata. The collaboratively developed International Image Interoperability Framework (IIIF), and the organizations contributing to the framework (e.g., linked.art) offer models for connecting scholars, artifacts, and knowledge to allow for a more comprehensive, accurate understanding of these objects and thus of late-Victorian artistic and literary culture. This chapter first explores the literary/visual/artistic intersections of the 1890s before turning to consider the ways that digital affordances can both simulate and illuminate those fin-de-siècle intersections, complementing previous modes of thinking about the 1890s while aiming to give us a richer sense of the varied visual culture of the period. Like ideals about the unity of the arts, these new transmedial approaches offer enormous promise but are not without their challenges and limitations.

Fin-de-Siècle Contexts

Artistic culture of the 1890s might anticipate the digital networks of the twenty-first century, but it does so through a deep engagement with the distant past. The origins of the British fin-de-siècle idea of the "unity of the arts" date from medieval and Renaissance models (especially the presence of artisan guilds), but their more immediate forebears arose in the mid-nineteenth century with the Pre-Raphaelite Brotherhood (PRB). By the 1890s, the mid-century genesis of the PRB might have seemed a distant memory: many of the founding members who were still alive had slipped into the seeming complacency of mainstream conventionality, and painting's avant-garde had moved well beyond the jewel-toned stunners by Dante Gabriel Rossetti that have since come to typify the movement. Nevertheless, another of Rossetti's hallmarks proved more resilient: working across multiple media – the visual and textual arts – producing poetry, illustrations, and paintings often drawn from the same sources or sharing titles and themes. This kind of textual/visual interface found an early, signal expression in Edward Moxon's 1857 illustrated edition of Tennyson's verse: in it, Rossetti along with John Everett Millais and William Holman Hunt – all founding members of the PRB – created illustrations that were as fresh in their visual vocabulary as they were revolutionary in their engagement with the poems they ostensibly illustrated. In retrospect, William Michael Rossetti cited the accurate depiction of nature and resistance to the conventions of academy-taught painting as the most significant of the Brotherhood's few ideological imperatives,[12] but perhaps more influential for the artists and movements that developed in the decades following the PRB's height was this commitment to a fundamental interdisciplinarity. Related complementary ideals – of the equality of the arts, the elevation of craft and design to the level of the fine arts, and the value of working across the text/image divide – did not come into their fullest fruition until the 1890s, as evidenced across an extraordinarily wide range of material objects, books, journals, fashion, civic and corporate institutions that privileged art, text, and craft in equal measure.

Among the best known of these efforts is William Morris's Kelmscott Press (1891–98), a press committed to the book-as-art, ensuring that the material aspects of the book were given the same attention and care as the textual contents. Bespoke fonts, intricate illustrations, and idiosyncratic typesetting were complemented by hand-laid papers and the finest bindings. It was and remains a high-water mark in bookcraft, expanding significantly on the example of Moxon's work of some forty years prior

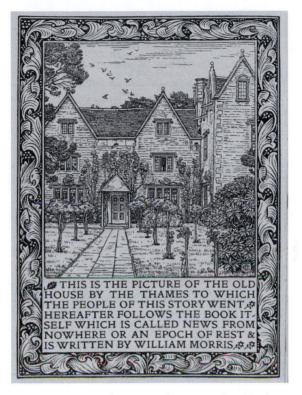

Figure 16.2   William Morris, frontispiece from *News from Nowhere* (Kelmscott Press, 1894). Public domain image courtesy of the New York Public Library. https://digitalcollections.nypl.org/items/8c63b298-401d-cca3-e040-e00a18063db8.

by raising binding, letterpress, and typeface design with illustration and text as equal elements of design and production (see Figure 16.2). The final products were incredible objects, and their cost ensured their exclusivity. When in 1899, a complete set of Kelmscott editions was first sold at auction, a gushing press detailed the sale: they were the "most remarkable volumes, it may be said, from a typographical point of view, produced this century," according to one account, which notes that "the majority of these fascinating books have doubled in market value since the previous year, some indeed have trebled, while most of them are now worth at least three times their issue price, and even more."[13] Still today, on the rare occasion that copies of the Kelmscott Chaucer become available, they list at over £100,000.[14] Termed the "magnum opus" of the press, copies were originally offered in 1896 for £21, already a princely sum.[15]

Other, less well-known manifestations of post-Pre-Raphaelite art and craft pushed the boundaries of generic divisions more fully, expanding the remit of the arts into more niche as well as more popular directions. The 1890s was also the decade when William Morris's more commercial enterprise, Morris & Co. (1875–1940), hit its creative stride, producing wallpapers, fabrics, and carpets that were sold, for example, at fashionable store Liberty's of London; when the Arts and Crafts Exhibition Society (1875–1935) reached its zenith; when artists Charles Ricketts and Charles Shannon undertook a cross-pollinated venture through their Vale Press (1896–1904), which published fine art books and magazines, often illustrated with their own idiosyncratic designs; and when architect, typographer, poet, and designer Herbert Horne would develop the foundations for the archive-based art history that shaped the study of art throughout the twentieth century, to name only a few examples.

Horne was, along with Selwyn Image of the *"Credo in unam Artem"* and architect Arthur Heygate Mackmurdo, one of the three founding members of the Century Guild. The group, like the Pre-Raphaelite Brotherhood, claimed no ideological imperative. Their organ, the *Century Guild Hobby Horse* (1884, 1886–94), embodied their ethos. It was a beautiful object, and with its hand-laid paper, bespoke headpieces, and idiosyncratic, medievalesque cover (designed by Image), it was a direct antecedent to Morris's Kelmscott Press (see Figure 16.3). But it was also the mouthpiece for the group's artistic philosophy, often rendered in flat-footed prose that makes clear that wordsmithing was not their primary occupation, giving voice to the earnestness of their commitment to the unity of the arts: "a very charming publication," one reviewer wrote, "in which an aesthetic company of artists, poets, and literary men in general embody their views—in very large type—of the unity of the arts."[16] In the inaugural issue, Mackmurdo devotes the opening essay to defining the group's aims:

> The common spirit that animates our work, the same fierce expectation that impels us each beyond the prose boundaries of simple craftsmanship, and keeps us undeviating in our art's progressive course, together weave the mind girdles that bind each to all. It being then, but unity of sentiment that bands us together—not fast fettering creed, or preventive code of practice— each stands free and firm to express this sentiment as he chooses; each stands alone responsible for the literary or pictorial form in which this spirit becomes incarnated.[17]

United then in spirit but free to follow their various artistic aims, the members of the Century Guild pursued architecture, stained glass, textile,

Figure 16.3   Selwyn Image, cover of the *Century Guild Hobby Horse* (1884). Public
domain image courtesy of the Getty Institute.

and furniture design, in addition to the verse and prose published in the
Hobby Horse. Though the Guild's three members were thus practicing
craftsmen, the outcome of their handicraft (as opposed to their literary
ventures) is not always clear from the letterpress of the journal. The closest

representation of their applied craftmanship can be found in the few pages
of advertisements that appear at the end of issues, listing their own work
and that of Guild-approved crafts. This context amplifies the commercial
aspect of production as opposed to the artistic.

An 1893 volume of essays by members of the Arts and Crafts
Exhibition society is more helpful in illuminating the range of media
covered by those devoted to this "unity," with pieces on – among other
things – textiles, decorative painting and design, wallpaper, metal work,
stone and wood carving, furniture, stained and "table" glass, printing,
bookbinding, book illustration and decoration, lace, embroidery, dye-
ing as an art, furniture, carving, intarsia and inlaid wood, cast iron, and
mural painting.[18] Among the contributors to the volume was Walter
Crane (1845–1915), whose body of work typifies the range of the 1890s
visuality far better than Aubrey Beardsley's. Like Morris and the members of the Century Guild, Crane worked across a remarkable range of
media. The son of artists, Crane was an accomplished engraver (including works by the PRB), painter, and designer of ceramics, wallpaper,
textiles, and stained glass. His biggest contribution to 1890s visual
culture was, however, as an illustrator of children's books, in which
he incorporated elements of the medieval illustration that inspired the
Arts and Crafts movement (to which he belonged) as well as more
contemporary visual influences, including Japonisme and – in later
works – elements of the burgeoning Art Nouveau. Consider two of
Crane's illustrations from the same period (see Figures. 16.4 and 16.5):
The Shepheard's Calender (1898) adopts the signature elements of the
Arts and Crafts style: hand-lettered font with cramped kerning; intricate, baroque border, with highly detailed natural elements; classical
and folkloric imagery; and an illustrated capital. An invitation card from
the following year maintains the monochrome and hand-lettering, but in
style seems decades away: spare in its line and sparce in detail, the font
anticipates the clean, sans-serif simplicity of the Art Deco style. The falling
crane – a bird long used by the artist for obvious reasons – is elegant in its
Japanese-influenced line. That they are both produced by the same artist
speaks to the variability of style of the period and the diversity of influence
(even within the same medium, by the same hand) informing visual arts of
the 1890s.

That there were other, highly contrasting movements in art and design
running concurrent with the Arts and Crafts movement was not lost on its
fiercest advocates. In the preface of the aforementioned Arts and Crafts
essay collection, William Morris reflected on his own artistic school (that

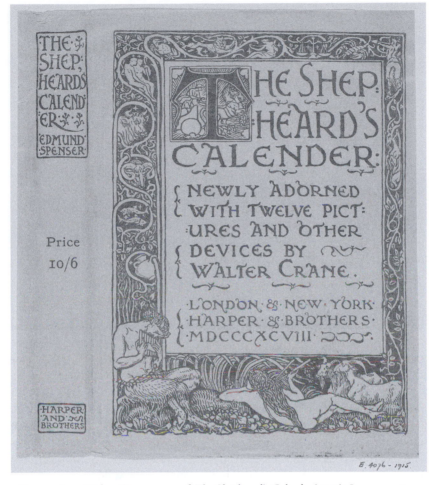

Figure 16.4   Walter Crane, cover of *The Shepheard's Calender* (1898). Image courtesy Victoria & Albert Museum, ©Victoria and Albert Museum, London, Department of Engraving, Illustration and Design, Accessions 1915. Given by Emslie John Horniman.

of the Arts and Crafts) in contrast to that of the Impressionists, whose work gained steam in France through the 1870s and 1880s: he acknowledged "a school of artists belonging to this decade who set forth that beauty is not an essential part of art; which they consider rather as an instrument for the statement of fact, or an exhibition of the artist's intellectual observation or sleight of hand."[19] To be sure, the Impressionist approach – "a school which is pushing rather than drifting

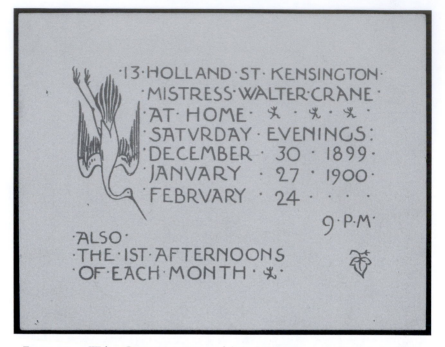

Figure 16.5   Walter Crane, invitation card (1899). Image courtesy Victoria & Albert Museum, © Victoria and Albert Museum, London, Department of Engraving, Illustration and Design, Accessions 1915. Given by Emslie John Horniman.

into the domain of the empirical science of to-day" – is at odds with his notion of Arts and Crafts – "which can only work through its observation of an art which was once organic, but which died centuries ago" (Morris, "Preface," ix–x). Selwyn Image also pointedly referenced the Impressionists in his "Unity of the Arts" lecture, as summarised by Wilde:

> The result at which [Image] ultimately arrived was this: the Impressionists, with their frank artistic acceptance of form and colour, as things absolutely satisfying in themselves, have produced very beautiful work, but painting has something more to give us than the mere visible aspect of things. The lofty spiritual visions of William Blake, and the marvellous romance of Dante Gabriel Rossetti, can find their perfect expression in painting; every mood has its colour, and every dream has its form.[20]

The "unity of art" as conceived by these artists, then, not only tolerates but depends upon an engagement with text or with the past. For his part, Morris concluded with some chagrin that variety of style and mode that he terms "genuine eclecticism" is "all that we can expect under modern civilization" (Morris, "Preface," x).

"Unity of the arts," in other words, might not in theory have meant a single unified style, though in practice the Arts and Crafts movement was most sympathetic to the ideal, with its inchoate multimedia orientation and its intended inclusivity. But ideological and practical tensions limited the full expression of those ideals. The skepticism meted out to the Impressionists was not the only limitation: unity was countered by eclecticism, exclusivity was countered by socialist ideals, and equity of access overwhelmed by a few predominating male voices. In the Arts and Crafts essay collection, for example, of the thirty-five essays only four are written by women: three are by May Morris (daughter of William) and one was written by Mary E. Turner.

In fact, women played a role far greater than is generally acknowledged in fin-de-siècle visual culture, including Arts and Crafts and related movements.[21] Digitized artworks can amplify their work by making it more accessible, but mere accessibility can risk replicating some of the biases that kept women's artwork marginalized in its own time. The *Yellow Book* itself makes the case for embracing an expanded notion of the many modes of illustration and design in circulation, yet illustrations by women remain scarce through all the early issues.[22] It is not until the seventh volume, October 1895, which featured pictures by the Cornwall-based Newlyn School (though this was less a formal site of instruction than a group of likeminded artists), that more than one artwork by a woman appears. In the ninth volume of the magazine, dated April 1896, all of the images that appear are by artists of the Birmingham School, a fact which helped to usher a significant increase of women artists into the pages.

Founded in the 1840s, the Birmingham School of Art expanded to become the first municipal art school in England in 1877.[23] From its inception, it drew from the ideological underpinnings of William Morris and the aesthetic underpinnings of Pre-Raphaelite legacies. The school was committed to instruction of handicraft as well as the fine arts, with particular strengths in jewelry design and book binding. It was also, to a degree unusual in its time, committed to the instruction of women. In the issue of the *Yellow Book* that made a feature of Birmingham School of Art illustrators, seven women artists contributed eight of the illustrations, showcasing the school as one of the premier sites of gender equality in art education. Of the seven, the majority adopted overtly literary subjects, despite the *Yellow Book*'s editorial philosophy that valued text and image equally and its insistence that it would not, like other journals, subjugate the visual to the literary. Taking the works together, the influence of Morris and of PRB notions of the relationship between text and image (and the concept of the "unity of the arts") are immediately evident, a starting point but not a final destination. Florence Rudland's illustration of Tennyson's "The Lady of Shalott" revived an evergreen Pre-Raphaelite theme and visually calls back to Holman Hunt's illustration of the poem for the Moxon Tennyson, though her use of black and the heavily stylized wood texture mark it as the work of the Birmingham School. Evelyn Holden offered "Binnorie, O Binnorie," a staging of a folk poem in an image that similarly recalls Kelmscott offerings, with her hand-lettered, tightly kerned text and innovative textures representing needlework (see Figure 16.6). As I have argued elsewhere, Celia Levetus's illustration of young women in a field reading a volume of Herrick's verse treads the line between sweetly pastoral – with the women in their child-like smocked gowns standing in a flower-strewn country field – and the edgy – as they are reading a volume that would have featured poems with frank sexual imagery as well as sacred verse.[24] Other contributions push the book/image boundary in different directions. Georgiana Gaskin offered a bookplate designed for Isobel Cave (a fellow illustrator herself). Gaskin was an accomplished illustrator – evident from the bookplate she contributed to the *Yellow Book*'s ninth volume (see Figure 16.7) – but in addition was, with her husband Arthur, among the foremost jewelry designers of the period. Their jewelry, as distinct from the artwork of either, is designed in a high Art Nouveau mode.

Gaskin, Holden, Levetus, and the other Birmingham School artisans earned their appearances in the *Yellow Book* through their affiliation with the art school, and their work is accessible online today because the *Yellow Book* is accessible online today. One enormously important illustrator whose work was not so featured in the *Yellow Book,* and is often excluded from accounts of fin-de-siècle illustration, is Kate Greenaway (1846–1901). Best known for her illustrations of young women and children wearing anachronistic Regency or Queen Anne dress, Greenaway tended to evoke a past in her illustrations that today seems idealized and nostalgic, the industrial and social innovations of her own period scarcely evident in her works (outside of their mode of mass reproduction). It is a vision of Britishness that inspired children's dress in its own time and proved remarkably persistent as a visual cue for book illustration, and children's illustration especially. Simplistic though her work might appear, she trained with leading artists of her day, including

Figure 16.6 Evelyn Holden, "Binnorie, O Binnorie," *Yellow Book* 9 (April 1896): 164.
Public domain image courtesy *Yellow Nineties 2.0*, Toronto Metropolitan University
Centre for Digital Humanities, 2020, https://1890s.ca/yb9-holden-binnorie.

Figure 16.7 Georgie (Mrs. A. J.) Gaskin, "A Book Plate for Isobel Verney Cave," *Yellow Book* 9 (April 1896): 257. Public domain image courtesy *Yellow Nineties 2.0*, Toronto Metropolitan University Centre for Digital Humanities, 2020, https://1890s.ca/yb9-mrs-gaskin-bookplate.

Edward Burne-Jones and Walter Crane. And though the soft coloration, lightness of line, and idyllic content choices of her work seem at first to share little with the overtly aesthetic or decadent stylings of Ricketts, Shannon, or Beardsley, it does have distinct imbrication with the Aesthetic Movement: her works speak to the Artistic dress moment in that, like the medieval fashion invoked in post-PRB paintings, their retrogressive design was simultaneously progressive, allowing for the jettisoning of the corset. So popular were her clothing designs for children that they were sold in Liberty's.[25] Moreover, when considered alongside some of the compositions from the Birmingham School issue of the *Yellow Book*, it is clear that Greenaway's illustrations draw on the same thematic choices as works by Levetus or Holden. Reasons for the exclusion of Greenaway being taken seriously as a fin-de-siècle artist include her gender, the apparent conventionality and conservativism of the content choices of her illustration, and, to be sure, the mass popularity of her work: it was antidecadent and thus anti-Yellow, having more in common with Walter Crane's oeuvre than with Beardsley's. She may have written the copy for the books she illustrated, but she did not formally identify with groups – Arts and Crafts or a school of Art – that would help to establish affiliation.

In a sneering 1893 review, G. R. Carpenter refers to the "fundamental unity of the arts, which it is now the fashion, following Mr. Pater, to introduce with a specious languor into the criticism of any subject."[26] But if the idea could be dismissed as a mere "fashion," it was a remarkably resilient one. Decades after appearing in the *Yellow Book*, Celia Levetus – now writing under her married name of Celia Nicholson – was still compelled by the notion. She wrote of the artist Elsie Henderson's etchings, "For who shall say this is an art, that a craft? Given a wide and questing spirit, the terms may well become interchangeable."[27] She went on, anticipating a future where this kind of unity could revolutionize the art scene: "The experimental mind rejects, of necessity, all established limitations of any craft, seeking, pioneer-wise, to arrive at new methods and effects; attaining empirical results which may broaden, if not revolutionize, existing conditions" (Nicholson, "Etchings," 335). Such a revolution of "existing conditions" of art production and reception, which was anticipated by models from the quattrocento past and revived in the 1890s through the Arts and Crafts, decadent, and related movements, still has yet to be fully realized, though the digital revolution offered a new means of achieving it.

The Promise of the Digital

If it was the fashion of the 1890s to introduce the "unity of the arts" into any discussion of fin-de-siècle artistic culture, just over a century later the digital likely presented a similar source of an alluring, if nebulous promise of working across media. And, as manifestations of digital scholarship in recent decades demonstrate, the range and scope of digital technologies and academic methodologies offer the means to recuperate and restore the eclecticism of that earlier period and exploit more fully affordances of a true "unity of the arts." For example, interoperability, the prospect of formatting data and metadata to ensure open access and usability across platforms or applications, is one analogue to the multimedia, multimodal artistic ideals of the 1890s. Echoing Oscar Wilde's notion that "all the arts have the same message, and speak the same language, though with different tongues," interoperable digital artifacts can be employed by different applications or users to different, individualized ends. Yet some of the most important aspects of 1890s visual culture are complicated rather than clarified by the digital. The exquisite material qualities that make art press productions such as the Kelmscott editions or the *Century Guild Hobby Horse* so special resist digitization: the touch of the paper, the impressions from a hand press, the feel of fine vellum bindings are tactile qualities that can be elided in even the highest resolution scan. Niche publications such as the *Hobby Horse*, not to mention the more costly Kelmscott volumes, were never intended for mass readership and thus reached a very different audience in their own time than today's open-access digitized editions can reach. Nontextual objects that typify the multimedia work of artists tend to be held in museum collections, subject to proprietary or closed search engines or catalogues. The ideal of interoperable, open-access digital artifacts is hampered by market forces and the practicalities of the institutions that tend to create them.

Within Victorian studies, digital engagement has tended to be defined by discrete projects as opposed to methodologies, and straightforward digitization is only one aspect, albeit the primary aspect, of the potential of the digital to make good on the ideals of the fin de siècle. In 2016, Adrian Wisnicki surveyed the field of what he termed "Digital Victorian Studies," noting that his focus was on large-scale, open-access scholarly projects.[28] Some of the projects Wisknicki describes remain active (e.g., the British Library's *Discovering Literature: Romantics and Victorians* resource; *BRANCH*, an open-access site featuring peer-reviewed articles, which has now been merged into the larger COVE enterprise[29]; or indeed *Yellow Nineties 2.0*[30]), while others seem to have been halted (e.g., the

Periodical Poetry Index) or retired. Other legacy projects, such as *The Rossetti Archive*[31] remain archived online despite no longer being updated; they maintain a digital presence through static archives or by working with other online projects to share data.[32] More to the point, the text/image/ object divide that fin-de-siècle artists sought to complicate has particular resonance for the digital sphere. All digital artifacts are ultimately code/text based. As is clear from Wisnicki's overview, early large-scale projects were almost all text-focused, with scans of manuscript or printed pages offered as a supplement to textual content (the quality of image scans, and the limitations of those scans, even in archive content providers' databases, is testament to the persistence of this dynamic).

Calls for interoperability, very much like 1890s calls for unity, indicate a desire to break down formal or conventional barriers to recognize shared goals across media. If we look to more foundational aspects of digital visual culture – not the content-focused projects but the format of digital artifacts themselves – we can see where this promise might be fulfilled. From its inception, for example, the IIIF has been framed less as a set of metadata protocols than as a community of users and programmers working to define a shared set of digital ontologies: deciding what information is useful, and in what format. Writing in 2015, Stuart Snydman, Rob Sanderson, and Tom Cramer – then all at Stanford – described the context that led to its development. Noting that "images are the primary carriers of global cultural heritage, and digital images are the medium by which important artifacts are shared with and interpreted by the widest international audience," the authors insist that "the infrastructures we build to store and manage digital images, as well as the online web applications that we build to deliver them, remain monolithic and institution specific: our images are trapped in virtual silos."[33] Those silos, which the authors term "walled gardens of technology," inhibit users being able to work seamlessly with images across multiple sites or platforms. IIIF was collaboratively developed with those working in cultural heritage sectors to define the kinds of metadata that would help increase usability and access, while facilitating curation, academic scholarship, and audience engagement. Rich metadata, formatted consistently regardless of the original medium of an artwork or its physical site in a collection, could make evident otherwise hidden links between works and collections.

How these goals might manifest in practice remains murkier, limited by mundanities of bureaucracy and institutional structure and finances as much as by technology. In a chapter in a 2018 collection on digital humanities partnerships, museum professionals detail the ways that curatorial and collections management staff of museums can enhance the metadata of their digital collections in order to facilitate collaboration with others outside of the museum context. Their summary of the then-current situation holds true some five years later:

> While the potential for collaboration between [Digital Humanities] projects and [Galleries, Libraries, Archives, and Museums] exists, a lack of cross-disciplinary methods for creating and sharing metadata is a significant barrier. Scholars and practitioners in both sectors acknowledge that sharing descriptive metadata practices is necessary; however, there are very few sustainable *and* generalizable methods for doing so.[34]

The very next chapter in the collection reiterates the issue: "A clear, focused emphasis on *collaboration* and *interoperability*, between both institutions and technical approaches, can provide significant relief from this conundrum" – the conundrum being siloed data and related practices – "and can provide value for organizational members and technological end-users alike."[35] Agreement in principal on the ideal does not ensure its implementation.

To turn to an attempt at implementation, Joris van Zundert wrote about Mirador, one open-source image viewer that allows for (among other things) zooming and annotation of high-resolution images, noting one of the myriad possibilities the platform affords: "In the case that a collection had properly added metadata, Mirador will also instantly display an index/contents, if so configured."[36] The rub, as van Zundert stated, is the condition of "properly added metadata," and its configuration. Exactly what metadata is required and in what format will vary by user. Van Zundert was considering Mirador and IIIF in the context of the scholarly editing of manuscripts, one of its more common applications, taken up with particular zeal by scholars of medieval manuscripts, where the digital image of the work adds inestimably to the information available to a user. But the information needed for the medieval manuscript editor is not necessarily the same as that required by an art historian, or a literary historian, looking at the same object.

One recent hope for addressing the sheer variety of interest and desires for digital artifacts is linked.art, an open-source community devoted to defining metadata protocols for IIIF. Echoing the language of IIIF, the linked.art project describes itself as "a community of museum and cultural heritage professionals collaborating to define a metadata application profile (the model) for describing cultural heritage, and the technical means for conveniently interacting with it."[37] Ideally, these practitioners, scholars, and coders could define a shared vocabulary for metadata – from the kind of data referred to as "tombstone" information – creator(s), media, date and place of composition – to more detailed provenance or exhibition history, to annotations or commentary; this would then, via linked open data structures, be accessible via searches regardless of visualization platform.

For an example of what this might look like in practice, we can consider the now-retired (though still online) *Rossetti Archive*, conceived in 1993 and completed in 2008, overseen by Jerome McGann. This extraordinary resource brings together all of the extant works of Dante Gabriel Rossetti, with high-resolution digital scans of images and notes on provenance and holding institutions. For Rossetti's 1871 oil on canvas *Water Willow*,[38] for example, the site lists two background studies (as printed in a journal), a chalk sketch (held at the Birmingham Museum and Art Gallery), the final work (held at the Delaware Museum of Art), multiple prints, and two landscape sketches; all told, sixteen artifacts, many with supplementary commentary or additional reproductions linked. The labor of compiling these many instances of *Water Willow*, annotating them, and providing scholarly commentary was performed by *Rossetti Archive* contributors, and the rich connections between those works are made evident only on that website: visit any of the Delaware Art Gallery's or the Birmingham Museum of Art's webpages and there is no information linking one work to the other. As long as the *Rossetti Archive* continues to function, the deep context of *Water Willow* will, one imagines, remain accessible. But nearly all of that connecting information could, in theory, be contained in the metadata of any of the digital images through IIIF, searchable by any user without the need for a separate website to present the links. No doubt, the scholarly insight of an editor or curator could enhance and explain that metadata, but protocols such as IIIF offer the prospect of sustaining information by attaching it to the artifact itself, ensuring its interoperability and its resilience. Similarly, connections between media – for example, William Morris's *Kennet* pattern worked out in design, in wallpaper, in textile, and as used in furniture – could be made without having to seek out individual instances across countless collections or digital repositories. Large-scale efforts by organizations such as Europeana (https://pro.europeana.eu) are seeking to unite digital collections across national boundaries for exactly these purposes.

Digital tools offer the tantalizing hope that we could maximize the network model that was imagined by the Arts and Crafts guilds of the 1880s and 1890s.[39] But the scale of the enterprise, and the methodological and practical limitations that inhibit the realization of the full potential of those possibilities, in many ways harks back to the limitations that inhibited their realization at the fin de siècle. The affordances of the tech carry the promise of incredible possibility, but it depends ultimately on the allocation of resources – time, human resources, data preservation, interpersonal and interinstitutional collaboration – that almost invariably depend upon institutions to make it possible. Digital tools, in other words, already exist that could maximize the ability for scholars, students, and the public to make connections between artifacts, to adopt them in their own applications (pedagogical, scholarly, popular). But while the tech exists, its application remains hampered by the usual issues that undermine collaborative, cross-disciplinary research in analogue contexts. These issues – inequity of access; resource limitations; ideological, sociopolitical, or personal biases – were, as this chapter has tried to demonstrate, existent in the visual arts and hand-icraft culture of the 1890s. Yet just as the difficulty of achieving a full "unity of the arts" did not dissuade the shared aspirations of that fin-de-siècle artistic culture, the practical limitations of maximizing the potential of digital interoperability are no reason to abandon its promise.

Notes

1 Oscar Wilde, "The Unity of the Arts," *Pall Mall Gazette*, December 12, 1887, 13; in *The Complete Works of Oscar Wilde: Journalism Part II*, eds. John Stokes and Mark W. Turner (Oxford: Oxford University Press, 2019), vii, 33–34.

2 Ibid., note on lines 7–9, 356.

3 In "School of Giorgione" (originally published 1877), Pater famously wrote that "*All art constantly aspires towards the condition of music*," separating the "matter" of the poetry or the visual arts from its form. The "matter" "should be nothing without the form, the spirit, of the handling, that this form, this mode of handling, should become an end in itself, should penetrate every part of the matter: this is what all art constantly strives after, and achieves in different degrees." Walter Pater, *The Renaissance: Studies in Art and Poetry*, ed. Donald Hill (Berkeley, CA: University of California Press, 1980), 106.

4 "What Sir F. Leighton Left Out," *Pall Mall Gazette*, December 4, 1888, 1.

5 "Notes on News," *East and South Devon Advertiser*, February 8, 1896, 6.

6 "Literary Notes, News, and Echoes," *Pall Mall Gazette*, October 20, 1888, 6.

7 "Arts and Crafts Exhibition," *Manchester Courier* (Suppl.), October 1, 1898.

8 Melanie McDonagh, "Aubrey Beardsley Review: Dazzling Originality in Impish Genius's Seven-Year Itch," *Evening Standard* 2 March 2020 https://www.standard.co.uk/culture/aubrey-beardsley-review-dazzling-originality-in-impish-geniuss-seven-year-etch-a4375686.html (Accessed January 28, 2022)

9 Laura Cumming, "Aubrey Beardsley; Among the Trees," *Guardian* 8 March 2020, https://www.theguardian.com/artanddesign/2020/mar/08/aubrey-beardsley-tate-britain-review-among-the-trees-hayward-gallery (Accessed January 28, 2022).

10 Tate Britain, "Aubrey Beardsley" exhibition site, www.tate.org.uk/whats-on/tate-britain/aubrey-beardsley (accessed January 28, 2022).

11 Max Beerbohm archly declared "I belong to the Beardsley period" in "Be it Cosiness" (*Pageant* (1896) 230–35 [236]), and Osbert Burdett's 1925 study of the fin de siècle was titled *The Beardsley Period*, taking its cue from Beerbohm. More recent references to the "Yellow Nineties" include "Selling the Yellow Nineties: The *Yellow Book* and the *Savoy*" in Koenraad Claes's *The Late-Victorian Little Magazine* (Edinburgh: Edinburgh University Press, 2018) and the web resource *Yellow Nineties 2.0*, https://1890s.ca.

12 See William Michael Rossetti, "Preface" to the reprint of the *Germ* (Elliot Stock, 1901), 5–35 (6–7).

13 "Sale of Kelmscott Press Books," *Dundee Evening Telegraph*, February 16, 1899, 3.

14 At the time of writing, used bookseller aggregator abebooks.co.uk lists a copy of the Kelmscott Chaucer, often considered to be the press's finest work, for £124,726.84.

15 "The Kelmscott Press," *Sheffield Independent*, November 25, 1899, 5.

16 "Here and There," *West Somerset Free Press*, February 19, 1887, 6.

17 Arthur Heygate Mackmurdo, "The Guild Flag's Unfurling," *Century Guild Hobby Horse* 1 (1884): 2–13.

18 Members of the Arts and Crafts Exhibition Society, *Arts and Crafts Essays*, (London: Rivington, Percival, and Co., 1893).

19 William Morris, "Preface," in *Arts and Crafts Essays*, (London: Rivington, Percival, and Co., 1893), v–xiii (viii).

20 Wilde, "The Unity of the Arts," *Pall Mall Gazette*, December 12, 1887, vii, 34.

21 This imbalance is beginning to be addressed in works such as Zoë Thomas's *Woman Art Workers and the Arts and Crafts Movement* (Manchester: Manchester University Press, 2020), which explores the Women's Guild of Arts, begun in 1907 in response to the predominance of the Art Workers' Guild, which had since its inception in 1884 been open to men only.

22 Vol. 4 features "Plein Air" by "Miss Sumner" and Vol. 6 "Padstow" by Gertrude Prideaux-Brune. While some scholarship has been devoted to the role of women writers in the journal, little has been said about the work of women artists featured in it; see, for example, Sally Ledger's "Wilde Women and *The Yellow Book*: The Sexual Politics of Aestheticism and Decadence" in *English Literature in Transition: 1880–1920* 50, no. 1 (2007): 5–26; or Linda Hughes's "Women Poets and Contested Spaces in *The Yellow Book*" in *Studies in English Literature, 1500–1900* 44, no. 4 (2004): 849–72.

23 It still operates today in its Victorian Gothic building designed by J. H. Chamberlain; it is now affiliated with Birmingham City University.

24 See "Rediscovering Celia Anna Levetus," *Burlington Magazine* 160 (January 2018), 31–37. Precious little has been written in recent decades on the Birmingham School. One exception is Simon Cooke's "The Birmingham School of Illustration," *Victorian Web* (2020), https://victorianweb.org/art/illustration/birmingham.html.

25 See Rebecca Perry, "Girlies and Grannies: Kate Greenaway and Children's Dress in Late Nineteenth-Century Britain," in *Fashion Forward*, eds. Alissa de Wit-Paul and Mira Crouch (Leiden: Brill, 2011), 111–21.

26 G. R. Carpenter, "Three Critics: Mr. Howells, Mr. Moore, and Mr. Wilde," *Proceedings of the Society of the Arts* (1891): 338.

27 C. A. Nicholson, "On the Etchings of Elsie Henderson," *Print Collector's Quarterly* (1928): 336.

28 Adrian Wisnicki, "Digital Victorian Studies Today," *Victorian Literature and Culture* 44, no. 4 (2016): 975–92 (976).

29 *BRANCH*: Britain, Representation, and Nineteenth-Century History, ed. Dino Franco Felluga, branchcollective.org.

30 *Yellow Nineties 2.0*, ed. Lorraine Janzen Kooistra, http://1890s.ca.

31 *The Complete Writings and Pictures of Dante Gabriel Rossetti* (*The Rossetti Archive*), ed. Jerome McGann, www.rossettiarchive.org.

32 Content from the *Rossetti Archive*, for example, has recently been integrated into the COVE project, ensuring that content from the earlier site can be accessed by later users, but also combined with other content, creating new applications and reuse options for the digital content.

33 Stuart Snydman, Robert Sanderson and Tom Cramer, "The International Image Interoperabiilty Framework (IIIF): A Community and Technology Approach for Web-based Images," https://stacks.stanford.edu/file/druid: df650pk4327/2015ARCHIVING_IIIF.pdf (accessed January 13, 2022).

34 Kristen M. Schuster and Sarah L. Gillis, "Digital Humanities and Image Metadata: Improving Access through Shared Practices," *Digital Humanities, Libraries, and Partnerships* (Amsterdam: Elsevier, 2018), 107–23 (108–09) (italics in the original).

35 Jeffrey P. Emanuel, "Stitching Together Technology for the Digital Humanities with the International Image Interoperability Framework (IIIF)," "Digital Humanities and Image Metadata: Improving Access through Shared Practices," *Digital Humanities, Libraries, and Partnerships* (Amsterdam: Elsevier, 2018), 125–35 (125) (italics in the original).

36 Joris van Zundert, "On Not Writing a Review about Mirador: Mirador, IIIF, and the Epistemological Gains of Distributed Digital Scholarly Resources," *Digital Medievalist* 11, no. 1 (2018), 1–48 (5). http://doi.org/10.16995/dm.78.

37 "About", *Linked Art*, https://linked.art/about.

38 "Instances of Water Willow," *Rossetti Archive*, ed. Jerome McGann, www.rossettiarchive.org/docs/s226.rawcollection.html. The *Archive* was an early testing ground for NINES, an online aggregator of nineteenth-century content and scholarship, and much of its data has now been migrated to COVE. For more on the theory behind the project, see McGann, "Imagining What you Don't Know," http://citeseerx.ist.psu.edu/viewdoc/ download?doi=10.1.1.457.5024&rep=rep1&type=pdf, or Andrew Stauffer, "The Rossetti Archive: Methodologies and Praxis," *RISSH* 33 (1997): 353.

39 For a discussion of the ways that Arts and Crafts movement anticipated network models, see Rebecca N. Mitchell, "*The Century Guild Hobby Horse*: Crafting Generic Networks in Fin-de-Siècle England," *PBSA* 11, no.1 (2018): 75–104.

Index

1890s (decade), 1–4, 7, 118, 194, 246–47, 264
  conservatism of, 246–47, 249, 250, 251–55, 260
  cosmopolitanism and, 6–9
  ecocriticism and, 133, 174
  gender and, 6–9
  history and, 4–6, 7, 177–78, 208–11, 223, 266, 332
  media ecology of, 250
  nature and, 165, 170, 171
  patriotism and, 255–60
  periodical culture of, 15–17
  realism and, 78–79
  religion and, 99, 285–87, 301
  sexuality and, 3, 6–9, 78
  spatial positioning of, 2, 4
  temporal positioning of, 1, 3

Abramović, Marina, 269
adventure fiction, 21, 61, 78
aestheticism, 14, 66, 68, 112, 113, 114, 121, 122, 126
  class and, 233
  cosmopolitanism and, 67, 69
  ecocriticism and, 112
  ethics of, 10
  industrialization and, 180
  japonisme and, 125–27
  morality and, 291
  nature and, 124
  politics and, 248
  religion and, 289
  science and, 293–94
  synesthesia and, 127
  theater and, 279
  urbanization and, 133
Afghanistan, 24, 28, 31
Agathocleous, Tanya, 10, 99
agency
  gender and, 274
  human, 133, 171

nature and, 176, 177
nonhuman, 189, 195, 198
race and, 28
Albuquerque, Alfonso, 80
Alger, William Rounseville, *Poetry of the East*, 101–2
Allan, Maud, 270
Allen, Grant, 69
  Woman Who Did, The, 298
American Library Association, Religious Books Roundtable, 108
Ames, Mrs. Ernest, *ABC for Baby Patriots, An*, 27
anarchism, 236, 249
Anderson, Katharine, 180
Anglican Church, 286, 288
Anthropocene, 14, 123, 148, 170, 171, 173–77, 178, 181–82, *See also* ecocriticism; nature
anthropology, 83–85
Anti-Jacobin (periodical), 251
Anti-vivisection Act (1876), 292
Arata, Stephen, 9, 21
Archer, William, 251
Ardis, Ann, 7
Arista, Noelani, 42
Arnold, Edwin, 105, 106, 107
  Light of Asia, The, 98
Arnold, Matthew, 114
Arrhenius, Svante, 173
Art Deco, 336
Art Nouveau, 336, 340
artifice, 116–17, 133, 170, 171–72, 233, *See also* decadence; nature
arts
  conservatism and, 343
  digitization of, 339, 340
  gender and, 339–44
  past and, 340
  socialism and, 339
  unity of, 328–44
  visual, 81, 195, 313, 316, 329–32, 336, 339

Arts and Crafts Exhibition Society, 334, 336
Arts and Crafts movement, 332–40, 347
Athey, Ron, 269

Baillie, John, 310
Baju, Anatole, 264, 276
Balfour, Arthur, 271
ballad (form), 150, 162
Barbauld, Anna, 311
Baring, Maurice, 313
Barish, Jonas, 264–65, 267, 268–69
Barlow, Jane, 156
  Irish Idylls, 157
Barrett, William, 287
Barrows, John Henry, 107
Bassnett, Susan, 274
Baudelaire, Charles, 171, 310
Bauer, Heike, 215, 216–17
Beardsley, Aubrey, 1, 3, 195, 311–14, 317,
  329–32, 336, 343
Beasley, Edward, 22
Beckett, Samuel, 269
Beckson, Karl, 4, 170–71, 248
Beddoe, John, 26
Beerbohm, Max, 1, 251, 255
Beetham, Margaret, 313
Bennett, Arnold, 251
Bentley, D. M. R., 121
Bentley, George, 296
Berlant, Lauren, 36
Bernstein, Susan, 148, 150
Betjeman, John, 17
Bildungsroman, 105–7
Bing, Siegfried, 65
Binyon, Laurence, "Summer Night," 115
Bird, Isabella, *The Hawaiian Archipelago*, 48–49
Birmingham School of Art, 339–43
Black studies, 13, 21–23, 28, 36, *See also* human,
  humanism; race, racialization
Blaikie-Murdoch, W. G., 3
Blake, William, 311
Blank, Frederike, 215
Blavatsky, Helena, 294
Blind, Mathilde, 134
  Heather on Fire, The, 134, 144–46
  "Manchester by Night," 118–20
  "Red Sunsets, 1883," 120
Blue Mountain Project (BMP), 306–7
Bodley Head, 231
body. *See also* gender; race, racialization
  degeneration of, 228
  eugenics and, 227
  gender and, 90, 139, 228
  impressibility of, 22
  modernity and, 230–31

race and, 23–25, 28, 33
  vital, 230
Boer War, 3, 251, 257, 258
Bonney, Charles Carroll, 107
book history, 306, 332–36, 339, *See also* digital
  humanities
Boone, Joseph, 45
Booth, Charles, 242
Bourget, Paul, 278
Bradley, Katharine, *See* Field, Michael
Brake, Laurel, 305, 319, 323
BRANCH (Britain, Representation, and
  Nineteenth-Century History), 344
Branch, Lori, 285
Brand, Adolph, 214
Branford, Victor, 320
Brantlinger, Patrick, 21, 45
Bristow, Joseph, 4, 7, 116
British Library, *Discovering Literature*,
  344
British Newspaper Archive, 331
Brook, Peter, 272
Brooke, Emma Frances, 5, 227
  Superfluous Woman, A, 228, 236–37
Bubb, Alexander, 101–2
Buchan, John, 251
Buddhism, 98–99, 100, 103, 105–7, *See also*
  religion
Buell, Lawrence, 190
Bühler, Georg, translation of *Dharmashastra*, 100
Bulson, Eric, 308
Bulwer-Lytton, Edward, 194
Bunyoro, 24
Burdett, Osbert, 1, 3
Burgess, Gelett, 125–27
Burke, Edmund, 253
Burnand, F. C., *The Colonel*, 53
Burton, Antoinette, 24
Burton, Richard, 217
Burty, Philippe, 65

Caird, Mona, 9, 227
Camée, Georgette, 278
Cannadine, David, 251
capitalism, 42, 55, 119, *See also* class;
  imperialism; industrialization
  class and, 144–46
  colonialism and, 146, 162
  industrialization and, 152
  nature and, 134, 135–40, 143–45, 175
Carlyle, Thomas, 64
Carpenter, Edward, 8, 210, 212, 219–23, 227,
  228, 229–31, 235
  Civilisation, 230
  England's Ideal, 230

"Smoke-Plague and Its Remedy, The," 181
Carpenter, G. R., 343
Catholicism, 151, 155–57, 161, 286, 288, 289
  decadence and, 289–90
  sexuality and, 289
Cave, Isobel, 340
Celtic Revival, 1, 309–10, 313, 319
Century Guild, 334
Century Guild Hobby Horse, 323, 334, 344
Chakrabarty, Dipesh, 175
Chamberlain, Fenollosa, and Basil Hall, 66
Chameleon (periodical), 15
Chandumenon, O., 5, 11, 82
  Indulekha, 78–82, 85–93
Chang, Elizabeth Hope, 171
Chang, Wo
  Britain through Chinese Spectacles, 63, 71–74
  cosmopolitanism of, 74
  identity of, 74
Chant, Laura Ormiston, 270
Charpentier, Louis, 272
Chatterjee, Ronjaunee, 11, 25, 41
Chaucer, Geoffrey, *Troilus and Criseyde*, 140
Cheah, Pheng, 62
children's literature, 27, 61, 308, 336, 340
China
  actors in, 268
  British writing on, 72
  cosmopolitanism of, 74
  imperialism and, 73
  literature of, 73
  Orientalism and, 62
Chopin, Frédéric, 112
Christian Science, 286, 296
Christoff, Alicia Mireles, 11, 25, 41
Claes, Koenraad, 307, 315
Clark, Nigel, 199
class
  aesthetics and, 120, 233
  capitalism and, 144–46
  eugenics and, 229
  exploitation and, 118–20, 139
  imperialism and, 25
  nature and, 143–47, 191
  race and, 25
  socialism and, 230
  utopia and, 230
classics, 102
Clifford, W. K., 70, 290
climate change, 5, 14–15, 171, 173–75, 180,
    189, *See also* Anthropocene; ecocriticism;
    weird fiction
Clive, Robert, 258
Clouston, W. A., 101
Cobham, Claude, 217

Cohn, Elisha, 290
collectivity, 25, 33, 84
Collins, Wilkie, *Moonstone, The*, 80
colonialism, 11, *See also* imperialism; nation,
    nationalism
  anticolonialism, 10, 11, 79, 144–46, 248
  capitalism and, 146, 162
  comparative religion and, 99
  dandyism and, 45
  decolonialism, 162
  degeneration and, 45
  gender and, 80, 164
  Hawai'i, 41
  historical record and, 31
  matriliny and, 86
  modernization and, 86
  nature and, 144–47, 149, 155–57, 161,
    163–65
  novels and, 83
  poetry and, 145, 163–65
  property and, 89–91
  race and, 45
  realism and, 5
  reverse, 21, 23, 28
  romance and, 62
  settler, 36, 124
  transnationalism and, 10
color science, 69
Commons Preservation Society,
    192
community, 63, 278, 293, 310, 345, *See also*
    world, worlding
Confederation of Canadian poets, 121
Conrad, Joseph, 251
  Heart of Darkness, 27
conservation, 190–92, *See also* nature
conservatism, 246–47, 249, 250, 251–55
  aestheticism and, 252
  arts and, 343
  decadence and, 254–55, 258–60
  imperialism and, 252, 255, 257–60
  modernity and, 252–53
Conway, Katharine St. John,
    228
Conway, Moncure, 5
  Sacred Anthology, The, 98, 102
Cooper, Edith. *See* Field, Michael
cooperativism, 229
Corelli, Marie, 13, 249, 287
  background, 296
  decadence and, 297–98
  Electric Creed of Christianity, 296, 300–1
  Mighty Atom, The, 285–86
  Praise and Prayer, 296
  religion and, 296

Corelli, Marie (cont.)
    Romance of Two Worlds, A, 301
    science and, 299–301
    Sorrows of Satan, The, 287–88, 295–301
    Ziska, 299
Corvo, Baron (Frederick Rolfe), 248, 286
cosmopolitanism, 3, 12, 62–63, 67, 71, 74, 248,
    See also liberalism
    aesthetic, 67, 69, 74, 75
    critical, 63
    decadence and, 6–9
    emotion and, 69
    ethical, 9, 70
    Eurocentric models of, 75
    evolutionary science and, 70
    genre and, 112
    globalization and, 75
    imperialism and, 74
    Indigenous, 120–22, 124
    liberalism and, 75
    music and, 69
    nation and, 75, 162–63
    orientalism and, 70
    religion and, 105
    self and, 70
Costello, Louisa, *Rose Garden of Persia,* 101
COVE (Collaborative Organization for Virtual
    Education), 344
Craft, Kinuko, 135
Craig, Edward Gordon, 273
Cramer, Tom, 345
Crane, Walter, 2, 336, 343
    Shepheard's Calendar, 336
Craven, Thomas, 272
Crawfurd, Oswald, 273
Crookes, William, 287
Croydon Brotherhood, 236
culture
    clash of, 72, 246, 260
    dissidence and, 78
    global circulation of, 11
    nature and, 179
    print, 305–8, 310, 313
    visual, 329, 339, 344, 345
Cust, Robert, 105

Daily Mail (newspaper), 251
Daily Telegraph (newspaper), 251
Dakyns, Graham, 217
dandy, dandyism, 11, 41, 42, 242, 272, *See also*
    modernity, modernization
D'Annunzio, Gabriele, 274, 276
    degeneration and, 46–51
    gender and, 208
    global circulation of, 43

    in Hawai'i, 44–57
    masculinity and, 41
    past and, 46
    politics of, 56
    race and, 51
Darmesteter, James, *Zend-Avesta,* 100
Darwin, Charles, 13
Database of Ornament, 323
Davids, T. W. Rhys, *Buddhist Suttas,* 100
Davidson, John
    "Nocturne," 115
    Testament of an Empire Builder, The, 258
Davis, Mike, 161
Davitt, Michael, 161
Dawe, W. Carlton, *Kakemonos,* 73
Day, Lal Mohan, 85
    Bengal Peasant Life, 81
decadence, 1, 6–7, 42, 113, 117, 163, 175, 177,
    265–68, *See also* fin de siècle; hothouse;
    symbolism
    Catholicism and, 289–90
    conservatism of, 254–55, 258–60
    cosmopolitanism and, 6–9
    critique of, 249–51
    degeneration and, 49–51, 241–43, 272, 274
    digital archives, 17
    East Asia and, 73
    gender and, 9, 227, 228, 232, 343
    genre and, 114
    imperialism and, 258–60
    individualism and, 241
    modernity and, 253
    morality and, 291
    nation and, 271
    nature and, 14, 132–34, 148, 171–73, 175,
    178–80, 182, 194
    poetry and, 132
    race and, 51
    scale and, 14
    sexuality and, 172, 272
    theater and, 5, 13, 264–68, 271, 272–80
    time and, 176, 182
    vagueness and, 126
    weird and, 194–95, 200
    women's writing, 7
Décadent, Le (review), 276
Dellamora, Richard, 7
Dénac, Lucie, 278
Denisoff, Dennis, 132, 148, 171
Dent, J. M., 102
Desrochers, Pierre, 190
Dharmapala, Anagarika, 106–7
Dial (magazine), 15, 306, 309, 313, 315,
    316–17, 319
diary. *See* life-writing

Diedrick, James, 120, 144
digital humanities, 15–17, 306
  access and, 330, 339, 340, 344, 347
  arts and, 339, 340, 344
  gender and, 339
  interdisciplinarity and, 331
  interoperability and, 344, 345–48
  materiality and, 344
  metadata and, 345–48
  nation and, 347
  networks and, 322–24, 347
  ontologies of, 345–48
  periodicals and, 308–10, 315, 322–24,
    329–32
  reading and, 322–24
  text and, 345
  Victorian studies and, 344
disability, 33, 228, 232, *See also* morality; race;
  racialization
discipline, disciplinarity
  interdisciplinarity, 331, 332–40
  undisciplining, 4, 11
Disraeli, Benjamin, 82, 252, 255
Dix, Gertrude, 227
  Girl from the Farm, The, 228, 231–36, 242
  Image Breakers, The, 231
Dobson, Eleanor, 294
Dome (periodical), 15
Dowie, Ménie Muriel, *Gallia*, 229
Dowling, Linda, 210, 213, 214, 227
Doyle, Arthur Conan, 287
  "Story of the Brown Hand, The," 23–25, 27
du Maurier, George, *Trilby*, 298
duan (song), 145
Dumas, Alexandre, 43
  dame aux camélias, La, 274
Dumergue, W., 82
Duse, Eleonora, 273–74
Dutt, Romesh Chunder, 103

East Asia, 61–64, *See also* China; Japan;
  Orientalism
  encounters with, 62
  Orientalism and, 62
  translation and, 64–65
ecocriticism, 14, 132, 171
  aesthetics and, 112
  capitalism and, 134
  dark ecology, 134, 143, 148
  gender and, 132, 133
  genre and, 114
  history and, 174, 176, 190
  poetry and, 134
  scale and, 14, 174, 177, 178, 181
  weird and, 189, 199, 201, 202–4

ecofeminism, 132
ecumenicalism, 13, 99, 101–2, 107, 108
  secularism and, 108
Eddy, Mary Baker, 300
Edkins, Joseph, 104
Edmond, Rod, 45, 48
Egerton, George, 9, 227, 251
Egypt, 24, 299
Ehnenn, Jill, 7
ekphrasis, 68
Eliot, George, 81
Ellis, Edith Lees, 228
Ellis, Havelock, 217, 230
Ellmann, Richard, 208, 289
Eltis, Sos, 266, 272, 277
Engels, Friedrich, 84
environment, environmentalism.
  See ecocriticism; nature
erotics. *See* sex, sexuality
essentialism, 67, 75
Esty, Jed, 79, 84–86
ethics
  aesthetics and, 10, 213
  cosmopolitanism and, 70
  daily, 230
  degeneration and, 228
  environment and, 191–92
  nature and, 165–66
  sexuality and, 213
  transnationalism and, 9
ethnic studies, 36
eugenics, 26, 227, 229
  degeneration and, 227
  gender and, 227, 232
  progressivism and, 230
  socialism and, 240, 242
Europeana, 347
Evangelista, Stefano, 9, 248
Evening Standard (periodical), 329
Evergreen (magazine), 15, 306, 309, 313, 319
Everyman's Library, 103
evolution, 69, 227, *See also* eugenics
exchange, exchangeability, 25, 28, 30–33, 42, 64,
  See also under race
exile, 144
extraction, 35, 133, 190, *See also* ecocriticism;
  fossil fuels

Fabian Society, 228, 236, 252
Federico, Annette R., 249, 295–97
Fellowship of the New Life, 228, 236
feminism, 7, 9, 42, 132, *See also* New Woman
  eugenics and, 227, 229
  nation and, 156
  nature and, 132–33, 156

feminism (cont.)
  sexuality and, 210, 219
  socialism and, 9, 227–30
  theater and, 274
Fenollosa, Ernest, 65
Ferguson, Christine, 286
Ferrier, David, 292
fetishism, 9, 23, *See also* race, racialization
Field, Michael, 16, 256–58, 286
  "To America," 256
Figaro, Le (periodical), 310
fin de siècle. *See* 1890s (decade)
Fitzgerald, Edward, *Rubaiyat of Omar Khayyam*,
  101
Flint, Kate, 122
FNL. *See* Fellowship of the New Life
folklore, 67, 162
Forman, Ross, 10, 72
Fort, Paul, 277
fossil fuels, 112, 114, 115, 116, 117, 129,
  174–75, 180–81, *See also* ecocriticism;
  extraction; pollution
France, Anatole, 313
Fraser, Hilary, 289
Free Churches, 286
Freedgood, Elaine, 35, 81
Freeman, Nick, 248
Freeman-Mitford, B., 101
Fried, Michael, 269
Friedman, Dustin, 194
Fuller, Loïe, 276

Gagnier, Regenia, 42
Galey, Alan, 315
Gallienne, Richard Le, 246
Galton, Francis, 26, 227, 229
Galvan, Jill, 286
Gandhi, Leela, 10, 107
Gandhi, Mohandas K., 106
Garelick, Rhonda K., 45
Gaskin, Georgiana, 340
Gautier, Théophile, 291
gaze, 62, 180
Geddes, Patrick, 310, 319
gender, 6–9, *See also* feminism; matriliny; sex,
  sexuality
  adventure stories and, 61
  agency and, 274
  arts and, 339–44
  body and, 90, 139, 228
  colonialism and, 79–81, 164
  dandyism and, 208
  decadence and, 227, 228, 232, 343
  degeneration and, 228
  digital humanities and, 339

equality, 93
eugenics and, 227, 229, 232
femininity and, 14, 132, 149–50, 214, 272
imperialism and, 25, 45
Indigenous people and, 41, 53
masculinity and, 41, 43, 53, 211
modernism and, 274
nature and, 14, 118, 132–35, 140, 146–47,
  149–50, 166
poetry and, 133–35, 146–47, 150, 166
progressivism and, 227–29, 237
property and, 90
realism and, 85
sexuality and, 7, 208–11, 212, 214–23
socialism and, 229
theater and, 272, 274
time and, 320
urbanization and, 116, 121
women's writing, 7
genre
  cosmopolitanism and, 112
  literary history and, 113–16
  popularity and, 78
  transnational circulation of, 113, 115, 129
Gerson, Carole, 122
Ghose, Manmohan, 10
Gilbert, W. S., and Arthur Sullivan, *Mikado*, 65
Gilchrist, Robert Murray, 189
  "Crimson Weaver, The," 199–201
Giles, Herbert A., 101
  Gems of Chinese Literature, 64
Giles, Lionel, 103
Gilman, Richard, 265
Gissing, George, 21, 251
  Private Papers of Henry Ryecroft, The, 259
  Whirlpool, The, 259
Gladstone, William E., 144, 251, 255
globalization, 10, 42, 62, 63, 73, *See also*
  cosmopolitanism; imperialism
  city and, 114
  cosmopolitanism and, 75
  nature and, 134
  trade and, 135–40
Gobineau, Arthur du, 26
Gollancz, Israel, 103
Gonschor, Lorenz, 54
Goodlad, Lauren, 26
Gothic, 21, 23, 27, 288, *See also* imperialism
Gourmont, Remy de, 276, 277
Grand, Sarah, 9, 227
  Heavenly Twins, The, 229
Gray, John, 286
Green Sheaf (magazine), 306, 309, 311, 319, 320
Greenaway, Kate, 340
Grein, J. T., 270

Guardian (periodical), 329
Guys, Constantin, "A Sketch," 310–14

Haeckel, Ernst, 290
Haggard, H. Rider, 287
  She, 85
Halberstam, Jack, 45
Hall, Jason David, 113
Halperin, David, 208
Hampshire Telegraph, 53
Hampstead Historic Club, 236
Handke, Peter, 268–69
Hanifi, Shah Mahmoud, 31
Hanson, Ellis, 7, 289
Hardy, Thomas, 5, 191
Harland, Henry, 317
Harrington, Emily, 143
Harris, Jonathan Gil, 31
Harrison, S. Frances, "Vie de Boheme! Or The
  Nocturne in G," 120
Hart, Ernest, 65
Hastings, Warren, 258
Hawai'i
  Bayonet Constitution, 54
  colonization of, 41, 42, 56
  dandyism and, 44–57
  gender and, 43
  leprosy and, 48–51
  periodical culture of, 42–43
  sovereignty of, 55
Hearn, Lafcadio
  Glimpses of Unfamiliar Japan, 66
  Kokoro, 63, 65–71
Hedstrom, Matthew, 107
Heilmann, Ann, 7
Hekma, Gert, 214, 216
Henderson, Elsie, 343
Henley, W. E., 112, 247, 250
Heravitharama, Don David. *See* Dharmapala,
  Anagarika
Herero and Namaqua Genocide, 22
Hermetic Order of the Golden Dawn, 99, 195,
  286, 288, 289, 294–95, 320
Hermetic Society, 99
Highland Clearances, 144–46
Hill, Octavia, 192
Hinduism, 80, 98, 102–7, *See also* matriliny
Hirschfeld, Magnus, 210, 214, 220, 223
history, historicism, 332
  art and, 340
  ecocriticism and, 174, 176, 190
  literature and, 16, 247
  matriliny and, 83–85
  print culture and, 305, 311
  realism and, 86

Hofmannsthal, Hugo von, 276
Holden, Edward S., 101
Holden, Evelyn, "Binnorie, O Binnorie," 340
Holland, Henry, 305
Hollinger, David, 108
Holmes, John, 258
Holocaust, 22
homoeroticism, 45, 289, 291, 298, *See also*
  Orientalism; queerness; sex, sexuality
Hopkins, Gerard Manley, 114
Hopper, Nora, 156
  Ballads in Prose, 157
Horne, Herbert, 334
Horton, William T., 15, 189
  Book of Images, A, 196
  Three Visions, 195–97
hothouse, 170–74, *See also* decadence;
  ecocriticism; nature
Housman, Laurence, 135, 310
Hultgren, Neil, 194, 255
human, humanism, 12, 21, *See also* nature; race
  artifice and, 117
  biological notion of, 22, 23, 27
  civilization and, 24
  emotion and, 69
  nature and, 14, 122–25, 127–29, 132–33, 150,
    170–72, 174, 187–92, 193, 198, 201–2
  nonhumans and, 187, 195, 204
  race and, 22, 24
  syncretism and, 98–100
  technology and, 309, 316
  universalism and, 103–8
  weird and, 195
  world and, 70
Hunt, William Holman,
  332, 340
Huxley, T. H., 290
Huysmans, Joris-Karl, 171, 276
  À Rebours, 293
Hyde, William, 154

Ibsen, Henrik, 267, 274
  Ghosts, 270
idealism, 67
identity, 7, 25, 26, 35, 51, 122, 149, 155, 162,
  209, 215–16, 223, *See also* gender; race,
  racialization; sex, sexuality
IIIF. *See* International Image Interoperability
  Framework
Image, Selwyn, 328–29, 334, 338
imagination, 14, 193, 201
imagism, 65
imperialism, 3, 9, 10, 21, 23, 25, 27, 29, 34, 45,
  72, 73, 190, *See also* colonialism;
  Orientalism; trade

imperialism (cont.)
  civilization and, 24
  class and, 25
  conservatism and, 255, 257–60
  cosmopolitanism and, 74
  decadence and, 9, 258–60
  gender and, 25, 45
  Gothic and, 27
  nation and, 79, 252
  nature and, 132–33, 155, 162
  networks and, 107
  poetry and, 155
  print culture and, 10
  race and, 12, 22, 26–27, 28, 34–36
  religion and, 104–5
  romance and, 85
  violence and, 34, 35
Impressionism, 65, 153, 179–81, 336–39
Independent Labour Party, 228
Independent Theatre Society, 270
India. *See also* colonialism; matriliny
  actors in, 268
  colonial history of, 79–81, 89–91
  gender and, 80
  matriliny and, 92
  nationalism and, 24, 79
  realism in, 85
Indian Rebellion (1857), 24
Indigenous people, 11, 36
  aesthetics and, 43–44
  cosmopolitanism and, 120–22, 124
  extinction discourse, 45, 46, 51
  gender and, 41, 43, 53
  literary form and, 122
  politics of resistance, 56
Indigenous studies, 36
individualism, 144, 180, 228, 241, 293–94
industrialization, 25, 113, 125, 129, 190
  aesthetics of, 118–20, 180
  agriculture and, 135–40, 151
  city and, 114
  modernity and, 152
  nature and, 134, 152, 154, 190, 191–94
  pollution and, 180–81
  religion and, 285
  time and, 317–19
International Image Interoperability Framework, 331, 345, 346–47
internationalism. *See* cosmopolitanism
interoperability. *See under* digital humanities
intersectionality, 14
Ireland, 24, 155–62
  Irish revival, 155–57, 309, 311, 320
Irish National Land League, 161
Islam, 98, 106

Ivory, Yvonne, 214

Jackson, Charles Kains, 253
Jackson, Holbrook, 1–4, 15
Jackson, Zakiyyah Iman, 21
Jamaica, 24
James, Henry, 5
James, William, 287
Japan, 68–69, *See also* Orientalism
  Europe and, 65–67, 71
  folklore, 67
  japonisme, 65, 115, 126, 336
  knowledge of, 67
  Orientalism and, 62
  romances and, 73
  spirituality, 70
Japon artistique, Le / *Artistic Japan*, 65
Johnson, Dominic, 269
Johnson, E. Pauline, 11, 115, 120
  "Cry from an Indian Wife, A," 123
  "Nocturne," 122–25
  "Shadow River," 122
  White Wampum, The, 121
Johnson, Lionel, 251
  "By The Statue of King Charles At Charing Cross," 254
Jones, Amelia, 272
Jones, Edward Burne, 343
Jowett, Benjamin, 212
Judaism, 103

Ka Nupepa Kuokoa (newspaper), 41
Kains-Jackson, Charles, 213
Kalākaua, David, 41, 52–55
  Legends and Myths of Hawaii, The, 53–54
Kamakawiwoʻole Osorio, Jonathan Kay, 55
Kapadia, S. A., 103
Kaplan, E. Ann, 45
Kaye, Richard, 7
Keats, John, 114
Kelmscott Press, 332, 334, 340, 344
Kerridge, Richard, 190
Kibble, Matthew, 251
King, Frederick D., 15
King, Rebecca Scarborough, 113–14
Kipling, Rudyard, 1, 2, 5, 255
  From Sea to Sea, 72
  "White Man's Burden, The," 27
Kittler, Friedrich, 323
Knight, Frances, 286
Knight, Mark, 286
knowledge, 62, 63, 180
Kodoth, Praveena, 90
Krafft-Ebing, Richard von, 214, 216, 217
Kuwada, Bryan, 43

Ladies' Land League, 161
Lamb, Hugh, 200
Lane, John, 73, 116, 121, 231, 254
Lang, Andrew, 162
LaPorte, Charles, 286
Lasner, Mark Samuels, 4
Lavery, Grace, 126
Lawrence, Henry, 149
Lawrence, James, *The Empire of Nairs*, 80
Le Gallienne, Richard, 1
Lecourt, Sebastian, 286–87
Ledger, Sally, 4, 7
Lee, Vernon, 6, 15, 67, 148, 189, 204
    Enchanted Woods, The, 201
    Hauntings, 202
    "Lie of the Land, The," 201
    "Oke of Okehurst," 202
    "Prince Alberic and the Snake Lady," 202
Leighton, Frederick, 328
Levetus, Celia, 340, 343
Levine, Caroline, 10, 16, 41, 307, 314, 322
Levy, Amy, 148
    London Plane-Tree, A, 148–51
liberalism, 21, 26, 42, 62, 72, 75, *See also*
    cosmopolitanism
    decadence and, 253
    optimism and, 63
    political crisis of, 251
    religion and, 99, 107–8
life-writing, 16, 41, 43–46, 48, 49, 54–57, 68,
    71, 217, 219
Lili'uokalani, Lydia, 42
    Hawaii's Story by Hawaii's Queen, 41, 54–57
linked.art, 346
Lively, Frazer, 277, 278
local color, 67, *See also* travel writing
Local Government Act (1888), 270
Lockerd, Martin, 289
Lodge, Oliver, 287
Logan, William, *Malabar Manual*, 82
Loomba, Ania, 22
Lord Chamberlain's Office, 269
Lorrain, Jean, 276
Loti, Pierre, *Madame Chrysanthème*, 73
Lovecraft, H. P., 15
    Supernatural Horror in Literature, 189
Lowe, Lisa, 35
Lowell, Amy, 65
Lowell, Percival, *Soul of the Far East, The*, 61–64,
    74
Luckhurst, Roger, 194, 204
Lynch, Hannah, 156

Macaulay, Thomas Babington, 24
Machen, Arthur, 15, 202, 253

Great God Pan, The, 203, 254
Hill of Dreams, The, 202–4
House of Souls, The, 187
Machin, James, 189
MacKay, Charles, 296
Mackmurdo, Arthur Heygate, 334
Macleod, Fiona. *See* Sharp, William
Macleod, Kirsten, 307
Maeterlinck, Maurice, 264, 276, 277
magazines. *See* periodicals
Mahabharata, 103
Malabar Marriage Commission, 86, 91
Mallarmé, Stéphane, 276
Marder, Michael, 149–50
marriage, 83–86, 91, 92, *See also* matriliny; property
Marshall, Gail, 4
Martin, Meredith, 113
Martiny, Erik, 114
Marx, Karl, 84
Mason, Emma, 147
Masters, Brian, 295
Masuzawa, Tomoko, 99
Matheson, George, 103
Mathews, Elkin, 116
matriliny, 78–82, 83
    anthropology and, 83
    colonialism and, 86, 89–91
    gender and, 90–91, 93
    modernity and, 92
    property and, 89–91
    realism and, 89
Maugham, Somerset, 310
Maxwell, Catherine, 114
McCracken, Scott, 4
McGann, Jerome, 347
McGuinness, Patrick, 277
McKittrick, Katherine, 23, 27
McLellan, John, 84
media, mediation
    cosmopolitanism and, 67
    digital humanities and, 344, 345–48
    form and, 307, 308, 311–14
    global, 306–7
    hierarchy and, 314–17
    materiality and, 315–17
    music and, 69
    perception and, 62
    periodicals and, 307–8
    remediation, 306, 308, 311–14, 315, 323
    technology and, 16, 316–17
    transition and, 305, 307, 308
    translation and, 67–68
    unity of arts, 332–40
melodrama. *See* theater
Melville, Herman, *Typee*, 43

memoir. *See* life-writing
Men and Women's Club, 227, 236, *See also*
    eugenics
Mendès, Catulle, 277
Menzies, Alan, 103
metadata. *See under* digital humanities
meteorology, 180
Meynell, Alice, 115, 147, 166
    Ceres' Runaway, 148, 152
    "Dead Harvest, A," 152–53
    "Grass," 152
    Impressions of London, 152–55
    "Threshing Machine, The," 151
    "Tithonus," 165
Mill, John Stuart, 24
Millais, John Everett, 313, 332
Miller, Elizabeth, 113, 118, 133
Miller, J. Hillis, 285
Miller, Joaquin, 125
Miller, Monica L., 51
Mills, Charles, 101–2
Milton, John, 297
mimesis. *See* realism
Mirador, 346
Mitchell, Rebecca N., 323
MJP. See Modernist Journals Project
modernism, 78, 85, 128, 251
    antitheatrical prejudice, 273–75, 277
    East and, 65, 99
    gender and, 274
    pessimism of, 4
    symbolism and, 275
Modernist Journals Project (MJP), 15, 306–7
modernity, modernization, 42, 73–74, 305, 310
    alternatives to, 115
    body and, 230–31
    colonialism and, 86
    conservatism and, 252–53
    decadence and, 253
    East Asia and, 73
    gender and, 274
    industrialization and, 152
    Japanese, 65
    nature and, 173
    past and, 125, 252
    poetry and, 118
    print culture and, 313, 316, 319–20
    religion and, 285–86
    resource extraction and, 190
    sexuality and, 253
    technology and, 118
    urbanization and, 154
Moine, Fabienne, 132
Moore, Jason W., 134, 172
morality

art and, 291
    decadence and, 291
    disability and, 232
    science and, 292–94
    theater and, 264, 270–71, 280
Morgan, Benjamin, 14, 172, 175, 177, 197
Morgan, Lewis Henry, 84
Morris, May, 339
Morris, William, 252, 332–36, 339, *See also*
    Kelmscott Press
    Kennet, 347
Morton, Timothy, 148
Moxon, Edward, 332–33, 340
Muddiman, Bernard, 1, 2
Mukherjee, Meenakshi, 81, 88
Mukherjee, Upamanyu Pablo, 161
Mulholland, Rose, 156
Müller, F. Max, 97, 99, 104, 107
    Lectures on the Science of Religion, 97–98
    Sacred Books of the East, 97–98, 100–1
    translation of *Upanishads*, 100
Municipal Corporations Act (1882), 253
Murphy, Patricia, 120, 132, 152
Murphy, Stephen J., 323
Murray, Alex, 113
Murray, James, 100
Murray, John, 103
Musgrave, G. A., 192
music, 68–70

Naidu, Sarojini, 155
    Golden Threshold, The, 163–65
    "Ode to H.H. the Nizam of Hyderabad,"
        162–63
Nair, Janaki, 93
nation, nationalism, 2, 9, 10, 35, 42, 152, 252,
    257, *See also* imperialism; patriotism
    colonialism and, 24, 79, 86, 93
    cosmopolitanism and, 75, 162–63
    decadence and, 271
    digital humanities and, 347
    feminism and, 156
    imperialism and, 79, 133, 255
    liberalism and, 42
    nature and, 133–34, 144–46, 149, 155,
        157–63
    periodicals and, 313
    poetry and, 157–65
    race and, 25
    realism and, 85
    sexuality and, 93
    world religion and, 106
naturalism, 115, 140–44, 267
nature, 14, 116, 196, 201, *See also* ecocriticism;
    imagination

agency and, 177
art and, 179
artifice and, 133, 170, 171–72
capitalism and, 134, 135–40, 143–46, 152, 175
class and, 143–47, 191
colonialism and, 144–46, 149, 155–57, 161, 163–65
decadence and, 132–34, 148, 171, 172–73, 175, 178–80, 182, 194
divinity and, 124, 151
ethics and, 165–66, 191–92
exploitation of, 118, 123
feminism and, 156
gender and, 132–35, 140, 146–47, 149–50, 166
human and, 14, 128, 132–33, 150, 170–72, 174, 187–92, 193, 198, 201–2
imperialism and, 132–33, 134, 155, 162
industrialization and, 120, 134, 152, 154, 191–94
modernity and, 173
nation and, 144–46, 149, 155, 157–63
Orientalism and, 125
poetry and, 132, 134, 140, 146, 147, 148, 150–66
politics of, 132–34, 152, 155–63
queerness and, 181
Romanticism and, 134
sexuality and, 132, 175, 181
time and, 151, 152, 177
urbanization and, 147–55, 191–94
weird and, 189
neoliberalism. *See* liberalism
networks, 11, 42, 306
digital humanities and, 322–24, 347
form of, 322
imperial, 107
literary, 64, 67, 129
periodicals and, 307, 309, 322–24
trade and, 64, 71
world, 62, 71
New Age (journal), 182
New Drama, 2
New Fiction, 2
New Hedonism, 2
New Man, 25
New Thought, 286
New Woman, 2, 6–7, 9, 25, 210, 219–23, 227, 229, 231, 236, 250, 274, *See also* Decadence; feminism
New York Times, 53
Newlyn School, 339
newness. *See* novelty
Neyra, Ren Ellis, 33

Nichol, Robert, 231
Nietzsche, Friedrich, 269
nocturne (genre), 5, 11, 14, 112–18
class and, 118
divinity and, 122–25
gender and, 121
Indigeneity and, 122–25
japonisme and, 125
nature and, 116, 123, 127–29
sexuality and, 116, 117
time and, 115
transnational circulation of, 113, 115, 120–29
urban setting, 118
Nogelmeier, M. Puakea, 43
Noguchi, Yone, 11, 115, 125
Seen and Unseen, or Monologues of a Homeless Snail, 125–29
Nōh theater, 65
Nordau, Max, 171, 233
Degeneration, 234, 250
Northern Art Workers' Guild, 328
novel
colonialism and, 82, 83
eugenics and, 229
feminism and, 227–29
in India, 81, 82
New Woman, 228, 229, 231
realist, 21
socialist, 5, 227–29
novelty, 2

occult, 189, 195, 202, 287, 295, 320, *See also* supernatural
Ó Donghaile, Deaglán, 248
Ōgai, Mori, 71
O'Gorman, Francis, 255, 257
Orient Press, 103
Orientalism, 9, 12, 25, 45, 62, 64, 72, 75, 83, 97, *See also* China; East Asia; India; Japan
O'Sullivan, Vincent, 251
aesthetics of, 66
ancient past and, 127
cosmopolitanism and, 70
nature and, 125
popular culture and, 101
romance and, 66
syncretism and, 99
world religion and, 98, 100, 102
Outlook (newspaper), 251

Pacific Commercial Advertiser (periodical), 46
Pagan Review, 15, 306, 309, 319
Pageant (magazine), 15, 306, 310, 311, 319
Pall Mall Gazette, 152, 328
Palmer, E. H., *Qur'an*, 100

Palmer, Julius, _Memories of Hawaii_, 48, 49
Parade (periodical), 15
Paranjape, Makarand, 163
Parkins, Wendy, 191
Parliament of Religions, 107–8
Parnell, Anna, 161
Parnell, Charles Stewart, 156
pastoral (genre), 14, 133, 143, 148
Pater, Walter, 9, 180, 233, 291, 328
    Marius the Epicurian, 297
Patridge, Bernard, 328
patriliny. _See_ matriliny
patriotism, 255–60, _See also_ nation, nationalism
Pearson, Karl, 227
pederasty, 8, 209–14, 217
Pemberton-Billing, Noel, 270
perception, 62, 66, 72
performance studies, 265, 269, 280
Periodical Poetry Index, 345
periodicals, 15, 42, 305, 309
    aesthetics of, 311
    design and, 315–17
    digital humanities and, 16, 308–10, 315,
        322–24, 329–32
    form and, 307–9, 311–14, 322–24
    hierarchy and, 307, 314–17
    history and, 311, 324
    international circulation of, 306–10, 314,
        322–24
    little magazines, 6, 15, 16, 305–17, 322–24
    materiality of, 315–17
    media and, 307–8, 311–14, 322–24
    nation and, 313
    networks and, 307, 322–24
    queerness and, 309, 317
    remediation and, 16, 306, 308, 311–14, 315,
        323
    rhythm and, 317–22
    self-publishing, 309
    technology and, 309, 310, 316–17
    time and, 317–22
    transition and, 307, 308, 310, 319
    translation and, 43
    urbanization and, 311
    whole and, 310–14
Perry, Imani, 22
Peters, Robert, 112
Petit Journal des Refusées, 15
Pilz, Anna, 156
Pinero, Arthur Wing, 274
    Gay Lord Quex, The, 271
Pittock, Murray G. H., 248
plants, 129, 133, 148–52, 155, _See also_ nature
Plato, 267
    Symposium, The, 211

Playfair, Lyon, 190
Poe, Edgar Allen, 126, 194
poetry. _See also_ nature; nocturne
    colonialism and, 145, 163–65
    form and, 140, 145–46, 150, 155, 166
    gender and, 14, 132, 133–35, 146–47, 150,
        166
    imperialism and, 155
    nation and, 157–65
    nature and, 132, 133–34, 140, 146, 147, 148,
        150, 156–66
    politics of, 133–34, 155–65, 166
    transnational circulation of, 113
    urbanization and, 152–55
politics
    of aestheticism, 248
    aesthetics and, 79, 152
    of cosmopolitanism, 12
    geopolitics, 79
    of literary form, 11
    of nature, 132–34, 152, 155–63
    of poetry, 133–34, 155–65, 166
    progressive, 8
    of queerness, 7
    radicalism, 12
    sexual, 249
pollution, 118, 125, 133, 148, 152–55, 180–81,
        See also industrialization; nature;
        urbanization
postcolonial studies, 23, 28, 33, 62, 72, 79
Potolsky, Matthew, 9, 175, 248, 278
Pound, Ezra, 65, 125
Pre-Raphaelite Brotherhood, 135, 200, 311, 332,
    339
primitivism, 45, 51, 72, 83–85, 134, 230
progressivism, 8, 249–50, 257, _See_ conservatism
    city and, 236
    eugenics and, 230
    gender and, 227–29, 237
property, 28, 33, 36, 80, 84
    colonialism and, 89–91
    gender and, 90
    individual, 86
Prynne, William, 269
Psomiades, Kathy Alexis, 7, 84
psychology, 69, 88
Puchner, Martin, 274, 276
Punch (newspaper), 251, 328
Pykett, Lyn, 7

Quarto (periodical), 15
queer studies, 7, 132
queerness, 43, _See also_ gender; sex, sexuality
    decadence and, 272
    Indigenous people and, 44

medievalism and, 253
nature and, 132, 181
periodicals and, 309, 317
politics of, 7
religion and, 289
theatricality and, 272
Quillard, Pierre, 277
Quilter, Harry, 272–73

race, racialization, 22, 24, *See also* imperialism
agency and, 28
anti-Blackness and, 22–24
biological notion of, 23, 25–27
body and, 23–25, 28, 33
class and, 25
colonialism and, 45
dandyism and, 51
decadence and, 51
degeneration and, 26, 45, 46–51
disability and, 33
exchangeability and, 25, 28, 30–33
fetishism and, 9, 23
human and, 12, 21–23, 24
identity and, 26
imperialism and, 12, 22, 26–27, 28, 34–36
national identity and, 25
Orientalism and, 72
plasticity and, 21, 24, 33
relationality and, 34
rigidity and, 25
scientific racism and, 26
slavery and, 36
Rachilde (Marguerite Vallette-Eymery), 275–76, 277
Madame La Mort, 278
Voix du sang, La (Voice of Blood), 278
Ragsdale, William, 46–51
Rahman, Abdur, 24
Raman, Shankar, 31
Ramayana, 103
Ramón y Cajal, Santiago, 293, 300
Rangajan, Mahesh, 164
realism, 21, 79, 83, 89
colonialism and, 5, 11, 79, 81–82, 85–86
gender and, 85
history and, 86
interiority and, 88
marriage and, 84, 91
nation and, 85, 93
Orientalism and, 66
socialist-feminist novels, 227–29
theater and, 267
waning of, 78–79
relationality, 10, 34
relativism, 62, 99

religion
civilization and, 103–6
colonialism and, 99, 105
comparative, 13
cosmopolitanism and, 105
fundamentalism and, 108
imperialism and, 104–5
liberalism and, 99, 107–8
modernity and, 285–86
nature and, 151
popular culture and, 98–108
science and, 13, 98, 285–90, 294, 295, 296, 299–301
syncretism and, 100–8
universalism and, 100
world, 12, 97–108
Religious Book Week, 108
Religious Tract Society, 104
Rhodes, Cecil, 258
Rhymers' Club, 42
Ricketts, Charles, 309, 315, 316, 334
"Marred Face, The," 317
Ridout, Nicholas, 264
Rimbaud, Arthur, 264
Ristori, Adelaide, 274
Ritvo, Harriet, 192
Roberts, Charles G. D., *New York Nocturnes*, 121
Robinson, A. Mary F., 112
New Arcadia, The, 134, 140–44, 147
romance, 78, *See also* matriliny
colonialism and, 62, 79, 81, 84
imperial, 85
Japan and, 73
Orientalism and, 66
utopian, 80
Romanticism, 67, 114, 127, 151, 192, *See also* nature
Rose Leaf (periodical), 15
Rosicrucianism, 296
Ross, Robert, 210
Rossetti Archive, 345, 347
Rossetti, Christina, 147, 162
Goblin Market, 132–40
Rossetti, Dante Gabriel, 126, 135, 313, 332, 347
Water Willow, 347
Rossetti, William Michael, 332
Roussel, Georges, 278
Rowbotham, Sheila, 219
Royalist (magazine), 255
Rudland, Florence, 340
Rudy, Jason, 10
Ruecker, Stan, 315
Ruskin, John, 81, 112, 135, 152, 252
Seven Lamps of Architecture, The, 191

Said, Edward, 35, 62
Sakai, Aya, 193
Sanderson, Rob, 345
Saturday Review (newspaper), 257
Savoy (magazine), 15, 306, 310, 311, 319, 324
scale, 14, 66, 119, 174, 177–78, 180
    reading and, 322–24
Schaffer, Talia, 7
Schechner, Richard, 269
Schreiner, Olive, 236
Schuller, Kyla, 22, 26
science
    aesthetics and, 69, 293–94
    morality and, 292–94
    race and, 26
    religion and, 13, 98, 285–90, 294, 295, 296,
        299–301
    sanitation and, 191
    supernatural and, 29
    weird and, 189
Scott, Heidi C. M., 172
Scott, Walter, 43
Scribner's Magazine, 49
Secker, Martin, 4, 17
Second Anglo-Afghan War, 24
Second Home Rule Bill, 251
secularism, 285–86, 301
Selborne Society, 192
self, selfhood
    cosmopolitanism and, 70
    individualism and, 293–94
    nature and, 123, 201
Senate (periodical), 251
sensation fiction, 78
Serano, Julia, 214
seriality. *See* media, mediation; periodicals
sex, sexuality, 6–9, 84, 213, 253, *See also*
    pederasty
    aesthetics and, 7, 45
    colonialism and, 79
    decadence and, 7, 172, 272
    dissident, 78
    gender and, 7, 208–11, 212, 214–23
    imperialism and, 45
    matriliny and, 90–91
    nation and, 93
    nature and, 118, 132, 175, 181
    politics and, 249
    power and, 209, 212–14, 217
    radicalism and, 3, 6, 21
    religion and, 289
    sexology and, 211, 214–23
    theater and, 272
    urbanization and, 116
Shannon, Charles, 309, 313, 334

Sharp, William (Fiona McLeod),
    147, 309
Shaw, George Bernard, 1, 5, 227, 247, 250
Shelley, Percy Bysshe, 80
    Cenci, The, 278
Sherry, Vincent, 275
Shiel, M. P., 189
    Purple Cloud, The, 177, 197
    "Vaila," 197–98
Showalter, Elaine, 6, 21, 122
Sigerson, Dora, 156
Silva, Noenoe K., 43
Simes, Sidney, 15, 187, 195
Simmonds, Peter Lund, 190
Sinfield, Alan, 208–9
slavery, 35–36, *See also* race, racialization
Sloan, John, 259
Smith, Logan Pearsall, 246
Smith, Pamela Colman, 309, 311, 320
Smith, Samuel, 270–72
Smithers, Leonard, 116
Snydman, Stuart, 345
socialism, 144, 181, 182, 237
    arts and, 339
    class and, 230
    eugenics and, 227, 229, 240, 242
    feminism and, 9, 227–30
    gender and, 229
    modernity and, 252
    novel and, 5, 228–29
    utopian, 9
Society for Psychical Research,
    287
sonnet, 118, 119
Sontag, Susan, 42, 46
Sōseki, Natsume, 71
space, 2, 35, 83, 91, 115, 176, 182, 191, 271,
    273, 275
    green, 133, 190, 192
Spectator (periodical), 74
Spencer, Herbert, 104
    Principles of Psychology, 69
Spillers, Hortense, 21
Spiritualism, 286, 288, 289, 294–95, 296
Spivak, Gayatri, 35, 133, 163
Staël, Madame de, *De l'Allemagne*,
    67
Stanford, Derek, 4
Star (newspaper), 251
Stead, Evanghélia, 307
Stead, W. T., 297–98
stereoscope, 62–63
Stetz, Margaret, 4, 7
Stevenson, Fanny Van de Grift,
    "The Half-White," 49

Stevenson, Robert Louis, 41, 49
  "Bottle Imp, The," 50–51
stewardship, *See* conservation
Stoddard, Charles Warren, 41, 53
  Hawaiian Life, 44, 45, 46
  South-Seas Idyls, 43–46
Stoker, Bram, 5, 287
  Dracula, 72
Stokes, John, 4, 275, 328
Strand Magazine, 23
Strauss, Richard, 214
street-lamps, 14
Stuart, Mary, 43
Stutfield, Hugh E. M., 250
subject, subjectivity, 21, 189, 195, *See also*
  liberalism; self, selfhood
supernatural, 29, 30, 204, *See also* occult
Swinburne, Algernon Charles, 257, 297
  "Transvaal, The," 257
symbolism, 126, 163–64, 265, 267, 275–77,
  279
Symonds, John Addington, 210, 211–14,
  216–19
Symons, Arthur, 112, 195, 267, 273, 279, 293,
  311, 324
  "Decadent Movement in Literature, The,"
  126
  London Nights, 116–18
  "Venetian Nights," 250
  "Violet," 170

taravad, *See* marriage; matriliny
taste, 265–66, 272
Taylor, Emily, 156
Taylor, Jesse Oak, 115, 116, 172–73, 255
Tchen, John Kuo, 31
Temple Classics, 102
Tennyson, Alfred, 192, 332
  "Lady of Shalott, The," 200, 340
Tertullian, 268
Thain, Marion, 16
theater, 65, *See also* Nōh theater
  antitheatrical prejudice and, 264–72, 273,
    274, 277, 279–80
  artifice and, 117
  decadent, 5, 13, 264–68, 271, 272–80
  decline of, 272–75
  feminism and, 274
  gender and, 272, 274
  morality and, 270–71, 280
  realism and, 267
  sexuality and, 272
  time and, 273
Théâtre d'Art, 275, 277, 278
Theosophical Society, 99, 294

Theosophy, 106, 286, 288, 289, 294–95, 296,
  299
Thomas, Chris J., 49
Thomas, E. J., 103
Thompson, Francis, 251
Thomson, James, 114
Thornton, R. K. R., 4
Tierney, Andrew, 156
Tildesley, Matthew Brinton, 270
time, temporality, 83, 115, 181, 191, 305
  decadence and, 176, 182
  duration and, 317–19
  ethics and, 1
  gender and, 320
  industrial, 317–19
  Japan and, 65
  nature and, 151, 152, 177
Times (newspaper), 257
transgender people, 7, 214–16, *See also* gender;
  sex, sexuality
translation, 42–43, 64–65, 68, 82, 100, 101
  failures of, 65–67
  mediation and, 67–68
  untranslatable, 68, 69, 126
transnationalism, *See* cosmopolitanism
trans-speciesism, 187
travel writing, 43, 48, 49, 66, 72, 84, 305
Tuck, Eve, 36
Turner, Mark, 311, 314, 328
Turner, Mary E., 339
Turner, Reggie, 251
Twain, Mark, 46
Tynan, Katharine, 155–56
  "Charity of the Countess Kathleen, The," 161
  Shamrocks, 156–62
Tyndall, John, 290
'Ūkēkē, 'Ioane, 41, 44, 45–46, 51

Ulrichs, Karl Heinrich, 210, 212–23
uncanny, 66–67, 69
undisciplining, *See* discipline, disciplinarity
Upward, Allen, 103
Uranianism, 210, 211–13, 253, *See also* sex,
  sexuality
urbanization, 114, 190, *See also* industrialization;
  modernity, modernization; nature
  aesthetics of, 118, 311
  gender and, 121
  modernity and, 154
  nature and, 147–55, 181, 191–94
  pollution and, 118–20, 125, 148, 152–55,
    165, 180–81
  religion and, 285
  technology and, 118
utopia, utopianism, 9, 80, *See also* eugenics; socialism

utopia, utopianism (cont.)
  rural, 227, 229, 230, 231, 236

Valance, Hélène, 112
Vale Press, 334
vegetarianism, 9, 229–30
Venture (magazine), 306, 309, 313, 319
Verlaine, Paul, 251, 278
Verne, Jules, 43
Victorian studies, 7
  imperialism and, 34, 35
  nation and, 4, 11, 41
  race and, 25, 34, 35
Visram, Rozina, 34
vivisection, 9, 292
Vogt, Carl, 26
Vyver, Bertha, 296

Wagner, Richard, 269
Waley, Arthur, 64
Walters, John Cuming, 300
Waugh, Arthur, 251
Weeks, Jeffrey, 221
Weir, David, 266
weird fiction, 5, 15, 187–90, 193
  aesthetics of, 195–203
  decadence and, 194–95
  ecocriticism and, 194–98, 199, 201, 202–4
Wells, H. G., 1, 5, 227
  Time Machine, The, 148, 176–77
  War of the Worlds, The, 176
Whirlwind (newspaper), 254
Whistler, James Abbott McNeil, 112–13, 247
White, Ellen, 300
White, Eric, 309
White, Gleeson, 313
Whitman, Walt, 114, 181
Wilde, Oscar, 1, 3, 6, 8, 14, 112, 172, 178, 208,
  209–10, 214, 233, 248, 270, 275–76, 278,
  286–87, 328–29, 344

  Catholicism and, 289–90
  "Critic as Artist, The," 213, 255, 294
  "Decay of Lying, The," 178–81
  "Impression du Matin," 112, 116,
    180
  De Profundis, 182, 289
  Picture of Dorian Gray, The, 174–76, 177,
    181, 233, 234, 287–95
  "Roses and Rue," 294
  Salomé, 181, 270, 329
  science and, 290, 292–95
  "Symphony in Yellow," 180
Williams, Raymond, 21, 134
Willmott, Glenn, 122
Wilson, Charlotte, 236
Winter, James, 192
Wisnicki, Adrian, 344
Wong, Amy R., 11, 25, 41
world literature, 62, 64, 67
world religion. *See under* religion
world, worlding, 62–65, 71, 74, 75, *See also*
  cosmopolitanism; networks
  humanism and, 70
  literature and, 67
  nature and, 132
Wynter, Sylvia, 22, 26

Y90s, See Yellow Nineties 2.0
Y90s Personography, 323
Yang, K. Wayne, 36
Yeats, Dylan, 31
Yeats, W. B., 65, 156, 195, 247, 251
Yellow Book (magazine), 15, 42, 251, 306,
  308–14, 316, 317–19, 329, 339–44
Yellow Nineties 2.0 (Y90s), 15, 306–10, 323, 330,
  344
Yeo, Stephen, 228

Zoroastrianism, 103
Zundert, Joris van, 346